For Better and for Worse

Memoirs of
Thomas Holland

By the same author
THE GREAT CROSS
MARY—DOCTRINE FOR EVERYMAN (with G. P. Dwyer)

ACKNOWLEDGEMENTS
Miss Eileen McCarthy, M.B.E., typed my MS.
Father Philip Caraman, S.J., prepared it for publication.
I owe them both more than I can say.

+ T.H.

03797812

ISBN 0 9514346 0 8

Typeset and printed in England by
John Roberts & Sons Printers (Salford) Ltd., Chapel Street, Salford M3 6BG.

To my beloved auxiliary,
Bishop Geoffrey Burke.

Contents

CHAPTER I

Home and School with Tram Sport

WE were seven children: girl, boy; girl, boy; (girl); girl, boy. The couplets are separated by three and six years respectively. Carmela, the one in brackets, opted out at the tenderest age and was buried in the cemetery behind the church flanking the school. The school, staffed by five devoted nuns (Selly Park) and one lay-mistress, was at a lower level. There were windows on one side only, high up and partly frosted. The transparent panes had room only for graves!

A dull school? Tough, yes, but not dull. Caning, of course, was in. We no more found it cruel or unjust than we thought the window view gloomy. There was a constant pressure of noses to the grindstone. We could parse and analyse Gray's Elegy, read Tonic Solfa, and recite the whole Catechism by heart before we were in our teens. That was not brainless parrot talk. At twelve in the seminary, our Christian Doctrine professor commented on the excellent understanding of Catechism texts somebody had given me.

Our school was in total harmony with our home. To attend it we travelled two miles on the tram; two miles back home for our dinner, repeating the two-way journey in the afternoon. There were reduced fares, by courtesy of the Tramways Manager. But even so, twenty fares a week multiplied by six is quite a sum. Our father had not inherited his uncle's estate and at this time his earnings were not big.

The old trams with their green maltese crosses to distinguish them from those leaving our village by another route, introduced us to the world of grown-ups. We came to know drivers and guards, regular passengers including the Recorder of Manchester and a Dickensian character (always accompanied) whose constant concern was to show us "An elephant on a shilling!" This was achieved by placing a finger on Queen Victoria's head, leaving only her hair-do visible. With a slight turn of the coin there indeed was an elephant's trunk and head. With childish cruelty I one day told him I was sick of seeing "an elephant on a shilling". My excuse now would be I was too young to realise the man was in mental care. Not good enough!

The trams were a schoolroom in their own right. Looking back I am convinced there were more "originals" around seventy years ago. There was more leisure in which to be oneself. Retired men of means would spend the whole morning on the open upper-deck as

7

the tram shuttled backwards and forwards, and there was also gallantry and gentleness among the tram guards. One in particular *sang* the names of the roads and helped his female passengers to alight with exquisite courtesy. I am sure they timed their return from town by his tram. One of the drivers, Harry Barlow, wore an enormous corsage of flowers, fresh each morning. He sang with the rhythm of his vehicle. He, too, was a hit with the ladies.

Came the war and the guards *were ladies*! One we loved, the "Sporty girl"—bulking large in her three-quarter length uniform and always ready for a lark with us. Blessings on them all! How well they served and cherished us! Seven years, four times a day! Well, not always four. In summer early afternoons we could save a fare by jumping on the steps at the back of the horse-drawn wagonettes, well out sight of the coachman. Coming home after school we would occasionally walk home; in fact on occasion we ran all two miles of it. Only later did mother discover we pocketed the fares. She was ashamed of us. It was a caddish thing to do. And only one of many ways we supplemented our Saturday spending money!

Who were we? The eldest of us was Hannah Fawcett born in 1900. She was "put to the piano" at a very early age and so came under the happy influence of a Miss Almond, her teacher—not only professionally but very personally. Miss Almond retained the custom of her recusant forbears of retiring to Holywell for spiritual refreshment. In penal days both the Inns of that ancient pilgrimage centre had a disguised Jesuit father as "mine host". From Lancashire went a steady stream during the period for Easter duties. Little Hannah Fawcett found her destiny there, and never wavered from it. At Pantasaph, Holywell, the Capuchin Fathers have spiritually inherited from the Jesuits. Their monastery introduced to a little piano-pupil the heroine who shared the Poor Man of Assisi's espousals to the Lady Poverty. Three score and ten years later our eldest died, Abbess and Foundress of a Poor Clare Monastery. Her predecessor as Abbess, Mother Columba, was one of the noblest ladies I have ever known.

The first-born son was John, two years younger than Hannah Fawcett. Probably the best brain of the family and the black sheep almost to the end. But a remarkable providence brought him into the fold again. In fact I doubt if he remembered he had ever been outside. For his last two or three years he recognised no one from the past, he was regularly at Holy Mass and Holy Communion and died while his two brothers were visiting him with just sufficient time in which to arrange and carry through the funeral on our last day. His son, too, and the son's wife were just able to be present and so was Sister M. Clare F.C.J. our sister.

The instrument of this fabulous denouement—the master-key— was Nazareth House, Plymouth. John had been indeed far from the household of Faith—far from the home in which we grew up together. There he was home again.

Powerful mind? Perhaps I exaggerate. But when John was teaching Greek in Cairo University, Culbertson and his circus came to play bridge at the Gezhira Sporting Club. He offered John a place in his team. (It's true we only have John's word for it!). His Arabic was good. Disguised as a native he spied for us in the desert for which he got 'mentions'.

Mary Winefride (Mamie), was third born in 1905, my elder half and mother's providential right hand in the long years ahead. She began with a new advantage. She was the first girl to go to boarding school: Lark Hill F.C.J. Convent, Preston. It was the beginning of a connection which lasted, I would say, from 1918 to this very day (1986), perpetuated in the person of the youngest girl who followed Mamie to Lark Hill and became herself an F.C.J. Mamie was no academic. She had a certain flair for maths and botany; that was all. She was never a really able musician, though she played the organ in our churches. She followed Hannah Fawcett as a sacristan. Daunted by the big festivals, she had her own method of attack: forget all about it, relax over a good meal and a "flick" the night before and then go in sharp and DO IT. The flowers and candles never mounted higher.

She was pious after her fashion. Capable of shocking the family with: "My only devotion is the Holy Souls!" Hard as agate, on occasion she was ready to dissolve when confronted with one's pain or worry. In this she was so like our mother. She never walked out with a suitor. There was, however, a supreme irony in her conviction that I came between her and a later marriage of convenience. I never denied it for the good reason that I was never formally accused.

I hesitate at this point to say more about our family. Three of us are still alive: Father Joseph, parish priest of Our Lady's, Lydiate, Sister Mary Clare, F.C.J., now retired after a lifetime's teaching, and myself.

I shall never cherish sufficiently the uncovenanted grace of good parents: great Christian people, whose only concern was to care for their family and to support the Church. One indication of this comes to mind. Our mother one day remembered in my hearing how she had prayed her children would always have pure thoughts. She was not making a big thing of it. It was said very much "by the way" in connection with something else which I have forgotten.

CHAPTER II

Parishes and Priests

I HAVE just been reading Alison Peers on Spanish Mystics, a non-Catholic scholar in an area you would think our monopoly—mysticism. As I write Gabriel y Galan's verse* comes back to mind:

"Light and shadows combine to make me.	De luz y de sombras soy,
To both I wish to give all that I am.	Y quiero darme a las dos.
I wish to leave of myself when I go	Quiero dejar de mi en pos—
Something of what I have of clay,	Algo que tengo de arcilla,
Something of what I have of God!"	Algo que tengo de Dios.

Parish boundaries did strange things for our home, shuttling it out of one parish and back again, *twice*. I was baptised before our original parish got its church, when Mass was said in a room above the school. Later, as a bishop in Lancashire, I was rather proud of that introduction to the community of Christ's faithful. So many parishes in my diocese began with church and school under one roof. A fair number remained so in my time and always, of course, the church at the top.

I count it a privilege that I was baptised in a parish which took its title from one of Leo XIII's great encyclicals: "The Holy Family". I read somewhere Cardinal Newman's tribute to that late harvest of mind and heart, the Letters of Leo. He was astonished, simply could not explain such vigour and penetration in a man so old, so sparing of nourishment as to be almost transparent. Others, of course, were equally astonished with Newman. In fact, Leo himself was one of them.

The new church, when it came, was worth waiting for. A little gem with a Norman tower that presented unusual difficulties. It was built on the edge of moss land. Whatever rafting or underpinning was adopted, clearly the extra weight of the tower took its toll. You came in under the tower to face a walk *up* the middle aisle. The parish priest, I believe, simply denied there was any gradient there at all. Thirty years later he recanted and undertook the puzzling task of levelling the church floor. He managed to do it despite the long-prevailing conviction we all had shared that the feat was impossible.

* José Maria Gabriel y Galan (1870-1905)

That sturdy Norman tower housed a very sweet Angelus bell which we could hear at home, a mile away, very clearly.

Should not my satisfaction at being baptised on the upper floor of Holy Family school logically involve regrets that I was never sent (nor any of the family) to Holy Family school, much the nearer? We should have been somewhat better-off as a family without the tram rides every day into the town. Moreover, there were excellent laywomen in charge of Holy Family school, with a superb record of success. Our parents, however, were determined we should profit by the presence in an elementary school and, in a rather non-Catholic corner of Lancashire, of Teaching Sisters. Since they could not aspire to the famous Convent School at the further end of the town, they sensed it a duty to do what they could. It was a good decision for all of us.

At the Holy Family church the parish priest was a rosy, rotund middle-aged gentleman who lived to advanced years always expected to be re-called as parish priest of St Austin's, Preston. He had done a long curacy there under a famous Canon. Clearly it was for him the unforgettable ideal. Even the division of Liverpool diocese which cut south of Preston along the Ribble failed to cut his hopes of returning. As a priest I was invited to his Golden Jubilee. Monsignor Dean, Rector of Upholland Seminary, preached at the Mass—on the Mass. It was Maurice de la Taille's theory—hook, line and sinker.

Father George Richmond, as English as his name, was the parish priest of Holy Family. He baptised me. By contrast, the two priests at the town church of St. Marie's, Dean Patrick Cahill and (believe it or not) Father Patrick Cahill, were regarded outside the Catholic community as father and son. And so they were in the bonds of charity. For the Dean was old, gentle, and, as I learned years later from his curate, extremely scrupulous. As a young priest, he had taught humanities in St. Edward's College, Liverpool which served two streams of pupils: boys aspiring to be priests and boys preparing for a secular career, many of the latter from South America. Of course the port of Liverpool hummed with traffic from those parts. Refrigeration of ships was a local brain-wave. The beef of the pampas stampeded into English ovens through Liverpool. And so did the rancheros' sons into St. Edward's and St. Bede's, Manchester, as boarders. The address of the Liverpool College, San Domingo Road, may have attracted some. The neighbourhood, however, was a rather unlikely one for a Catholic Seminary. It was in the very heart of the Orange District. Student crocodiles issuing from the high-walled, ample precincts of "Ted's" ran many a gauntlet. As if being Catholics were not provocation enough, the boys wore bowler hats. Hence, I presume, the phrase: "I'll knock your blocker off!"

But back to our priests. At the very time when a new deanery was built it came Dean Cahill's time to go home to the Lord. It was 1914.

11

I was six and remember his death. I treasure too the memory of his curate. It seems they asked me once—it was a Good Friday—why I came to church. The answer came pat: "To see Father Cahill!" He was in all truth worth seeing. Well over six feet, his leonine head mounted on broad shoulders, his face lit with the brightest smile. The sun, moon and stars shone into my little world from that face. Even a boy could tell men do not come better than that giant from Mullingar, so splendid in vestments, so full of fun, and yet so shy at heart. Such clergy, of course, had a profound influence on the shape of our lives.

Recently I was asked to do a couple of interviews on radio. Each one raised the question of my early commitment to the priesthood. I was just twelve when I joined the diocesan seminary at Upholland in 1920.

My elder brother, too, offered himself for the priesthood. That influenced me. He proved, however, a refractory element and was "bunked"*. There was sorrow in our home when the news came. I was on the point of saying I would give up, too, when the eldest sister like a flash said: "Don't let this stop you, Tommy!"

Father Pat Cahill Jnr. swopped places with Father John Turner who thus became our parish priest. (We were now out of Holy Family parish in virtue of another boundary revision.) John Turner's family honeycombed Preston and the surrounding countryside. Three of his nephews were priests. Another more remote relative, Monsignor Joe Turner, was to become a well-loved president of Upholland. He was apparently made of india-rubber. His nickname "Dives" (no connection with the Rich Man in the gospel) neatly epitomised a whole range of impossible contortions and projections into space. He was conscripted into the First War as a P.T. instructor. His performance on the parallel bars, I suppose, would thrill no one today. We have seen what little Russian girls can do, but he thrilled *us*. And so did his mastery of the Latin poets in the schoolroom.

Despite my frequent failures to please authority (one serious indeed) Canon John Turner stood by me. Not that he failed to censure. He kept things to himself, however, which was remarkable given the close, almost daily, contact he had with my father who was his chief apparitor.

The day came, thirteen years after my entry at Upholland, when Archbishop Downey ordained me in St. Marie's church. I can only hope the joy of it compensated in some way for all the old man's loyalty and care. He was "old school" at its best. Silvering black locks curled to his neck in undulating waves. His shovel hat was moored to the lapel of his Chesterfield coat. Under the projecting brim sheltered one of the most winsome, joyful countenances you could meet in a day's march. With his springheel walk and welcoming approach, he appeared to be entering always into a happier world.

* Local argot for "expelled".

Many, however, who would have wished to attract his attention, refrained. It was another world, they felt, in which he was moving, beyond their everyday experiences.

That impression was true but only so far. Canon Turner's joy, though firmly anchored elsewhere, thrilled with appreciation for the good things of this life. I have rarely known wittier conversation than his. Good music was a passion with him as with all his family—the family business was music. In all the parishes entrusted to him, Lydiate (where tradition has it he visited his farming community on horse-back)), St. Teresa's, Birkdale, and St. Marie's, Southport, he trained the choir and got the best out of his singers. In St. Marie's choir there was a contralto of truly phenomenal power. With her he had his problems. She would counter the curb he sought to impose on her volume, by leaving the choir, joining the body of the kirk, and from there drowning the twitterings from above.

As a young priest the Canon had been sent on a Mediterranean cruise for his health. He died at the age of 89! I was thousands of miles away—Royal Naval Chaplain at Colombo, Ceylon.

Once the Canon invited me, still a raw student of the humanities, to join him for a day by the sea at Blackpool, forty miles away. On the train, as he lit his cigarette (a brand he always referred to as "Golden Flake") he explained this was a comfort he never allowed himself on trains going south towards Liverpool—too many people knew him in that direction. They might be offended. Going north it was different, though we had to pass through his native heath round Preston. The difference was clearly this. He had had pastoral responsibility in two parishes to the south: none to the north.

That day opened all manner of "magic casements on the foam" for the schoolboy. We lunched at the oldest and still the most decorous hotel in the town. Nothing was omitted from the ritual. The claret carefully chosen, the port sipped into the golden afternoon.

The Canon's conversation never flagged. The raw schoolboy looked up and was richly fed, spiritually and corporally. Lightly, even hilariously, the musical voice moved gently backwards and forwards over the years—then a good forty of them—in the priesthood. The schoolboy, perhaps already slightly elevated in a golden mist caught glimpses of long-dead bishops *, the dome of Santa Sofia, the masterpieces of distant art galleries, heard the music of the spheres as the soft, rhythmic voice, occasionally interrupted by a generous smacking of the lips over the port, discoursed on the most spiritual of the arts, music.

During his thirty and more years as our parish priest, the Canon had a remarkable succession of assistant priests. Eight or nine of

*e.g. Archbishop Errington, Wiseman's coadjutor (with right of succession which Pius IX annulled in favour of Manning). The Canon recalled as a deacon groping his way into the dark chapel for his breviary, and stumbling over the Archbishop prone before the altar in prayer.

them come back vividly to mind, all worthy of most honourable mention. They will not take it amiss if I record only one of them, John Wilcock.

When, in 1964, I was drafted from Pompey to be Bishop of Salford, he, sole survivor of those distant days, was now a Canon of the Metropolitan Cathedral Chapter of Liverpool, and long-serving parish priest of St. Elizabeth's, Litherland. He gallantly travelled to Salford for my installation despite his four score years. Forty-one years earlier he had attended my eldest sister's final profession as a Poor Clare in Levenshulme, Manchester.

He had graduated from Cambridge with a brilliant classics degree in the early years of this century. When I went to Upholland in 1920, he was Prefect of Studies. I don't remember his teaching me either Latin or Greek. Certainly we had a year's English from him, He was a fastidious scholar and held our noses to that then popular grindstone, Nesfield's *English Grammar*. It was not popular with us twelve-year olds. Nor in fact was he, though we had a healthy respect for him, not only as a fine scholar, but more endearingly as a pioneer photographer, an art in which he relentlessly sought perfection, as in all things else.

He moved after about a year to his first curacy with John Turner. There he brought the same faultless perfection to his pastoral duties. He had verbally belted me for sloppy work at Upholland. He rightly blamed the expression on my face for spoiling a superb group photograph in early colour. At Southport he so far overcame his repugnance as to suggest we might visit a cinema together. We never did: he was too shy. I wonder what his reflections were in Salford Cathedral that 12 September 1964 when his Archbishop sat me in the chair.

CHAPTER III

The Provost went to Spain

THE President of Upholland College, Provost William Walmesley, was twice the age of any of his colleagues, even of his vice-president and procurator, Dr Joseph Dean, whom we boys, from his baldness and heavy gait, took for a very old man. He was, in fact, no more than in his early forties.

Of course we resented anything our limited vision judged to be unfair. Our mentors too were human. But their total dedication to the one purpose of forming raw lads into likely candidates for Sacred Orders was firmly based on their love of the Church, the Priesthood and Christ's faithful. Since we were in two of those categories and aiming at the other, there can be no doubt of their love for us. I say that now with utter conviction. But I am sure they would have been the first to recognise that such fair reasoning was beyond us adolescents.

With "Old Bill" Walmesley, however, I had a unique chance to learn the truth. It came at the end of my seven years at Upholland. I was a young philospher of nineteen and he had been replaced by Dr. Dean as president.

The Vice-Rector of the Upper House was Dr. Downey, later Archbishop of Liverpool. Diplomatically he informed me at the end of the scholastic year 1926-7 that I was destined for a foreign seminary. "When plants fail to come to their best in one soil," he said, "nurserymen move them. You are to be transplanted to the English College in Spain." A student one year ahead of me had just left the vice-rectorial carpet with the same destiny. So we did a fandango together outside the Doctor's door.

The summer vacation came on. We could not have been entirely without grace. Both of us felt we should not leave England without returning to Upholland to take farewell of the Old Provost. He was reading St. Teresa of Avila with a large magnifying glass and, characteristicauy, raised his hand to peer at us. He was already deep in his eighties. Our little courtesy visibly transformed him: the years fell away, as he remembered his years at the seminary at Valladolid. When we knelt for his blessing, he gave it, still seated, with a fumbling hand. It wasn't from any physical infirmity I assure you. Most masculine of men, he did not want us to see the tears. *Sunt lacrimae rerum!*

I must not forget the other Upholland priests of the 1920s. For the most part Dr. Joseph Dean ("the Bean") viewed me with a cold

15

disapproving eye. He had every right. Yet when I visited him years later in retirement, he made me smoke his last cigar. There was also Father William Finnessy, ("Pa Fin"). Of all the professors, he warmed to us scallywags and we to him. His nickname derived approximately from his exquisite pronunciation of the French word "parfum". It also chimed in with our schoolboy argot of naming professors. He was our first Latin master. I still have the certificate (a holy picture) attesting *in dorso* in his fine handwriting that I had accurately recited all parts of the four Latin verbs in the Active and Passive voices!

Dear Father Cuthbert Wareing opened our minds to the beauty of our English language. He had graduated at Cambridge in the days of Sir Arthur Quiller-Couch and vibrated with enthusiasm for Kipling, Stevenson and the other stylists of the time. Thirty years later I was sent to give a mission in one of the Chorley parishes. Dear "Cuddy" was the parish priest. He expressed appreciation of my work. I was only giving back what he gave me as a lad.

The "Profs" together, as I have said, provided us boys and young men with a harmonious pattern of the priesthood. Easier for them to do that than for today's priests. It was a point of honour, in the tradition of the nineteenth and the early decades of this century, to stay within a highly disciplined code of external behaviour. Archbishop Whiteside, for instance, when rector of Upholland in the eighties and early nineties, did not return the salute of his young men when they lifted their birettas to him. That was judged extreme, I think, even at the time. But the dangers of over-familiarity were recognised by all; and the duty of honouring the "cloth", and the status. Today, neither preoccupation cuts much ice. "The cloth" has largely gone. Openness is all part of the pastoral approach as exemplified in John Paul II. There is a considerable gain. We were in danger of becoming Kantians—not intellectually (God forbid!)—but behaviourally, set on "saving the appearances".

This gives me a chance to honour the "Minor Professors", young men who had finished their humanities, some with external degrees at London University, whose approach to the priesthood was interrupted for three years to serve us as "Minors". Perhaps a dozen of them over the six years taught my class. They were for the most part in their early twenties, with no acquired skill in the art of teaching, and no sanction available to them but "impots". Priest-professors' reports to the Prefect of Discipline activated the "tan"—vigorously, six or twelve times, all on the same hand, if you so wished. But "Write out three pages of Dickens!" or Scott (in small print editions) was about the toughest a "Minor" could impose.

The man who alerted me, perhaps more forcibly than any other, to the need for change was a former "Minor". He was in fact the doyen of the five with whom my studies began in 1920. Even as boys we sensed greatness in him. I remember one of us saying: "He's a future Archbishop of Liverpool". Nobody disagreed. He had been born in South America and like so many young Englishmen in the diaspora returned for active service in World War I. He became a stoker in the Royal Navy. I can't think this pleased his academic father who had invented a new World Language competing with Esperanto.

At Rome he achieved a flawless academic career, returned to become President of Upholland and later Rector of the English College, Rome. He was well on his way to the peak honour we lads had marked out for him twenty years before, when he made the statement which impressed me so much. It was simple but all-embracing. He said: "We pretend too much!" It was true! The old public image to which the man in authority conformed certainly involved more than a degree of play-acting.

Yet I am grateful for that united front which priests presented at considerable personal cost. The result was coherent and for youngsters, on their way, reassuring. Now, with the decline of "Noblesse oblige!" and the slackening off of all such constraints, priests can no longer give public expression to an *esprit de corps* such as, for example, still inspires young men to choose a certain unit of the Services. It's true, of course, that even before secular priests and religious men and women began "doing their own thing" in habit and manners, Monty and others were at the same fragmentation process in the Services. But we have gone further.

At the end of term in Underlow (Upholland's first form) it was of immemorial custom for our teachers to wind up reading a story. As the Provost entered we chorused: "Last Class, Provost! Read us a story!" He mounted the dais and turned shading his eyes. "I can't read a story with these eyes!" We sensed deviousness, but were ready: "Then you've got to tell us one!" Good humouredly he took his seat and began. Should I try to repeat it as he told that story? It made a lasting impression. I think I can be tolerably faithful. It was the story of his going to Spain from Brindle, a Lancashire village ever true to the old Faith, where the yeomanry were men enough to frog-march their Squire out of church one Sunday when he expressed loud disapproval of the Vicar Apostolic's pastoral letter. William Walmesley's father was one of those men.

To put the story into its historical setting, I calculate the Provost went to Spain in 1853. He was fourteen and had been held back for a couple of years until his younger brother was old enough to join him. "We sailed from Liverpool, six of us" he said, "in a sloop with white sails. One lad's mother had him clothed in a long white smock. She gave him a large bag of biscuits. Then all said goodbye and we went aboard. One of our companions had a very queasy stomach. We told him the cook made the eggs for breakfast by spitting in the frying-pan. So we had an extra egg each morning. We landed at Santander. It was the month of May and all the church bells were ringing for evening devotions to Our Lady. They called them 'Flores de Mayo' 'Flowers of May'. During the night I was awakened by the

17

'Sereno' (night-watchman) as he went his rounds each hour calling: 'Ave Maria Purisima, y una noche serena!' ('Hail Mary, most Pure! and a quiet night!') As there were no railways, we made our journey down to Castille by road.

"The College of St. Alban, Valladolid was on the other side of the street from a military barracks. We could look into the detention cells from our rooms. Their windows were covered with a wire-mesh between the iron bars. But the wine seller carried with his skin of wine a sheaf of long straws. The soldiers detained in the guard-room got their fill by suction after slipping their coins through the wire netting.

"Our part of the city was called St. John's, after the parish church. The College gave onto a little square called Plaza de S. Juan. There was a silly fellow who wandered round the square holding a big stone over his head. Asleep on one of the stone benches was a fowler. His dog slept at his feet. The silly fellow stood for a moment looking at them, lifted the stone higher and dropped it on the dog. Howls from the dog—imprecations from the fowler! He caught the silly fellow. 'My pointer! Take that!' Wallop after wallop! The silly-billy learned his lesson.

"The father of one of the students paid a visit to the college. He was a military officer and arrived mounted and in uniform. He was on his way back to England. In front of all of us he asked his son: 'Would you like to come back to England with me, son?' Of course the lad said, yes! His father looked him in the eye. 'Be a man, son! Stay the course and come back a priest. We need you.' He stayed and became a very good priest."

That last little episode makes one wonder whether after the Peninsular War, we continued some kind of a military presence in Spain as a gesture of good-will. Wellington received a dukedom with estates near Cuidad Rodrigo for his services. His heirs were still in possession in 1940 when a curious ceremony took place in the palace of the Archbishop of Valladolid.

The British Ambassador, Sir Samuel Hoare, with his suite came bearing gifts for the new National Sanctuary of the Sacred Heart. The Archbishop had just founded this in what was once the Jesuit university church. One of the Faculty, the Venerable Padre Hoyos, a sixteenth century Jesuit, experienced in that church all that St. Margaret Mary Alacoque experienced in Paray-le-Monial—perhaps, in Spanish eyes, much more.

The gifts came from the Duke of Wellington's estates. It seems the family had decided to withdraw, leaving the Iron Duke's original rewards, at least in part, to be returned to Spain at the Ambassador's discretion. His choice was singularly well advised. Samuel Hoare's was a brilliant and sumptuous gesture, well calculated to off-set the enormous German propaganda then swamping Spain.

The students of the English and Scots' Colleges were invited to the delivery ceremony. The Ambassador's address was sweetly rendered in Spanish by one of his aides.* The Archbishop beamed happily as he reminded us all that Catholic Empancipation at last came to England under a Wellington administration. But did he realise how much the Duke hated what he was doing?

The Ambassador and Archbishop faced each other across a long table. When did any table ever glitter with such a load of treasure-trove? Ranged full length lay altar furnishings of every kind, all solid silver: ciboria, chalices, monstrances, candlesticks, Blessed Sacrament lamps, cruets, thuribles, gradines, ewers and basins, altar-cards, missal-covers: the King of Spain's provision for the celebration of Mass in the chapel on the ducal estates. Was the Duke ever present there? I can think of one occasion when it could have been possible. Suppose a troop of his Irish Catholic soldiers turned up and bivouaced on the *finca*? The warm praises he gave them in his despatches must then have gained a third dimension had he joined them at Mass.

One final memory of the old Provost. Ordained in 1865 in Valladolid, William Walmesley was retained on the staff as a professor. One of his students was Henry Brewer, later a priest in the Salford diocese who built St. Joseph's church in Halliwell, Bolton, in 1879. In 1979 I had the privilege of assisting as Bishop of Salford at the centenary celebrations. How *do* you come to grips with a continuum in which the same teacher has two pupils, one of whom presided over the centenary celebrations of a church the other one had built? No wonder St. Augustine admitted that the concept of time had slipped from his grasp "like a fish"!

*Bernard Malley whose unrivalled knowledge of Spain was, I believe, acquired as a student at the Escorial with the Jeronomite Fathers. Our present Ambassador, Lord Lennox, remembers him.

CHAPTER IV

Classmates and Shipmate

LET me now leave Rectors, Professors and Minors and come to my own classmates, my *commensales, coheredes et sodales*, the Underlow of 64 years ago. This very spring, two have gone of the seven who became priests; Frank Reilly and Bernard Dickinson. Frank was my fellow townee. Indeed he was baptised as I was, but a year or so before me, above the Holy Family school by Father George Richmond. His father ran the famous Oyster Bar across the Promenade from Southport Pier. Monsignor Joseph Dean, again a fellow-townee, and no mean authority, held him to be a Catholic Apologist in the great tradition.

These were the days before Ecumenism dawned. Pat Reilly was of supreme value to his employers. His witty repartees drew many "regulars", some for the sheer fun of it, perhaps even more for the chance of hearing him matched in religious controversy. This could be a fairly constant occurrence. Professionals and amateurs alike felt the menace of what they could only regard as a sounding-board for Irish papistry. Mr. Reilly had a loud and brogue-ful voice.

One day after breakfast, college routine soared into the stratosphere. We were packed into a charabanc for a day by the sea at (of all places) Southport! We were, however, decanted on the shore well away from the town. The order of the day was *stay* on the shore, but Frank and I had other plans. No sooner were we allowed to disperse than we crossed the railway (carefully avoiding the live rail), caught a lift into town and separated, each homeward-bound. There was a deadline for the charabanc. In late afternoon when we met, it was all too clear we could only make it by a non-stop conveyance. No taxis appeared. We took a cab, clamoured for speed and, alighting at the strategic point ran hell-for-leather over live rails and what is now Hillside Golf Course, to arrive unobtrusively as the charabanc was boarded for the return.

Not a praiseworthy exploit, nor worth recording for itself? But at least thirty five years later, Frank was sent as parish priest to Hillside with the obligation of building the long over-due Church. He built it, a beauty in the Lombard style, where only some months ago I attended his Requiem. Then all came back to me. Though they have made a new road and bridge over the electric railway, Frank's building stands pretty well at the point where two highly apprehensive schoolboys leapt out of the cab and hared across the dunes to the shore.

Bernard Dickinson, "Dickybird", was brilliant. Obviously he was made for a "Minor" Professor. After his three years' stint teaching French and English, he resumed his studies for the priesthood at the Dominican University of Fribourg. It was midway through his course there that I met him again after six years. I had just been ordained and was attached at sixth curate at the Sacred Heart parish, Liverpool. The enterprising Rector had billed me for a course of sermons on Sunday evenings. Dickybird spotted this world-shaking event in the press, and turned up, not to scoff, as of right, but to hearten with a generous accolade. We took the tram down to the Landing Stage and caught the evening breeze coming up the river, then still full of shipping. The bonny liners—White Star, Cunard, Pacific Steam N.C., Yeowards, Booths and Alfred Holt.

I should not have mentioned our meeting at the Sacred Heart church but for our final meeting there after fifty-one years. He died a few weeks after Frank Reilly. His last appointment as parish priest was the Sacred Heart and there we gathered for his Requiem. Ill-health withdrew him from teaching and later parochial work. At Cambridge he was awarded a stage at the Sorbonne and there picked up a virus which, it seems, had lasting effects.

I said he was brilliant. Here is a sample. For such English Literature conundrums as: "Give dates and authors of the following passages", Dickybird bequeathed a key fashioned from his own sensitive mastery of styles and periods. My brother used it when he was "up", and found it excellent. Dicky was too ill to sit his finals. The University had no difficulty in awarding him his degree.

Strange! We never met over the recent years and corresponded only twice. Once when he read something of mine in which I quoted, as from a nebulous past: "In the bright lexicon of youth, there's no such word as FAIL", he wrote at once to tell me where we had heard it together—in Pa Fin's elocution class. The second time was his last Christmas: he sent me the first-ever card. I replied at New Year with a little booklet illustrated by our local artist Harold Riley: "Seven Prayers to Our Lady". He was quite ill at the time but at once capped me with his rendering into English verse of the *Salve Regina*. It was admired, he shyly noted, by Alec Jones of *Jerusalem Bible* fame. (Alec was a year ahead of us and "no slouch" at rendering.)

I must add one other classmate in the robust shape of "Ham" Cunningham. Ham hailed from Lancaster and could give an eye witness account of the tremendous explosion at the White Lund Chemical Plant in 1915. More memorable, however, were his renderings of sea songs in a rollicking baritone: for instance "Shipmates" which still vibrates on my inner ear. Did his vocation as a sea chaplain germinate out of these early successes? As a student of the English College Rome, no man, I believe, "rose and shone" more idiomatically with R.N. shore-parties visiting Rome from the Mediterranean Fleet. His command of Lower Deck argot was already well developed.

We had met in Rome in a rather unusual way shortly after I arrived there in 1933. News reached me that Ham was to say his first Mass at the Tomb of St. Peter. I got there just as he began, and at the end of the Mass, lined up with the others for his blessing. He gave it with a beatific smile, I kissed his hands and stole away. He had not recognised me. True, it was six years since we had met and he was well up in the clouds.

A dozen years later and the near-miss of all places in Sri Lanka, the Pearl of the East. In Colombo I heard some ratings discussing the R.C. naval chaplain in Trincomalee. In their view he was "mustard". He said the 9 o'clock Mass every Sunday in Trinco Cathedral. His sermon was not to be missed. He leaned back on the altar to begin his address with: "Now you skates!" I pricked up my ears as they went on to describe his seven minutes' *tour de force* in the sustained idiom of the Lower Deck. The ratings could not name him. But I was sure I could, and thumbed a lift to Trinco in the daily Expediter—a comfy little "kite" if you didn't mind squatting on the floor. But Ham had "flown" the previous day, typically taking passage to the U.K. in a submarine. It took me another six years to catch up with him; alas, in the cancer ward of the University Hospital, London. Throat surgery had reduced his once vibrant voice to a whisper. But the spirit was more than willing. Only on the day of his final discharge from the Navy, his old enemy, "the noonday devil" of depression, plagued him greviously. He was convalescing with us at the Headquarters of the Catholic Missionary Society. I found him in his room hunched in a chair, his naval cap on his head for the last time. But God's grace was sufficient for him. Laboriously he mastered the art of preaching to a full church without the benefit of vocal chords, and served St. Bernard's parish, Knott End, single-handed until his death.

Bishops *can* make good appointments! Ham's name is Bernard and his parish was surrounded by the sea.

And the other classmates of 1920? I know only two to be still earthbound, Joe Brown and I!

*Vita mutatur non tollitur!** How often we youngsters together heard those reassuring words! Lord, grant that the transformation of those already called from earth be in a place of "refreshment, light and peace". Grant the same to those of us who remain until You call. We never had a class reunion here below as Ushaw men do. Let us celebrate the first with You!

I fear we shed no tears as the Dover train left Victoria and our families in September 1927. My stable-mate, Tony Joyce, was twenty-one to my nineteen, and Spain was before us. Spain—then the great unknown, long before the mystery was shattered by "Chips

"Life is changed not ended!"

with Everything" and "Lancashire-by-the-Med"! Our excellent elocution master, Parker Lynch, had capitalised on Chesterton's ballade "Lepanto" that year. We sought seats in the dining car chanting "Love-Light of Spain Hurrah, Domino Gloria!" The five course lunch cost 4s 6d and we drank wine. The Calais porter failed, however, to share my sense of political economy. He raised a hullabaloo in which I missed everything but the oft-repeated: "Grandes Baggages!" Shamefully I doubled and quit.

We stayed two days in Paris at the Jeanne d'Arc (recommended by our old Prefect of Discipline, Tom Turner) and "did" the churches, galleries and the opera. (Tony's comment on the Louvre was, "Too human! Fleshy!") We also played billiards in the Bar across from the Jeanne d'Arc. The barmaid's only comment here was "C'est loin!" when she learned we were for Spain. The poor lady suffered from spots.

We left Paris by the 20 hours Rapide from the old Quai d'Orsay Station to the lilt of a sweet cantilena: "Monsieurs les Voyageurs—en Voiture! Tours, Angoulême, Bordeaux, Dax, Hendaye, L'ES-PAGNE!" Sheer *vox humana*, unadulterated by Public Address Systems. (Vive Jacque Tati for his supreme squelch of P. A. Systems in "Vacances d'Eté"!) Once aboard the Rapide we discovered two others bound for the English College, Valladolid: Jim McCarthy, a student from Rome who masterfully created room for us in his Second Class compartment, and Father C. C. Martindale, S.J., whom we discovered wandering in the corridor. He was to give the annual eight-day Retreat which inaugurated the College year.

Jim's mastery of good order in human relations was to be amply demonstrated during the next four years as College Master of Ceremonies. The old High Mass Liturgy under his guidance flowed as a "river rejoicing the City of God". The multiple "orationes" of those days unerringly met the eye of the Celebrant as Jim's silver stylus, permanently attached to his wrist with a silken cord, came to rest in the exact spot on the revolving pages. Fine, healthy six-footer though he was, radiating charm and distinction from his auburn curls to the soles of his feet (once so firmly planted in the scrum), alas, poor Jim agonised and died in a single night.

I cannot forget Cyril Grice's lament after his funeral in Derby. We met in the car-park. Cyril, a senior contemporary at Valladolid, released his pent-up indignation: "What utter waste! It needn't—it should not have happened!" Cyril was a holy man, a very worthy member of his diocesan Chapter. He was not railing at divine providence. It was human improvidence that cut twenty years off the normal span of a highly gifted parish priest.

CHAPTER V

The Problem of Divine Providence

SO MANY times I have to note the early eclipse of our brighter luminaries. Yet dull men (I know only too well) live on beyond their span. I can't be the only one to be puzzled by this. Yes, *Vita mutatur non tollitur*. Life is changed not taken away. And "eye has not seen nor ear heard what things God has prepared for those who love him!" Jim may be doing far more for his parish now than ever he could knocking on doors or thumping pulpits. In terms of the ultimate purpose of anyone's existence, we pray that he now ministers to God's glory to the joy and profit of the whole Church more continuously and splendidly than ever before.

*"Nobis quoque peccatoribus!"** We here below need the light to lead us and the ardour to sustain us if we are to make harbour. Of course, we have the wisdom and example of the saints and more than everything, we have the Lord, the Word and the Sacrament. But all is veiled for the ultimate greater happiness of those who have not seen yet have believed.

We do rely on living people, flesh and blood who are sent us at critical times to keep us believing. When the Reformation fractured Europe—and alas, England—we were given our Martyrs and the phalanx of Founders and Foundresses of the Counter-Reformation. We could not have survived without them. Nor are we left today without the same sovereign remedy in the confusion master-minded by the Enemy in the wake of Vatican II.† Popes John, John Paul I and II and Mother Teresa, are among the first of another phalanx of leaders whom we need, should be praying for, and surely will be sent. Most of all we need a Saint-Theologian of Aquinas quality (no less) who will reconcile and harmonise Existentialism and Essentialism. Or is that beyond hope?

Why so often is the light of these fine men and women withdrawn by untimely death, or dimmed by disease? Providence is co-terminous not only with Time (St. Augustine's 'Fish'!) but with Eternity, ranging from end to end mightily, disposing all things sweetly. Nothing can happen outside or in conflict with Providence. Even the rebellion of Satan and his wicked spirits (which is not in Time since angels are in another system of motion) fell within Providence. And so did Adam's fall. This is my prayer.

* "Also for us sinners", from the old Canon of the Mass.
† e.g. men like Von Balthasar, de Lubac, Hamer, Ratzinger.

So You, Lord, all-powerful, ever-loving God, hating nothing You have made, are equally source of Evil as of Good—Physical Evil and Moral Evil alike? If so, Lord, can You wonder there are atheists who simply deny You exist? Or others who can only credit You with a limited Providence—like the religious broadcaster in the dark days of the Second War who begged us to remember *You* were "up against it" as well as us! Don't dismiss them, Lord, as "bone-heads". Cicero held pretty well the same line, and so did Abelard. Of course that contentious genius had to be different. He saved Your face, as he thought, by a subtle distinction. Your Providence, yes, was limited, but only because You had sportingly abdicated part of it to give us total mastery.

There are others, Lord, so many of them—like Spike Milligan the other night in that winsome self-portrait of "The human soul by nature Christian". They know You exist and not just when they are in a jam (as atheists do!) And, Lord, they are definitely on Your side, i.e. they love You. But they simply can't understand why little children die, and all efforts to "justify God's ways to man" remain for them like Milton's verse—blank.

It is no use my pretending to any original line of argument. On the other hand, it's I who have broached the problem. I must offer a personal answer—personal, however, only in that I hold it with every fibre of my being. It demands an effort. But so does every exercise in humility. The problem before us burns like the bush in the Sinai desert and is not consumed. We are on holy ground. We face Mystery, as the old theologians used to say, "with the eye of a bat on the noon-day sun". But only one science has shaped us to this Mysterious Reality, not on the basis of experimental research, but on information disclosed by the Subject of this science, God. But is the source really genuine?

For centuries Society built its whole civilisation on the conviction that the Transcendent Reality was the genuine source of information. No other civilisation has so closely, or so advantageously, bound together so many different peoples. As we plough our way from League of Nations, to U.N.O., to E.E.C., how many look back and wonder is something now missing? Are the foundations firm enough?

Anyway, I know no other way out of the problem I have posed than the way of the Queen of Sciences, Sacred Theology, together with her Handmaid. Am I an ass to venture upon it?

Nothing, I have said, happens outside of God's Providence—or in conflict with it. But first let us get our eyes (bat's eyes) somewhat accustomed to the Light, with a pair of blinkers, to save us from looking sideways instead of upwards.

First, God is not composed of parts. Everything in God IS God.

Second, since we are not on the same level of existence as God, we must qualify everything we say about Him with a reminder that we speak "according to our way of thinking". Our way of thinking, like every other action we perform, is conditioned by our way of being. We are, we exist. Don't ever get called the "Great I am". You would be somewhat above yourself. You would be God. His perfect definition, provided by Himself is: "I am Who am!" You and I HAVE being. A part share has been given to us. It need not have been. God *has* to be. He IS being.

Now our Prince Theologian, Aquinas, fastens on an undeniable cosmic datum—the element of order, design. Order, both the making of it and the perception of it, can be the work only of intelligence. Cosmic order only of Supreme Intelligence, God. In God's mind, therefore, before creation the design is present in every detail. That design, pre-vision and pro-vision, is God's Providence.

Then what about disorders? They occur at every level of creation: floods, earthquakes, volcanic eruptions at the inanimate level; blight, bad harvests at the vegetable; tzetze flies, predators at the animal; and at the human, we are still raiding the Greek vocabulary for names to describe what can go wrong in our bodies. All that is in the physical. But what about the moral order? Every phenomenon previously mentioned has its counterpart in the human conscience but uglier and more sinister for our peace.

Should not a Supreme Being, infinite in all perfection, have created a perfect universe? In fact He did, but relatively. The universe perfectly responds to the degree of glory He sought in creating it. There is no discrepancy between the design in his mind, His Providence, and what has come into being. But clearly it is not the most perfect of all possible worlds. God was under no more constraint to produce that than he was to create at all. The "liberrimo consilio" of Vatican I is vital.* It was not to increase His goodness but to manifest and communicate it to us that He *"with the utmost freedom"* decided to create.

God and his universe no more add up together than the Queen and her portrait make two Queens. They are in different orders of reality. What is gained by the portrait is, however, not to be despised, namely, clear knowledge, and (we hope) praise. Clear knowledge and praise, in the strict theological definition, are Glory.

God is his own artist. His self-portrait reveals just so much of his goodness as He freely determines. Both knowledge and praise are His free gift. We, too, are free to accept or reject it. Does it sound selfish to say of Him: He, God, created for his own glory? Scripture is even more forthright. "God made all things for himself" (Proverbs 16, 4 cf. Isaiah 43, 7.)

But though God is not constrained to produce the highest results in his handiwork, He is constrained to act always from the highest motive. There is none higher than Himself. It so happens, must happen, that nothing could be better for us. This is most clear at the apex of His design, the final provision of his Providence, the Beatific Vision. There precisely, in the face to face sight of God as He is,

* Sess. III 24.4.1870; Dz. 1783; 13th Ed. 1920

comes God's greatest glory—the clearest knowledge of His goodness with the resultant greatest possible praise. That precisely coincides with the highest possible degree of human or angelic happiness. "Eye has not seen, nor ear heard what things God has prepared for those who love Him." (1 Cor. 2, 9)

*"Elevamini portae aeternales!"** Our own happiness grows as the gates of mind and heart open on God. Our joy grows as He reveals— what? Only Himself. Nothing can take his place! His greatest thinker Aquinas (whose ABC for beginners I have gauchely sought to paraphrase) gave the perfect theological answer to His Lord's question:

"You have written well of Me, Thomas—what would you have in return?"

"None but Yourself, Lord!"

There could be nothing greater.

So to return to the problem of premature recall of those who could do so much for us here. And to sharpen the point—the recall even of babes from their uncomprehending parents.

We know that a catastrophe overtook our human family from the beginning. We might all of us be still in a Garden of Delights. God might have walked with all of us there in the cool of the evening. But that only shifts the problem back to the beginning. Adam, without God's co-operation, could not have made the fatal choice. God foresaw it? His providence covered it as surely as it covers all that follows from it? Why then did He not prevent it? Surely if He did not, either He could not, and that is the end of His universal mastery of creation. Along with us, He is "up against it" and Cicero, Abelard and Company (including Spike Milligan) are right. Or God Himself willed it. He would then cease to be our Abba, Father. We are forced to the unforgiveable sin of blaspheming the Holy Spirit who inwardly teaches us to say just that.

Why should we ever be tempted to conclude that God's bountiful Providence involves Him in willing the abuse of it? He has shared free will with us. Ours to choose good or evil. He can turn hearts this way or that. But must He always turn them one way? What then remains of His fine gift of free will? This is what He wills, a supreme manifestation of His glory which coincides (as always) with the ennoblement of His creature. We are not marionettes. We are free! We really are made in His image and likeness.

Yet He has not abdicated. The too subtle Abelard got it quite wrong. God allows us the choice of evil. He foresees it and continues His mastery. His foresight does range from end to end mightily, disposing all things sweetly—not indeed for the production of the best of all worlds, but in shaping the world which perfectly corresponds with His design for the degree of clear knowledge and praise He has chosen to offer us.

* "Lift high eternal gates!" Psalm 24(23), 7.

What of the other evils outside of our human control? The earthquakes, the bad harvests, the starvation? Surely He could have chosen to create a better regulated universe?

Yes, of course! Leave out all the predators? No lions, tigers, bears, lynxes. That might not have pleased all of us. I think Wild Life Associations might have something to say about the balance of Nature. Perhaps the Weather Men might demur at eliminating storms and floods for the same reason. Do we know enough to want any part of creation cancelled? We don't seem to be able to save the assets we know are vital to us: pure air, clean rivers and seas, and so on.

We have already agreed that the world is not the best possible. What needs a final emphasis is the universal responsibility God has for every part of it. If he were Lord only of lambs he would have to starve all the foxes. But He is Lord of foxes, too. The whole of creation falls within his Providence.

We do better marvelling with the Psalmist at the splendour of His universal Providence than nursing resentment at the inevitable subordination, in a highly complex system, of certain elements to others for the good of the whole.

CHAPTER VI

Journey's End in a Patio

IT IS time to resume our seats on the 20 hours Rapide from Gare Quay d'Orsay, September 1927.

Our seats? In fact I spent most of the night standing in the corridor. It was well worth it with C. C. Martindale standing by me. What a night! As we got deeper into France, his yellowing bald head went out of the window to listen to nightingales. "They sing so beautifully in the Midi" he recollected from his Tertian Year. But what chance had they against the bucketing carriage-wheels?

C. C. Martindale was a boyhood hero. I treasured a postcard written in response to a fatuous letter I had once sent him. He had also included Upholland in his whirlwind promotion of the two young Jesuit Saints canonised by Pius XI. It was one of seven whistle-stops that day. We talked English Catholic novels. I was avidly reading Compton McKenzie and Maurice Baring. You couldn't mention one he had not read and constructed theories about, Baring's ladies with grey eyes, for instance. He had written to the author about his particular syndrome. I forget what it was. The author acknowledged it. He had never noticed it!

I quoted to him the verses in his biography of Father Charles Plater at the head of the chapter on ordination to the priesthood. My room-mate in that last year at Upholland raved about them. C. C. Martindale was delighted and with good reason. The name they appeared over was one of his pseudonyms.

We got to Irun in nice time to miss the morning Rapido for the South. The next train left in mid-afternoon and would reach Valladolid at 1.30 a.m. It was a slow "Tranvia". So we drifted about the station until Passport Control called us in for a courteous check. Several policemen were present. Father Martindale whispered in my ear: "Stand between me and the one with the prominent teeth. He makes me nervous." Was he serious? One had heard of his almost sleepless industry and need of stimulants. His Jesuit colleagues will judge better than I.

He was no feckless dreamer. It was he who shepherded us an hour later into the Fonda. There he had a table for four, covers already laid and wine in place. It was my introduction to the genial stack of plates before each diner, five of them, I remember. A magnificent meal "by courtesy of Almighty God", as the little girl said, and C. C. Martindale!

Three Spaniards shared our compartment on the Tranvia.

Martindale chatted with them from the outset in superb, animated French. He was soon on a first name basis. One was Henri. "What's the Spanish for Henri?" "Enrique". Martindale pronounced himself an ass for forgetting. He had just finished a cigarette (the same "Golden" brand dear Canon Turner smoked) when Enrique handed him a Spanish replacement, neatly rolled out of its coarse container into rice-paper. Once it was lit and puffed, we witnessed a lightning example of Martindale's resourcefulness. With a commanding gesture he drew the Spaniards' attention to a feature of the landscape on their side of the compartment, flung the cigarette through his window and lit one of his own before they turned back to converse.

A grinding of brakes! Voices in the night: "BYADOLITH". Sure enough, it was Valladolid and 1.30 a.m. as we came to our feet. The College Rector, Canon Edwin Henson was there, cassocked, cloaked and hatted á la espagnole, with a bustling welcome. We mounted the Station omnibus from the step at the back. With a crack of the whip the tumbril rumbled into the night. "A la derecha!"* bawled the Rector. I was to know that commanding voice for twelve out of the next fifteen years. This time, as I realised later, it meant our journey and fare was half what it would have been had we gone to the left instead of the right.

Twenty minutes later, quieter but equally final, the Voice squelched Jim McCarthy. We were now seated in the Professors' dining-room round a decanter of yellow wine and a flat loaf of incredibly white Spanish pan. Consulting his watch in a rather marked manner, Jim announced he would not partake since he would be going to Holy Communion that morning.

"You won't", the Voice affirmed, lisping slightly. "You'll drink a glass of wine and eat some bread." He did.

In fact we only surfaced for the late High Mass. It was Sunday. The same evening Father Martindale's retreat began. We were incommunicados for the week.

Why did it get me so down in the mouth? A dozen crack preachers from England gave retreats in my time—Grimley, Arendzen, Knox and others. I doubt whether any of them knew how to speak to young men as C. C. Martindale did. Was it the sudden plunge into silence? Yet that was preceded by an afternoon at Top Ribera, a College property on the River Pisuerga and we swam. There was no problem in acclimatising with one's fellow-students. Twenty-one of the forty-two were from Lancashire. Or was it the physical atmosphere of the house—a strange blend of olive-oil and Spanish tobacco smoke, at the unaccustomed altitude of six hundred or so metres?

On an afternoon midway in the retreat I went into the patio for a furious walk, very close to deciding to pack up and go home.

Blessings upon all Patios and Quads Collegiate, Palatine, or humbly domestic! "Sweet especial places" safe from roaring traffic,

* "To the right."

polluted air—safe for minds to think, lips to converse, feet to pace with due respect for our almost angelic dignity! Why didn't Horace give the Patio of his Sabine Farm the same exquisite treatment he gave to his beloved Bandusian Fountain? (I think Latin Farms all had a Patio.)

I've read and re-read R. A. K. Mason's quirky translation of *"O Fons Bandusiae"*. In the same mood and somewhat on the same model (though far short of Mason's neatly concealed art) here is my effort:

The Patio of the English College
VALLADOLID

My darling mignon Patio
   For thee no Ichabods!
Whatever be the fate of
   Those famous College Quads.
For thee I fondly bond these
   Few dactyls, trochees, spondees
In hope of saying daintily: "How good it was to know Thee!"
And after fifty-seven years: "How very much I owe Thee!"

Most sweet to me of Patios!
   Eschew all airs and graces.
You only looked your best, dear,
   With spring on Winter's traces.
O then the sweet aroma
   (Soon quenched by Castille's summer)
Of quince and lilac blossom
And the shapely pinnacled bloom sprung from the Yucca's bosom
Once only in each quinquennial, beauty so rare and awesome!

No more than a cricket-pitch square,
   At your midmost under the chestnuts
   (Deny it if you dare!)
An ugly old pump protruded
   And fatally, alas, precluded
All hope of a prize but the booby at the Concours d'Elegance
For Quadrangles in England, Portugal, Spain or France.

But let me, I beg, pert Patio
   All envy fast forestall!
Laurels are not thy line, dear!
   Too soon they shrivel and fall.
From thy soil sprang a timeless briar
   Impervious to dungeon, sword and fire:
Once glimpsed in thy corner-casement a single rose of thine
Drove blood back to a coward's heart from my County Palatine!

That corner casement gave onto the passage from the front door to the Professors' corridor. Through it you looked straight at a grim portrait. Out of the corner of your eye you could see the "oak" sealing a professor's suite. (Nine years later it would be mine.)

George Borrow in *The Bible in Spain* recalls his visit to the College about 1850. He needed nerve to chance it, given the frankly proselytising mission he was on. He notes the College "with true English exclusiveness is surrounded by a high wall". True of the bounds only, and then not to keep people out, but to keep footballs and raquets balls in.

He was taken aback by the portraits in the corridors of former students who returned as priests to England and were hanged, drawn and quartered. Half a dozen of them were canonised by Pope Paul VI in 1970. It was all too much for George who was prompted to grim reflections on the invasion of England by these "pale grimalkins" skulking from the light of the Gospel. My namesake, Blessed Thomas Holland, along with the others, wears the martyrs' livery, a rope round his neck, a knife in his midriff. There is reason to believe the seventeenth century artist produced authentic likenesses in some cases. A legend in Spanish at the bottom of each canvas records the martyrdom in oddly abbreviated black lettering. My namesake's, the one glimpsed through the corner window, runs (near enough): "Ven. Thomas Holland . . . natural de Lancashire en Inglaterra . . . murió por la fe Catolica 12 diciembre 1641 a Tyburn siendo ahorcado, destripado, y hecho quartos." I had never in my nineteen years come across any other of my name. That glance through the window stopped me in my tracks. With the Spanish and Latin I already had and a guess or two at the abbreviations, the message went home, whole and entire. There was no coward's way out—only the way of the "pale grimalkins"—now no longer heroic, hard, short and supremely glorious.

In the next six years I came to know one Rector, two Vice-Rectors, two Priest Repetitori and about one hundred fellow-students; one Señora housekeeper (Esperanza) and a dozen housemaids, one butler (Felix with forty years service) and half a dozen knife-boys. All of them within the house though not all at the same time.

But I have left out one of the household. Strangely, that seems often to have happened to him though we all loved him: Don Justo Miguel del Campo, priest, convent-chaplain, one-time journalist, our Spanish tutor and the Rector's wise 'corregidor' on all matters pertaining to Spanish protocol, ecclesiastical, civil and social.

He was in his late forties in 1927, shy, never strong I think, grey-haired and constantly subject to bilious attacks. I fear our outrageous conduct in class did nothing to alleviate that condition. He must have been heartily sick of us. Yet to our shame he was supremely a gentleman, indeed an hidalgo (son of "something"), I stood by him once at his family tomb. "Buena gente" ("Good folk") he murmured and added: "I can't remember a single day in my life when we did not say the Rosary."

Later, when I was a professor we used to play "tresillo"along with the then Vice-Rector, Edgar Hardwick. One learned a totally new dimension of Old Castillian living and thinking. It was of the Faith—of Europe, in the sense of that famous (ridiculed) phrase of Belloc's: "The Faith is Europe: Europe is the Faith."

I was in India when I heard of Don Justo's death. He had moved from the English College to die in a Spanish home. He gave me the supreme accolade. He said he remembered me as "the Ingles who knew me best". No credit to me! If, after twelve years, man and boy, I had not come to know him and his loyalty to a great Catholic heritage, I should have been, in his own phrase, "Un payaso"—a clown!

CHAPTER VII

Pictures tell Stories

THE College of St. Alban, Valladolid, began in 1589. Was Father Robert Parsons S.J., the founder? Our young and vigorous Rector would have none of it.

At that time a Jesuit historian was understood to be working on a definitive Life of Parsons. That was sixty years ago.

There is no doubt (though our Rector might challenge this) that the College, however it was founded, owed a considerable debt to Parsons' shrewd diplomacy at the Spanish Court. Philip II was born in Valladolid. It remained his favourite residence until the Escorial was ready to receive him. (Yes, little College Patio, it was beside you in our still unroofed refectory, that the son of Emperor Charles V and brother of the hero of Lepanto, sat to hear Psalm 71 recited by our students in many languages. Were your white roses all turned pink by the King's acid comment on those who had failed to get their text "by heart"?)

It was Parsons who turned down the prestigious offer to the College of a Castle in Spain—Coca Castle, some miles to the east of Medina del Campo. In 1938, when I biked there, you could, at your peril, climb all over the gaping ruins, and dream of the vanished outlines of a palace in sunset stone.* Rightly Parsons saw our need to be in the City. Where otherwise find regular alms and lectures in the sacred sciences? That decision alone placed us in Parsons' debt for the next four hundred years—and beyond.

He knew well our first "grimalkin" to die for the Faith, Father Henry Walpole, S.J., one of the Forty canonised by Pope Paul on 28 October 1970. Let me briefly digress to relive the moment in that canonisation ceremony when a single treble voice (or so it seemed) soared into the dome with: "Nisi gramen frumenti . . . " ("Unless the grain of wheat falls into the ground and dies, it remains a single grain." John 12, 24).

Henry Walpole, English to the backbone, could claim to be a European, as all Englishmen could spiritually, before England was cut off from the Continent by the royal peasouper which fogged up our Faith. But broadening Walpole's English background (Norwich Grammar School, Peterhouse Cambridge, Gray's Inn) came studies

* Recently I was assured Coca Castle has been restored to its pristine, pink, fairyland splendour.

in Rheims and Rome, an army-chaplaincy in the Netherlands, imprisonment in Flushing, teaching posts in Spain and Flanders. He served our Valladolid College as procurator for a year or two but was scarcely at ease. The example of Father Gerard S.J. was too much for him. England beckoned. His Jesuit Superiors saw in him a likely successor to the anchor man of the English Province, Father Henry Garnett.

Father Walpole landed at Flamborough Head 4 December 1592. Freedom lasted less than 24 hours. From York prison he graduated to the Tower. The full torture treatment—fourteen times hung for hours by the wrist—failed to extract information about his fellow Catholics at home or abroad. The offer of life and liberty made at his York trial likewise failed to win his acceptance of the spiritual supremacy of the Queen.

He was hanged, drawn and quartered at York 7 April 1595. Strictly illegal! He was apprehended before his statutory 24 hours' allowance for reporting his presence in the realm had passed.

Poignant indeed is this extraordinary sequel dated April 1597 from Father John Gerard: "The next morning I walked round my cell. In its dim light I found the name of the Blessed Father Henry Walpole cut with a chisel on the wall. Then close to it, I discovered his little oratory, where there had been a narrow window. It was now blocked with stonework, but on either side he had chalked the names of all the orders of Angels. At the top, above the Cherubim and Seraphim, was the name of Mary Mother of God, and then above it the name of Jesus; above that again the name of God was written in Latin, Greek and Hebrew characters. It was a great comfort to me to find myself in a place sanctified by this great and holy martyr, and in the room where he had been tortured so many times—fourteen in all, as I have heard. And as they tortured him more often than they wanted known, they did not do it in the ordinary public chamber. And I can well believe that he was tortured that number of times, since he completely lost the use of his fingers. For when he was taken back to York to be executed in the place where he was arrested on his landing in England, he wrote out with his own hand an account of a discussion he had with some ministers there. Part of it was given to me later with some meditations on the Passion of Christ which he wrote in prison before his own passion. I was hardly able to read what he had written, not only because he had written in haste but because his hand could scarcely form the letters. It looked like the writing of a schoolboy, not that of a scholar and gentleman. Yet he was a courtier before Campion's execution and while he was still a layman wrote beautiful English verses in his honour, telling how the martyr's blood had brought warmth into his life and many others' too, inspiring them to follow the more perfect way of Christ's counsels.

"So I was very glad when I found myself in Father Walpole's cell: but I was too unworthy to inherit the place where such a noble soul had suffered. The next day the warder moved me to a cell on the floor above."*

St. Henry Walpole's portrait had hung in our corridors, I suppose, 250 years before his and others plunged George Barrow into deep depression. He can't be the only one. Nor need one have a Protestant bias to feel revulsion. My peep through the Patio window lit on a dark visage, black gown, rope-round-neck, knife in breast, a gallows, and no artistic merit. The black-letter legend at the foot of the canvas revealed name and shire. That rang up the curtain on a transformation scene. My cafard went up with the curtain. Mercifully I was home and dry of self-pity.

C. C. Martindale's retreat and personal advice of course clinched everything. His main theme was the wounds of Christ's Mystical Body through which his life-blood drains away. It all sounds very sad, but how could the author of *Words of Life, The Difficult Commandment, What are Saints?* fail to exhilarate and give one heart of grace?

Slim volumes, but each taken on its own ground—has anything before or since better bridged the gap between the savant and the simple faithful? To get the measure of C. C. Martindale's scholarship and gauge the sacrifice he made in the service of the simple faithful, look only at his treatment of the Apocalypse in *A Catholic Commentary on Holy Scripture.*

* *John Gerard, The Autobiography of an Elizabethan,* trans. P. Caraman, Longmans, Green & Co. 1951, pp. 104-5

CHAPTER VIII

Seven go to School

CASSOCKED, caped, shovel-hatted and in crocodile, seven second-year philosophers left the College at 8.40 for Don Mariano's first lecture of the 1927-28 Academic Year at the Universidad Pontificia ("Pont" in student slang) in the Calle Cardinal Sanz y Fores.

Well over two thousand times we would make the journey together losing midway in the course one only of the magnificent seven, gaining none. The way led across our street, still unpaved, deeply rutted in winter, and clamorous with herds of sheep at the time of the "trashumada". You could hear their bells from far away: "a tintinabulous single thing" in Francis Thompson's phrase. I could only think of a lake. Even, now the inner ear registers the music, yes, as a "single thing"—a lake.

Our street, Calle Don Sancho was a Cañada. One of Spain's traditional staples is merino wool. Sheep had right of way on tracts of the Royal Highway marked Cañada. Watching from above was an unforgettable experience. First came the pace-makers, shepherds moving stiffly with staff and scrip, careful not to overtire the flock. Not a great difference in dress from the days of Goya or even Murillo. Then the moving patchwork quilt of a thousand merinos the width of the street, from the Intendencia Barracks to the English College "high wall". At the rear, the pack-horses, Pyrenean sheep-dogs with spiked collars and more shepherds. I once quickly rolled a cigarette and tossed it to the rearguard. It was observed. But the stiff march continued uninterrupted and the cigarette lay where it fell.

Once across the street (we have left the sheep for our own crocodile of seven) we crossed the little Plaza S. Juan unchanged since Provost Walmesley's time. We turned into the Calle de Velardes. I forbear to reveal our nickname. The street was as filthy as the word suggested. A broad crossroad led us along a convent wall which enclosed the tomb of Christopher Columbus (Cristobal Colon in Spain). His house and garden are still preserved elsewhere in the city. We turned left passing the ancient and magnificent church of La Madalena. The Medical Faculty of Valladolid University and the City Hospital faced us. 'El Estundiantil' (the Students' Bar) on our left beckoned in vain.

Mine host at the Bar greeted us as we passed. He never got us inside, alas! He informed us once that his Queen, Alfonso's consort, "had to be baptised to come to Spain". She was the ill-starred

37

Victoria of whom a recent biography records little but misery. She lived her last separated years in Lausanne. In her biographer's view, Lausanne's social life was pretty deadly.

I remember, however, a queenly gesture well calculated to enliven it. A protest against an enclosed community of nuns was being organised. It seems their bells calling to early prayer disturbed citizens whose bedtime failed to coincide with that of the nuns. Victoria had a sense of tradition. "They have rung those bells", she proclaimed, "for centuries before those now out to silence them came to live in this city." I wonder whether that silenced the protestors?

Once past the City Hospital (staffed by nuns) we turned into Calle Cardinal Sans y Fores and came to the high gates of the "Pont" (Universidad Pontificia). The gates peaked in a metal shield bearing the letters U.P. I remember one of the first year philosophers perilously climbing the gate with a lump of chalk. Above U.P. he scrawled a number, 30.

The Scots' College in 1927 had a likely group of first year philosphers but none for our second year. We ingleses alone entered Don Mariano's hall. The twelve Spaniards occupied the wall bench on the Professor's right, we on the left.

I came out of the inaugural lecture somewhat depressed. My classmates, with a year's advantage over me, had overplayed the difference of Spanish pronunciation of Latin from ours. On emerging I grimly remarked to a companion: "Scarcely a Latin word came through to me." "You fool", he said, "he was speaking Spanish. They always do at the Inaugural."

Old Don Mariano wisely adopted the Socratic teaching method. From a little black book he extracted a name. If it was yours, you were "up" for the duration. Deft questions elicited how far you had prepared the subject of the day. The nearest Don Mariano ever got to my name was, "Jollanth". The first time he used it he called me to deal with the philosophy of "Creatio ex nihilo".* Did it involve anything repugnant to reason? For a laugh, like a fool, I used the English 'varsity' pronunciation—w's instead of v's. The row of Spaniards facing us rocked on their bench. Felix Ramirez Conde, petit, dark, oval-faced—straight out of El Greco's "Burial of the Conde de Orgaz" (as I tried to tell him afterwards) simply sparkled with irrepressible mirth. After all, it was only tit-for-tat! Where I said "inwolwat", they all said "inbolbat". Spaniards cannot do otherwise!

We had one other lecturer that year, Don Juan del Valle. Alongside Don Mariano's Cosmology he dispensed Physics. His laboratory was equipped with instruments of all kinds. Exhibit No. 1 was his "Maquina Wimshurst". What it did, I fear, is now beyond recall. It was said that one of Don Juan's earlier lecture programmes excluded aerodynamics and double-decker buses as physical impossibilities. Certainly his science was of an earlier vintage but

*Creation from nothing.

38

scarcely as old as that. But I would not have changed him for all the Galileos in history. He taught me something far more precious. A simple instance will suffice. We treated his subject largely as a joke but it went far beyond that on this occasion. He had in his hands a long glass tube. No word escaped him but suddenly the instrument snapped. It was one of his favourites. He bent over the fragments for a few moments and rose to say: "God forgive me for failing to control myself". Was it a subtle way of saying: "What cads you are!" It would have been the whole truth. But Don Juan del Valle was without guile. He meant what he said and no more.

In one of his classes it fell to my neighbour, 'Flan', to discourse on the electrolysis of water. I got ready to prompt him. He managed copper-filings off his own bat, and stuck there. "Zinc!" I whispered as Don Juan waited. A longer pause. I hissed "ZINC!" Flan rounded on me, "I *am* thinking, you ass!" Z in Spanish is pronounced TH. Don Juan later became a Canon of the Cathedral designed by Philip II's architect Herrera but never finished. We genuinely shared the joy. Generations of English students might claim to have contributed to form that mellow forbearance which made him beloved of everyone. Somehow he always looked different, though in no way departing from the regulation clerical dress. His cuffs were whiter, his cassock, manteo and hat more carefully brushed, and peace was in his face.

Don Juan del Valle was parish priest of San Salvador in the heart of the city. His present successor is Felix Ramirez Conde, my classmate "straight out of the Burial of the Conde de Orgaz". His jet black hair is slightly grizzled. Otherwise, there is no change! He is of all our contemporaries almost the only one with whom some kind of contact continued. Three years after we were both ordained, I returned to Spain to find him by chance in the Village of Boecillo. The Scots' Country House, where they grow such a splendid clarete, is near-by. It happened to be the feast of St. Agatha, patroness of Young Wives. These were prancing round the church square, levying alms to pay their hired piper and other festive expenses. A priest emerged from the rectory, angelic oval face wreathed in smiles—it was Felix. I met his mother Dorotea who died fairly recently aged one hundred, and Felisa, his sister. It was the custom then in Spain to take the name of the saint on whose feastday you were born. But what happened with twins of the same sex? Some years later, I rediscovered Felix. He was Arch-priest of Portillo where our college once had a country house and also produced an excellent wine. Portillo crowns a steep hill. The only source of water was a well of incredible depth. No wonder our country house moved elsewhere. Felix's predecessor, the powerful Don Benito, was a close friend of our Rector.

In December 1985 I returned to the College to celebrate a thanksgiving Mass on the twenty-fifth anniversary of my episcopal ordination, December 21st, formerly the feast of St. Thomas,

Apostle. It so happened that professors and students all left at 3 a.m. that morning for their group-ticket flight from Madrid to England, booked well in advance of my arrival. Seven of my 1927 classmates, all like myself retired after fifty years in the ministry, rallied to concelebrate with me before the shrine of Our Lady Vulnerata. We dined together at Laguna and drank the sound and simple wines we all knew from our youth.

CHAPTER IX

Mitres Three!

I SHOULD say more about the Rector. He took over at the age of thirty-two in 1924, and at once ran into trouble over his appointment. Protocol required the choice of rector by the Bishops in England to be endorsed by the King of Spain. The omission of this perhaps less-than-Right but more-than-Courtesy, meant Edwin Henson's withdrawal from Spain. He returned, but seven years passed before the King regularised his position.

That must have been one of Alfonso XIII's last audiences. It was February 1931. Elections in the cities produced a strong anti-monarchial vote though on the following Sunday the country returns were overwhelmingly pro-monarchy. But the King had had enough and boarded a British warship.

On the edge of tragedy, however, there was light relief. Alfonso courteously pulled up a chair for Henson and the back came off in his hand. This was in the Pardo palace.

I believe he told the Rector he had made him wait for so long for recognition because the Church was elsewhere eroding the rights of the Spanish Crown. Hadn't they appointed bishops in Ceuta and Melilla without consulting him? In view of what was to happen in a few days, however, his declared intention to preserve the rights of his ancestors was not without irony nor perhaps pathos.

Edwin Henson was rector of our Spanish College for thirty seven years—about five times as long as rectors today in any of our colleges. His best years were the early 'wind of change' when he blew cobwebs out of the library, the liturgy, the archives, the diet, the country house, and doubled our numbers. Typically he turned down the British Government's offer to evacuate us at the outbreak of the Spanish Civil War. The chance came for him to play an inconspicuous but useful role in the service of truth with a daily broadcast from Spain to England.

Truth was a constant casualty throughout those three violent years. I remember saying rather sententiously about the news we got from England: "If there's any compensation in being here on the spot, it's having one's eyes opened to the tripe that passes for truth." The experience, I think, comes best in early manhood though the risk is there of life-long cynicism.

Our three beaks—Henson, Petit and Healy—all got mitres in due course: Henson as a Protonotary Apostolic, Petit as Bishop of Menevia, Tim Healy in Gibraltar.

John Petit was Vice-Rector and ran the ship as Henson's first lieutenant. Not an easy task under an explosive autocrat. On the whole we admired but scarcely warmed to him. His clipped southern accent grated on our broad Lancashire sensibility. He could be devastating: he could say, for instance "There's a yellow streak running right through you, Holland!" But he had guts. Realising our year had "got across' with him, he suddenly arranged in mid-winter a whole day with us at the shuttered Country House. Lashings of food and drink and a huge fire in the kitchen provided the decor for several hours of eye-ball confrontation. The sight of "the other side" was a salutary, mutual experience. I recommend it to all vice-rectors and prefects of discipline, though in these palsy-walsy, egalitarian days, aren't we all supposed to be "see-throughable" all the time?

At the very end of the first session of Vatical II John Petit had a massive heart-attack and was rushed into hospital. I followed and anointed him, helped, I remember, by a young chaplain who clearly thought I had never done it before. The prognosis was bad. I stayed on in Rome until he was in better trim.

"Tom", he said (we were now on first name terms!). "My diocese is a poor one. Don't fly me back. Bury me in Rome. We are all at home here."

He was still recumbent months later when I returned to Rome for a meeting of the Unity Secretariate. I smuggled in a couple of bottles of white wine. I suppose I should have had more sense? Anyway, he lived another eleven years. About half-way we were side by side in the stalls at Westminster during sung Mass. His elbow thumped my ribs.

"Will you bury me, Tom?"

"So long as you bury me if I go first."

He snorted and resumed his devotions.

Bury him, I did, at Pantasaph and at his requiem I read his last statement forbidding any panegyric and calling upon his people, as a last favour, to promote Catholic Schools against all odds. This was precisely what he had done for twenty-six years as their bishop. Guts to the end!

Tim Healy came up from Gibraltar to be one of my co-consecrators. He was my confessor as a student for the three years he remained for his degree in Canon Law. He was a superb violinist and orchestral leader, but not so good at alloting instruments to new-comers. I got the drums. Shortly before the Christmas concerts I had to miss a rehearsal and a former drummer stood in. Father Healy was not a man to beat about the bush. "Dutchy", he said, "the drums were so much better last night. You know what I mean?" I did exactly and was given the harmonium with which to fill in parts for which we had no instruments.

One of the most robust looking men, Bishop Healy died prematurely. His successor and former secretary, Bishop Rapallo, spoke to me once of that fatal illness, finishing, not without tears: "I loved him."

It would be absurd to say that I would not have missed a moment of my twelve Spanish years in peace and war. There were many bad ones due to my own folly for which I blush, not so many for which I have to feel aggrieved towards others. All in all, rough and smooth together, I do honestly thank God for Spain. There was little enough peace there from the outset. The dictatorship of Primo de Ribera was chafing a lot of stiff necks when I arrived. Plots and Pronunciamientos were in the air.

I remember a pathetic revolution led by a young officer in the garrison town of Jaca under the Pyrennees. His defence at the court martial contained such phrases as: "An officer of Spain can have no other motive but The Ideal." Sheer Lyricism! They shot him even so. Primo himself got the assassin's bullet in Paris. It was the lifting of the sluices on a turbulent flood which swept out the King and mounted giddily towards lawlessness of every kind including the political murder of Calvo Sotela, which sparked off the Civil War in July 1936.

Still I had experienced the old Spain, Catholic, strong in loyalties, courteous, maddeningly inefficient! Horsemen still swept through the city streets in colourful blankets, reckless of the then infrequent internal-combustion machine. In fact the Rector's car was one of the earliest. He soon gave it away to one of his farmers.

My first Holy Thursday, 1928, we visited thirty-seven altars of repose in under two hours in a city no bigger than my native Southport. All but shank's pony traffic ceased during the Triduum of the Lord's death (Thursday, Friday and Saturday morning of Holy Week).

Children ran to us as we made our way to the 'Pont' begging "Una estampita!", a Holy Picture. They kissed priests' hands and even our own un-consecrated hands. A rather bitter-sweet melody often accompanied us on our way. Children chanted it at the French during the Peninsular War:

"Los Franceses comen cacueses
Agua fresca y melocoton."

"The French (in our case, English)
guzzle peanuts, cold water and peaches."

On May 3rd, feast of the Holy Cross when in all towns and villages the Spaniards rose against the French, the children demanded "una elemosnita" (a little alms) brandishing their tiny wooden crosses.

There were more solemn events: the Holy Week processions when the polychrome statues of the 17th century Valladolid wood-carvers were carried. Perhaps even more endearing and entrancing was the procession in the dark on September 8th, a river of lamplight and black mantillas. Indoors, the Cathedral supplied a solemn and splendid background to the life of the city: full Divine

Office daily, great festival High Masses when the Canons paid homage to their Archbishop trailing their choir cloaks. To one who had known no other instruments in church but organs and harmoniums, Saint Cecilia's Day 1927 was a surprising ear-opener. We sang a Perosi Mass under the baton of Maestro Blanco to an orchestral accompaniment. A brass band played the National Anthem at the consecration. Paolino, one of the Spaniards in our year, had the sweetest silver-tenor voice I have ever heard 'uncanned'. His "Tu es Petrus" (again Perosi) rippled through the gaunt, grey Cathedral.

But in the streets and among the children I sensed the change as the years passed. Something was simmering, a strange alien frenzy. One learned that the once demure and smiling Lorenza, a girl living next door to us, was a leading Communist. She had graduated as the local Pasionaria. Governmental crises led to violent eruptions. Churches and convents were burned. "Casas del Pueblo" (Communist Headquarters) were built. The rumours ran they were arsenals. As usual Barcelona led the riot list.

The Spanish Civil War began. I had been in Rome at the Gregorian University for the three years leading up to the outbreak. Since I was to return to Spain, I despatched my trunk via Genoa and Barcelona with Thomas Cook and Sons. It arrived in Barcelona for the first air-raid on the docks there and has never been heard of since.

Cooks apologetically pointed out that the insurance policy did not cover loss in war. Later, under some pressure from my younger brother who had replaced me in Rome, they yielded so far as a £5 grant *ex gratia*. The trunk contained three years of student's notes, all my thesis material and books. It also contained a Roman cloak self-designed in the style of a Sherlock Holmes ulster, greatly admired by a fellow Beda student renowned for sartorial elegance. Looking back, I can see some kind of comeuppance was due!

I have done my old College scant justice. But there are another six years to come after Rome. George Barrow was right—we were an "exclusive" English community. Our contact with Spaniards ceased at the "Pont" except, of course, for those who served us in the College itself, and for occasional visitors.

May I first salute our servants: Felix and his forty "Vulneratas" He counted the years by the feasts of Our Lady Vulnerata; Señora Esperanza, housekeeper for perhaps as many years but with interstices; Marcelina, seamstress, and saint; the long line of maids and boys whose names if recited in order would rival any sung page of the old Roman Martyrology.

A salute then to our Professors at the Pont: Don Gregorio Alastruey, prince theologian from Aragon, later dean of the Faculty at Salamanca, a pioneer in Mariology; Don Felix Gonzales, the saintly ascetic and confessor of his fellow priests whose set features scarcely moved as his sudden flashes of humour dissolved the hall in laughter; "Bull-Pup" (I've forgotten his name) whose General Introduction to Sacred Scripture was so widely acclaimed; Don Lucio, Fundamental Theology and *De Ecclesia,* Roman trained, capable of astonishing express deliveries of faultless Latin; Don Florian (Hebrew) whom our year treated so badly be refused to sit on the Board of Examiners; Don Daniel de la Cruz (Ethics). Such was his reverence for Thomas Aquinas that he required us to get off by heart the copious quotations from the *Summa* in our text-book. And our Morals Professor Don Cipriano, the Canon Penitentiary. As a younger man with a cure of souls he never missed a day giving his people a Catechism lesson, as the Council of Trent required 400 years ago.

I recently came across letters I received from Archbishop Downey as a student in Spain. (It was he who "transplanted" me there.) More than once he states his admiration of Spain's theologians with the hope that I shall benefit his archdiocese with what I have gained from them. Alas, apart from a short curacy, parish supplies and a few missions and retreats, my only return to my roots was for holidays.

All our Colleges abroad now spend the lion's share of vacations in England. There are today, of course, good reasons for abandoning the old rule of four of your half-dozen vacations spent where you studied. The Villa (Rome), Quinta and Luz (Lisbon), Viana Casa de Campo (Valladolid) were Country Houses available for the odd break during the year and for the Long Vacations.

I certainly would not have wanted to be twenty years away without seeing England as probably Provost Walmesley was. But I give hearty thanks for the long vacations at Viana as student and professor, for all eight of them. You came to know your fellow students in a new way. Unsuspected resources of appreciation and inventiveness enriched the enjoyment of our three rivers, our games, picnics, libraries, and wine. Good Spanish wines (Rioja, Valdepeñas etc.) now circulate here at a moderate price (two to three pounds). We could fill a bota (wineskin) for pence. All wine is good drunk where it's made.

You came to know Spain and the Spaniards as you wandered on donkeys, bikes, buses and shanks' pony. Perhaps best of all there was a chance simply to sit back and drink in the long views across the pine forests and the cornfields rolling away to the flat-topped hills. Even now when I think of heaven, distractions will crowd in of a certain clump of pines above our Country House, a deck-chair, a pipe, a book and the long view to Simancas Castle nestling above the River Pisuerga.

CHAPTER X

"And so we came to Rome." (Acts 28)

"YOU are not going to Rome to bury yourself in books. Finish off your degree, if you feel you must. But it's Rome you must soak in— Rome! You will be free to do that at the Beda College under Monsignor Duchemin."

Did ever a student-priest set out with such generous briefing? And the speaker, Rector Henson, as I learned to my surprise only later, cleared the way ahead by opposing the alternative of an English University in preparation for teaching French at Upholland.

My debt to Upholland was and remains very great. Ten years later, my younger brother was sent to Cambridge and later taught French (and English) at Upholland for eleven years. Family ties, I hope, are strong enough to warrant a measure of vicarious substitution. There must have been times when Joe felt he was doing two men's work. He was, and I am grateful.

Rector Henson waved me off to Rome mid-May 1933. I arrived there October 15th. A good day for anyone from Spain, for Teresa of Avila, "undaunted daughter of desires" and "daughter of the Church" (to cap Crashaw's famous line with her dying words) then had her feast day on October 15th.

Unlike baptism, ordination is not a sacrament you receive primarily for your own benefit. The Fathers are very clear on this: *Christianus propter se, Sacerdos propter alios* (You are baptised for your own salvation. You become a priest for the salvation of others.) Precisely that service of others demands and exercises the love of Christ and never more so than when, at your priestly peak, you say Mass for the living and the dead. But there is another personal benefit in becoming a priest. Shrewd laymen can see it. The bolder ones give it you straight from the shoulder. "Thank God, Father, you became a priest. You would have been a mess as one of us."

Priesthood is unlivable without responding to the pressures it imposes on soul and body. Like most other people, I prefer to live. But how much more alive one would be with a more generous response to those pressures. My three months at the Sacred Heart certainly introduced me to the Church in Liverpool. I recognise the absurdity of paralleling this with Paul's rendez-vous at *Tres Tabernae*—though there is a three in both! My main activity (as wisely insisted on by the old Canon-in-charge and firmly enjoined by diocesan statutes) was visiting people in their homes. Certainly I found it hard. A baker's dozen of years in seminaries, then still faithful to the old *hortus conclusus* (enclosed garden) model, endowed you with a certain *esprit-de-corps* which was judged to be unobtainable without some insulation from outside influences. The extreme version was voiced (before my time) from on high in the statement: "There would be no going home at all for holidays but for the needs of the domestic staff." So highly prized was the indefinable sense of belonging together as men set apart, trained for a unique service! It went under the name of "the Ecclesiastical Spirit".

Clearly you paid the price for the treasure. In my own case, no doubt due in some measure to the nature of the beast, communication with strangers was the casualty.

I could take you now to the house (in Kensington Fields estate) where, visiting-book in hand, I raised the first door-knocker, my heart deep in my boots. Three or four young men lodged there. One of them was clearly very unwell. All were without work. None was practising his faith. That visit should have blown all the cobwebs and butterflies out of my system, their response was so heartening. It didn't. I remember prolonging an errand I had to make for the Canon at the Philomena Book shop, browsing among the shelves with an aching conscience, until there was no time left for going back on the knocker.

When one did respond to this particular call of duty, the reward continued to be exceedingly great—and manifold. Marriages to "put right", baptisms to be arranged, instructions to be provided etc., etc. Hours on the knocker spun a web of priestly duties which brought grace and joy to homes where both were in short supply.

I've hinted earlier at the dead-hand which fell on Liverpool with the Wall Street Crash and the recession of the early 'thirties. The poet, Tom Hood, could alone do justice to the "poverty, hunger and dirt" in which you ministered to the sick and dying in their homes. There were no home-helps. The people were their own social workers.

But how could they cope adequately when the bread-winners could not even find the penny-a-week for heating their C.Y.M.S. rooms? The total "take" at the Sacred Heart with its seven priests and multiple packed Masses on Sunday was seventeen pounds. Daily we doled out tickets (worth 1s 6d at a local grocer's) to a queue assembled behind us as we knelt for the post-prandial visit to the Blessed Sacrament.

We had orders from the Canon never to give more than one ticket per client, but what could you do? Even discounting the embellishments, their stories were only too firmly based on what one had seen for oneself in their homes.

One client, a man in his early forties, produced a deeply creased paper with the words: "I suppose I should have done something about this years ago." It read (in Latin) after careful un-creasing:

"I, Maurice de la Taille, chaplain to the Canadian Expeditionary Forces, have summarily instructed the bearer in the truths of the Catholic Faith, baptised him and given him Holy Communion, *imminente praelio* (on the eve of battle)." It was dated 1917. I had admired this powerful theologian for his writings on the Mass. Here was another side to his priesthood.

The famous Sunday Outdoor Collection, when priests, accompanied by a lay collector, sallied forth after the last Mass and returned from combing the district for a 2 p.m. dinner, was gruelling enough for the priest. How much more so for the people! When they saw the priest with the collector, the modest pile of coppers ready on the mantel-piece would be deftly capped with a piece of silver. Something suffered—the gas? Tomorrow's dinner? You dare not in mistaken compassion pass any door. That was for them, whatever Canon Law might say, the equivalent of ex-communication from the Church.

But it was not all so sombre. For instance there was Miss McEvoy. She gathered the human cock-sparrows off the streets into an old empty house riddled with holes inside and out. The noise, the slithering of small bodies through cavities, down banisters, round corners, in and out of windows, left circus and cinema far behind for sheer quicksilver entertainment. Neither Miss McEvoy nor the lads had a penny to bless themselves with. No doubt she would be reprimanded by any Local Authority today for exposing Youth to loss of life and limb. She was, however, in full control. The lads respected her—nay, loved her. I salute her over the years, a brilliant brave woman, and thank her for coaxing at least one sustained outburst of *joie de vivre* from a rather sad city.

And what price for this tragi-comedy? The *mise-en-scene* is Hall Lane, Saturday night, our breather in five hours' of hearing Confessions, and the noise of a brass band approaching.

It used to be said that Archbishop Whiteside, of saintly memory, and the spiritual head of the Orangemen and women in Liverpool, Mr Wise (or was it Councillor Longbottom?) had agreed in the interests of civic peace, to keep all provocative demonstrations off the streets, particularly outside their own territory. The truce was no doubt an uneasy one on both sides.

But lo! here was an Orange Band parading past a Catholic Church at the very hour on Saturday night when penitents in considerable numbers frequented the Church. It was too much for one old lady. She snatched off a shoe, plunged across Hall Lane and hammered the heel into the tail-ender of the band. He was the big-drummer and it must be recorded to his credit that the drum-beat did not falter despite the equally vigorous rain of blows on his person. Did the old lady return to the box for further penance and absolution, I wonder? I fear the penance would have been a light one . . .

Later in Rome I would do a special course in Pastoral Theology under Father Vermeersch. But neither lecturers nor their textbooks could condition the beginner for the heart-breaks or the side-splittings of the real thing: for instance, the sick person accepting the offer of Holy Communion because "it might do my breathing good"; the desperate housewives who after confession beg you for a prayer that: "The Megantic (White Star liner) comes in tonight so the old man gets a bit of work"; and the lady, at your Mass only the day before, who welcomes you as a strange priest because "You look so different in your vestibules!"

But forward! Rome awaits . . .

The College in the Via S. Nicolà da Tolentino was about to shroud itself in the silence of Retreat. Shades of my debut in Spain! The Rector had invited as director a Jesuit Father, Sam Myerscough, from Wimbledon, well remembered in later years as Rector of Holy Name, Manchester. He gave us a latter-day version of a medieval classic, Gerson's "On bringing little ones to Christ". Physically you could scarcely call us little ones. Someone had recently referred to the Beda as "An Ecclesiastical Whipsnade". Even that scarcely prepared one for the species assembled in chapel that first night.

The statutory threshold for entering the College was twenty four years. There was no ceiling. The lamps shone on rows of bowed heads—heads bald, grizzled, raven, curled, sleekly parted. The best iron-grey thatch was undoubtedly the Rector's.

Two staunch Catholic families and their fortunes came to their close in Charles Duchemin and indeed their peak. Newman's definition of a gentleman was surely made with him in mind. For once, a childlike candour hid no cunning. He was transparently good, and comely to behold. As he appeared at the end of a Beda year leaving for England, I challenge all generations of churchmen to rival his unstudied elegance. His three-quarter length "De Dom", perfectly cut and buttoned only at the collar, allowed just a sliver of purple stock to betray his rank. *"Simplex munditiis!"** Why did Horace launch that exquisite phrase in such a sleezy context?

The Rector's first lieutenant, Monsignor Joe Moss, loyally complemented his captain's broad policies with a capacity for fussy detail which he exercised under a variety of hats. We all had to bow to Joe's dedicated service of both the Rector and College. The Beda was a happy ship. Joe's intensely serious handling of his manifold duties only added to the merriment. He died within a year of his return to England as parish priest of St Mary's, Wigan.

There was one other resident professor, Dr. Cornelius Schut, from the Mill Hill Missionary Society. Beda men were unanimous in awarding him full marks for his theology lectures. As a student at the Gregorian University, "The Burgher" as he was known to his contemporaries, swept the board. So went the legend. But I heard him come down like a load of bricks on a Beda man who suggested that he was the finest Hebrew scholar of his generation. His were the days of the prince theologian Billot (Prince, too, of the Church for a time) and, though I was never present at his lectures, I am sure Dr. Schut in his long years at Mill Hill and the Beda, and Dr. Downey at Upholland, based their teaching on Billot.

*"Unstudied elegance" is the best I can do.

CHAPTER XI

The Gregorian University

NO ONE in my time at the Gregorian had quite Billot's reputation, except Father Capello in the Canon Law Faculty. Along with Capello's scholarship went the fame of sanctity. People lined the Piazza Pilotta to touch his garments. I slipped into one of his lectures. Phenomenal! He appeared to read the Code of Canon Law off the ceiling. There were over 2,000 Canons. A lift of the head and down they came word perfect as needed. Vermeersch had just vacated the chair of Moral Theology. Harry Lennerz, Filograssi, Bernard Leeming, Arnou and others lectured in Dogma. Old Van Laak was on his umpteenth voyage round the Greek and Latin Fathers.

De La Taille, whose war-time note from 1917 had turned up at the Sacred Heart, Liverpool, only the month before, had just died. I had been an ardent admirer of his theory on the Mass, *Mysterium Fidei*, since student days in Spain under the famous Professor Gregorio Alastruey. On my first attendance at the Gregorian University for the formal inauguration of the Academic Year 1933-34, the Public Orator, Father Filograssi, S.J., recording the memorabilia of the previous year, mentioned the death of Maurice de la Taille. "Whatever may be the final verdict of theologians on *Mysterium Fidei*," he said, "we may confidently hold this work to be one of the finest theological achievements of this century." I wonder how far it is remembered that his masterpiece began in the presbytery of the Sacred Heart church in Accrington? Indeed, I wonder how far his masterpiece is now remembered?

I must pause a moment to salute Harry Lennerz. His lectures were delivered with index finger following the printed lines of his book which we already had. He changed the odd word for an equivalent but, at least for me, failed to alleviate the tedium, if indeed that was his intention. Until one day drama supervened.

Harry interrupted the flow with a mild "Taceas!" ("Shut up!") addressed to someone high up on the top tier. Harry resumed, finger on page. Then suddenly and more sharply: "Aut taceas aut exeas!" ("Either shut up or get out!") Harry again resumed. But minutes later explosion! "STATIM EXEAS!" ("Get out at once!") He did. He was from a house on the Via Sistina where I used to stick any periodicals I received from Spain through the letter-box. It was a convent of Spanish *Recollects*!

Harry's capacity for work was colossal even by German standards. His only break was a couple of weeks per year on the beach at Rapallo reading English "bloods".

Bernard Leeming, I fear, was not at home in the seventy-strong community of Jesuit Professors living at the Gregorian. Who was it told me that Christmas Day only differed from other days, humanly speaking, in the provision at the refectory door of "take-away" fruit? Academically Bernard was well worth houseroom under a roof which covered more high thinking and plain living than any I had known. The most frequented Senior Common-room in this seat of learning was the Chapel.

As a fellow-townee of Bernard's from Southport, I rejoiced to hear praise of his work, *Sacramental and Ecumenical Theology* from his peers on the rostrum. Two occasions when I visited his room come to mind, perhaps because of the contrast they pose. On the first occasion his door opened to reveal Bernard closeted with a bearded oriental priest. Bernard introduced him at once in French. I mumbled my pleasure at meeting him, hand extended, in the same language. The voluminous black bulk hooted with laughter. "Don't be a fool," he said, "I'm from Blackpool". So he was—name of Wilcock, a Jesuit from the Russian College. The other occasion was minutes before Bernard was due on the rostrum. He had a telegram in his hand. His sister had just died leaving four young children. Down he went to the lecture hall. How he got through that hour tells something of his inner resources.

I should have done my thesis under Bernard. The subject (The Holy Spirit and the Anglo-Catholic Movement with special reference to the Anglo-Papalists) was very much his line of country. Had he already bowed to "Mr. Johnson's" (Mussolini's) "invitation" to "get the hell out of here"? That would explain why.

Anyway, Father Sebastian Tromp, Professor of Fundamental Theology, agreed to be my obstetrician. He ran a special course entitled the Mystical Body in the Greek Fathers. Only a dozen of us were taking it. That alone was a relief from the anonymous battalions of the main lectures, and Trompy was at large in his happiest hunting ground. Much of what I had in notes from this course appeared half a dozen years later in Pius XII's encyclical *Mystici Corporis Christi*, when in Europe all the lights had gone out and there was nothing for our comfort. St. Augustine, dying in 430 A.D. as the Vandals encircled his city of Hippo and Arians enjoyed imperial favour within it, consoled his people and himself with the same theme—the indestructible Body of Christ which is the Church.

Trompy in happy mood could sparkle. For instance, one morning snow lay on the ground and our hopes shone bright, for in the Greg. tradition, snow and lectures were incompatible. But this day the edict went forth "Docetur!"—"Lectures as usual!" Trompy smilingly intoned "NIX" (Latin for snow). "In my language", he added, "Nix means "Nihil" (nothing)—which is precisely what we've got". But

Trompy's glum moods were deadly. Time and again I returned to his room to pick up sections of the thesis I submitted for his supervision. He hadn't seen them. "Impossible, caro! Look at this lot." He pointed to the full In-tray.

Time was running out. I had to get the stuff read. There was much more to come. Luckily he was out when I deposited the next instalment on his table and topped it with a modest box of Dutch cigars. I don't know if they had anything to do with it but I got treatment from then on. What I do know is that Sebastian Tromp gave up what could have been a life-long solace when Pius XI suggested smoking was not for Jesuits. Was that one good reason why he was so crotchety when we met thirty years later at Vatican II?

At this point it may appear that contrary to the Rector's instructions I buried myself in books and scamped the major mission "to soak myself in Rome". The Rector did say, finish the degree if you feel you must. I did feel I must, for the sake of the College in Spain to which I was destined to return and for the honour of the bereaved "Pont" in Spain where I had got halfway with a theological degree and would have finished it but for the Roman decree *Deus Scientiarum Dominus* which drastically reduced the number of papal academies awarding degrees.

I had felt badly about that. After putting in extra lectures and studies from which my classmates were exempt, with the assurance that whatever was in the wind would not prevent my graduating, in the end the cupboard was only too bare.

I felt even worse when I first matriculated at the Gregorian. The Prefect of Studies, Father Filograssi, went through my scholastic record with a fine comb. In addition to the full range of theology courses, I found myself loaded with extras in Canon Law and Scripture to supply *lacunae* in the "Pont" curriculum of studies.

CHAPTER XII

Soaking in Rome and elsewhere

THAT first year in Rome did tend therefore to stretch mind over legs as did the thesis later. But by no means exclusively. Many, many mornings I was out from the Beda by 6 a.m. on my way to celebrate Mass at the basilicas and churches of Rome. At that time of day it was possible to read your breviary as you walked the relatively quiet city streets. I always boned up beforehand on the background with Chandlery's indispensible *Pilgrim Walks in Rome*.

I took out a season ticket for the Augusteo. The Rome Orchestra played under Bernardino Molinari, Leader, Principe, first cellist Chiarappa. The trio toured England on a 'bury-the-hatchet' mission after the war and were tumultuously received. I was delighted to get, among visiting conductors, Sir Henry Wood and others whose music I only knew on records.

With a companion, usually that year Cyril Copsey, a deacon from Oscott, and Joe Moss's Thursday picnic lunch, (two hardboiled eggs, *pane* and a large wedge of Gruyère) we covered the Capagna north and south of Rome, from Veii to Genazzano. At Christmas we had a week in Assisi, (eighteen lire a day all-in at the Poor Clare Convent of S. Quirico), Perugia, Todi and other places.

I must say a word about the last day of 1933, my year of Ordination. We left Perugia by train in late afternoon and were decanted at Todi station to climb up to the city in darkness. The hotel was excellent. After dinner our host accompanied us to the large double bedroom. "What about heating the beds?" we asked. "Ci penso io. Metto fuoco!" he replied. ("Leave it to me! I put fire in them!") Well!

Greatly marvelling we made our way for coffee to the Cathedral Square and the Corner Bar, despite Vermeersch's "Non licet clericis intrare in BAR!"* Were we not travellers? The place heaved with highly animated humanity, all squeezing the pips out of the last hours of the Old Year. Out from the bright lights into the dark, freezing Piazza, flanked either side by a Palace, Ghibelline left, Guelph right, outlined against the stars with the distinctive crenellations of each feuding family. At the far end of the Piazza the Cathedral faced us with a long climb up steps to the dark portico. A pull on the "baby-crusher", a push on the swing door, and we stood within rooted to the spot. From a high pulpit, in cope and mitre, the

* "A cleric is not allowed to enter Bars."

53

Bishop leaned over the congregation, raining fire and brimstone on the misdeeds of the Old Year and, with the active participation of his crozier, driving home lessons for the New.

The fury died away and lovingly the Bishop blessed us. Everyone rose happily as the organ crashed into *Te Deum Laudamus*. They sang their hearts out—in Latin. My Ordination year closed in a very grand crescendo.

On return our host again accompanied us upstairs to open the door with a proud gesture towards the beds. They had bellied towards the ceiling. We watched wide-eyed as he extracted glowing braziers from under large wooden frames. "Get in *subito*". "E Buona Notte!" Both agreed we never slept so well.

Subterranean Todi is, I believe, rich in Christian antiquities still largely unexplored. My interest, I fear, was only marginally ecclesiastical. I had long wanted to salute a city which, when in Spain we chanted the Office of Prime at 6.45 a.m., never failed to win a titter. In the Roman Martyrology, the phrase *Tuderti in Umbria* ("At Todi in Umbria") often introduced the names of martyrs of the early centuries. Unfortunately *"Tuderti"* coincides with our "Too Dirty" in Church Latin pronunciation. Thirty years later I sat near the Bishop of Todi at Vatican Council II but never attempted to tell him why I first visited his city. Italians have a phrase for mad dogs and Englishmen.

My knowledge of the inner working of the Vatican Congregations* was minimal. That, I think, says a lot about the personnel's "tenacity of the secret" for I came to know quite a lot of them: even (but only by sight) Cardinal Pacelli, Secretary of State, supreme after the Pope. We passed him frequently *passeggiando* on the Pincio. No sign of recognition was allowed. He went wholly in black, always with a sheaf of papers in hand, which, however, did not prevent his penetrating glance going through the passer-by. I, for one, shall never forget it.

Cardinal Lepicier, Prefect of the Sacred Congregation for Religious, came to the Beda every Monday to lecture on Sacred Scripture. My only contact with him was in my last year when the Rector insisted I act as Dean, despite being what was called "knife and fork Beda"†.

Poor "Leppy" had made a mistake for which he was taken to task by Pius XI, a martinet even with his Cardinals. I had to meet him the following Monday. He lay slumped in a chair on the ground floor. Gone were the days when he joked about the five flights up to his lecture room. ("I'm going to ask His Holiness for a plenary indulgence each time . . . ") Gone, too, the colour from his cheeks. The following week I said the Beda Mass of Requiem by his bier. His superb tribute to Monsignor Duchemin on St. Charles' Day at the Rector's Feastday lunch, November 4th 1933, was unforgettable.

* The ministries of Government
† Students, usually priests, attending courses outside the Beda.

Among those present that day was a Monsignor William Theodore Heard, Auditor, and already tipped to become one day Dean of the Sacred Rota, and a Cardinal. John XXIII completed the process a quarter of a century later.

A weekly visitor to the Beda came from the Black Pope's H.Q., the Casa Generalizia of the Jesuits. Promptly at 11.45 every Friday, Father Joe Welsby began his spiritual conference, always finishing as the clock struck 12 noon for the Angelus after which we filed into lunch. There was a gemlike quality about the man and his words. In conference or confession they were clear, spare, hard, but never harsh.

Mention of the miraculous draught of fishes (153 in number) in one of his talks, drew from him a rare personal aside: "Today I am giving my 153rd Beda Conference!" A Beda wit later remarked on the miracle of his being still alive after 153 Beda fish-dinners. He himself once, not in conference, spoke of never having had a day's illness, adding: "The Lord probably has a rod in pickle for me." In fact He had. Cancer killed him within a few months. His skin drew tighter though how that was possible again bordered on the miraculous. Monsignor Smith's magnificent tribute in the *Venerabile* magazine, adopted as the official Obit for the English Province, quoted someone as saying: "He seemed to be made of mortification."

He soldiered on during the hot summer, walking from the Villa Rufinella to hear Confessions at Palazolla, a distance of about eight kilometres. In him the Father General Ledochowski had a saint to accompany a saint, and if I seem to be guilty of uncanonical anticipation, let me recall what Father Welsby himself once said of Archbishop Whiteside of Liverpool: "He would have been canonised by now (1936) had he been an Archbishop in Italy."

CHAPTER XIII

The Rock

IF ANYTHING could win credulity for the disputed, or discredited, "Prophecies of St. Malachy" it is surely the mystical titles therein allotted to recent popes. Pius XI's *Fides Intrepida"** was every bit as just as Pius X's *"Ignis Ardens"*.†

Let Father Welsby, a chip off the rock of Lancashire Martyrs, tell of his encounter with the Rock which is Peter, the sole occasion, he said, when he spoke to Pius XI.

"It was mid-morning when Father General Ledochowski told me the Vatican had just 'phoned. The Pope wanted to see me! I at once reached for my hat and made for the door. Father General with greater experience in these things, gently guided me to the refectory and made me take a bowl of soup.

"It was, however, gone three o'clock when the Pope appeared. Our conversation was:

"Lei Welsby?" ("Are you Welsby?")

"Si, Santità!" ("Yes, Holiness!")

"Parla Tedesco?" ("Do you speak German?")

"No, Santità!" ("No, Holiness!")

"That was all, no less, no more, four words each, and he was gone! I wonder where and what my future might have been? I had earlier resolved to learn German only if I were appointed to teach Scripture."

Could there be a link here with the brilliant Father d'Herbigny, S.J., a former Roman Professor, whose treatise on the Church impressed me almost as much as Cardinal Journet's *Church of the Word Incarnate* . . .? Again there was a sudden call, followed in Father d'Herbigny's case by ordination as a bishop and an underground mission in Russia.

My first sight of any Pope was at the canonisation of St. Bernadette, December 8th 1933. We dashed across Rome from the old Beda to arrive bedraggled, but early enough as we thought. The Basilica was crowded to the doors. Somehow we inserted ourselves mid-way up the middle near the route of the papal procession. My parents had brought back from the Canonisation of the Little Flower in 1925 a composite ollograph entitled in block letters: "The imposing pontifical Cortege in the Basilica of St. Peter's Rome." The

*Fearless Faith †Burning Fire

picture was twice as long as the title, mounted on wood and sealed in shiny transparent material.

There before my very eyes was the same Holy Father aloft in the Sedia Gestatoria preceded, flanked and followed by *"L'Imponente Corteo"*. The vivid picture came alive in three dimensions and with it centuries of Vatican history. Triumphalism? Fifty years ago, I think the main emotion might have been rather joyful gratitude for the timeless permanence of the Rock (Matthew 16, 18), so vividly dramatised before our eyes. In fact, as the Pope passed and the vivas increased, I found myself muttering over and over again: "The Fisherman! The Fisherman!" A rather strange way of expressing victory, especially when accompanied with tears. Anyway, what's wrong with glorying in Our Lord's victory over the Gates of Hell or over the last enemy, Death? His Church is committed to the celebration of Victory and has never kept quiet about it in the Liturgy.

One ceremony, I am sure, Popes were glad to be rid of. With a certain reservation I'm glad I made it: the kissing of the feet. Candlemas 1936 as usual assembled representatives of Parishes, Religious Orders, Pontifical Colleges etc. at the Vatican. Monsignor Duchemin was accompanied by his dean and sacristan. Improvidently I had remedied the loss of the last rear button on my nether garment with a safety-pin. We advanced three abreast. Monsignor handed the decorated candle to be touched by the Pope, knelt and kissed the cross on his slipper. My turn to lean far over from the right to do the same. At the peak moment there was an audible 'ping'. It had to happen, but thanks be to God, the retreat took us in single file huddled against the wall to make room for those advancing three abreast.

Did His Holiness guess? If so, I can only hope he reacted as he did with the rubrical cage of birds presented at one of his many canonisations. For once I was only yards away from the throne under the Gloria, seated with the basilica canons. The birds began singing their heads off as they approached the Pope. This cannot be rubrical because Monsignor Respighi, ceremoniarius-in-chief, showed unmistakable signs of annoyance.

Pius, so often wearing the set face of the warrior, dissolved in smiles and wagged his finger at the cage. I can time it. It was 12 noon and the gun on the Gianicolo went bang. My neighbouring canon who had favoured me with a running commentary rose. "Mezzogiorno!" he said taking my hand: "spaghetti!". Was this what Rector Henson meant by "soaking Rome"?

CHAPTER XIV

Roma Ave atque Vale!

I HAD completed Father Filograssi's daunting programme of lectures and exams by the end of my second year but the thesis was still in embryo. Father de Guibert, better known for Ascetical and Mystical Theology, was giving a Special Course in Methodology designed precisely for thesis-writers. I put my name down for it hoping to be guided out of my self-created labyrinth. In his first lecture the professor invited us to state the themes we had in mind but only the essential point and in few words.

I gave him: "The Action of the Holy Spirit outside the Church, not on individuals but on a corporate movement". He pondered a moment, then out it came: *"Non commendarem"* (I wouldn't recommend it.) Why? Little work had been done on the subject. True. Father Marechal at Louvain tried his hand on Eastern mystics. But otherwise "Dickybird" couldn't recollect any treament. It was not a subject for tyros!

I was committed too far to drop the idea. Two of the Americans at the Beda, both former Episcopalian clergymen, had served together at St. Mary the Virgin's in New York until the senior fired the other for being too Roman. Dr. Delaney, the Firer, had a string of books to his name. The Reverend Pearse had something better, a whole library of publications on a single theme, Anglo-Catholics, Papalists included. Father d'Herbigny, of secret mission fame, implored Pearse never to allow it to be dispersed: it was unique.

When I approached Tromp about my thesis he had demanded: "First construct a bibliography". Here was the way ahead in Pearse's treasure-trove. Tromp was so impressed he accepted my compilation as the Practical Exercise required for qualifying for his course.

Two birds with one stone! Orders then came, not from the Rector in Spain but from Archbishop Downey, that I return for a third year and complete the thesis. I remember rushing from the Beda and floating "lonely as a cloud" through the highways and byways of the city. Errand-boys swayed past on loaded bicycles whistling me aside; bustling markets screaming fruit and veg., lottery-tickets, gelati, "Oggi trippa"* all asserted their claims. Even Albrecht's and the Dodici Apostoli (legitimate filling-station for clerical students en fête) failed to distract. I trod the empyrean. Rome was still mine! Late, but not too late, I knew how much I loved her. I was at last fairly "soaked"?

* Tripe today!

That last year mainly free from lectures nailed me to my Beda desk, trotted me round libraries, registering historical data or grimly wrestling with theological principles dimly discernible in the action of the Holy Spirit, Lord and Life-giver, Who unites us in Christ's Body, which is the Church.

As the manuscript grew, and laboured across Trompy's desk, dactylography succeeded pneumatology: typists followed the Holy Spirit. Two vivacious English girls clattered away at the end of a narrow passage in a gloomy palace, at so much per page, carbon-copies extra. (I needed four). Clearly they had no shortage of work, but they could have given Professor Tromp a lecture in punctuality. Nor were they slow to comment on the uncovenanted snags. The clatter of their machines gave way to a kindred clatter of high heels on the uncarpeted passage way as one or other rushed to tell you how many different languages they had to cope with in your MS. I think my famous Bibliography broke the record.

Despite all efforts to maintain the production line, I got miserably bogged down. Another fifty pages would do the trick—I just could not do them! De Guibert was right. I should never have touched that theme.

The last weeks before the deadline for submitting theses I was remorselessly prodded to write, and re-write, verify the facts and references, and turn in typist fodder. The day before submission I picked up the last typed instalment. Sports to their heroic finish, the girls must have rejoiced that a corner of that foreign thesis was for ever done with!

There lay the statutory number of copies on my desk, beautiful but unbound. There was no hope of their naked acceptance by the Greg. It was late evening. No hope either of interesting any book-binder. Someone, probably Dicky Foster, remembered the the Beda cellars rented by a hard-working paper merchant. He was still there after our 8 p.m. supper. Could he cover these piles of paper in stiff boards? He would look around. Could they be ready tomorrow by 8 a.m.? They were, but alas, encased in grey sugar-bag paper. Ominous! He had done his best and charged buttons.

Four of us, Dicky Foster, Tim Healy, Alec Jones and myself, hurried down to the cab-rank in the Piazza Barberini at the end of our street. We mounted and sat face to face each holding a slim grey volume as the deacon holds the Gospels. Down the Via Tritone, past the Trevi Fountain, to the Piazza Pilotta! We mounted the Greg. steps moving ceremoniously to the Secretariate guichet. There in a modest queue were the thesis-writers. Before me an English College man "Tiny" Marsh consigned his *magnum opus* bound in brown and white calf. Carmelite colours! The thesis dealt with a medieval English Theologian, the Carmelite Thomas Waldensis.

My own offering slid gently under the raised window. The clerk sharply slid it back again. "Won't do," he said. I eased it back again. "It won't stand up". He demonstrated with the top copy. Could this be the end of my Burmah Road? Every fibre resisted. Desperately I plunged my pockets. There was a five lire piece left from paying the cabby. This I placed firmly on the grey pile, looking him hard in the eye. "Eh, be!" he said. "Proviamo!" ("All right. We'll have a go!")

The Greg. accepted the thesis, sugarbag (very literally) notwithstanding. About twenty came to its public defence. Nobody came to the specimen theological lecture except the judges, among them Trompy and Bernard Leeming. The thesis had yet to be printed, at least the substantial guts of the thing, before the Greg. would post you S.T.D.* That could wait—in my case nine years. The final professional touches were made by courtesy of a theological library in Kandy, Ceylon, while I was naval chaplain at Colombo.

Neatly and nostalgically, between grey but stiffer covers, the Bombay Examiner Press brought the overdue off-spring to the light. The Greg. received the regulation number of copies. I doubt if they were dazzled, but I was duly "renunciatus"—an odd word for being home and dry! It can mean "abandoned".

The Beda year peaked with the Patronal Feast, May 27th. Most men were away as soon as internal lectures and exams were over. "Knife and Fork" Beda-men, mostly student-priests, soldiered on at the universities. Their oral examinations continued throughout July. At the Greg., the first letter of your surname decided the batting order. Fair enough, since the letter changed each year in strict alphabetical sequence. There were even lots of Z men!

My first year luckily it was not "I". The delay was minimal. But another factor intervened. My youngest sister then at the FCJ novitiate in Brussels was in retreat prior to her profession. I was expected there for the great day.

What about synchronising with Belgian students en route for home? Such inspirations are too precious to be frequent. Four students *were* leaving on the right day, intending the right numbers of days' travel. Emile de Smedt, pilgrim-in-chief, would put me up for the night before the Profession at his home in Opwyk, a short ride from the Capital.

These were the days before anything like a Students' Union emerged at Róme. You made individual contacts "spreching" (i.e. swapping English for somebody else's German etc.) Needless to say, the continentals were the eager beavers. We finished usually speaking just English! Inter-Collegiate affinities ensured a few sports fixtures and exchanges of concerts. On the whole, very little was made of a unique social opportunity. In lecture halls or occasionally at Mass the five continents fused, but rarely elsewhere.

Of course in 99.9% of cases the main reason for being in Rome at all is successful study. That could be a daunting and devouring occupation. You survived at the Belgian College on a minimum score of eight marks out of ten. Monsignor Maximilien de Furstenberg was rector in those days. Thirty years later Cardinal

* Doctor of Sacred Theology.

Max joined us on the Secretariate for Unity. I can't imagine he made many exceptions to the rule.

Judging by my four companions on the Brussels trip, I doubt there was ever need of them. The youngest, Heuschen, born in 1915, had just performed brilliantly in philosophy. Forty-five years later we were to meet again for the first time of all places in Dublin. It was during the Papal Visit of 1979 and in a rather dim corridor. "Tom"—"Jos"—our names collided in mid-air. He is now Hasselt's first Bishop, but at the Vatical Council as Titular Bishop of Drua he single-handed researched both Greek and Latin Fathers for the vital evidence of "Collegiality". One good reason perhaps why we never met during Vatican II.

The only Walloon in the party, Jean Delvaux of Liège, I ran into thirty years later at Annecy. The tall Greek god had lost his curls and put on weight. Years as Rector of a diocesan seminary render most men hairless.

"Fons" (Alfons) I have not seen again. It was he who later chose the very special bottles of claret I was to discuss on a hillside among pines with John Carmel Heenan and Emile de Smedt of Bruges. We were on our way to a meeting with Cardinal Bea and the Secretariate for Christian Unity in Germany.

I have called "Mil" pilgrim-in-chief. In no time you knew the man was born to lead. He masterminded our four days in Brussels. We almost arrived with more money than we began with. The first night we were guests of the Rosminians at Domodossola, the remainder with the Franciscans on Rigi mountain overlooking Lucerne. Mil's flair for ordering cheaper midday meals left inn-keepers very pensive. On Isolabella in Lago Maggiore he queried the price of the fish. "*Possono soddisfarsi!*"* fenced the Patrone. "Fine!" said Mil, "but you throw in the bread!" (Bread was extra). She took it with good grace, her tribute to a bonny swordsman. What she did not know was student capacity for the staff of life.

At the Monastery on Rigi a fellow-guest proposed that we should all rise before dawn and climb to the summit with our breviaries. He promised an experience, as well he might, being the Monsignore in charge of Youth in the diocese of Lucerne. I agreed along with the rest though at twenty-six scarcely within the Monsignor's scope. His promise was amply fulfilled in both ascent and descent. For me scaling mountains in the dark was an experience. Coming down in a stampede of Monsieur Nestlés cows was terrifying.

We were at the top by first light. Our gaze was expertly directed N.E. Silence! We waited. Suddenly the darkness split. A shaft of gold flew from the region of St. Gallen to hit the bull's eye, smack in the middle of Lake Zurich, forty miles away as the crow flies, burnishing it into a shield of gold. Even as it did so, the Monsignor's strong baritone voice intoned the "Deus in adiutorium meum intende"† of

* "You'll get as much as you want."
† "O Lord come to my aid."

Lauds. TONO FESTIVO!* We took it antiphonally. As the five psalms and "Benedictus" rose from Mt. Rigi, the world flooded with a tide of colour and small fowls made melody with us.

A *veritable* experience, we all agreed. Lucky Lucerne Youth! But Lord deliver us from prancing cows on "1 in 2 gradients". Going up, one proudly responded to Jean Delvaux's example of what he called: "les pas longs et lents des montagnards".†

Brussels broke up the party. An inescapable "esprit d'escalier"‡ destines always the best things to return too late to record. I salute the Land of Flemings and Walloons. Would they could live always together as my companions did during those four days, one in mind and heart, alternating in songs. Tunes come back: "Avete Studia", "Jean de la Lune" (Delvaux, tenor) and others. I still hum them. Four lasting friendships from four days fifty years ago

Emile de Smedt's home in Opwyk wraps all memories in a warm cocoon. We lined up for the last ceremony of the day. Bearded paterfamilias formed the sign of the Cross on each of our foreheads. I stood first as priest and guest, then Mil, then his nine brothers and sisters in order of seniority, materfamilias embracing us with loving smiles the while.

Mil was on his inevitable way very soon—Rector at Louvain, Auxiliary Bishop to Cardinal Van Roey of Malines, Bishop of Bruges, dominating figure at Vatican II, inventor of the ecclesiastical term "Triumphalism" and main architect of the *"Declaration on Religious Liberty"*.

After my sister's profession in Brussels, it was homeward bound to England. A few weeks later as I cycled back to Isleworth presbytery from hearing confessions, my eye caught a placard: "Civil War in Spain". It was Saturday July 18th 1936.

I was on the eve of returning to Spain for the next six years.

---

* In festive tone.
†"The long slow strides of the mountaineers".
‡The staircase syndrome, i.e. On your way out remembering what you should have said.

CHAPTER XV
Civil War

BATTLE locked the Hendaye-Irun frontier. For us the only approach to the Peninsular was by sea. We sailed from Liverpool to Lisbon in S.S. Alca, a Yeoward Line banana-boat. The youngest of the party, a sixteen-year-old, has lately (1985) emerged as Vicar General of his archdiocese. As a canon lawyer he has for some time been recognised and used far beyond it. The other three were mature students returned from a long vacation in England.

Our sister college, Sts. Peter and Paul Lisbon, welcomed us. She is, or alas was, our junior by thirty three years (1622). Perhaps the greatest of her rectors, Monsignor John Cullen, used his considerable influence at the embassies to get us the special visas which we needed to enter a country at war. In fact the battle lines swirled near our point of entry. The Alcazar of Toledo was still under siege. Merida was taking a heavy beating.

A word about both those places. There are few more heroic sieges in history than Colonel Moscardo's. Battered by gun-fire and down to their last resources, the men in the Alcazar survived by strategic withdrawals deeper into the heart of the fortress as outer bastions fell. Telephonic communications were still intact. The moment of truth came when Moscardo's young son spoke to his father: "They say they will kill me if you don't give in". "Then son, die with a 'Viva Cristo Rey!' and 'Viva Espana!' "

Maria, a girl shot by the Reds, makes Merida for ever memorable. She fell modestly smoothing her skirt in the tradition of St. Agnes of Rome and other Holy Virgins.

We entered Spain in time to make Salamanca by nighfall and threw ourselves on the mercy of the great Dominican College of San Esteban. A Moorish tercio was bivouacked in the Patio. Lights from the house glittered on coffee-cups as the men relaxed after their meal. I asked the officer, a Spaniard, what their discipline was like. They looked a casual lot squatting in the dust. Bridling somewhat the officer said: "One word from me and they would be in marching order. Like to see how soon?"

We excused ourselves. Upstairs an old Dominican professor was waiting. He wore dark glasses and sat ruminating at his desk. He warmed to us and we to him at once. Gran Bretaña was dear to him for a number of reasons, but in the final analysis, mainly one—G. K. Chesterton. "Este Chestertón!" He repeated the words with reverence. "For me, a true revelation! In one page—in one sentence—he opens up a view so clear, so new, reaching so far!" The old man had forty years lecturing on the *Summa Theologica* behind him but "this Chesterton" threw light even on his own beloved "realm of gold".

We reached our destination by train the next day. With us, on the hard seats of a third-class carriage, travelled another much younger Dominican, Professor Venancio Carro. His work was known to me from *Ciencia Tomista*, Salamanca's theological quarterly. Conversation, however, was mostly confined to unscholarly comments on the War. One diversion comes back vividly: Father Venancio's apology for scandal which I found rather consoling. He was rolling and consuming cigarettes all the way to Medina del Campo. "I know," he said, I should do something about it but—!" He needn't have worried. Ration cards for tobacco were on their way. It wouldn't be long before men like Monsignor Humble, Rector of the Scots College, who, when parish priest of Wishart had imported his own cigars, would be filling his pipe with a home-made mixture smelling like a gardener's fire.

In Valladolid the Reds had surrendered the Casa del Pueblo after three days. It became clear it had in fact been an arsenal. The only violence the city experienced afterwards came from the air in the shape of fifty kilo bombs. One of them fell on the Campo Grande as children came out of school. Sirens sounded so many air-raid warnings at this time that the Rector drafted all our students out to Country House. Professors of course went with them and grim study seized our holiday home in its unrelenting grip. The ample cellars of the Town House had become the compulsory "Refugio" for the neighbours. We were constantly up and down with them. Students of course were delighted with the interruptions. Delighted, too, when the local lads indulged their talent for mischief, drumming their heels against zinc sheets that happened to be behind their bench with the effect of approaching gun-fire, soon followed by panic among the females.

Gun-fire reminds me of yet another metamorphosis of our Country House, this time from academics to ballistics. A requisition order turned Holiday Home into Italian Artillery Barracks. An archiepiscopal nod turned me into their part-time chaplain.

Students and Professors by this time were back in town ten miles away. A hit and miss service was all I could give the Gunners. They would fix a time for Sunday Mass; I would mount my horse Malaga—so named since I bought it the day Malaga was relieved. I was literally taken for a ride by the horse-coper from whom I bought it. It proved to be a barely animated hearthrug of a horse. Horse and I would arrive miraculously on time to see the soldiers on the point of leaving for duty elsewhere. Expostulations and protestations would ensue.

The years in Rome, however, were not without their influence somewhat in schooling my impatience, more so in understanding Italian temperamental hang-ups. There were fine men among them; a Major Fonda, for example. His men trusted their lives with him and so should I. I regret never having looked him up in later years along the road to Tivoli. Many of them had served in the Abyssinian Campaign. The comment was "That was a biscuit compared with this one!" There was in fact a repetition of the First World War disaster at Guadalajarra. I fear it did the Italians no good with the girls in Valladolid. Their "Una parola, signorina!" met with a fiercely ejected "Guadalajarra"!

"Fanciullismo", a juvenile sense of humour, showed itself rather engagingly among the officers. Towns and villages on their route produced a crop of self-conferred Spanish titles: Conde de Simancas, Duque del Valdestillas and so on with which they hilariously addressed one another.

Country House was not the only students' building to be requisitioned. The "Pont", erstwhile our lecture halls, became a barracks for the duration of the War (July '36—March '39). All lectures ceased. The English College faced a problem which was not foreseen when Rector Henson declined the British Government's offer to evacuate us. Academic training in Theology and Philosophy had now to be provided within the College for students ranging from First Phils to Fourth Theology. A few dioceses had held back students in England on vacation. Only Cardiff had sent out a new one, later joined by one from Hexham and Newcastle. So numbers were reduced, not however the courses to be provided. There were only two of us to provide them.

Our Vice Rector, Father James Turner, who had studied at Valladolid from 1923 to 1930, returned after ordination to graduate in theology. Together he and I mapped out the courses: four lectures each every morning, five days a week. Thursday morning Academy. For the Vice, Sacred Scripture, Moral Theology, half the Tracts in Dogmatics, and Ethics. For myself, the other half of Dogmatics, Logic, Metaphysics, Cosmology and allied disciplines. I'm no longer clear who took Fundamental Theology, perhaps each half. We dropped subsidiaries such as Church History and Hebrew.

One bargained on an early finish to hostilities. They lasted three years, for only one of which we on the rostrum had a third shoulder to lean on. If, however, we had known the work-load of some of our predecessors in the 18th century, we should certainly have hung our diminished heads. One man single-handed for a period taught Phils and Divs with humanities thrown in and could still present students for the prestigious Public Act at the University of Valladolid which with Salamanca and Jaen ranked as Spain's best.*

Had the Civil War been fought not only in Spain but by Spaniards and with Spanish resources, it could have been a matter of months rather than years. But the International Brigade, Mussolini, Hitler and Stalin joined in. Rumours of a Russian strategy to grip Europe

* See *St. Alban's College, Valladolid: Four Hundred years of English Catholic Presence in Spain,* by Michael E. Williams, C. Hurst and Co., 1986.

5

in a pincer-movement were in the air at the time, and, I believe, have not been dissipated by later research. *

Franco, of course, became the big bogeyman for bringing in the Moroccan troops. You were led to believe another Hannibal had invaded Europe with a horde of bloodthirsty avengers. In fact the Moorish tercios were the most disciplined fighting unit on either side. They belonged to the Spanish Army as the Gurkhas do in ours. Franco had commanded them in battle. They were utterly devoted to him and not only for his generalship.

Long before the Civil War split Spain geographically, indeed well over a century before, down to the tiniest village people were irreconcilably at loggerheads. Is it fanciful to look for the origin of the Two Spains in the contrasting strains, Visigothic and Hispano-Roman, which blended into the peninsular people? What is more to the point is that the battle-lines of the Civil War in no way coincided with the cleavage of minds. *Hinc illae lachrimae!* All too surely blood was to flow not only on the battlefield but in the rear. The outbreak of hostilities reaped a predictable whirlwind.

Red violence had erupted in Asturias two years earlier (October 5-14, 1934) with the murder of priests and seminarists. Calvo Sotela's speech in the Cortes in July 1936 detailed an appalling list of subsequent crimes which the Second Republic had allowed to go unpunished. His own murder, two nights later, with or without her complicity, proved La Pasionaria a true prophetess when she declared that speech the last he would ever make. Cannot she also claim a significant place in Spanish history for ringing the bell which from eye-ball confrontation plunged the two Spains into battle? Franco flew at once from the Canaries to raise the revolt.

Valladolid was the first mainland city to declare for him. Law and order quickly returned. Not quickly enough in the outlying villages to prevent a period of Lynch law. Even allowing for the pent-up resentment of five years' misrule, who could endorse such savage reprisals in which, along with the laudable effort to restore law and order, went the payment of old personal scores?

"To know all is to forgive all"? Only "Up to a point, Lord Copper!" if I may use Waugh's phrase in such a tragic context. Remember this is Franco's zone, in the first days of the Movement. It serves however, to illustrate the "stop-at-nothing" strain in the Spanish temperament common to Iberian saints and sinners, "church-mice" and anarchists.

Has any country known such a series of head-on collisions? Between 1812 (the Cortes de Cadiz, and the first inroads of liberalism from France) and 1876 (restoration of the monarchy after the brief First Republic 1872-4) ten Constitutions appeared each radically opposed to its predecessor. Monarchy and Church each drew the fusillade; the Monarchy first for its absolutism, then for its legitimate succession (Carlist Wars 1833-39, 1847-49); then for its

* In fact the liberal historian Salvador de Madariaga later confirmed them.

extinction (1872). The Church, so closely enmeshed with their Catholic Majesties, shared the onslaught. For instance, in one day, July 17th 1834, one hundred religious were massacred in Madrid. Twenty years later Espartero, newly returned from exile in England primed with Masonic principles, stopped the publication in Spain of Pius IX's Bull defining the Immaculate Conception of Our Blessed Lady. Spain which of all countries had done most over the centuries to promote the devotion, became the only country to reject the definition.

How explain such hatred? One may trace its organised appearance to the same source as the opposition to monarchy, namely the kind of "enlightenment" brought in by Iberian masonry. The Conde de Aranda founded the first Spanish Lodge in 1760. I fear contact with English merchants in the seaports had a lot to do with that. (The first lodge in England was in London in 1717.) This would account for the anti-Roman *animus* of Spanish masonry. The dogmatic dismissal of throne and altar as archaic shackles on the nation's progress was an added bonus from the French Encyclopedists.

Neither masonry nor the other secret societies which sprang up on the same model explain the successive waves of anti-clericalism which peaked during Barcelona's "Tragic Week" with the anarchist riots of Francisco Ferrer in July 1909 and smashed all breakwaters in the Red Zone during the Civil War of 1936-39. Deeper and earthier convulsions than the brain-storms of intellectuals were needed to raise such tides. Undeniably men of the Church, clerical and lay, must share responsibility.

Priests were not slow to recognise this. At the height of an earlier wave which swept his neighbourhood clean of every sign of religion one of them wrote: "Have we not been living in a fool's paradise? We had enough going on in churches, the wherewithal to organise a procession, and took no account of the constant stream of dropouts."*

Manuel Ballesteros in the official report on the diocese of Guadix wrote in 1936: "Negligence, self-satisfaction, and indolence of those whose sacred duty it was to defend their flock, deprived them of any solid Christian formation, and left them defenceless to the storm of sophisms and blatant travesties of the faith that rained upon them." The Valladolid diocesan report cuts even nearer the bone with this indictment of the Catholic bourgoisie: "Life was grim indeed for farm-workers. This was in large measure due to the lack of elementary justice on the part of employers trading on their reputation as devout Catholics and their alleged fidelity to Catholic principles. No wonder the poor people were confused and identified the Church with social injustice."†

* *Jesuits in The Red Levant*, pages 59-60.
† *Latifundia* in the provinces: in Badajoz 50% of the land was in the hands of 1% of the population; Andalucia roughly the same, e.g. the big landowners in Seville (5% of the population) held 72% of the area's wealth.

Ballesteros' report of 1936 goes on: "The unpardonable neglect by the Church of the moneyed classes in power, year after year, became the spark which burst into flames of passion, hatred and crime. Starvation wages, sickness and helpless old age awaited those who had spent a life-time of blood and sweat in the service of people who despised them and abandoned them in their greatest need."

In justice to the clergy it is only fair to see the odds they faced in the cities where rich people largely resided. Take for instance St. Raymond's in Madrid (1934), a parish by all accounts buzzing with pastoral activities and regarded as one of the best equipped in the metropolis.

Population within the parish   80,000

Population at Mass (Sunday)   7%
(inclusive of the children in the parochial schools)

Parishioners married outside the Church: 20%

Parishioners living in concubinage: "innumerable"

Parishioners married in Church: 40% unable to say the Our Father

Parishioners unbaptised: 25%*

The first Church effort to organise the workers resulted in *"Circulos Catolicos"* in 1864. The two main anti-Catholic unions came later: the General Union of Workers (U.G.T.) in 1888; the National Confederation of Work (C.N.T.) in 1910. By 1900, "Catholic Circles" had 80,000 members to U.G.T.'s 26,000.

What went wrong? Shrewd observers foresaw the collapse long before it happened. The Catholic formula brought workers and bosses together, capital and labour under the same banner. Ideally right perhaps but practically disastrous. The workers at last had access to a considerable range of social services and met in splendid premises. But the influence of the bosses was bound to prevail. They paid the piper. Workers had no independent voice as against bosses who solidly resisted the introduction of the eight hour day. Inevitably the *Circulos*, however abounding in works of charity, were politically mute on social issues with the exception of those affecting religion.

It was precisely for the big voice in politics and progressively the big stick, indeed in some cases the stick of dynamite, that the purely worker-syndicates of the Left emerged. The *Circulos* withered. Perforce many members looked elsewhere to articulate their grievances and were lost to the Church.

The Catholic reaction came in 1897, came in fact from the Madrid *"Circulo Catolico* of St. Joseph" with a genuine workers' trade union, the *"Sindicato catolico de Tipografos"*. Within five years the mustard seed was branching in Madrid, Valencia, Barcelona and Burgos. Four years later Bilbao had already federated a forest of member branches.

* Statistics in *Razon y Fe* 1934 by Father Peiro, S.J.

Farm-workers' syndicates owed their origin to Antonio Mone-
dero, a pioneer who had the sense first to make a close study of
Catholic Syndicalism in other European countries and secondly
harness as his team-mate the Jesuit Father Sisinio Nevares, who had
been in the *Circulos Catolicos* from the beginning and had first-hand
experience of the pitfalls. They began in Madrid and in 1917 at
Valladolid the Agrarian Confederation of Farm-workers was
founded which within two years represented, workers and families,
about two million people—roughly half the farming-class of Spain.
They went to the heart of the problem with three main objectives:
the replacement of the *latifundia* with small-holdings and collective
leases, the promotion of agricultural loans and savings-banks, and
the social teaching of the Church.

Earlier in this narrative evidence may well have seemed to prove
the total non-existence of any social conscience in Spain. For a true
balance however one or two facts could be relevant. Some consciences *were* deeply disturbed. The official diocesan reports of Guadix
and Valladolid I have quoted placard the worst features of clerical
and lay Catholic life. I doubt if the Left could have made a more
trenchant analysis. At the same time it would be a mistake to look
elsewhere even in Europe for the highly developed social teaching
which from *Rerum Novarum* (1891) onwards has sensitised, or should
have sensitised us, to our social duties as Christians.

Yet even so, in the earlier days of the industrial revolution, voices
were raised within the Church unerringly calling for the right
remedies. One of them, *"Pan y Catecismo!"* (Bread and Basic
Christian Principles) must have grated uncomfortably on the ears of
gradgrind bosses and indolent clerics. If only they had all responded
earlier! As it was, even *Rerum Novarum* was blocked in some areas
and not only in Spain. The great Catechetical Congress in Madrid
came at last early in this century.

CHAPTER XVI

The Misery of Spain

MARTIAL LAW goes with a State of Emergency, the acutest form of which is Civil War. The acutest form of that can only be incubated in Spain, the land of the fiercest sundering of minds.

I had personal but mercifully long-range experience of the operation of Martial Law in the early days of September 1936. The Circumvallation Road to the east of Valladolid passes below the San Isidro plain with square-topped Mount Cristóbal in the background. There by chance in the sandpits below the plain I stumbled on visual evidence of events which had made an aural impact at 6 a.m. as I struggled from bed. I found the crown of a man's head. So Martial Law dispenses justice, not (*Pace* Roy Campbell) from a "Flowering Rifle", but from "adamantine lips" whose kiss is death. My innards rebelled as I fled the spot praying for the victims of such rough justice. In both zones the chance of instant retaliation proved irresistible. There was however a difference. The difference is vital. There could have been no Civil War without it. Franco struck against the "Loyalists"? Loyalists to what? The first duty of any government is *"Salus Populi"*, the peace and protection under law for all the people. Five years of unpunished crime, not just petty theft or disorderly conduct, but systematic murder, arson, sacrilege suffi- ciently document the infidelity of successive administrations to their primary responsibility. As for "Law", the first Constitution of the new regime (1931) was later described by Niceto Alcala Zamora, prime minister of the Republican government that passed it, as an "invitation to Civil War".* Parties of the Left, without a smile, voted God out of existence—by a majority of 7!

Franco at once restored justice under Law. It was rough justice, as I have been at pains to make plain. The back-log of crime was cleared. Who wouldn't have hoped for gentler methods than the Military Tribunals and the firing-squads in the sandpits of San Isidro? Martial Law and a dicey State of Emergency make grim demands? A long campaign whose issue was far from certain lay ahead? Yes, but even so . . . even so!† In the other Zone unpunished illegality simply continued as before with this difference: the engines of crime roared into top-gear.

* *Defectos de la Constitucion* by A. Zamora, p 51.
† Jose María Peman foremost playwright and spell-binding *"charlista"* (off-the-cuff commentator before huge audiences) and Manuel de Falla both urged Franco to soften stark justice with mercy. Only recently I came across their correspondence.

How on earth could decent men like Clem Attlee identify themselves, fist clenched aloft, with the mayhem wrought by P.O.U.M. (Workers Party of Marxist Unification) and Anarchists? Take Andrew Nin, President of P.O.U.M., writing in his *Vanguardia* on August 2nd 1936: "The working class has solved the Church problem very simply, leaving not a single church standing." Or days later declaiming in a Barcelona theatre: "The problem of the Church . . . we have resolved . . . by suppressing its priests, churches and worship." Or again Solidaridad Obrera (Workers' Solidarity) on August 15th 1936: "We have to pull the Church up by the roots . . . bishops and cardinals must be shot . . . " Galarza, Republican Minister of the Interior in the early days of the Civil War, confessed to more than 20,000 "illegal executions", or rather murders, in Madrid of which a quarter were still to be identified. The first fruits of this initial holocaust were of course Catholic priests and laymen.

The Republic shaped up to the problem with the decree of August 24th 1936 creating the famous "Popular Tribunals". The Attorney-General of the Republic issued an official circular* to his local subordinates explaining their *raison d'etre*. "The Republic is a regime of justice and justice emanates from the people . . . ; if this noble and great people is giving its life for a regime of freedom and justice, let us give them the justice they want in harmony with the rhythm and tone which is our style . . . "

So along with the "Popular Trubunals" came the "Chekas" masquerading behind official titles such as "Committee of Public Investigation", "Special Services of the Ministry of War", "Special Posts of Vigilance". There were 226 of them in Madrid alone. In them torture was the order of the day and night.

I was in Barcelona in time to tour the grisly premises of one of these torture chambers. The speciality of this one was "neveras", ice-boxes, into which you could just about cramp a human being. It is hard to think of one's own countrymen giving their lives for freedom, as they fondly believed, in alliance with this lot. Harder still to view recent TV presentation of the war, screened with all the aura of authenticity and objectivity yet entirely blind to this dimension. Hardest of all, of course, to remember the stream of Catholic propaganda condemning Franco, particularly in France, from Maritain, Bernanos, François Mauriac and others. The Dominican Father Venancio Carro who shared our journey from Salamanca was quick off the mark with "*The Truth on the Spanish War*". He had good reason to be. The French Dominican review *Vie Intellectuelle* in the same year published a high-toned theological dismissal of the rising. Later, I was told, the French brethren apologised to the Spanish Dominicans. Their *amende honorable* recognised that while they were theorising in their ivory towers, in Spain the sons of St. Dominic were shedding their blood. One

* Later published in the Madrid Journal *El Liberal* September 3rd 1936.

hundred and thirty-two Dominicans were massacred in hatred of the Catholic Faith during the pogrom.

Pius XI within a month of the outbreak of war received five hundred Spanish exiles in audience, and before any episcopal pronouncement in Spain, saluted them in these terms: " . . . We can and we must apply to you the beautiful divine word: 'The wise son rejoices his father' (Prov. 15, 20) who, embracing with sight and heart all your companions in tribulation and martyrdom, can and must say to you, as the Apostle said to your first predecessors in the glory of martydom: my joy and my crown (Phil. 4, 1) and not only mine but God's . . . ' " (Allocution 14.9.36).

Thirteen diocesan bishops were executed during the Civil War.* I knew personally only Bishop Florentino Asensio y Barroso of Barbastro who was in charge of catechetics in Valladolid during my student days. He was martyred August 9th 1936 shortly after 3 a.m. on the Sariena Road by the 3rd kilometer stone, less than five months after his consecration. He was herded on 23rd July 1936 with ninety priests, Escolapians, Claretians and Benedictines, and three communities of female religious into a college on the town square. The Anarchist commander, Durruti, demanded his death from the Town Hall balcony. The Bishop heard him from the nearby college window. He was cited to appear before a "popular tribunal" on the night of August 8th and put in custody. There is evidence that he suffered physical torture of the most revolting kind. Everything recorded of his last days is in perfect harmony with the man we knew. "They took him from the gaol at 3 a.m. As they drew back the bolts, he moved towards his executioners with a mild, untroubled gesture."

Barbastro was decimated, more than eight hundred of a population of eight thousand being killed, not in battle but in the rear. No profession or social group suffered as badly as the diocesan clergy of Babastro: one hundred and twenty-three out of one hundred and forty died. Lerida diocese comes next in the scrupulously compiled list of victims amoang the secular clergy with two hundred and seventy out of four hundred and ten. The total number of diocesan priests massacred in fifty-four of the dioceses in the Red Zone is four thousand, one hundred and eighty-four. Religious priests and brothers two thousand, three hundred and sixty-five. Religious women two hundred and eighty-three. A total of six thousand, eight hundred and thirty-two secular and religious, brothers and sisters. Among the male religious: Claretians two hundred and fifty-nine, Franciscans two hundred and twenty-six, Escolapians, Marist Brothers one hundred and seventy-six, Dominicans one hundred and thirty-two. Among the female religious: Daughters of Charity of St. Vincent de Paul thirty: Adorers of the

* Siguenza, Lerida, Cuenca, Barbastro, Segorbe, Jaen, the Auxiliary Bishop of Tarragona, Cuidad Real, Almeria, Guadix, Barcelona, Teruel, and the Apostolic Administrator of Orihuella (in full charge of the diocese but not yet consecrated).

Blessed Sacrament and Carmelites of Charity each twenty-six: Capuchin Sisters twenty.

Before leaving this tragic but glorious roll of honour, I feel it a duty to return to one other bishop of the thirteen who died because of hatred of the Faith, Don Diego Ventaja, Bishop of Almería for almost exactly one year. At the end he had two clear days in which he could have escaped. He refused to leave his flock. From an unusual source comes a document which illuminates his decision in all its splendour. I transcribe it in full:

"The undersigned, Geoffrey John Wesdale, single, engineer, British subject, living in the Square of Saint Leonard, 10, Exeter, England and William James Smith, married, retired, residing at Seven Gables, Beech Avenue, Exeter, Devonshire, England, British subject, wish to give testimony of the circumstances of our last meeting with the late Very Reverend Diego Ventaja, Bishop of Almería, Spain.

"In July 1936, when the civil war had broken out in Spain, we were both employees of the Fuerzas Motrices del Valle de Lecrin, an enterprise dedicated to the production and distribution of electricity and gas; W. J. Smith, as resident adviser of the company in Almería, residing in the Villa Maria, Almería and G. J. Wensdale, as engineer of the same, living at the Villa Anita, Almería.

"On the 25th of July we were informed by the captain of an English destoyer anchored in the port of Almería that he would take on board all British subjects and conduct them to a safe port. We promised to join him on board before midnight when it was his intention to depart.

"On the afternoon of that day we were in the street which comes from the "Four Streets" when we met the bishop, and expressed our concern for his safety. We asked him if he knew that the priests were being hunted by the armed mob and we begged him to go into hiding. With a sweet smile he said he had duties to his diocese and as long as possible must continue to attend to its needs. He was dressed in his ordinary clothes and in no way disguised.

"We then further insisted and said that as we were going to get away on the English destroyer, we would arrange to take him with us and assure his safety and in the meantime we would keep him in hiding. We had no success in persuading him to let us do so. We pleaded with him to come with us, because we feared the people would do him terrible harm. To this he replied that these poor souls were near, but could not do him harm. "Of course," he said "they can destroy this body (and he beat his breast), but they couldn't do me harm." And so, at the same time that he thanked us for our concern for him, he said: "Go with God," and he gave us his blessing there on the street.

"This was the last we saw of the Very Reverend Bishop Ventaja. May he rest in peace!

"Signed by each of us in the presence of the other and of the witness whose signature follows:-

G. J. Wesdale, A.C.G.M.I.E.E. (with seal)

W. J. Smith (with seal)

Dr R. C. M. Coke-Hervey, M.A. (Oxon) Bachelor of Chemistry (Oxon) (with seal)."

Visum et approbatum

+Cyril, Bishop of Plymouth, 16th August 1955.

"This is a literal copy of the original which is kept in the Vicariate of Almeria" signed J. A. Tapin (Diocesan Report of Almeria, doc. 12).

There is a sequel. The destroyer's doctor was a Catholic. He learned that the bishop had refused to go aboard and went with a naval uniform to the palace. Already the mobs were suspicious and aroused. All new efforts to save the bishop while there was still time came to nothing. The doctor returned alone to his ship, carrying the naval uniform and in admiration of the bishop's courage.

Footnote on Church property destroyed:

Churches totally destroyed: 1,624. Valencia diocese tops the list with 800. Oviedo diocese next with 354. No other diocese lost more than 40, though Cuenca without giving a figure reports "nearly all".

Churches partially destroyed, profaned and sacked: Seven dioceses report simply: "TODAS" (all), Five dioceses report simply: nearly ALL, e.g. Toledo was left with seven intact, Cuenca three. Valencia reports: More than 1,500; Jaen 95%; Barcelona: all but 10; Palencia: the majority in the deaneries of the red zone.

Liturgical instruments *(chalices, ciboria, etc.) and* **Furniture** *(reredoses, statues, altars etc.):* Valencia, Solsona, Barbastro, Oviedo: Everything. Burgos: Everything in 175 churches. Leon: Everything in 132 churches. Avila, Cadiz, Granada, Jaca, Mondonedo, Palencia, Sevilla, Tenerife, Vitoria, Zaragoza: Everying in the churches attacked.

This is a selected list. For full details, see *Historia de la Persecucion Religiosa en Espana: 1936-1939* by Antonio Montero Moreno, Madrid 1961 in the B.A.C. (*Biblioteca de Auctores Cristianos*) published in connection with the University of Salamanca, pp. 627-658.

CHAPTER XVII

'The Flame which Quickens'

VALLADOLID swarmed with young troops from Navarre on their way down to the Guadarramas. A thin wind blows there in winter which Spaniards say "doesn't put out a candle but kills a man". The lads wore the rose-red beret their grandfathers wore in the Carlist Wars. On their tunics was another emblem of the same colour, a Sacred Heart badge. There were so many of them that Don Cipriano wrote: *"No es tanto una cruzada, es una 'corazonada!"* ("Not so much a Crusade as a Heartade!")

A number of lads in Valladolid joined the Requetes, as the Carlist Regiments were called, among them three sons of Dr. Igea, an ear, nose and throat man. They died with so many others in the assault on Altos de Leon, the pass commanding the road to Madrid— wearing yet a third rose-red emblem on their tunics, their heart's blood. Don Felix was in the College shortly afterwards. We tried to offer our sympathy. His answer was: "My sons were brought up to know I would rather see them dead than in a state of mortal sin. As things in Spain were going it was evident they would need heroic virtue to live in grace. God chose they should have it to die."

We also lamented their General Mola, killed in an aeroplane accident. To him, under Franco, we owed the rapid rally of Castille and Leon to the movement.

Around the same time the Civil Guard General Sanjurjo died in similar circumstances. If there is any truth in the story which circulated at the time of Alfonso XIII's abdication, that enigmatic commander must be seen as a vital link in the chain which dragged Spain into the Second Republic, five years of misrule, and inevitable Civil War.

General Queipo de Llano's nightly commentary in the early days of the campaign in the South stopped everything in Franco's Spain except the recitation of Divine Office in religious houses. How many times dear Don Justo called me to his room to hear that husky, port-wine voice ad-libbing on the fortunes of the day! Valladolid knew him well in his salad days when he hurled a bottle of brandy from his box in the Calderon Theatre into the hands of a comrade-in-arms in the box facing. It was in the same theatre that Franco addressed us one unforgettable night. It was the only time I saw him. He sat to the left of the stage, resting one leg on the other knee and occasionally slapping his leggings during the earlier speeches. There was no *braggadocio* about his. He thanked Valladolid for its vital support. He also went to the root of Spain's malaise naming the Encyclopedists and the free-thinkers. I recall one phrase "And not one of them could produce a big bouncing baby with all their Godless thinking!" The women rose and remained standing for one of the longest rounds of applause I have ever heard.

The *Catholic Times* published a translation I made of his inaugural ceremony as Generalisimo. It took place in one of the chapels of Burgos Cathedral and was immediately followed by the Red Mass of the Holy Spirit. One may differ about some aspects of Franco's campaign. We found his cautionary tactics hard to understand and his delays intolerable. His peace-time regime is no doubt questionable on a number of heads. I am convinced, however, he never swerved from the solemn duty he swore to God to serve Spain to the best of his ability. Who in the last two hundred years of the nation's history has given Spain forty years of peace?

At last his death was announced. I sent a Latin telegram of condolence to a dear friend, Marcelo, Primate of Toledo.* Courtesy, and perhaps a well-developed sense of timing, moved him to have it passed into his hand as he pronounced the funeral oration at the Valley of the Fallen. Luckily for me, he used the name of the previous diocese I had served. At the Bishop's House, Portsmouth, I believe telephone bells rang all day. The hunt had gone cold by the time I got home from the usual Sunday Visitation.

To and fro washed the wave of hostilities, bringing into our community priest-refugees from the Red Zone, and recruiting from our reduced student body three of the brightest into Franco's tercios. One, whose departure halved the strength of a Philosophy year, became a standard-bearer. Another, with the name of one of Nelson's admirals, became an Alferez (second lieutenant). He died in our war as rear-gunner of an R.A.F. bomber-plane.

The first of the three to leave died in the Spanish War. He appeared in my theology class for the first time on St. Andrew's day 1936. Living in Ireland, he had difficulty it seems in arranging his return from long vacation. I asked his name. It was Patrick. "Lucky for you it wasn't Andrew! You would have been 'up for class' giving your understanding of today's thesis in Latin", I said. He was both brainy and dreamy, and in remarkable intimacy with nature. Fish attached themselves to his hook in the most unlikely places. Birds knew him and led him to their nests. He was deeply read in the Spanish poets and found it hard to get up in the morning. One could not see him as a priest. Yet it was difficult to see him as anybody else. So he worked his own way out of the dilemma on the Sierre de Espadan where he was found propped against a tree with

* Don Marcelo Gonzalez Martín, ordained a priest of Valladolid, taught Sociology and Ethics in the old "Pont", and applied his social teaching in three dimensions to the creation of a new estate of economic houses for working class families. He became bishop of Astorga (1960), archbishop of Barcelona (1967), and Toledo (1971).

his *Imitation of Christ* on his knees and a bullet through his chest. Later details confirmed that his tercio was dislodged in a counter-attack from its position on the heights. Paddy had a leg wound, and was carried down by a couple of his comrades. He insisted for their own safety they should leave him and go. The position was recaptured within days and Paddy was found where they left him.

One of our guests from the other zone brought home to us at first-hand the peculiar horror of Civil War. He went into hiding and somehow filtered his way through the Red Front to safety. He was a priest but I gathered some of his family were front-line soldiers for the other side. One heard so many stories of inter-family encounters at the front. Here was one that could have been fratricidal.

Two or three times in later years my brother, sister and I stayed at a farmhouse pensione on the coast near Mataró, north of Barcelona. The staple crops were carnations and early potatoes. In the near-by hills fourteen Claretian fathers met their martyrs' death, all due to a little child's babbling when certain strangers came asking questions. Of this, as of so many other tragedies elsewhere, we had first-hand acccounts.

Slowly the Red Zone shrank. The Republican Government moved from Madrid to Valencia then to Barcelona and onwards through the passes into France, some of them like "El Campesino" to pastures new in South America.

Outside the Spanish consultate at Perpignan in August 1939, five months after the final dissolution of Red resistance, we met a man typical of many Spanish expatriates. He was a "wanted man" on both sides of the conflict. *"No hay justicia!"* ("There's no justice") he incantated looking at us appealingly. Was he hoping we might hide him in the boot? There was then fine-comb treatment for travellers into Spain. During the conflict my occasional goings and comings involved the British Consulate in Bordeaux, where I was informed by H.M. Consul I was the first of many to prove I had a right to enter Spain since I had proof of a job to which I was returning. At the Spanish Frontier all my ten fingers were printed on more than one occasion. When Father Jim Turner's books were taken back to England months after the hostilities had ceased, every single book had to be taken out, carried to an officer on an upper floor who scrupulously went through many dozens of Latin tomes on Theology, Scripture and so on. The result was another night on the Spanish side of the frontier with all Spanish currency already exhausted.

It is shameful indeed to bring this part of one's life to an end with small-talk. The Spanish War all of which, apart from the first month and a couple of breaks, I experienced in Spain taught me many things. I mentioned one earlier, namely a certain reserve about media news. It appears inevitable that even the sharpest gatherers come abroad equipped with blinkers imposed either by the people who fee them or their own pre-judgment, not to say prejudice.

Picasso's "Guernica" proved a most powerful engine of propaganda because of his overwhelming vogue. It absolved millions from any further need to think or enquire. Father James Turner debated that grim event publicly in Wales with the Communists. He had studied every aspect of it. From all accounts he had the better of the encounter. But did anyone paint the desecrated tombs, burning hospital chapels, enclosed nuns hauled out to die, the mob playing football with the head of Pachal Baylon, Saint of the Blessed Sacrament, or the murder of any one of the six thousand priests and brothers?

War fever is literally hate-full. Comrades-in-arms in our 1939-1945 war solemnly repeated: "The only good German is a dead one!" I remember our fire-eating Commodore exploding at some bungling delay with: "Look at the time you're wasting, time I could give to killing Germans!"

And yet Spain still has a message. She was more herself in relative poverty when Valladolid, capital of old Castille, had 80,000 people and the characteristic old houses stood only two stories high. Now with 400,000 a concrete jungle has sprung so high they can comfortably look into the inmost heart of our College—even into the patio I have already described.

The streets swarm with students—carbon copies of boys and girls everywhere and anywhere. But I remember, I remember, an older modesty and gentleness such as flowered in Mary of Merida. Dear old John XXIII meeting the Cardinal of Tarragona in January 1959 to receive the canonical processes of those who died *"in odium fidei"** in his diocese, said: "The sufferings of the priests, religious and laity who in your diocese (as in all the Catholic Spanish Nation) gave proof of the love they had for the Faith and the little esteem in which they held earthly things are still recent . . . Their example, as is true of the Martyrs we this day commemorate in the Church, will be the flame which quickens the fervour of this beloved flock into a life of constant holiness . . . " May his words come true!

* "In hatred of the Faith"

CHAPTER XVIII

'Twixt Civil War and World War'

SIX months after the end of the Spanish War, the "Pont" reopened and our students, only slightly increased by a minimal inflow of new-comers from England, resumed lectures there in the normal way. Our own war had broken out. Three English students from seminaries in France moved in, all later to become excellent priests in the diocese of Salford.

Our doughty chain-horse, Vice-Rector Jim Turner, returned to England. He had written considerably on the Spanish War during his years as vice-rector. When that was over, theories of Social Credit engaged his brilliant mind. He was a disciple of McNair Wilson but, as always, had his own ideas.

He was succeeded by Father Edgar Hardwick from Newmarket, a born disciplinarian and a natural philosopher. Though a couple of years my junior, as students we had found ourselves strolling together after supper, smoking the best pipe of the day, night after night, year after year.

Rector Henson, once received by the King in that unforgettable interview, became at last a Domestic Prelate by grace of Pope Pius XII. Years passed before he received due recognition for his broadcasts during the Spanish War and was welcomed by Franco into the Order of Isabel the Catholic.

The delay was in the circumstances entirely understandable. On the surface, at least, and certainly in the mind of the average Spaniard, England had been all for the "loyalists", contributing generously to their fighting units, interposing R.N. units between Franco's ships and their sea-borne targets. And wasn't there an English comic, Captain "Potato" Jones, ferrying cargoes of grenades, lightly masked under a top-dressing of King Edwards, to the Basques?

The Spanish War finished with Germany and Italy on the crest of the wave in Spain, ourselves sunk full fathoms five. That was to register bitterly when as usual the College celebrated the annual Mass for the farmers in the Chapel of San Isidro, their Patron. At the *"Vino de honor"* after the Mass, there were the usual toasts. Someone in his cups called for a *"Viva Inglaterra!"* There were acid voices of dissent, which were much harder to take once we were at war with Germany. Personal friends of the College remained true as ever. So did the clergy of Valladolid. Don Justo, our resident "*corregidor*", left his colleagues in no doubt about our position during the war and that of Catholics in England.

Suddenly we at the College in Valladolid were in great favour in high diplomatic circles. Sir Samuel Hoare had arrived to hold the line in Franco-land where Germany and Italy both rode so high. Someone at the Madrid Embassy must have alerted the Ambassador to our unique position as the oldest English institution in Spain, and one known in government circles to have worked throughout the war for a fair hearing of Franco's side of the "argument".

Sir Samuel and Lady Dorothy arrived at the College one Saturday evening for supper and stayed with us for the Feast of Christ the King the following day. The Rector had copies of the Mass specially printed and bound for them. Sir Samuel joined us in the choir-stalls. Lady Dorothy, appropriately mantilla-ed, sought the privacy of the "tunnel".* They occupied the Bishop's Suite during their stay. In the interest of our English image, Monsignor Henson had ordered the removal of toothpicks from the comedor table looking hard at me the while, a known addict to their use. I sought his eye in vain when, at the end of our first meal, the Ambassador drew a gold toothpick from his waistcoat pocket and went elegantly into action.

I found it strange when the Rector informed me that the Ambassador would like me to become the chaplain to the British Catholics in Madrid. Stranger still, and somewhat deflatingly, he appeared quite ready to let me go. I had said Mass for the said community on one occasion. The main body, Irish and English nannies, were refreshingly bright and devout. They met on Sunday afternoons for tea and a sing-song in which Father Faber's hymns mingled with "Daisy, Daisy" and "A Bicycle made for two". The Rector accepted my excuses and passed them on.

Walter Starkey, author of *Raggle Taggle Gypsies* and other picaresque wanderings, came out as head of the British Institute in Madrid and, *inter alia*, played his well travelled fiddle (Silent Night!) at Midnight Mass. He invited us to lunch at the Gaylord hotel, and complained of the difficulties he was meeting in his cultural mission to the Spanish nation. "They're trying to destroy me!" he ingeminated with intense pathos. It was too much for Henson who burst into laughter as Walter's twenty stone trembled with the pity of it all. He joined in the laughter, I think, with a certain effort.

I like to think that the famous meeting of Hitler and Franco at the Hendaye-Irun border failed in its main intent, namely the opening of Spanish frontiers to German troops, not without Hoare's carefully orchestrated approach to the civil authorities during his mission to Spain. One instrument, albeit a minor one, was certainly the English College, Valladolid. It seems to be agreed that Franco was under pressure from the Führer. With Gibraltar and other fat

* The Tunnel opened through the buttress nearest the altar; had its own light, prie-dieu, cushions, chair—all hidden from view of the congregation but affording the best view of the sacred ministers at the altar.

prizes beckoning, one might conclude it was considerable and firmly applied. To the surprise of so many, Franco held the line. Hitler later said he would rather have all his teeth out than go through that interview again.

Sir Samuel's diplomacy was crowned with a richly deserved coronet. You could say, without exaggeration, that he laid a corner-stone of our final victory when there was little or nothing for our comfort. At the time of his visit he interested himself in the lighter books I was reading. I forget now what they were—Scott or English Essayists, perhaps. "When I'm out of politics," he said, "that is just the reading I hope to take up". Diplomacy again? Anyway, I hope he got the leisure he looked forward to, and lots of it!

CHAPTER XIX

Great Rector goes to God

NEWS came from Lisbon, grievous indeed for Monsignor Henson his close friend, that the English College rector, John Cullen, was about to have major surgery. One result was a range of subjects from Theology to Latin verse would indefinitely lack their hard-working preceptor. This was early in 1942.

My duties at Valladolid were now largely suspervisory. The Rector asked me to stand in for Monsignor Cullen without delay.

In fact there was considerable delay in getting the travel permits—time enough to make a retreat at the nearby Jesuit house. (At that time, average weekday communions at the Jesuit Church where I celebrated each morning numbered two thousand). I was piloted through my retreat by an old Basque Father whose Spanish was anything but easy. One sentence, however, comes back very clearly: "If you felt the call to become a Jesuit, you wouldn't resist?"

I shall never forget the journey to Lisbon. Trains were unpredictable. We got as far as Zamora where the train "died". It was night. Four of us, a German, a South American and a lady whose nationality remained obscure, made for an isolated house near the station. There enthroned like a queen sat a middle-aged lady wearing a medal, obviously communing with a grief too deep for words. The husband explained why and clearly not for the first time. The medal was Franco's "Sufrimientos por la Patria" (Sufferings for the Fatherland), awarded for the loss of near relatives, in their case the loss of a son. I hope I am not insensitive in wondering whether such an award had not set the old lady's subsequent existence in the wrong mould? The war was now two years over.

An obliging guard unlocked a couple of apartments in the "dead" train where we slept full-length on wooden seats. Breakfast consisted of apples of which the German seemed inordinately fond. I wondered why he felt it necessary to explain to us his exemption from active service on one or other of the German fronts. I gathered his mission in Portugal had to do with trade and had the Führer's personal blessing. But what was the "trade"? He left the Lisbon train at an unlikely minor station.

The "Inglezinhos" (our English College of Sts. Peter and Paul) crowned a steep rise and commanded a superb view of City, River Tagus and Alentejo (Southern Bank). It was, I think, this spaciousness of land and water, and the sudden changes of height which I found a relief from our tight, flat neighbourhood in

Valladolid. You dropped by cable-car or lift from College level to the Avenida in a matter of seconds. There were also the spacious open areas like "Blackhorse" Square and Pombal Circle paved in billowing black and white setts.

As expected in the capital city of our oldest ally, a certain cultural osmosis made one feel much nearer home here than on the high Castillian *mesa*. At the quayside you had Corpo Santo church and the Irish Dominicans; down river, close to Palos, the point where Columbus weighed anchor for the New World, Irish Bridgettine Sisters; inland our Embassy, Consulate, Hospital, golf course (the greens were oiled sand) and all manner of British commercial interests and professional services, including the Club.

At the other side of the College was the French Hospital. There Monsignor Cullen awaited surgery by the well-known specialist Pinto Cuello. I was present for the operation. In more than one sense I was the patient, who through an angled mirror watched the whole thing. It took four hours. His later comment was characteristic of a sound Thomist. For the first time he saw what Aquinas meant by the "constricting" nature of the pains of hell.

John Cullen, a student from boyhood at Lisbon, graduated after ordination in Rome and became Rector within very few years of returning to his old College. Few men could have carried their workload so long. Apart from the late night half-hour over a glass of wine with his staff, one rarely saw him relax.

His convalescence lasted four months, most of it spent at Senhora Maria de Mello's house in Lumiar. She was a devoted benefactress of the College and Monsignor's lifelong friend and penitent. In her lovely house she had often gathered groups to share his spiritual guidance. We priests visited him often. He was determined to be back on the rostrum for the autumn term. One usually found him valiantly exercising round and round the rose garden. Man and boy he had been more years in Lisbon than any other member of the British community at that time. He knew the city's magic and misery, the glamour and the gloom. There was nothing of the elder statesman about him. Yet I found myself returning to Lisbon on the Lumiar train with a lot to think about.

My last visit to Lumiar was to a house in great distress. Monsignor had appeared to be gaining strength to his own and everyone else's satisfaction. In mid-summer he began to experience extraordinary changes of temperature. His whole body shuddered violently. It was unbearable to watch. He was back to the French Hospital where the Sisters *tout court* said: "He's dying!"

The duty of alerting him that he was dying fell to me. The other professors, all of them former students of his, stood in reverential awe. "Monsignor, you are not going to get better!" Did he know? Anyway the command came tersely and to the point. "Get out and send in Holmes and Crowley." They witnessed signatures and received his last instructions. Our greatest Lisbon Rector in three centuries died that night, early on Saint Isabel of Lisbon's day. John Cullen's sustained effort was in the service of priests for England and Wales. They are still there, in many of our dioceses. They and their doyen, the Archbishop Emeritus of Cardiff, John Murphy, witness to the success of a good and faithful servant.

College routine had continued that summer. We were out at Luz, a large farm property to the north of Lisbon, where again it fell to me to break the news, this time to the students. That early morning Senhora de Mello drove me there from the hospital. Her husband, a brilliant surgeon, had died in a road accident. As I stepped out she whispered: "Pray for me. I have had this kind of grief before." She kissed Monsignor's feet as he died.

Years later in the port of Colombo, on the heels of the War in the Pacific, a troop ship cast anchor. As Port Chaplain R.N. I was soon aboard. To my surprise and joy the captain proved to be Monsignor's brother. When he left port he also left me a memento of our mutual hero—Monsignor's gold cuff links.

The Luz term ended. Students and professors crossed the Tagus for a month at the Quinta de Pera. It was vintage time and the season for glorious bathing, exploring castle ruins, long walks to Cape Espichel along the "Charmaker Road", an area which figures somewhere in Shakespeare as the source of a wine clearly well-known to Elizabethan theatre-goers.

I stood in for a spell down in the Algarve as chaplain to the rice growers. Malaria was endemic. The locals even said of the rice shoots when they looked less than promising: "They have malaria!" The local saint's day there in the Algarve came with great excitement and peals of bells. The school-mistress was to sing solos at the Mass. The excitement and distinguished (?) company clove her tongue to the roof of her comely mouth. Not a sound emerged as she stood music in hand, organ vainly intoning the first notes.

After Mass children's dances on the square were presided over by Donna Lina the supervisor's wife. Dust rose in columns as nimble feet battered the clay with fast and incredibly intricate steps. It was all too much and energies began to flag. Donna Lina, from a huge tin, plied the dancers with sugar biscuits. The effect was like rain on flowers. The magic returned. The king of the dance was a small, freckled urchin in white shirt, blue *faja*, three-quarter corduroys and alpagatas. Cervantes has a tribute in verse to Preciosa, the Gypsy girl and her dancing. It begins: "The soul is wonder struck and the judgment amazed by her sweet and super-human movements."

Regretfully so soon after mentioning local vineyards, I must record the unneighbourly opinion of Portuguese wine which prevails in Spain, as exemplied in the old jingle:

"De Aire Burgales,
De Vino Portugues,
De Hombre Sanabres,
Dios nos libre de los Tres!"

"From the air of Burgos,
Portuguese wine,
A Man from Sanabria (a district of Spain)
God deliver us from all three!"

Travel broadens more than the mind. The palate also benefits. I stand by my earlier statement that there is no such thing as bad wine, IF you drink it where it is made. "Where" in that context means in the neighbourhood of its own vines. Thus Colares wine, perhaps hardly a classic, when drunk on the plain below Cintra, greatly enhances even the fairyland vision of the palace on the heights. Vinho Verde comes from Minho, the most northerly province separated from Spain by the river whose name it bears, but you could drink that anywhere with profit, especially if you had a lobster to go with it.

I have the final comment for Portugal's best. It's very clear green-eyed jealousy must have beguiled Spain into heresy. Once the Duero becomes the Douro and is well clear of Spain, then, (ah, then!) Portugal has Port. I went to pay homage at the great river's mouth. Ron Symmington dug me out of my modest hotel to stay with him. He introduced me to the firm's cellars at Vila Nova de Gaia where they produce a number of well-known ports. Ron also instructed an ardent novice in tasting and blending. Somewhat to his surprise the novice learned: a) You don't have to use a famous brandy to fortify even the best vintages, b) The taste of any port is best discerned by shaking the glass (half-empty) sharply beforehand, c) The wine needs moving occasionally and may be conveyed from vat to vat in rubber pipes without affecting the taste, d) The vats at Silva and Cozens (their trade-names) were the largest in Oporto, e) They undoubtedly contained at that moment the wine in which England would celebrate Victory but they were all full, since wine-shipping was at a standstill and trade with it.

I must not leave Ron's hospitable home without recording a snatch of after-dinner conversation. A dozen people were there including a survivor of the First War Flying Corps. We had rejoined the ladies. The news at the time was bad from all our fronts. Heavy casualties were mentioned. The RFC man chimed in with losses in the flimsy box-kites his lot flew in the First War. I can only hope *"in vino veritas"** goes for what he said:

"Quite a few one way or another died in my arms, in flight or shot down. I can't remember one even among the scallywags, going without words like these, 'Christ Jesus, have mercy on me!' " I treasure the remark. As chaplain in World War II I found greatly comforting the Lord's words: "Greater love than this no man has, than to lay down his life for his friends." To die in defence of one's country surely qualifies?

Braga drew me north from Oporto. The ancient cathedral was being restored. Visitors were not admitted. So I scaled the heights of

* He had drunk liberally!

the Bom Jesus Basilica on the hilltop, with the help of the rack and pinion. A jolly crowd of young men, all wearing peaked white caps, sang their way up and down to banjo accompaniment. Riotous laughter met those who found themselves going in the wrong direction. The legend on their caps read "Os Inseparaveis"—"The Inseperables".

Later, when Bishop of Salford, I discovered that one of the Roman cohorts garrisoned at Manchester was from Braga. A recent discovery on a site near Deansgate proves that Christians were in Manchester as early as 175 A.D. Could they have come from Braga?

CHAPTER XX

Fatima

NO REAL victory had come our way after many months of war. Early in 1942 the English community in Portugal organised a pilgrimage to Fatima to pray for better times. Two trains assembled us, one going north from Lisbon, the other south from Oporto.

On May 17th 1917 a sudden flash of light at noon alerted three little shepherds to another world. They and their flock were in the Cova de Iria. Twenty-five years later there were still few buildings: a hostel on the west side of the hollow, a Carmelite monastery, and little else. A simple shed still canopied the spot where the Lady appeared over the scrub-oak.

We sang there a melody which has haunted me ever since. The first verse runs (in straight translation):
"Immaculate Queen of the Heavens
Under your mantle woven of light,
Bring all war in the world to an end.
Refrain:
For the sake of the children, flowers in bud,
The old people without home or bread,
The soldiers who go to war,*
Give us the alms of your prayer."

Our improvised procession was followed by Midnight Mass. I preached on Eccles. 24, 24.† We numbered about seventy. There were no other pilgrims: Fatima was all ours.

High summer came. The last lectures were delivered and it was holiday at the English College, Lisbon. I set out alone from the house on a second visit to Fatima, this time on foot. The Archbishop of Mitylene, Vicar General of the Patriarch of Lisbon, personally blessed my solo effort and insisted on dressing the pilgrim for the part. He produced a long yellow dust-coat. All my instincts rebelled. But on reflection why not be a fool and go the whole hog? Not surprisingly, I fairly reaped the whirlwind *en route*. I had rounded off the Archbishop's extravaganza with a broad-brimmed reaper's straw hat of the same colour as the dust-coat.

There are pleasanter memories. I can still recall a sturdy boy, his blue jelly-bag Tam o'Shanter over one ear, whistling like a linnet as he clattered by with two buckets yoked across his shoulders; a dark valley of tall trees where I sheltered from the storm and heard a

* Portuguese troops fought with us in the 1914-18 War
† "I am the mother of fair love, reverence, knowledge and holy hope."

dialect totally alien to any Portuguese I knew—analogous, perhaps, to the survival of Ladino in the Tyrol?; many a dappled stream into which I plunged; bride and bridegroom in traditional country finery timidly holding hands at the head of a happy procession of villagers; and a poor village shop where they invited the pilgrim to take what he wanted without paying because his Portuguese proved he was English!

Blunders are sweet now to recall: not at the time, however. I had soaped the insides of my socks. An old soldier who had served in India had assured me it was the best way to keep your feet fit for marching in heat. By the second day I had blisters, large ones, on both; they didn't improve.

Barbers' shops, so I heard, were a fount of local information. I gave up shaving to place my custom at the end of the day where I might best discover a bed for the night. At least on one occasion the intelligence service must have broken down. I bedded down for the night behind a hedge in a rather rocky field. Knapsack-research came up with only a lump of hard sausage coated with green mould, a strict modicum of which I devoured after stripping away the rind. That rind must have transmitted a powerful scent. I had no sooner closed my eyes than something warm and soft passed over my forehead. It belonged in the mouth of a hungry spotted dog. He sheered off as I came bolt upright. No doubt a friendly dog! The shock of his introduction, however, put an end to any further chance of sleep and I took to the road again in the dark. There was a large house at the entrance to the next village with carts drawn up outside—a Teamsters' Rest. A bed, even for an hour or two, seemed advisable. Alas, there was to sleep that way either. The huge sack of straw was alive with fleas. I was off on the road again before cockcrow.

At least I was allowed to say Mass that morning after a careful scrutiny of my papers, signed by the Archbishop of Mitylene. In another village the priest took one look at me in my saffron get-up and slammed the door. Who could blame him? "A Buddist monk? Where's his begging-bowl?"

Further along the road there was a wayside chapel. A young priest was preaching to a fair-sized congregation in the open air. He hammered them hard. After Mass I resumed the march to be passed a little later by the same young priest flying along on a bicycle. I had given up tobacco for the duration of the pilgrimage, but unmistakably there was a large pipe in his mouth, fuming away. I promptly lit a cigarette. It ill became me to refuse the example of so strict a censor of morals . . .

The fifth and last day of the march I abandoned roads and relied on my own fallible bump of direction. A goat track through the trees looked likely. Though it swayed from left to right, the line was consistent, and I confidently followed it mile after mile, until hunger and fatigue called a halt. The knap-sack yielded a final stub of sausage which I gnawed at with distaste, realising, however, I must stoke up. I could be hopelessly off target. Not a bit of it! I was in the last belt of trees to the south of Aljustrel, the village within the parish of Fatima where the three children who saw Our Lady were born. In fact I debouched alongside the Cemetery where the two younger ones, Francis and Jacinta, lay buried. (They have since been re-buried in the Fatima basilica.)

The legend above the cemetery gates ran: "The Bones waiting here are waiting for Yours too!"

Forty odd years ago "Tia" Olimpia, mother of two of the little shepherds, Jacinta and Francis, still sped like a bird barefoot along the road I now took from Aljustrel to Fatima. She and her husband, tall spare Senhor Marto, later welcomed me with great courtesy into their home. Manuel Pedro Marto loved to talk about the children, taking his time, gently lingering over their early deaths (Francis 1919, Jacinta 1920). As he told the story, his wife busied herself with little cheeses for my refreshment. From time to time she darted from the kitchen to interrupt the old man with additions and comments. Senhor Marto tolerantly disagreed here and there, insisting he had the right angle. He was emphatic that neither child gave any sign of being different after their experience in the Cova da Iria. But neither did their elders! On the 13th June the parents went as usual to St. Anthony's Fair at Porto de Mos. That was the day their children were to return to the Cova to see Our Lady for the second time. Parents wisely went elsewhere.

I was greatly amused at Olimpia's comment on the modest fact that I was born on the same day as her son, Francis, 11 June 1908. "Then you are the lucky one"—meaning, still earthbound. The lucky one! And Francis had seen Our Lady in both worlds, this one and the next!

My guides on that visit to Fatima were two seminarists from the diocese of Port Alegre. The clergy of that diocese were "in retreat". I was kindly lodged in the same hostel with them. Silence was assured at meals. The Bishop patrolled the refectory. He looked a martinet, though later we met on Fatima station and he was manifestly not what I had thought.

I have twice visited Fatima since 1942. The inevitable transformation has taken place: roads sweep up to the Cova de Iria leaving broad open flanks and every arrangement for easy dispersal. The old hollow in which the oak-tree once grew is now encased in concrete with space for the million pilgrims who rally there half a dozen times a year on the 13th of the months between May and October. But Fatima will never perhaps experience the same sustained affluence of pilgrims so characteristic of Lourdes every day of the season. Fatima's glory is in its unsurpassed peak-events and the heroic, old-style confluence to the shrine of a million faithful peasants on foot, sleeping rough, carrying babies-in-arms, singing and praying on the way.

What about the credibility of the apparitions at both Lourdes and Fatima? "Surely both have a common source in the credulity of a backward peasantry?" suggest the critics who, I suppose, can't always be blamed for their ignorance of Church procedures.

Fatima may not ever equal even the modest number of cures attested over a whole century at Lourdes, those which have passed scrutiny at the Bureau des Constations. The criteria in force there could not be more rigorously demanding: full medical documentation of the disorder *beforehand*; automatic disqualification of any disorder attributable to nervous causes; proof positive of the permanence of the alleged cure gained by repeated year-by-year appearances of the patient for examination at the Bureau; unanimous agreement of the experts that the cure could not be attributed to any known natural agency and so on.

I was once present in 1928 at a Pilgrimage when a girl in an advanced stage of consumption rose from her only possible prone position at the Blessed Sacrament blessing. She was hurriedly wheeled away.* Enthusiasm led her fellow-pilgrims to sing the *Magnificat* at the Grotto. It was a fatal anticipation of the privilege only conceded after the final verdict of the Bureau. The case was, I believe, again summarily dismissed from all further consideration.

Fatima, however, can claim an event unique, as far as I know, in the history of all our miraculous shrines—the Miracle of the Sun!

The children had predicted that on a certain day, at a certain hour, the sun would dance down towards the earth. Sceptics of all persuasions gathered to witness their total discredit. The press was there in force complete with cameras. A huge crowd gathered to the spot. The Lisbon evening papers recorded the whole event with photographs that same day.

Exactly as the children had foretold the sun went through the most unusual motions. A wild cry went up as finally it hurtled down towards the multitide. This is not to be attributed to mass hysteria. Isolated witnesses at considerable distances from the spot recorded their own stupified experience. They saw what the crowd saw and testified to its truth.

I have seen copies of the newspapers which carried the event. At that time of anti-clericalism and disaffection from the Catholic Church, testimony coming from such a source as Portugal's national press can only be judged as (in the legal phrase) *omni exceptione maior*—totally unprejudiced by any form of self-interest.

---

*Footnote: By John Traynor, the famous Liverpool "*miraculé*". He was a "total disability pensioner" from the First War as a result of a shrapnel wound in the brain. He went to Lourdes and was cured. Even the silver plate covering the wound disappeared. John called it "Our Lady's tip!" Pain and helplessness, he said, were never worse than during the night before the cure. His return to Liverpool produced an enormous reception party at Lime Street Station. All Scotland Road turned out to welcome a friendly convivial man always in a wheelchair pushed by a friend who also received a pension for his full-time services. When John reported his cure to the War Pensions authorities, they refused to budge from their original verdict of "Total

Disability" and continued his pension. John started a modest trade delivering coal, carrying sacks of it on his own broad back.

He returned every year to Lourdes with the Diocesan Pilgrimage as chief brancardier (organiser of the men responsible for moving the sick from place to place in wheelchairs, ambulances, etc.) It was under his genial direction I served my apprenticeship in 1928.

Never had it entered my imagination that the human body could be heir to such a legacy of diseases. (Lupus, e.g. was common in those days.) I think John realised how callow and squeamish I was. I had my share in the latrines. A word of praise from him worked wonders.

Looking back (and begging pardon for this over-long digression) may I record a conviction that this experience saw me finally across the bridge into manhood.

CHAPTER XXI

Lusitanian Valedictory

LISBON was a war-time "neutral" city seething with espionage, propaganda and counter-propaganda, yet totally devoted to our final victory in arms. One of the mainstays of the College, I later discovered, was a Secret Agent. If Franco, in that rendez-vous with Hitler at Irun-Hendaye, had let the Wehrmacht into the Peninsula, this man, with others, was entrusted with blowing up the bridges in Portugal.

Returning from my younger brother's ordination* in England, I landed at Lisbon airport alongside a plane identical with mine. Both planes were K.L.M. Dakotas. "Mine" had escaped the Netherlands invasion, the other hadn't: it was manned by Gerries. Off Ushant a member of the crew brought me a cup of tea. He pointed upwards on the port-side: "Messerschmits!" There were four of them cavorting around the sky some distance away. One flew high out to starboard of us. "Isn't there a Gentlemens' Agreement about this flight?" I asked, for I had been told something to that effect before embarking. He laughed as he repeated my phrase. "Nothing to put your money on . . ." he added. The tips of my fingers, I regret to say, went quite wet . . .

Not so long afterwards on a return flight, the Lisbon plane was in fact shot down. Among the victims was Leslie Howard. Lisbon had packed the Teatro Nacional for his soliloquies from Shakespeare. Alone and dressed in a lounge suit, he held us spellbound for an unforgettable evening. His death was, I suppose, a grim recognition of his immense value to our cause in "neutral" countries. He too "laid down his life for his friends". Lights were still going out in Europe.

In the meantime the good life in Lisbon opened up bright vistas of Catholic pastoral work: days of recollection for the British community, catechism in the English School at Carcavellos, Mass at a Portuguese enclosed convent—even the odd sermon in Portuguese. Whereas I can't remember a single evening spent in a Spanish home, doors opened in Lisbon so hospitably as to menace one's duty to the College. Golf and sea-bathing were instantly available and so much else I had come to associate exclusively with holidays in England. Guests apeared at the professors' table *en route* for or return from Rome—Monsignor Hugh O'Flaherty of the "Vatican Escape Route"; D'Arcy Osborne, British Minister to the Holy Sea, then a guest

* 14.2.1943

92

within the Vatican, and others. Flying-boats from Lagos decanted military personnel to await their next flight on to Poole harbour or Foins. Neutrality demanded their brief stay ashore be passed in "civvies". Gerry propaganda, it was said, took over another shop-window on the Chiado for every reverse they suffered. (We were at last turning the tide in the desert.) The sight of our military top-brass from Africa pacing that famous thoroughfare in borrowed, ill-fitting plumage must have excited certain *schadenfreude* behind those plate-glass windows.

Part of Monsignor Cullen's teaching legacy was Classics. The year of Poetry, the sixth of the seven-year division of Humanities, involved the students in composing Latin verses according to the strict and intricate rules of Latin prosody. I have never composed a single line though I must have read thousands of them. I found myself correcting hexameters. It was a pleasant exercise akin to "doing the crossword" and a welcome interlude between Hurter's Scholastic Theology, Monsignor Cullen's text-book, and Liturgical History, to name the two other components of his work-load which fell to me. There were others still within his role as professor.

Much of the Douai tradition lived on in the daughter college on the Tagus. The game of Cat (or is it Quat?) a French sixteenth-century base-ball game, in a different version from the Ushaw tradition, was played during the weeks of early summer when students and professors transferred *en bloc* to the out-of-town house at Luz. A hit which cleared the perimeter fence of the large playing field automatically earned a full day off from studies and lectures. I don't remember it happening. I doubt if any of the star Yankees could do it. Another Douai survival was the pedagogue system. A junior seminarist† was assigned on arrival to a senior theologian for whom he performed certain tasks, such as tidying his rooms. The boy's study desk was in a corner of his pedagogue's room. He had the right to consult his pedagogue on any difficult point in his lessons.

Lisbonians also inherited a tradition of scholarship continuing into later life. Several of them had proved doughty champions of the Church in the religious controversies of the 17th and 18th centuries. John Gother's *A Papist Misrepresented and Represented* (1685) brought the redoubtable Bishop Stillingfleet into the lists along with a host of lesser Anglican theologians. Gother, single-handed, more than maintained his position throughout an endless series of charges and counter-charges. He wrote very clear trenchant prose. In fact Dryden saluted him as the only other man, besides himself, who knew how to write English. Perhaps his early upbringing as a strict Presbyterian played a part here. But undoubtedly his fourteen years as a mature student at Lisbon (1668-1682) account for his theological acumen. His devotion to the College moved him to return there by sea in 1704. It was to be his last resting place. He fell

† Boys of 12-13 were still being admitted as late as 1940.

ill on the voyage and died at sea 2 October 1704. There was a priest on board who gave him the last rites. Impressed by his holiness, the captain preserved the body and delivered it to the College for burial.

Gother's output in twenty-two years as a priest was phenomenal. He was appreciated not only by Catholics. There were many converts from his controversy with Stillingfleet. Despite his retiring disposition he was proposed as bishop of the Western District shortly before his death.

In the College Chapel against the wall flanking Gother's grave, there is the head-stone of another remarkable Englishman, Francis Tregian of Cornwall (1548-1608). His vast estates brought him an annual income of £3,000. He chose, however, to reside at court as the strategic point for being of assistance to persecuted fellow Catholics. He hid St. Cuthbert Mayne when the hunt was on for this intrepid missionary priest from the English College, Douai*. Elizabeth was furious, confiscated all his properties and gaoled him. Tregian's biographer, however, has another explanation of her fury in the old adage: "Heaven knows no fury like that of a woman spurned."

After twenty-eight years in prison Tregian was released by James I and banished overseas. He stayed at Douai, the haven of many Catholic exiles besides the seminarists. He moved later to Madrid, where the King granted him a pension, and died at Lisbon on 25 September 1608. Seventeen years later Francis Tregian's body was found free of all decay. Incorruption is not accepted by the Catholic Church as alone a sufficient criterion for canonisation. Normally she requires more than one miracle rigorously proven to be beyond any natural agency and clearly attributable to prayer for divine intervention because of the candidate's holiness in life.

In the case of Francis Tregian remarkable divine favours are not wanting and the significant title "Confessor" has been coupled with his name, with what authority, however, is not clear. I would welcome an official enquiry into his credentials for sainthood by the highest authority. He has a lesson for our time, in marital fidelity, and not only that of spouse to spouse. If his biographer's explanation of the Queen's fury is correct, he made that one very clear. Equally relevant, however, is the fidelity of the spouses to the demands of their privileged act of union in one flesh. Of its nature, as the expression of mutual self-giving, that privilege is both unitive and open to life. Here also are two elements God has joined together which may not be "put asunder".

Were Francis Tregian's cause pursued as far as canonisation, he could perhaps be the first Saint to have eighteen children. At the same time I think the Holy See would have to face a female lobby

---

* St. Cuthbert Mayne was in the end apprehended and hanged, drawn and quartered at Launceston on 30 November 1577. Of the many martyred priests from the continental Colleges, he was the first to suffer the penalty for High Treason under the 1558 New Act of Supremacy 1 Elizabeth. c. 1 and the Act of Uniformity 1 Eliz. c. 2.

claiming equal, or rather prior, rights for Mary, his spouse, to share the honours of being raised to the altars of the Church. Surely she, too, practised virtue to a heroic degree.

I cannot let Lisbon go without saluting once again the as yet unrecognised saints and maybe sinners, both British and Portuguese, who in those early war years cherished and supported the College and would have continued to do so, war or no war, *in saecula saeculorum*. In 1961 I was sent by the Holy See to visit both Valladolid and Lisbon Colleges and report. Monsignor Henson had died some months beforehand. Valladolid College has healthily survived under three successors. *Floreat!* Alas, Lisbon has gone forever. *Saudades!* to a precious portion of our Post-Reformation heritage.

Let me take leave of a country and College I came to love dearly in those two privileged years. They were my last of twenty-four spent as student and professor in English Colleges for priestly studies in Lancashire, Spain, Rome and Portugal. Students' loyalty to their Alma Mater was strongest, I must record, to Sts. Peter and Paul's, Lisbon. That College after three hundred and fifty years has changed hands, and I, *contre coeur*, with another bishop who is an alumnus of Lisbon College, was in at the final decision to close. I greatly treasure the honorary life-membership of the Lisbonian Society granted so generously on my departure in 1943.

A new rector was then due to take over at Lisbon. It was time I moved on. Archbishop Downey graciously authorised my volunteering. Monsignor Dewey, senior R.C. Chaplain R.N., welcomed it warmly: "I'd almost come to believe our bishops had put an embargo on us." He had had no reinforcements for months. A surprise awaited me at the medical. Did the young doctor take me for a conscript as so many have presumed I was for the priesthood at the age of twelve? "You don't really want to join up, do you"? The suggestion was he could fix it for me. I reassured him. He must have passed me: an appointment duly arrived.

CHAPTER XXII

"Destination: R.M. Small Arms Training Camp, Dalditch, Exeter"

THE three-tonner at Exeter station was already loaded with Marines returning from their "run-ashore" among the blacked-out city lights. They eyed the new recruit uneasily as I flung in my gear and climbed aboard. There were no doubt plenty of good reasons for that. I prefer this kindlier explanation. The only recognised R.N. outfitters in my native town had rigged me impeccably in all things save the cap. That they encircled with a black band carrying what they assured me was the current insignia of chaplains R.N., a black gun-metal Maltese Cross. On the unsophisticated marine this could have acted like the skull and crossbones on Kaiser Bill's death or glory cavalry in the early days of the First War. From the ensuing conversation I gathered the last transport from Exeter was crucial to life at Dalditch, the alternative being a mid-winter's five-mile walk. The country road we travelled, so far from being the brilliant red colour constantly attributed to it by the marines, was white with hoar-frost.

I made my number on arrival with the mess president, George Underwood, a major promoted from the ranks after deeds of derring-do in the Zeebrugge raid of the First War. He was not the only Royal Marine on the camp to have been honoured for that desperate exploit. Our victualling officer, a captain, had the Victoria Cross. He introduced me here and there and conducted me through the pitch-black night to my nissen hut. Topography was far from clear as I had reason to lament later when, sallying forth in response to a call of nature, I landed myself full length in a ditch. "Ice and snow bless the Lord" (Daniel 3, 80). Mercifully the ditch was frozen.

I had inherited my predecessor's M.O.A. (Marine Officer's Attendant). Though I shared him with another officer he was to all intents and purposes my full time treasure, a devout Catholic and like all in his branch of service, the only reliable source of information among the "buzzes" or rumours as to our future movements. Later he shyly asked me to teach him to read.

There was a handsome R.C. Chapel at Dalditch, in which we reserved the Blessed Sacrament. My predecessor had left everything ready for this, but jibbed at taking the risk. He needn't have worried. But there was one valuable hint I picked up from him concerning confessions. They mostly occurred before Sunday Mass and in full view of the assembly. "Make sure they leave you with a smile on their faces" said Father Harry. He was right. How many waverers were heartened by those smiles to come forward is anyone's guess. I should say a pretty fair number. But my chief disappointment at Dalditch was reserved for Good Friday.

The parish priest of Exeter, Father O'Malley, enjoyed a great reputation at Dalditch where, I think, he served as officiating chaplain for a time. Captain Lesser, whose father was a judge, was so taken by Father O'Malley's wit, he had his family down from London to pass an evening in his company. It was this charmer who launched the idea of a living tableaux of the Stations of the Cross at 3 p.m. on Good Friday in the open-air Cattle Market at Exeter. Catholics were, I gather, few on the ground in that once Catholic Cathedral City. Hence the rub! Chaplains were to marshal *their* flocks. The grand finale would be confessions for the troops with priests stationed all round the market precincts. Shrewdly the charmer went first to work on Father Freese, Principal Chaplain U.S.A. At this point, the Cornish-Devonian peninsula was credibly reported to have sunk six inches owing to the concentration of arms and men on its surface. This was the build-up for the invasion of Europe. Freese, Father O'Malley informed me, had promised seven hundred men. I was next. "How many? R.M.s at Dalditch number over 3,000. Aren't we the usual 10%? So, three hundred? Just right for the 1,000! You'll get transport laid on, of course."

He was gentler with Father Barry, the Ack-Ack man. The peninsula was dotted with Ack-Ack as England now is with petrol pumps. Father Barry could never get them together. I think he settled for thirty.

The day dawned at Dalditch. Long lines of three-tonners were drawn up. Colour sergeants were on duty to see the gallant three hundred aboard in an orderly manner. I had made every effort to get the event home to the men. Thirty-seven turned up: one and a half three-tonners. Father Barry fielded ten. But Freese's seven hundred were all there, fine and dandy as promised.

The decor was well done. Fourteen of Father O'Malley's altar-boys were spaced evenly round the cattle-market perimeter, each holding a framed "Station". Processional cross-bearer and acolytes preceded the parish priest as he moved from Station to Station for the meditations. His choir tunefully intercalated the Stabat Mater stanzas. All went well. The seven hundred and forty-seven men sat on the ground for the next feature. They filled a good half of the arena. By this time local citizens were three deep on the rails. I was to speak first, Freese followed. He really went to town. My effort, by contrast, sounded like a pep talk for convent school girls. But even Freese's splendid declamation paled beside what followed. Chairs and stoles were supplied to the five priests. Our turn to be distributed strategically round the market. Long files of penitents

97

lined up for our services. Ropes and handcuffs were never less needed. Later in the Normandy landings I got used to Yanks demanding confession as soon as I set foot on a quarter-deck.

The locals gazed and still the wonder grew as the men knelt at the priests' knees, off-loading their burden and receiving absolution. I can't, however, honestly say I did much to "Have 'em on their way smiling." There was no need. The men were willing and 'raring' to come. Invasion was in the wind.

I could scarcely bear to look at my own "Dog and Basket" troops in the next few days and mentally added five words to their motto *"Ubique."**

Our colonel at Dalditch was an inspiration to us all. I would love to recall his name but it may be enough to identify him as the darling of Pompey† in the Saturday night boxing ring before the War? A somewhat middle-aged Captain Carey was one of my Catholic stalwarts. He belonged to a well-known recusant family in Devonshire. That he got through the R.M. Officers' toughening-up course does him considerable credit. One exercise involved being submerged some distance from the shore at Dawlish (I think) and being dragged in along the sea-bed. I asked him once what was his line in "civvy-street". Was he pulling my leg? With a very straight face he answered: "Before the War I was rather mixed-up in cement." The "Schooly", Lieutenant Singleton, came from the Lancashire Fylde where whole villages held on to the old Faith through the penal days. I suppose in Kings Regulations he should have taken on my M.O.A. for reading lessons—no doubt with much better success than I did.

Relations in the chaplains branch were frankly cordial. The Church of England padre, M. A. P. Wood, now (rtd.) Bishop of Norwich gave all he had. In the best sense of Shakespeare's phrase he was also "the glass of fashion and the mould of form." The O.D. chaplain (whose name I can't recall) was very different from both of us. If not born there, he was brought up in Plymouth Naval Dockyard where his father held a position of trust. He spoke pure golden Devonian. An eternal pipe rested in the corner of his mouth, which curved nonetheless into a permanent welcoming smile. He talked a lot of sense and knew Dalditch Camp, every nook and cranny.

Not a word so far about the fair countryside from which the camp site had been gashed out. A reasonable walk to the cliffs and you were down in Budleigh Salterton where, I believe: "Colonels speak only to Generals and Generals speak only to God." On Sunday evenings I spoke to the people of God in the local Catholic church. Father Fanning, parish priest of St. Peter's, was an alumnus of St.

---

* The Royal Marine badge is a lion mounted on a globe. *"Ubique"* (Everywhere) refers to world-wide zones in which they have served. My sardonic addition was " . . . but where you should be."
† Portsmouth.

Alban's College, Valladolid, a contemporary of Rector Henson's, from whom I had often heard of this talented priest. Ottery St. Mary's, Collerton Raleigh and other delectable towns and hamlets prompted me to get my bicycle sent down from home. I did not get much chance to use it. The "ubiquitous" Marines filled in most of my days. Officers told me of farmhouses where strawberries and cream teas were still available free from all ersatz ingredients. I never got there. Time at Dalditch was running short. May came and was half-way gone when Monsignor Dewey informed me a new appointment was in the offing. My replacement was due any day. I should go on leave at once.

By now everyone was aware the Big One was imminent. The build-up in our corner of England was not exclusively material. All R.C. chaplains gathered for a spiritual retreat. Fathers O'Malley and Freese assembled about three dozen of us in Exeter. Ack-Ack Father Barry and I were, I think, the only Limey participants.

Father Barry was quite certain he would die. No badinage could shake him out of this conviction. No doubt he made all the better use of our brief spiritual refresher which again did nothing to change his premonition. In fairness to him I must here anticipate events four or five weeks ahead. Father Barry did die. The manner of his death no one, not even he, could have anticipated. He had moved up that day with his unit to a position behind the main advance where they occupied a damaged and deserted farmhouse. He was in his room, writing, I think. There was a hole in the wall probably made by one of our shells. Through that hole came the Gerry shell that killed him.

The night that followed our retreat in Exeter was his last with fellow-priests. It was a *"Gaudeamus Igitur"* such as our particular fraternity alone can celebrate. Frankly I remember more of the night than the preceding day. Luckily the "Charmer" had transport laid on for getting us back to Dalditch in the small hours.

My snatch of leave (or "leaf" as the matelots called it) came abruptly to an end with a signal requiring me to report at Combined Ops. H.Q. in London the following Monday. My brother and I were in Liverpool on the Saturday and paid a good-bye visit to St. Mary's Highfield, the Benedictine Church near Exchange Station. I had never made a will. Together we cobbled up a formula and wrote it down sitting in the pews. The Benedictine parish priest was just emerging from his confessional. My brother neatly intercepted him. Somewhat reluctantly the old man witnessed my signature. As he handed me the pen after appending his own, he said very gently: "I hope I have not witnessed a death warrant."

CHAPTER XXIII

J for Juno

COMBINED Ops. H.Q. interviewed, equipped and drafted us chaplains as one by one we were called up an outside stairway. Our Commander's propitious name was Commodore England. Three vessels were involved as accommodation ships: *Ascanius*, an Alfred Holt crate that once sailed the China Seas; *Thysville*, a Belgian liner from the Antwerp-Matadi run; and *Cap Touraine*, a reparations prize extracted from Germany after World War I, and presumably "borrowed" from Vichy France.

Our job as chaplains was primarily with Royal Marines manning L.C.P.s*. In addition to R.M.s there were Royal Navy and Merchant Navy crews on the three accommodation ships. Any other vessel in our area without a chaplain would also look to us. Transport was waiting outside Combined Ops. H.Q. to take us to our ship, the *Ascanius*. At last were were afloat but not at sea. We lay incommunicado alongside the Pool of London. After two days aboard a crowded ship someone must have got permission to give us a breather in the interests of both our physique and our morale. It was, however, a very different "run ashore". We were marched from the ship, forbidden to break ranks, to a country estate somewhere in Essex. I remember a house or fort surrounded by a moat, which in turn, was surrounded by a barbed wire fence.

Back aboard I made my number with the Merchant Navy crew of the *Ascanius*. The home port for the Holt liners and crews was Liverpool. The men were mostly Catholics from St. Malachy's parish where a famous Father Murphy ran a boxing club and ran it very well to judge by its popularity and the champions it produced. Does "Ginger Foran" still ring a bell? That's where he learned to box. One of the youngest members of the *Ascanius* crew could scarcely have qualified at quite the same level. He had taken a terrific pasting in his last fight and could scarcely articulate a word of two syllables. It was touching to observe how the old hands in their own rough way were nursing him along.

The day came for meeting our Commodore England. He boarded *Ascanius*, the mother ship, and from us spoke to the other units under his command. He was a tall, white-haired, choleric gentleman. Somewhere in the 'thirties I imagine, he had fallen as a captain

* Landing Craft *Personnel*. There were various craft initialled L.C.: LCT (Tanks), LCG (Guns) etc.

under "Geddes' Axe", that devastating reducer of World War I naval officers. Decently enough, they were on axing promoted to a higher rank. Their name, on recruitment into World War II, was "Dugouts". They were Legion and thank God they were still around. From his fire-eating address we gathered that Combined Ops were supremely vital to the Operation shortly to be mounted. He called us, I think the "Build-Up".

We three chaplains were presented to him. I was Number Three and found it hard to keep a straight face when the O.D. chaplain, next after the C. of. E., was presented. His name was MacRurie. He was a Scottish Wee Free, and found it just too much when the Commodore, obviously confused with "McRory", saluted him as the R.C. chaplain. The correction, I need not say, came at once and sharply. But both my colleagues became good friends. I met Mr MacRurie years later when I was civvy Port Chaplain in Bombay. He was returning from the China Station, still chaplain R.N. His wife was with him and a sweeter lady you would travel very far to meet. In a rather different way, you might also call the Anglican chaplain a "Dugout". He had entered the Navy as a youth and trained in gunnery. Like all graduates from the Gunnery School at Pompey he had the right to wear the "shin-leggings" which he did throughout the present campaign. He had interrupted his naval career to become a parson and was likely to be chosen for a living somewhere in Salop after the War, if, as he put it, "my face fits" with the patron whom he had still to meet. That patron would have been an ass not to find his face "fitted". He was a very perfect, gentle padre. Though I cannot recall his name after forty years, I salute him, grateful always for his comradeship and example.

I had a neat but tiny cabin aboard* and stowed my gear decorously. As recommended, it was down to the minimum: only two books—breviary and a Charles Dickens. I had of course my Mass kit which more or less fitted into a haversack. Boarding other vessels by means of the scrambling net, you had to be pretty sure of your hold. You carried the right weight for direct transit to Davy Jones's locker.

My "action-station" reasonably enough was near the sick bay where all the casualties would arrive. We drilled with fire-protective covering on our hands and face. All this was under the direction of "Number One", our commander's senior officer. I award him in retrospect a richly deserved accolade. He was, in contrast to his chief, of a mild and forbearing temperament, nonetheless efficient and totally loyal to his superior. He accompanied him on "Captain's Rounds" carefully recording his comments.

Somehow the Captain of the *Thysville* alongside us had kept his cool, despite the peace time complication of Congolese deckhands

* As we hit the Normandy Beaches, I surrendered my cabin to our first casualty. I'd little choice in fact. Even so, I vividly remember being overwhelmed by the ecstacy of possessing nothing—a totally unmerited Franciscan thrill of joy.

and the wartime addition of an R.N. crew. He was Belgian and the secret of his urbanity may well have been his love of music. He had a massive collection of records aboard which he played throughout Mass in the main lounge. Few priests, I imagine, have celebrated to the coloratura accompaniment of Signora Galli-Curci. But more pertinently to his good relations with our naval top brass, he had a considerable crate aboard of Angostura Bitters. This vital element of all Pink Gins (best drunk East of Suez, they say) was unobtainable at this stage of the war in our theatre of operations. A feature of the R.N. presence off Normandy was to be the courtesy calls paid to the *Thysville* in Senior Officers' barges, and the small parcels nestling closely to the heavily-ringed sleeves as the great men later descended.

The *Cap Touraine* must have been a pleasant ship for peace time voyaging. I had my own reasons for gratitude to her. I had seriously miscalculated the number of communion hosts I was going to need. Already the imminence of battle was having its effect on the men. Now they were beginning to come after me. There was still a lot of hunting to do, and already I had met a classical reluctance which in a way one had to admire. The formula, more or less, was this: "I never bother with religion in the ordinary way. I'd be a skunk if I changed because now I'm in some sort of danger." The best I could do was invite them to say what they'd do if they were haring along a road in the blackout and sudden lightning showed they were on the edge of a landslide or a cliff? It didn't always work but certainly some started thinking.

But to get back to the *Cap Touraine*, and my shortage of hosts. We had moved from the Pool down river and were anchored off Southend. Very reluctantly our Number One agreed to let me ashore for essential supplies. A boat was lowered and I stepped on to the pier. That was as far as I went. The Red Caps and the civvy police absolutely refused to let me go any further. They had their orders. Any attempt to go higher was certain to meet with a peremptory refusal, I was assured. But the chief steward of the *Cap Touraine* at least temporarily solved my problem. He unlocked one of the elegant glass cupboards in the main lounge and produced a large tin hermetically sealed. He gave me his honest expert opinion after sampling. The hosts were in perfect condition.

It was late evening that same day when we weighed anchor. *Ascanius* trembled as the engines turned over. Over the loudspeakers came the Commander's voice. More trembling? Never! "Our destination is J for Juno, the toughest of the beaches. God save the King!"

Somewhere between Folkestone and Dungeness we drew fire from the iron nostrils of Cap Gris-Nez. There Gerry had his heaviest guns. It was a forenoon of fair weather and fine visibility. The troops were battened down under hatches. They could, of course, hear the boom of the guns. Perhaps they could also hear and see the shells as they splashed around us. To make sure that they missed none of the "fun", the loudspeakers broadcast expert information from the Bridge.

"That one—five cables adrift."

"This one—three and a half."

"The last one—not a bad shot."

This, I suppose, is all in the tradition of stiff-upper lips and true British phlegm. But I thought differently and with men crowded and cooped up below, decided it was my turn to get into the act.

"Where the hell are you off to, Padre?" I was well on my way to the bridge.

"I'm going to broadcast General Absolution."*

It was his turn to think differently.

"Belay there at once! You realise we are fighting this ship?"

No doubt "General Absolution" was double Dutch to the watch-dog. So was his "fighting ship" to me. I can't remember a single reply coming from our guns: we were miles out of range. In fairness, however, to the watch-dog, I have since tardily taken his point. Technically, they were at action stations for whatever reprisals Gerry might get up to—gun-boats, submarines, the lot! He, Gerry, seems to have reflected it could be counter-productive to launch his units in seas peppered by his own mammoth shells. But once past Dungeness we were clear of trouble all the way down the Courseulles. There we dropped anchor opposite J for Juno, the middle beach of the British assault area, flanked by Gold and Sword.

Helen of Troy's face, we read, "launched a thousand ships". The Combined Services, Royal and Merchant, had done rather better, and without the need of poetic licence. Indeed, with a touch of brâvura, they had actually sunk a couple of dozen. These sat on their bottoms, stem to stern, in three elegant half-moons, the "Gooseber-ries", D.I.Y. harbours, behind which the sinews of the assault were initially unloaded. Everyone has heard of the Mulberries which arrived later, their sections riding the waves like huge inverted grand pianos with their legs in the air. Few know of the crucial service of the Gooseberries in the early days of the landings.

Lord Haw-Haw swooped like a hawk on their undeniable position on the bottom of the sea. Naming the sunken vessels one by one with scrupulous accuracy, he neatly diverted credit for the sinkings to the Gerry Luftwaffe and shore-batteries. His trump-card was the *Jean Bart*, the pivotal unit of the Sword Beach Mulberry. My introduction to this old battlewaggon, once the pride of the French Navy, came curiously enough. The extreme left of our assault area was under constant fire from across the River Orne. Why did we delay cleaning up the nuisance? Rumour ran that the Navy had offered its services, but met with Monty's decision to keep our assault area strictly this side of the Orne. Anyway it was clearly my duty to get to Sword

* The faculty of clearing consciences without individual confession in crisis circumstances.

103

Beach at once. Gerry was throwing a nasty high fragmentation shell, the kind that bursts above the target into a lethal hailstorm.

The *Jean Bart* was the H.Q. ship of the Sword Mulberry. I was ferried over to her from the shore after a rather odd experience. There was a little café not so far back from the shore. Surprisingly it was not only still there despite our cannonade and bombs, it was actually open for custom. We paid a visit as to a shrine. I can't recall what they had on offer but behind the bar hung an old coloured calendar showing the *Jean Bart* in all her glory. We left for the beach. There was the *Jean Bart* up to her waist in the drink half a dozen cables away. The old fellow behind the bar had fished out a fifteen-year old calendar to honour a Great Lady now in somewhat reduced circumstances. Once aboard her I had plenty to hear about those H.F. shells and a lot to do. On a return visit days later, I had a full house for Mass preceded by confessions. The only entry to the chapel area was through a lobby in which I sat with my stole on and bagged the lot, all individually shriven. All is fair in love and war. I could claim both.

I told them at the Mass of a young girl* who died a few miles inland from us in the Carmel at Lisieux. She promised she would shower favours ("roses", she called them) on people in need. In view of the prevailing havoc on Sword I decided to enlist for a "rose". I can't think what got hold of me but at the end of the homily I found myself saying: "There will be no more casualties aboard this crate. St Thérèse has it all in hand. In the name of the Father . . . " There *were* no more casualties. Within half-an-hour the order came to evacuate the *Jean Bart*.

It was not the end, however, of High Fragmentation. An L.C.G. patrolled our flank, pumping the odd shell across to Gerry. He didn't like it and with deadly accuracy put his reply slap into the ratings' messroom as they were at tea. The only living creature to emerge unscathed was the ship's dog.

Gerry even so hadn't finished chucking his canisters. A burly chap in a blue gansey paired me in moving a stretcher-case off one ship to the adjoining L.C.T. We were half-way there when the H.F. burst above us. Down we went but with a difference. The burly chap fell so that his body entirely covered the wounded man: I with my hands protecting my own head. I never met the man before or since. I don't think we exchanged a single word. Had he ever heard of the parable of the Good Samaritan? That day he lived it heroically.

My base was still J for Juno where they gave me a tent ashore next to a Beaufors Gun. It sounded as though it was fired inside the tent. I can't say, however, I lost any sleep. I remember bedding down one night knowing Gerry had our range (he had well proved it) but too tired to bother about whether I'd be there in the morning. The same

---

* Marie Françoise Thérèse Martin: the "Little Flower"; born 1873, same year as my mother who was present at her canonisation in 1925 and lived 17 years longer to pray to her.

insouciance could take over in broad daylight. We were bowling along in an L.C.P. this time. Gerry was firing in salvos of three. Numbers one and two hit the drink. Three would be smack on our way ahead. The helmsman held his course amidships. Should I tell him? Why bother? He knew his job. Number Three, for once, never came.

Juno Beach remained my H.Q. though many a night I dossed down on the last ship I'd visited. Let me pay a warm tribute to the top brass and especially the Anglican chaplains of our cruisers. It seemed that I was the only R.C. chaplain in the area. I couldn't have been received more kindly. C. of E. chaplains appeared to be all High Church and made me free of their altar facilities. I met on the troutline* an Australian chaplain who was Low Church and in rather low spirits. He told me why. During the previous night they had caught a couple of Gerry frogmen in the act of sticking a limpet mine onto their cherished Hunt Class Destroyer. It seems they were welcomed aboard in a manner which the padre judged inconsistent with the Geneva Convention governing the handling of prisoners-of-war. The chaplain in duty bound felt he should register his protest with the captain. It was not well received. In fact the Captain was still seething with fire and brimstone when I made my number with him. I offered him a cigarette. More flames! His noble father never smoked before noon, nor did he! I registered three cheers for the Chaplain Courageous and (in Runyonese) a "mild hello" for the Captain Conflagratious.

It is bitter-sweet to recall now being piped aboard Polish vessels†. I shall ever remember Mass and meal on the *Slazak* (pronounced Slonzak). But one Polish unit, a cruiser (Danae Class) piped no pipes. She was the *Dragon*, victim of a human torpedo. She limped into Sword Beach on one auxiliary pump and cradled between two destroyers into our Mulberry Harbour on Gold. Thank God I got aboard her well before that. The magazine flooded with oil. Nothing one could do for the victims engulfed there. I worked through the ship. Was it the engine-room? or the magazine? I there saw sights that killed for ever the "glamour of war", if that ever existed.

But let me relieve the tension. One of my three original ducklings the *Thysville* of the Antwerp-Matadi run, whose Captain achieved high-level popularity with Angostura Bitters and won my own somewhat reduced favour with his inter-Mass disco, also ran into a spot of bother. She too took an offensive shell aboard. There were structural damages, but, if I remember rightly, no serious casualties. I got aboard more or less level pegging with Commodore England. In fact we usually collided where there was trouble.

At the captain's request I met the head serang of the Congolese crew. They had been somewhat disturbed by Gerry's attentions.

---

* A screen of destroyers anchored "line-ahead" of our eastern flank.
† The Polish Navy in the days of freedom welcomed chaplains aboard and saw them away with the bosun's shrill salute. Honours don't come higher in any navy.

Formally, and with some emphasis, he proposed on behalf of the crew that I should receive the unbaptised members into the Catholic Church. This was a tricky problem. Were they victims of highly-wrought nerves or responsible human beings? So I told the head-man to assemble them on deck. They paraded in a long line. There could have been somewhat more than two dozen. Most of the native crew were already Catholics judging by the attendance at previous Masses. Pidgin French was our only medium. I put searching questions about their present desire and future commitments it would engage them in. One by one they asserted they understood and were ready and willing. A brief catechetical interlude followed: Did they believe in One God (one finger up)? Did they acknowledge three Persons (three fingers up)? Did they believe in God the Son, their Saviour Jesus Christ (both arms extended as on a Cross)? Did they undertake to live as His Church gave guidance? Emphatic acceptance all along the line.

Then I directed the serang to bring a large jug of water and baptised them, giving to everyone the same Christian name, Peter. It took much longer to write for each man a personal certificate to be shown to the priest in the Congo as soon as they got home, if ever they did.

I copied more or less the same formula used by Father Maurice de la Taille in the First War except that I could not at that point give them Holy Communion. All were clear they had to contact their priest and show him the paper at their first opportunity.

CHAPTER XXIV

Runs ashore from Bayeux to Blighty

ASHORE again at J for Juno by way of the Beachmaster, Commander Maud! Fashioned in the mould of Earl Beatty of Jutland*, his stolid presence complete with bull-dog, either pacing the strand or shooting seawards in his skimmer, telegraphed "Everything under Control".

Mines were cleared, rolls of steel netting laid down for traffic up the beach. Back in the shelter of the Gooseberry, unloading continued with supreme artistry. I could not take my eyes off one of the artists, a huge hulk of a man, poised on the gunnel, one hand gripping a stay, the other orchestrating winches. A Sir John Barbirolli of stevedores! With exquisite legerdemain he persuaded three-tonners and gun-carriages to descend and nestle on the floats below within inches of their neighbours.

Houses on the sea-front were in no shape for receiving visitors. The parish church had lost its tower on the pardonable presumption it was a Gerry look-out. Bad luck! M. le Curé took it in good part, but wryly testified, *"Aucon Allemand dans l'eglise ou dans la tour."†* I came to know and respect him greatly. The thousand ships off-shore he accepted as a perfectly normal enlargement of his little parish. We were strolling seawards one day when the Admiral happened along. I had great joy in introducing him to his parish priest. May I record for the honour of the Navy that C.I.C. could not have been more gracious. I must also record in fairness to the Army the passing-by of Monty one morning. I was alone on the roadside. He stood up in his jeep and saluted me!

One way and another I saw a lot of the Curé. He filled me in on the situation in France. Of his own flock he remarked sadly: "They have lost the will to work." At this time our sappers were beavering away on the river Courseulles which gives the place its name, freeing the estuary from years of silt and bridging it with a high-level Heath Robinson contraption which got you easily across—if you didn't look down. The oyster beds were all caput. I've seen them since in form again. What gave me greater satisfaction on that visit was to see they had re-named the street by the church after my saintly friend, the Curé: "Rue de l'Abbé Bourdon."

* As a lad I lined up in Lord Street to cheer him as he passed in an open landau the day he received the Freedom of Southport. Behind me a lady remarked: "I don't like her—she paints". A recent biography suggests she gave him as much as his cruisers gave Ad. Scheer at Jutland.
† "No Germans in the church or in the tower."

Work ashore grew as it dwindled at sea. Our Mulberry took over from the Gooseberries. One of my later memories is the landing of half a Polish Motorised Cavalry Division. On the first tank up the ramps sat two chaplains, each wearing the distinctive *Virtuti Militari* ribbon. I ran along side of them, shaking hands.

"What's the equivalent British decoration?"

They laughed exchanging glances.

"The Victoria Cross of course," and with a sharp acceleration of the whole column, were on their way.

In a forest some miles further on, all hell was let loose on them . . .

My land parish began stretching east and west as more naval units took root in the coast and the ships departed, mission completed. There was much to thank God for. Of the expected overall R.N. casualities*, only a tiny fraction were called upon for the supreme sacrifice. Some few of them it was my privilege to prepare for the Last Enemy, Death†, though neither they nor I foresaw his imminent arrival. A flotilla of L.C.P.s manned by Combined Ops. Royal Marines under Captain Downey sailed for Pompey, mission gallantly completed in the Assault Area. Great care was taken meterologically to pick the right day. L.C.P.s with their wide, flat bows were suckers in high seas. However, an unforeseen swell developed and swamped them in mid-Channel. I pray for them and commend myself to their prayers. They qualified, I firmly held and hold, for the guerdon due to those who "lay down their lives for their friends."‡

Since my lines ashore now reached from Granville on the west of the Cotentin Peninsula to Ouistraham on the Orne, I clearly qualified for personal transport and was awarded an Ariel motor-cycle after two minutes instruction how to ride it. The instruction ended with these words: "Padres are replaceable, motor-bikes are not. Remember!"

In the area of Port-en-Bessin, stuffed with our small craft, I remarked one morning extraordinary excitement converging on Bayeux. Next to where I pulled up, a small over-crowded car was parked. The kepi grazing the roof could belong only to one head, Charles de Gaulle's!

A couple of hundred yards along the road I met the Town Major.

"I've just seen de Gaulle!"

"And about time! Where?"

I pointed. "Thank God! He should have been here days ago."

I joined the crowd in the main square. They were playing the Marseillaise, endlessly as the hubbub grew. A huge tricolour was draped across a balcony on the east side of the Grande Place. Miniatures floated above the crowd in many hands. Not so long before, I suppose, you might have had a bullet past or in your ear

* I was given the figure for officers alone of 6,000. Clearly a wild exaggeration.
† 1 Cor. 15, 26.
‡ John 15, 15.

for that. At last he appeared and spoke. The gist of it: "France must now liberate herself." At that moment General Jacques Leclerc (more popular, I fear, than de Gaulle with the troops)* was no doubt meditating his lightning drive on Paris.

Shortly before this, in an L.C.P. I had come astern of the cruiser carrying Churchill. Now I'd seen the two, both well-matched in-fighters—with a difference. Churchill waved his cigar at us and made the V-sign. My lads shouted: "What about some 'leaf'?" De Gaulle perorated and the audience raved. British phlegm! French *élan vital!*

I awoke one morning determined to take the day off and pushed along the coast through Langrune, Bernières (Benares to the troops) and somewhere north of Sword Beach shot inland through forest land. Miles away guns rumbled. After what I calculated was a prudent advance, sleep, the business of the day, could now begin. I jacked up the bike and fell full fathom five, awaking, however, not to the guns but to an odd refrain: "Searle-Ern! Searle-Ern! Ern-Searle!" The sound came from behind a farm wall. The gate was open. A mobile Field Hospital H.Q. had taken over and there was the dentist with his mobile drill. After introductions, I joined them in a cup of cha. The dentist was a Mancunian, in fact a Bedian†. I broached the subject of the "odd refrain". "That was me in my Bedian French," he said. "The farmer's wife asked me to do her daughter's teeth. The patient came back with a dozen eggs. I'd only had to work on one of her teeth. I was pointing at the eggs repeating 'Only one!' One tooth, one egg seemed fairer." Mancunian business integrity!

Every morning I was treated as I prepared for Mass to another kind' of farmyard medley. A fervent Catholic lad from St. Helens had the early duty of going the rounds with "Wakey! Wakey! Rise and shine!" tent by tent, with a hearty slap on the canvas. Off his own bat he added: "R.C. chaplain about to say Mass in the canteen." You should have heard the sulphurous applause, tent by tent, seasoned with unusual advice for the R.C. padre. I should perhaps have restrained the lad. I rather enjoyed it and it did bring in a few worshippers. "Wakey, Wakey!" was at 6.30 a.m. You can't hold anything against any man for what he says at that hour.

I was sharing censorship duties at this time. A letter came up from one of my flock I did not like one little bit. I had him in. It was a risky thing to do and by service regulations strictly unprofessional. Holding the letter, I said: "That's no way to honour any decent girl and you know it." We looked hard at one another. He could of course assert his rights with dire consequences for me. "She *is* a decent girl, isn't she?" He softened. Later, in various ways, he showed his thanks.

* I heard one of Leclerc's men describe de Gaulle as: *"Ce bougre de capitaine!"*
† Alumnus of St. Bede's Catholic Grammar School in Manchester. Half my year in Spain were Bedians. After six years together one felt one had been there too.

FOR BETTER AND FOR WORSE

Came the morning it was announced on the 6 a.m. short wave that we had taken Lisieux. I was due once again for a rest and resolved to join our men in Lisieux. My Ariel was equipped with a "governor" which held the speed down to 40 m.p.h. Not, however, on that day. How or why it happened I have no idea but the bike answered all the way to 70 m.p.h. It was exhilarating to move along those empty country roads, and be waved to from fields and windows. The fifty miles were going to finish under the hour. I would have a good long day revisiting the city I'd liked so much in August 1939.

Man proposes, God disposes! It was on the tree-lined road from which you turn right over the bridge into the city that the Red Cap stopped me, no more than a cricket pitch only from the bridge.

"Where do you think you're going, Padre?"

"To Lisieux. I heard on the radio early this morning we were in."

"He's got us out again. Look, Padre, he's aiming at that bridge. Salvoes of three. You've got five seconds in between. If you feel you have to go, I suppose I must let you."

I stopped the engine to weigh things up. Astraddle the bike, I remembered: "Padres are expendables, bikes are not. Remember!" But bike apart, I knew the trip was just not on—either for me or for anybody else. I had a smoke looking at the cathedral spire. Bishop Cauchon who condemned St. Joan of Arc is buried there. I, too, felt a bit of a Quisling funking the bridge. Off the road among the trees on the other side of the road a VHF truck was humming away. Perhaps the Red Cap should have moved me out of earshot. I could hear a commentary on the battle in our vicinity, and certain instructions being given, as I thought, from somewhere in England. Could it have been the War House in London? Was there that kind of link-up in 1944? Can battles be fought from hundreds of miles away? Should they be? One thing is clear: the Red Cap cannot have thought I was a collaborator. Small comfort as I mounted for the return journey. It was to prove very nearly my last, for about half-way, twenty or thirty kilometres nearer the sea, I moved out from behind to pass a three-tonner. At the same moment the driver pulled sharply to the left across my path. I had accelerated to overtake. Instinctively I pulled over too and with handle-bars and shoulder rubbing the truck went through the hedge on the other side of the road. The bike left me and I landed head first in a manure-heap. The three-tonner, too, I discovered later, came through the hedge but the more orthodox route, by way of the open gate. I heard voices: "He's dead isn't he?" Slight pause—manure heaps don't immediately invite manual exploration, nor do bodies plunged into them. I hope, by the way, I never acquire the manure-heap addiction. Withdrawal symptoms are deadly.

Well and truly extracted by heroes who, I am afraid, got no other decoration than normally supplied by the medium in which they were working, I was carried out from the field across the road into the house opposite. It was the only one for miles, otherwise I can

110

well imagine being shuttled from door to door. They laid me down flat in the little hall behind the door, feet inboard pointing to the stairs. That gave me a privileged view of the next development. I wouldn't have missed it for all the pitchforks in Normandy. My hosts, an old man aided by his noble consort, opened a secret chamber under the stairs to extract sparkling treasure. A bottle of very old brandy! Smartly I voluntarily abandoned the prone position and took nourishment. No bones were broken and after a reasonable but far from easy clean-up, I insisted on an inspection of the inexpendable Ariel. The bike had cunningly avoided all man-made traps to continue its own career a considerable distance into the field, and quietly lie down.

I got safely home to the sea-shore despite the advice of well-wishers and retired to my tent. The full Lisieux story belongs to exploits in a later phase of the liberation of Europe. I did get there, three times.

Operation Fortitude* must for ever command grateful homage to the planning genius behind it and the total commitment of the men—British, American, Canadian, Polish, Free-French, Dutch, Belgian and the others who carried it through. I have never seen men work so hard, or so heroically against such odds, combining their relentless determination with supreme charity towards those who fell. This goes for all branches of the Services including the Merchant Service. Each Service and regiment no doubt has recorded its Battle honours, its share in the achievement—except, perhaps, the Merchant Navy?

May I be allowed a collective, personal salute to chaplains of all Services whom I met on land and sea in those early days? Already I have in duty bound honoured chaplains C. of E. and O.D. A mention of R.C. padres, I hope, will not come amiss.There was Father Peter Firth, shot dead as he waded ashore. Also Father Rick Slevin whom I met for a brief moment on the coast. Twenty-two years later I presided at his requiem. He died in the confessional which, in quite another context, is also a bridge-head in Enemy Territory. And a Franciscan and a Dominican whose names are now beyond recall, not, however, the O.F.M.'s light-hearted *bonhomie* nor the O.P.'s crusading devotion to the rosary. His stock of beads was exhausted. Not, however, his resourcefulness. His men, I gathered, were firmly assured the Lord had endowed them with ten fingers for just such emergencies. Then Father Terence Quinlan whose versatile service career employed him as Army Chaplain, Chaplain R.N. and Chaplain R.A.F. And finally, in the briefest of all encounters with my colleagues, the two laughing Polski chaplains on the first tank up the beach. (That barrage in the forest—did they live through it? I should long ago have sought the answer.)

Release from the beaches and the long-drawn line of naval parties came with a surprise "spot of leaf" in U.K. An L.C.T. from

* The Normandy Landings.

Arromanches, and an interminably slow train from Pompey to the North, got me home before nightfall. I managed to telephone my sister from Pompey. She promptly begged a bottle of whiskey from the village wine and spirits purveyors who had served our family for over fifty years. Alas, in vain! The young Pharoah now installed there, in all the plenitude of his wartime insouciance to customers, knew not Joseph: "I don't care if King Peter is coming home—no!" (About this time Roumania ejected its playboy sovereign and his famous lady, Madame Lepescu.) Nonetheless those few days and nights in an unbombed village were sweet indeed. I slept impartially through both, and on a day of boisterous winds sailed to rejoin the main naval party at Rouen. It was deep December. The tin crate we sailed in did everything but climb trees. Our "rig of the day" testified to a prevalence of flying *mal-de-mer*.

CHAPTER XXV

The "Godams" return to Rouen*

NAVAL H.Q. at Rouen was a providential Christmas present from Gerry. Why he failed to destroy this immense underground command-post of the Narrow Seas remains a mystery. I cannot remember being given an explanation for its survival. At the north end of the long precipitous climb from the heart of the city by way of Mont S. Aignan et Mont Aux Malades, any movement in the Channel, by air or by sea, was recorded on sensitive screens. It seems there is no doubt now that Hitler first guessed we would land in Normandy. If any proof were needed that he was at the time taking no chances with the Pas de Calais, the installations at Mont Aux Malades, Rouen are more than ample.

I had a room in one of the campus bungalows, and quickly chose the disused chapel of the former Junior Seminary (then a hospital) for my operational H.Q. It was there, in the evacuated hospital, the ship's Company were accommodated.

Our Captain Whittaker was a rare naval phenomenon, and a very decent Christian man (C. of E.). Rare for having achieved the prestigious ascent from the Lower Deck, "via the hawse-pipe", to the rank of Four-Ringer. Decent for his immediate concern to provide his men with a fitting place of worship. He at once consulted me on the propriety of taking over the chapel of the former seminary.

Having already moved in with my own flock, I stonewalled.

"You would, I think, need authorisation from the Cardinal Archbishop."

Four-Ringers from the Lower Deck are, however, unmoved by that kind of evasive badinage.

"Then I put you under orders to approach the Cardinal for his permission."

The sequel reflects a kindly light on Cardinal Petit de Julleville whose motto was *In Pace et Caritate Christi.*† Though born in Paris where his father was a professor, he was of ancient Burgundian stock and had been Bishop of Dijon before becoming Archbishop of

---

* St Joan of Arc was burned at the stake on Rouen market-place May 30th 1431. We English ("Godams" to the French including Joan) were mainly (but not solely) responsible. Does anyone remember the Battle Hymn to the Maid sung everywhere in England in World War I? Climax: "Come lead your France to Victory" (opening bars of the Marseillaise): "Joan of Arc they are calling You" (High note and cadence on "calling").

† "In the peace and charity of Christ." The Cardinal's father was a recognised authority on St. Joan of Arc.

Rouen in 1936. I was unprepared for his appearance. He entered between two priests, each holding one of his arms: later I learned of his First War service at Verdun as combattant and chaplain which in some way impaired his balance. (Perhaps the effect on the inner-ear of continuous bombardments?)

I stated the Captain's request précisely as he had made it. The answer came after the briefest pause: "This is an unusual request. In the circumstances, however, I feel we owe it to our allies to say yes." At this point a harsher light falls inevitably on the Captain's envoy. All I can offer in fairness to myself will in no way soften the glare. These, however, are the facts.

Forty years ago ecumenism at the official level existed neither in name nor in fact. Archbishop Fisher's warm recommendation of an offensive pamphlet "The Roman Catholics"* was still to come. "Continuity" of the Anglican Establishment with the pre-reformation Church of England was still being vigorously asserted. So I felt it my duty, a greater duty than I owed to Captain Whittaker, to invite the Cardinal to consider the effect of his decision on my Anglican colleagues and their flocks. As usual, they would conclude continental Catholics understood, far better than the native breed, that we are essentially one and the same.

The Cardinal was clearly disappointed. "I would dearly wish to accommodate your Service in every way possible but I cannot disregard what you have said. You spoke as your conscience demanded?" I nodded. "Then I have no other recourse but to decline your Captain's request. You will inform him I do this with the deepest regret." Whittaker's reaction was predictably violent. "I thought we were fighting this war for freedom!" The voice of a simple, honest man. If I may be allowed a similar voice, it would be to say that if such a problem faced me today, I would have welcomed the Cardinal's first judgment and communicated it with joy.

Rouen widened my ministry in ways unthinkable in the assault area. There dear Abbé Bourdon was almost my only civilian contact. Here I formed friendships ashore which have lasted a lifetime.†

My first call on arriving in the city, somewhat worn after threading the Ariel through heavy military traffic and bombed-out towns still smelling of death (Caen was a nightmare), presented an altogether different challenge. A Red Cap halted me in the main square.

"Are you R.C.?"

"Yes. Anything I can do?"

"In that courtyard," (he pointed to an open carriage-way) "there are a few dozen P.O.W.s They appear to be all R.C.s. They want a priest."

I have rarely seen such misery, such starved, broken men in

* Written by a C. of E. dignitary in the West Indies.

† e.g. I am at this moment in Normandy staying with a retired priest whose family honoured me with their friendship 41 years ago.

tattered rags. Not one of them was a German, or a combat soldier. All of them, Poles, Czechs, Lithuanians and others, were conscript slave workers and either Orthodox or Catholic Christians. What could I do? Using Latin interspersed with the few mid-European words I could muster, I slipped on a purple stole. At least they got the idea I was a priest. One by one I absolved them, adding what words and gestures I thought might convey comfort—not mine but the Lord's. Many were clearly in such physical and mental distress, only Gabriel's trumpet could have lifted them.

That same day came news of a wounded Irish nun in a convent* at the heart of the city. This was the Mother Superior's story: "It was the night of the heaviest and highest bombardment. As usual we all lined up under the refectory arches, the older sisters on one side, the younger half on the other. The bomb fell on the side of the young. Thirteen were killed outright. The youngest, our Irish sister, at the end of the line, survived with a broken arm which so far refuses to mend."

"Might I see her, Mother?"

"She is here beside me."

The grille opened. There she was smiling at me. They arranged for me to meet the Irish Sister occasionally for the pleasure it gave her to recapture her native tongue. It was indeed gone almost beyond recall, but mended slowly. The use of her broken arm was not so easily restored.

The garrison was by this time relaxing in the sunshine of a warm civic welcome. Entertainments were laid on. ENSA appeared. Regimental musicians performed. Mistinguette was announced. But there were ugly contrasts with the general euphoria. One witnessed in the streets flashes of the back-lash on collaborators and the bare-faced attempt of the Left to monopolise total credit for the Resistance.

I had a personal whiff of both. I now had a car at my disposal. I learned to drive. The first day I sat at the wheel a couple approached me with honeyed words. "Would the gallant British aumonier do us the honour of dining with us tomorrow at midday?" They were loaded with parcels.

"Where do you live?" It was half a mile down the same street.

"Jump in. I'll take you."

On the way I confided this was the first time I was driving alone. A certain chill then pervaded the atmosphere. They insisted they were practically on their doorstep and dismounted. I was conning the gears preparing to re-start when a citizen advanced with a message. The gist was to warn me against the couple who had just left my car. "They are notorious collaborators," he said. "They are now ingratiating themselves with the Allies. You should be more careful."

My brush with the Resistance began late one night as I drove back

* The home of English Poor Clare Nuns in the 17th and 18th centuries.

from a distant Naval Party on the coast facing an endless column of American trucks. Their headlights blazed away. Mine were the merest glimmer. A slight metallic click indicated contact on my right flank. It could have been a stone thrown up by the front wheel. I had no view ahead: the trucks were rolling within feet of each other. I pulled up and shoved my head through the window. Twenty yards back in the glare of the headlamps lay a body and a bike. With death in my heart I ran to the spot and lifted a lady of advanced age from the hedge. Mercifully she was alive, and very brave despite abrasions and shock. The car wing had grazed the left pedal of her bicycle.

Somehow I managed to get her into the car, and with the bicycle on the bonnet drove gingerly, under her direction, to her home. It was a large chateau outside the city. I left her with the doctor. He made it clear there was nothing serious. A day or so later I was invited to lunch with a companion.

I returned with the bicycle on the bonnet in mint condition thanks to the resources of our transport officer. In fact I invited him to join me for the lunch. At the last moment he was forced to stand down and with me went a Leading Hand R.N.* This was a fatal error. For the chatelaine was not alone. Her daughter, alerted, no doubt, to the maternal mishap, had dutifully returned home. She was a heroine of the Resistance and an astonishingly beautiful woman.

I cannot blame the mother for the total uneasiness of that event. She, from the moment I lifted her, had agreed I had no chance of seeing her in the blinding ferocity of those headlamps. But who was it resented my maladresse in introducing to her table a companion of less than officer rank? Surprisingly in one who must have shared supreme danger with heroes of humbler clay, I felt it was the Resistance heroine. For that very reason I felt out of collar from the outset. There could also, frankly, have been a praiseworthy reaction against myself as the agent of her mother's present distress. But I wonder? Were the Left correct in this particular case? Was this heroine at least undeniably one who could claim to be body and soul their kith and kin? Was I, as a Catholic priest, the skeleton at the feast?

Shortly after arrival in Rouen and before graduating to four-wheel status, I at last accomplished the ride to Lisieux. Whom should I meet on dismounting but a hero who one day, I hope, will be recognised by the Church as a saint, Bishop Pierre Falaize O.M.I., pioneer missionary in Alaska among the Esquimaux. I have the excellent biography by the author of "Inuk".† Snow-blindness had at last forced the Bishop to retire. He could at least distinguish a clerical collar and naval uniform. He spoke first. "Good afternoon, Father. You are English?" We embraced and from there on he

* Lower Deck but expert in his own *metier*.

† I defy anyone—certainly any Englishman or woman—to read the chapter on the husky dogs without tears. "Inuk" was followed by "Inunuak". The author, Pierre Roger Buliard, O.M.I., sent me a copy signed and dedicated in memory of my meeting Monsignor Falaize in Lisieux on this occasion.

became my guide. First to the Basilica. Our bombs had splashed the perimeter. There were no direct hits. This the Bishop noted as one indication of the special protection of the Saint in whose honour the huge edifice was raised. It was the same story at the Carmel. Two of the Saint's sisters, Leonie and Celine, received me. It seems I was the first priest, in fact their first visitor, from England since 1939. Their first enquiry was for news of Monsignor Vernon Johnson, for whom they had the tenderest regard.

They informed me their little Sister had taken care of her Carmel. It was untouched but for the roof. "Could M. l'Aumonier find perhaps a large tarpaulin with which to cover it?"

The *devout* female sex had joined our Naval Party by this time, the Wrens being accommodated in a Villa named "Les Roitlets". Some weeks later I married one of the inmates in the chapel (so meanly kept for R.C.'s only) to a Surgeon Commander*, nephew of the famous Canon Sheehan, author of *Luke Delmege* and so many other clerical novels now forgotten but still supreme in their genre.

Female interest was, I think, crucial in securing a very large tarpaulin from Army Stores. A transport sergeant provided and drove the truck. The Sisters at Carmel were duly grateful. Now, I thought, one will carry away a treasured word on the Mystical Life as a reward. But war is relentless in its assertion of earthy demands. "M. l'Aumonier will know that the town's electricity is caput? Could he perhaps supply oil for the Night Office? Otherwise we can't see to read our breviaries." Oil, lashings of it, was acquired via the same agencies.

I have often returned to Lisieux in the piping times of peace, but never to seek audience at the grille. It would, I think, be an impertinence to distract Carmelites at a time when one could be of no help.

* I had the joy of meeting the menage years later when he was Surgeon Captain at Hasler and I was Coadjutor Bishop of Pompey. They lived up the hill from the city, close neighbours of Surgeon Captain Rory O'Connor, of Colombo days. Both families throughout Lent 1961 assisted at my early Mass in the Cathedral of St. John.

CHAPTER XXVI

Advance into Agony

TIME to move on again. Time for farewells to good companions, speeches and songs in the wardroom of the Gerry bunker. Out rolled the barrel, joy was unconfined.

My appointment this time ran "R.C. Chaplain, Holland and Belgium. Admiral Dickens. H.Q. Antwerp. H.M.S. Athelstan".

I had recently come under censure for approaching Admirals. My car had been withdrawn. An R.M. Major whom I consulted was very clear on how to get instant justice. "Go to the top. Pitch it firmly." He traced out the kind of signal I should write. All right for Majors! He, an Irishman who had achieved fame for successful but highly unorthodox methods in one of the M.N.B.D.Os,* had got away with it. I was cited before a senior officer—not the Admiral—and strips torn off me for by-passing normal channels. Transport, however, was restored.

We were quartered in an Antwerp hotel at the heart of the city. The Barracks, H.M.S. Athelstan, was a short tram ride away. Servicemen by courtesy of the City Fathers travelled free. In fact people, mistaking my uniform, even forced money on me.

The Free Belge Navy shared our barracks. Their chaplain, Father Delbare, became a cherished father and friend. As a boy on the family farm near Poperinge† he had the experience of World War I behind him. How vividly he recalled the day the R.F.A.‡ Sergeant Farrier offered his father a horse. It was a beauty. Service Regulations demanded its death. All horses maimed in any way were to be put down. The Sergeant pleaded with the farmer to save it. The injury was slight. "It's yours if you hide it. I can't bear to see it killed." Inexorably the moment of truth came when he had to sign a statement that he, the Sergeant, had despatched it. His conscience would not let him and back he came in great distress. The horse was put down. Not before the boy had come to love it. He wept bitter tears.

Antwerp was captured with all its docks intact. Gerry, too late, poured in V1s to rectify the error. One destroyed a cinema packed with our troops.

I was wearing a new duffle coat for the first time when one crashed alongside me hitting a Servicemen's Club. We got the

---

* Two of these overseas operations were manned by Royal Marines. I can't now recall what the initials stood for—something to do with the construction of docks?
† "Pops", he recalled, in 1st War army English.
‡ Royal Field Artillery

hostesses out down broken staircases. One young girl, bleeding from a leg wound, left gallant stains on my new coat. Please God she survived.

There was considerable anxiety in the city at the time of the Gerry counter-attack through the Ardennes forests. People remembered their General's valedictory words when they evacuated Antwerp: *"Wir commen zurück"* * "He is a damn fine general" said my informant Father Seeldrayers, a Jesuit priest who befriended me in many ways, and a genuine savant. He wrote for the Bollandist series†, and was at that time doing work for the Larousse Encyclopaedias. I supped occasionally at his home. The father was a clock maker of very stern aspect, sporting a huge spade of black beard. The mother was a honey: the daughter somewhat rebellious to paternal rigours.

At Antwerp I saw two plays of Shakespeare, both regal, Richard II played by Laurence Olivier in the flesh and Henry V played by the same on film. The second was remarkable for the number of troops leaving the cinema once, I suppose, they realised it wasn't a leg-show. The irony was our Bishop-in-Ordinary to the Forces had just circulated a pastoral letter to be read at all Masses in which he made much of the night scene in the film of Henry V. There in a tent an early Mass is being said in the English camp before the Battle of Agincourt.

The whole Dutch coast was now within my parish. I shrink even now from facing the appalling deprivation and destruction of the Netherlands. Four years' occupation had seared both minds and bodies. It was the physical effects which surfaced first. A faint greenish pallor, so it seemed to me, was discernible in the faces of many whom I met. Starvation! Even more dramatic evidence of scarcities made one weep for shame. Wedding rings for instance were traded for cigarettes.

There were consolations. The chance came my way of dropping sacks of food where they were sure to be wisely distributed. A very thin Franciscan Brother opened the door of the monastery at Ijmuiden. With his little beard and ragged habit he might have just stepped out of one of Giotto's murals. I had a few words ready in Dutch and announced my name. Presuming too much, he rattled into a wordy welcome which became a hurricane when he peered into the sack. I said "Whoa!" which is, I hope, in general circulation. "But you are Dutch—your name!" (How nearly right he was. It's been my nick-name for over sixty years.)

Gerry had cleared a wide sweep of dwellings in that coastal area. The purpose was to create what the artillery call "a field of fire" for the guns commanding the sea-approaches. He hadn't touched the Franciscan monastery.

One night I holed up in a village in company with the C. of E.

* "We shall be back."
† Scholarly research volumes on the lives of saints. Internationally regarded as supremely authoritative.

chaplain. We had an early start the next morning and were on the street shortly before 7.30 a.m. just in time to observe a veritable phenomenon. At 7.25 all the house doors opened, the garden gates clicked and the whole village went to Mass. It was too much for my colleague. He announced his intention of coming over.

We were very much in and around Breda, Harlem, S'Herthogen-bosch and met with wonderful kindness. R.C. chaplains of all services gathered one night in Breda at the Catholic Centre. How the folks managed to decorate the hall and provide ample food and drink remains a mystery. There was a lot of singing and games. Shall I ever forget the incomparable Father Sidney Lescher's* verve and vigour as we circulated in a chain dance, holding hands to the accompaniment of a Dutch folk-song. The nearest he got to the refrain was: "My father was a bookie." He was repeating this endlessly every time we passed on the chain. In fact his father was senior partner in the firm of Lescher, Evans and Webb.

My old Professor, Father Sebastian Tromp, popped up in conversation at the Jesuit house in Rotterdam. Old Trompy was to be created a Cardinal. A circular from Rome had gone round the Jesuit houses of his native land, apparently inviting reactions. I wonder what killed it? He never became a "porporato" (a wearer of the sacred purple). My guess is that he himself was the axeman.

How, and for what purpose I found myself in Cleves I cannot now remember. Our armies were across the Rhine by now. I was in Naval Rig. Though I approached the river, I did not cross it. I felt I had no right. On our side of the frontier a huge placard bore the legend: "The Penalty for Looting is Death". How then explain the brisk auction, back up the road, of furniture and all manner of household goods? The kindest explanation, I suppose, is that all of it was traded in for cigarettes and allied scarcities which again is not very kind.

Moral standards, I am afraid, dipped well below the horizon. The Dean of Flushing remarked that there were more sexual offences in his bailiwick during the first three weeks of our liberation than during the four years of the German occupation. One must make allowances for the ecstatic euphoria and the sense of owing everything to the liberators.

In May 1985 I was back in the Benelux countries for the visit of Pope John Paul II. How greatly the scene had changed from what I remembered of Holland forty years ago! The years of famine had indeed yielded to the years of plenty. Pope John Paul from the moment he alighted at Eindoven met with demonstrations. It would be supremely unjust to get this phenomenon out of proportion as, I believe, our media tended to do. The truth is that in Eindoven,

---

* "Lesch", as he was known to my generation in Rome, was a fine batsman, a member of the famous Venerabile knock-about song and dance trio and one of the best-known chaplains in the British Army. He ran a Retreat House in Germany after the accident which paralysed him from the waist downwards.

Utrecht and one or two other areas, a concerted effort was made to assert the compatibility of paganism* with Christian morality. The challange was singularly counter-productive. All that came through was the ugliness of decadence. The post-war years of plenty, as John Paul said, have achieved what earlier centuries of religious wars and persecution had failed to do in damaging Catholic Unity.

Did those four years of famine, however, prepare the way? Church law could scarcely escape scot-free when the moral law was in jeopardy. What in other circumstances was criminal-theft, murder and so on—had become virtuous under the German occupation. Concentration Camps, not surprisingly, removed all obstacles to full participation in worship with obvious dangers for distinctive principles of belief. The results are foreseeable in the theories of Situation Ethics: nothing is right or wrong in itself; everything depends on circumstances. In peacetime, why refrain from filling the passing moment with maximum self-gratification?

The memory of doors opening and gates clicking in the village forty years ago, along with memories of the un-equalled record of Dutch Foreign Missions over centuries, are not dead letters. The vital spark is there under the stubble. Confusions will clear. The Maas will flow again with the waters that rejoice the City of God.

St. Ignatius, in his quest for recruits to carry the Faith across the seven seas, wrote: *"Da mihi Belgas"* (Give me people from the Netherlands). We have even greater proof than he that there are none better and for long years none readier to answer the call.

* cf Rom. 1, 23-27.

CHAPTER XXVII

Farewell to the West

MAY I quote from a letter dated 5 August 1945 from HMS Royal Athelstan, Antwerp to M. l'Abbe Maurice Graindor, Ecole Join Lambert, Rouen:

" . . . I was sorry to have missed you that evening. I journeyed on to Calais where a tearful nun, standing in front of her ruined convent, addressed me: "Look at it, M. l'Anglais! Our once beautiful mother-house! So this is 'La Liberation'? Bombed to smithereens." I tried to comfort her. Not a chance! Later I pushed on to Ostend, Antwerp, Brussels etc. and so on right up to Den Helder, covering all my naval parties. Now I am finishing my last days at Antwerp and shall be moving out to the Far East with an assault force soon. Still I pray I shall do whatever I can for the boys. Perhaps we shall see one another in the good days ahead . . . "

In fact we did, but only by courtesy of the Japs who capitulated before our assault forces went into action. Our destination was Port Sweetenham on the Strait of Malaya. The story goes that Naval Intelligence assured a landing there on hard beaches. Later, however, thanks to a dummy exercise on the site, "hard beaches" revealed themselves in their true character. They were mangrove swamps. Amphibious assault craft would have bogged down tight, presenting the shore batteries with a covey of sitting-ducks.

A posting to Alexandria was next in the wind. Tropical kit was issued. I was at home on leave in August '45 when speculation gave way to official command: "Sail in M.V. *Strathnever* for duty as R.C. Chaplain H.M.S. Lanka, Ceylon."

No Strath can ever have carried so many passengers. Aboard was a multitude of all the Services, male and female, plus civilians. The Goan stewards soon got on my trail. We settled for daily Mass at 6.30 a.m. October devotions (Rosary and Litany etc.) were intoned by the crew throughout. A conducted tour of the Goan bunks proudly demonstrated the simple but profound piety of their occupants. *Bondieuserie?** Yes, I suppose so, but a refreshing change from Western pin-ups.

Amenities aboard were cramped. Quizzes, tombola, etc. filled the huge dining-spaces of an evening: comedians, a hypnotist, the theatre. I tangled with one of the comedians over his tasteless smut, and argued fiercely about the morality of extracting total submission from the stooges to the will of the hypnotist.

* Mass-produced objects of piety.

My talks on John Henry Newman were of course a drug in the general market, but among the handful who came one or two lasting friendships emerged. Susan Bliss, manager of the Bombay Examiner Press, would later print my doctorate thesis and prove a tremendous support during the two years I spent after demob as civilian R.C. chaplain to the port of Bombay.

Tropical clothing came out once we were in the Med. It was a grim moment of truth for me. My sister had deftly prepared and packed everything, adding her own artistic flourish. Down the front of six pairs of white shorts my name appeared in bold indian ink. There was nothing else for it! No man could live in doeskins in that torrid heat. I had to grin and bear the inevitable raillery.

From the Med. we slipped into the Indian Ocean via the Suez Canal. For R.C. chaplains R.N. the Indian Ocean still broods over an unsolved mystery. Father Thomas Brennan R.N. was last known to have sailed there alive. Apparently none of the ship's company would offer any explanation of how or when he was lost overboard. There are rumours of a celluloid clerical collar washed up somewhere. These are shark infested waters. Years later, as bishop of the diocese to which Tom belonged, I met his father and sister. They have added his name to the family tombstone in Wardley Cemetery. I went there from time to time during my years at the Hall* to pray for the repose of his soul.

In Bombay I lunched and supped at the Cathedral, Woodhouse Road. The young administrator, Father Valerian Gracias, kept open house. Archbishop Roberts (whom Father Gracias later succeeded to become the first Indian Cardinal) was where he always longed to be, voyaging the seven seas in his capacity as Bishop Delegate to ships in Eastern waters.

Late evening saw the *Strathnever* at sea on the last leg of her long voyage. I must salute her 'ere I leave her. A fine steady mountain of a ship, working to full capacity, mastered and crewed by a remarkable breed of seamen, mainly Scots I should think, but serviced by Lascar fire-men and Goan cabin staff, Muslims and Catholics respectively. Their fidelity to prayer, I fear, offered both contrast and challange to us western passengers.

I have no memory now of entering Colombo harbour by day or by night, or of how I came to the presbytery of St. Philip Neri's church in the Pettah where I was to be based for the next twelve months. My host was a Father Brennan O.M.I., son of a Tower of London beefeater. The missionary Order of Mary Immaculate goes in for extremes. They opened up Alaska, an enterprise only men of heroic mould could ever have compassed. Naturally, ranging "from frozen North to torrid South"†, they also took on Ceylon where they were well-established.‡

* Wardley Hall next to the cemetery is the Salford Bishop's home.
† Wiseman's hymn "God bless our Pope".
‡ The Archbishop of Colombo, Masson, was O.M.I.

123

My predecessor at H.M.S. Lanka had wisely chosen to lodge at St. Philip's in the Pettah. It was the noisiest corner of Colombo, but nearest to the harbour—a five minutes rickshaw ride. The parish priest was an "officiating chaplain R.N." who varied his white cassock with naval rig, and his parochial duties with trips to Ceylonese ratings in the Andaman Islands. As a cult figure in the service and civilian life of Colombo, he proved the perfect drago-man for a greenhorn like myself.

H.M.S. Lanka covered a multitude of shore establishments includ-ing St. Peter's O.M.I. College, now a Military Hospital, gunnery stations like H.M.S. Anderson and the vast Transit and Rest Camp in the interior at Diyatalawa. From the outset, I decided the Port was No.1 on my worksheet. Ashore I had a huge grey station-wagon at my disposal, afloat any number of water-taxis to whistle up from the jetty. Signals poured in from visiting ships requesting the services of the R.C. chaplain. Often enough, in the case of our larger units, it would the C. of E. chaplain to alert me. With U.S. traffic, chaplains of denominations hitherto unknown would make the approach.

From an R.N. Air Craft Carrier returning to England came this classic signal: "Request R.C. Port Chaplain report tomorrow 1100 hours celebrate Mass for R.C. personnel and brides." I complied with a wild surmise. The reality was wilder than any surmise. There were hundreds of them, of every degree and age. One was said to be over sixty. Bridal accommodation aboard had cost the Admiralty considerable expense—nothing was spared. What it cost in headaches for those in charge of discipline aboard during the voyage was another story.

In the large airy O.M.I. Church we had Midnight Mass at Christmas 1945. I started to hear Confessions in good time, as I thought, but only chipped the edge of the queue. General absolution simply imposed itself. For once I had no hesitation. The old carols clove the firmament. "See amid the Winter Snow" on a tropical night is no problem . . . at Christmas.

Shortly after Christmas, as a mild break from the Harbour and the City, I took a few days up-country at the rest camp, Diyatalawa— "Diyat" to the troops. Despite the undeniable amenities and the copious presence of the female Services there is an ominous aura about the site. Goering once replied to a deputation of critics from abroad in this wise. "Concentration Camps, Gentlemen? You object. Let me read a passage from a standard encyclopaedia on that particular issue. He read: 'Concentration Camps were first used by the British during the Boer War.' " The evidence still subsists in the Pearl of the East, at Diyatalawa. There are the remnants of the installations which accommodated the Boers eighty odd years ago. The Geneva Convention is, of course, posterior to the Boer War. They were careful, however, in that document to forbid the deportation of Prisoners of War outside of the continent (maybe it is more stringent than that) in which they were captured.

There was another phenomenon at "Diyat" which I found hard to take. Ceylon is the homeland of Buddhism. Very close to the camp, however, there was a Hindu shrine carefully arranged, it would seem, to coincide with Christmas. It appeared to be a copy of the Bethlehem scene. Who lay newly-born in the crib? Ganesa, son of Siva, the Elephant Godling!

The main Transit Camp in the Island was Mayina, where hundreds of officers and ratings awaited passage home. During hostilities I suppose it was the reservoir for replacing crews. It was not without amenities. Witness the theatre-cum-cinema, said to be the largest structure of its kind in Ceylon.* Inevitably, however, men waiting to go home tended to think of the place as a penal settlement. Some acted accordingly. Organised theft and mayhem precipitated almost siege conditions.

The Camp Commandant had me on the carpet after one of the more serious outbreaks. "Padre," he said, "I'm going to allocate you a cabin next to the cells. All of them in there at this moment are your flock—Glaswegians. Get weaving! They are monsters!" In fact they were a lamblike bunch of black sheep. All they wanted was Glasgow and "hame". The remedy was obvious; obvious, too, in whose hands it lay.

Cricket flourished particularly on the excellent ground at St. Peter's O.M.I. College (then our Hospital). An official invitation to join a Services Eleven came round. I rose to the bait only to sink like a stone: "Only players of county standard need apply." I had missed the small print. But better luck prevailed with British civilians. The President of the Tea Planters that year was Harry Hurst, whose hobby was the study of Catholic Apologetics. Harry could have qualified for a chair in the Gregorian University. He brought to theology the same care and insight which distinguished his blending of teas.

He invited me to stay at his up-country estate which thanks to Harry's own provision you reached by a fine upland road. I was not the first serviceman to enjoy the incomparable view from his verandah. Tea-gardens sloped down to a deep gorge in which a tumbling river gashed the greenery against a rising background of hills. They peaked in a skyline which centuries ago gave to the area the name "Spreading Eagle".

A Father Soubry Mathews O.M.I.† opened up for me a chapter of Ceylon's religious history. I wouldn't have missed it for all the tea in Harry's warehouse.

* When Mayina closed, the then Archbishop of Colombo, Cardinal Cooray, O.M.I. invited me to accompany him to the Admiralty Assessors who were disposing of the properties. He expressed an interest in the theatre as a future church. I was extremely proud when the Assessors at once proposed a very modest figure which he had no difficulty in accepting.

† Father Mathews was a native of Rouen where he was a student at the College Join Lambert where I had often spent an hour in Father Maurice Graindor's study listening to his inspired reading of Peguy.

European rule in Ceylon covers 450 years in fairly equal layers: Portuguese 1505-1658, Dutch 1658-1796, British 1796-1947. Portuguese missionaries from Goa, including the greatest missioner of all time, St. Francis Xavier, planted the Catholic Faith too firmly and deeply for the Dutch Calvinists to uproot it despite their enthusiastic efforts. They declared the Catholic Church illegal, banned Catholic priests from the Island and handed over their churches to Calvinist pastors. Both Sinhalese and Tamils conformed outwardly in large numbers.

Father Mathews' invitation opened the magic casement on an event which could be traced back precisely to that period. It was a pilgrimage celebrated annually in May in the remote recesses of a northern forest. Spain has its famous Romerias and none more famous than that to the shrine of our Lady of the Dew in Andalucia. Ceylon's began secretly, with the added zest of danger at a time when civil laws grievously violated freedom of conscience.

The road north from Colombo to the venue was tedious, but trust an Anglo-Frenchman to mastermind the amenities. At the halfway mark we pulled up at a convent of French sisters for lunch. Father Mathews had 'phoned ahead. Maxim's could not have done us prouder.

It was late afternoon when we arrived, threading our way through a colonnade of trees into a long, wide clearing. All manner of vehicles except the motor car flanked the approaches to a large hut in front of which an altar was erected. To the right of the altar was Our Lady's statue. We had come to work. No time was lost. I was ensconced on a raised dais alongside the statue and confessions began. Two hours later a halt was called for May Devotions.

My elevation commanded the full length of the clearing. It was dusk. Men, women and children, hundreds of them, knelt by their vehicles intoning the Litany. The silvan cathedral was arched with tree-tops and filled with the incense from twinkling fires and cooking pot. In the dry swamp, just beyond the right-hand column of trees, the crocodiles lay uneasily, longing for the rains. Nobody gave them a thought. You could approach quite close with no other reaction than the lifting of a wary lid from dreaming eyes.

The climax came the next day with High Mass. Melodies softly sung in Calvinist times rose full-throatedly from the kneeling throng. Donkeys contributed their graceless descant. Far back in their lineage one of them carried the Lord we were adoring in flight from persecution, in the arms of the Mother we had all come to honour. Egypt moves around the globe. Three hundred years ago it was here in the forest with the crocodiles and the hunted humans.

Again to the north of Colombo but much nearer to the city, three places forming a slim isosceles triangle drew considerable numbers of servicemen and women. The apex was Negombo with its long palm-beach and fishing boats constructed of unsinkable logs lashed together. Between them the sea "boozed" up and down.

Two inland communities of sisters formed the base of the triangle. One had become famous among Wrens and nurses who were on the eve of returning home with marriage awaiting them, for the Sisters specialised in exquisite bridal trousseaux at fantastically low prices. I ferried a bevy from St. Peter's hospital there in my grey station wagon. One of them was inclined to greater familiarity than my state of life warranted. Perhaps it was no more than innocent practice for the young men in England. I remarked gravely and truly: "I'm rather worried about the car. The guts could fall out any moment." Arctic winds blew from then on.

The other baseline convent was Hendala. I took many a shore party there from visiting ships but never a Wren or nurse. Hendala is a Leper Colony in the care of the Franciscan Missionaries of Mary; their superior, Mother Rosary, one of the greatest women I have ever met.

There were 600 patients within a compound surrounded by high walls. In addition to the hospital wards there was a mosque, a temple, a Catholic church, a church for other Christian denominations and a police station-cum-cells. The Japs managed to drop only a single stick of bombs on Ceylon. They hit the Leper Colony at Hendala.

On my first visit Mother introduced me to both the youngest and the oldest patient. The first was a little Tamil girl with a sweet name I can't recall who danced for me. She was delighted with herself and so was I. Such turnings of the hands and synchronising with the feet! *Joi de vivre* was vibrant despite the grip of the fell disease. "Lebbay", the oldest inhabitant—I can only write his name as I heard it—had been there seventy years.

I learned that the government were subsiding experiments with a "cure" claimed to have been revealed in a dream to a women with remarkable psychic powers. In later years further "cures" have been claimed, I hope on sounder evidence. The disease strikes, it seems, in two ways—externally on the epidermis, and internally at the nerve-centres. The neural kind is the deadlier.

I asked Mother had any of the sisters contracted leprosy over the years. The community was a large one and, as I believe is the custom in Franciscan Missionaries of Mary houses, composed of sisters from a wide range of countries. "Yes, but only one. She worked in the linen-room. It is thought she pricked her finger with a contaminated needle." Mother was careful to tell us not to put knee to the ground in the chapel.

One of the by-products of leprosy is discontentment. Mother had gradually sieved the worst offenders into a special ward where they were safe from disturbing others and could neutralise one another.

I shepherded a couple of dozen American sailors there. There could be a few "barber-shop" harmonisers among them. We entered the ward of the chronic malcontents.

"I want you to cheer up these patients with a song. They get mean with one another if the next fellow has three more grains of rice in his curry."

"What'll we sing?"

The answer was never in doubt: "Pack up your troubles in your old kit bag!" They obliged at once in harmony. The patients loved it.

On that occasion a tragic error was made. There was a young American sister in the Hendala community who had a brother in the American Navy. She was elsewhere when our truck unloaded and we trooped into the Colony. Mother Rosary and another sister accompanied us. I think Mother's companion on our tour was an Italian with an imperfect command of English. It seems one of the crewmen informed her he had a sister who was a nun. On returning to the convent she met the American member of the community with the news that her brother had arrived in Colombo and was actually in Hendala to see her. She ran over to us, breathless, as we emerged from the Colony, looking from one to the other. I have rarely witnessed such a drop from supreme exhilaration to utter misery when the truth came home.

There was a more spectacular case of mistaken identity connected with Hendala which Mother Rosary confided to me. I hope the interval of forty years releases me from keeping the facts "hush-hush". Archbishop Masson had retired from Ceylon to his beloved Midi. The Holy See chose as his successor Father Thomas B. Cooray, O.M.I. a Sinhalese and, I believe, the first native Archbishop. Throughout the Island joy was unconfined. Great crowds converged on the Cathedral of St. Lucy for his consecration. Mother Rosary, as befitted her responsible position and universal prestige, was seated with the notables in the gold and crimson chairs quite close to me. At some point in the ceremony she chanced to turn round. There behind her, in gold and crimson chairs, were three of her lepers. They had scaled the walls at Hendala determined to see their man, one of their very own, inherit the fulness of the sacred priesthood. It is anyone's guess what might have ensued in those seats of the mighty had their presence been revealed. That was Mother Rosary's reaction. They spent a night or two in cells—not for being at the Consecration, but for breaking bounds.

My last week in Ceylon I spent at Candy putting the final touches to my doctorate thesis in the splendid Jesuit College library. The Silvestrine Benedictines staff the Cathedral there, one of them being the Bishop. At lunch there one day I asked who's the Bishop?

"That's him, the little man over there against the wall." It was the first time I had seen an unidentifiable bishop, all in black, ringless and without a pectoral cross. Monastic communities are great levellers.

My last day at Candy, and nearly my last in Ceylon, climaxed with the procession of Buddha's Tooth, a blaze of fire-crackers and gaily caparisoned elephants.

Sic transit gloria maris! It was curtains for a Naval Chaplain R.N. (H.Q.)

CHAPTER XXVIII

Sea Chaplain Civilian

THE dismantling of our wartime naval presence in Ceylon was well under way when I received a signal from Archbishop Roberts of Bombay. H.M.S. Lanka's days were numbered. His proposal was neatly timed and reflected his boundless concern for men of all services and nations who go down to the sea in ships whose business is in deep waters.

Chaplains R.C. R.N., he noted, would shortly be returning home from the East, "mission completed". Many ports in the East were opening up again to civilian traffic. They lacked port chaplains. Would any of us consider accepting local demobilisation and serving for a year or two as an Apostleship of the Sea chaplain in an eastern port?

I felt I should make the offer. My last home leave was only a year ago. Many of my colleagues were much longer away. Apart from the Normandy landings, my own war had been fairly free of shots fired in anger. People at home had had much more experience of V1s and V2s. I could well understand other chaplains thinking twice about the proposal even if they were assured of their bishop's approval. In many dioceses that would be highly unlikely.

In my case approval came with what might be construed as almost indecent haste. I informed Archbishop Roberts that I was available.

There was a brief spell for speculation before he replied. Whither, I wondered, was I destined? Scenes from Conrad crowded in, especially from his nostalgic short story *Youth* which I remembered being publicly declaimed one Upholland speech day. The great sentences came rolling back: "By all that's wonderful it's the Sea, Youth and the Sea! Or is it Youth alone?" "Judea London, Do or Die!" and the unforgettable awakening of her shipwrecked crew as the East looked down on them from the jetty at Bangkok. Would Bangkok be mine?* Or Port Sweetenham sheltered by those two long Mango Islands where one might have "had it" but for Hiroshima and Nagasaki? The Archbishop's appointment cleared

* Twenty-seven years later I did get to Bangkok. But only for a couple of days *en route* to the 1973 International Eucharistic Congress at Melbourne. My secretary and I boarded the dream boat built by an enterprising American on the lines of the "King and I" royal barge. The Siamese waitresses, so he said, were thrilled to see two "Holy Men" come aboard at last. (Long live the clerical collar!). They served us three curries—each hotter than the last. The third floored me—my only defeat in many such encounters. We sped down to the Port in a skimmer. The ghost of the *"Judea* London. Do or Die!" was not there. The *City of Belfast* was.

all doubt. None of these fabled harbours was to be mine. It was Bombay, the only Far Eastern port I already knew outside of Ceylon.

The Navy courteously provided sea-passage from Colombo to Bombay. A thousand miles lay between my service and civilian life, allowing three days of meditation on the past and speculation on what lay ahead.

Farewells ashore fulfilled all justice and protocol. Father Brennan*, my kindly host, assured me the room I had occupied in his presbytery would always be known by my name. The Admiral was neither gracious nor gruff. This was a new experience. We simply sat together chatting as old friends do. Earnestly straining every nerve to understand, he asked me to explain why his dear brother, a saintly member of an Anglican religious order, had changed over to become an R.C. priest.

Abreast of Goa with three-quarters of the voyage behind us and the Western Ghats already lining the skyline as they continue to do so nobly for Bombay Harbour, the gauntlet hit me full in the face. It was thrown by the greatest missioner of all time, Francis Xavier. His incorrupt body is preserved at Goa, and regularly exposed there for the veneration of the faithful. He was a Basque Pyrrenean, a student of the Sorbonne, pioneer in Rome of the Society of Jesus with Ignatius Loyola. This great-hearted European gave his all to Asia.

Could this chicken-hearted European funk his own minimal commitment and still live with himself?

Bombay Harbour opens to the sea-farer with outstretched arms. I know no other port so physically welcoming and reassuring.

For the second time I stepped ashore on Ballard Pier bound for the Cathedral Clergy House on Woodhouse Road in the Fort area. A significant change had taken place in the meantime. Father Gracias, the former administrator, was now an auxiliary bishop. It was clear the Archbishop was grooming him to take over. From Rome the Archbishop had obtained full powers for his auxilliary to run the diocese during his protracted absence.

We were a community of eleven at the Cathedral: Bishop Gracias, two Catalan Jesuits in key positions (vicar general, Father Balaguer, and diocesan financial secretary, Father Dominech); Father Angelo Fernandez (later Archbishop of Delhi) Cathedral administrator; Father Joseph Cordeiro (now Cardinal Archbishop of Karachi); Father Ignatius d'Souza (now Bishop of Baroda); Father Joe Lobo, editor of the Bombay Examiner in succession to Father Roper; Father Willy Gomes, Archbishop's secretary (later Bishop of Poona); the chaplain to the Goan Clubs† in Bombay, a dear diminutive man

---

* We were to meet fifteen years later in the Channel Islands, he in a parish served by O.M.I. clergy, I as Coadjutor Portsmouth to which Catholic diocese those delectable Channel Islands now belong.

† Large residential units catering for seamen, seasonal employees, musicians etc.

always on the job whose name escapes me; and Father Frank Lobo, in many ways my closest friend and mentor.

Concentrated under one roof there were two future Cardinal Archbishops, a future Archbishop, and four future Bishops all sleeping easily o' nights on the huge open verandah encircling the second floor, untroubled by noisily revolving fans or the ominous shape of things to come.

Anyone serving the Cathedral in whatever capacity needed all the sleep he could get. From the earliest Mass until late evening devotions, the Cathedral hummed like a beehive. The Catalan Jesuits were first to celebrate and first to hear confessions at the crack of dawn. But everyone had times and turns of duty. I was the odd man out, lending a hand only when clear of duty in the Port. It was, I am sure, in fidelity to the Archbishop's instructions that everyone was so careful to leave me free. "Archbishop Thomas" who had ordained many of them, enjoyed their total loyalty.

Appropriate introductions ensured good, indeed cordial relations with the Port Authority and launched me on the maritime equivalent of house-to-house visiting: systematic boarding, ship-by-ship along the quays, taking note of arrivals and departures with the aim (alas, far from realised) of making my number with all the crews in harbour before they sailed away. Broadly speaking, the work was a continuation of the Colombo routine without the burden of shore establishments or the many advantages of belonging within an outfit which recognised both your duties and your rights. Though by now I had a club (the "Heart and Anchor") going on Ballard Pier, complete with chapel, library and other amenities, I was now working from the outside. So to reduce that particular handicap I continued to wear tropical naval rig, head and shoulders sporting respectively the cap-badge and epaulets of a R.N. chaplain. After all I was still a few months away from my official demob on Christmas day 1946. Maturer reflection however, and a certain amount of experience advised a compromise. Wartime can and does unite the two services, R.N. and M.N., often in the same ship, but rarely without a certain amount of stress and strain, and never merging the two distinct areas of command. Service traditions, and much that goes under the word "ethos", vastly differ. Chances to serve R.N. crews in Bombay were rare indeed. The Royal Indian Navy, trained to a remarkable standard of efficiency by an R.C. British Commander, appeared to be self-providing.

My compromise replaced the senior service version with a civilian cap badge* but retained the R.N. epaulets which, being mainly metal crosses, after all are nobody's monopoly. Generally my visits aboard were cordially welcomed. Indeed there were skippers who would gladly have kept one for the duration, not by any means because they were Gospel-greedy. Any visit is a relief from the boredom of

* The Heart and Anchor of the Apostleship of the Sea, exquisitely woven in the appropriate colours at the convent next door to the cathedral.

days, perhaps weeks, in port. I met remarkable men proof against this prevailing miasma from their own inner resources. Rarely creative, they excelled in their mastery of disciplines allied to their trade—astronomy, maths and of course navigation.

Warm commendation of the skipper once came from an unusual source—half-a-dozen apprentices on a large freighter. Hers was a regular but intricate run around the southern seas. Her master's concern for the wider experience of his apprentices, some of them on their maiden trip, had led him to indulge in some fancy variations on the normal schedule. The cadenza, it seems, was played entirely from memory. The lads were wide-eyed. One of them said very simply: "He just knows the way".

Ship visiting can also involve its unscheduled variations. I boarded a Soviet merchant-man largely for the fun of it and was told to wait where I was for a senior officer. The chief engineer appeared, a very large woman in uniform. We made little sense of each other but I was left in no doubt which way to go. One quaint vessel with a crew of three never left harbour: the fresh-water carrier, which supplied in-coming and out-going traffic. How many years and miles this specialist trio had voyaged round the docks, I never discovered. What did become available was a fund of knowledge about the port, shipping lines and personnel generously shared over a mid-morning cuppa afloat.

Customs and Excise were in large part recruited from Jesuit schools. Officers were friendly no matter what world religion they professed. This, I believe, was a telling point when the future Cardinal Lépicier returned to Rome from India after visiting Catholic schools in the 'twenties on behalf of the Holy See. He is said to have reported somewhat critically on the large number of Jesuits teaching non-Christians who rarely embraced the Faith. This theme of course invited colourful popular embellishments: thus the speech on prize-giving day in which an O.B. Mayor of Bombay, a Parsee, congratulated the Fathers on the fact that he had never heard the name of Christ mentioned in all his years at the school! Pius XI, whose pitiless scrutiny and impartial judgment of major issues are not likely to have nodded in one of such magnitude, gave his verdict: "Jesuits carry on". Preparation for the Faith, however remote, justifies the exercise.

Down at Colaba Point, the cantonment area, the chaplain, Father Harold Roper, S.J. was about to take home leave. He had been five years there without a break. Once again the diocesan man of affairs, Father Dominech, came up with a solution. The question was put to me: "Would I, could I?" Of course I accepted. If the Archbishop had been there I doubt if the question would have come my way.

Colaba Point was a couple of miles further away from the Port than the cathedral. The man of affairs had anticipated that snag. He was on the track of a second-hand motor-bike. I tried it on the curving Marine Drive. At speed something was wrong and I turned it down.

By then I was already installed in the chaplain's bungalow, commuting by push-bike. The man of affairs was engaged with other problems. There was stabling for the chaplain's horse at Colaba. Dare I? Alas for Victoria's glorious days when horse-power came only from horses. I daren't!

I had two servants, Joseph the church "boy", a middle-aged Eurasian, and the Mali. Meals came in from the Officers' Mess. Early on, the Major General from the posh bungalow next door paid me a call. Passing my place daily, he explained, he was affronted by the lack of what he called "conservancy". He looked for a general "smartening up", for instance, those bits of paper round the house. I repaid his call wearing No. 1s and sporting my campaign ribbons. The censorious tone of voice underwent a remarkable sea-change. Sweetly he enquired into "my war". We parted at his gate very good neighbours.

I had no need of an alarm-clock. The regiment, Gloucesters, were drilling on the parade ground by 6 a.m., bugles blaring sometime earlier. Already the sun was at work.

A handful of Italian prisoners were still in residence in the nearby Military hospital. One of them in the sick-bay had a problem. He was all set on marrying a lady from the Bombay stews, whom he had come to know through a liaison with her sister. I was pulled in by a kindly medic to talk him out of it. But all my efforts came up against the stony phrase: *"Ma ci amiamo".** Impossible to budge him. Hadn't he thought he loved her sister? Same answer. Did he realise it was goodbye for ever to Italy? All this apart from consideration to do with his faith. In a way it was heroic, legendary—the stuff grand opera is made of. With anything like a decent libretto, what couldn't Mascagni have made of it?

Father Roper, a life-long cat-lover, among other amenities (as he thought) left his cat, a temperamental animal, somewhat disturbed, I agree, by the absence of its master. I have no allergies, but there were moments when I could have knocked this cat cold. One such was when mother-rat in tandem with half-a-dozen baby rats, each with the tail of the fore-runner in its mouth, swivelled round the cat and disappeared unchallenged.

There were other creatures both great and small one had to get used to. The white walls of the study, once you were settled in of an evening and the lamps lit, were policed by geckos. Each had its own beat and woe betide the trespasser. I was used to wall lizards outside the house in the Peninsula. These were inside and much larger. One soon learns to appreciate them. Any flying insect landing in the gecko's precinct is summarily liquidated. Our fly-catchers were obviously not in the same league.

For attractive habits neither are the vultures or the kites. One of

* "But we love one another!"

the latter managed to nest in a tree close to the bungalow. I'm sure a pukka sahib like Father Roper would have prevented this had he been there. Once the eggs hatched I dare not mount the outside staircase to the gazebo where one might sleep a-cool o'nights, without creating a protective screen for head and shoulders with a revolving walking-stick. The swoop was instant and deadly, corrected just in time to clear the circular trap and flash out through the open verandah on the other side. Vultures, stodged with the offerings of Parsee temple-roofs, settled on the nearby tussocks where the land ends. You could approach them in all their loathliness without provoking more than a slow evasive waddle.

As well as Port chaplain and acting military chaplain, I was now a parish priest with a winsome parish church and several hundred parishioners. Bombay converses in twenty-five different Indian tongues. Colaba residents mostly and mercifully spoke English. For the sake of native servicemen I had a crack at learning Urdu, the esperanto-type *lingua franca* of the Indian Army. I did not get very far. No occasion comes to mind when it could have been of importance.

Father Roper was a man of considerable culture. His *History of the Church* was the standard text in Catholic schools throughout India. His carefully prepared sermons were delivered in flawless English. British residents in Bombay, and not only Catholics, attended his Sunday services from all over Bombay, particularly Malabar Hill (pronounced "Nob Hill" by non-residents). I came to know all sides of our civilian presence in India, military, administrative and business. It was a mixed blessing. On the one hand there emerged distractions which menaced an already complicated round of duty; on the other, opportunities for necessary mental and physical recreation which in several instances have developed into lasting friendships.

The balance between Port chaplain and parish priest was not always delicately achieved. It was clear enough in principle: in doubt, I decided, Port wins. In practice, people's approach to the Church (little people for baptism, star-gazers for matrimony, late people for burial) can wreck your schedule. Relatives can't come at any other time, celebrations are booked, and so on. One's efforts to maintain a rational pattern calls, perhaps, for further scrutiny and illustration.

CHAPTER XXIX

Twilight of the British Raj

JOHN MOON may very well represent the British trade presence in India, as well as a significant sector of my own whereabouts off-duty. He was a senior clerk in Mackinnon Mackenzie's* prestigious water-front offices close to Ballard Pier. He first approached me at Colaba. He was interested in the Faith and asked me to help him get the hang of it. We soon became close friends. Along the jetty in front of M. and M.'s I had often admired a handsome row of yachts and wondered who were the Nabobs in command. They were of course M. and M.'s, for the use of their employees, a word from one of whom alerted a boat-boy to have his craft ready to sail when the Sahib's office-day was done.

I have earlier praised Bombay harbour for its "reassuring" embrace of the new-comer. It amply fulfilled the promise. I can never forget those Saturday afternoons when, John at the helm and the boat-boy poised to luff at the word of command, we slipped through miles of glittering water, this tyro braced practically upright across the thwarts with his feet against the gunwale and his heart in his mouth. John's superb handling gradually allayed all fears. At whatever angle we lay, I found myself thrilled and wanting more. But the inevitable day came when hubris evoked the anger of the gods. It was latish evening. John emerged from M. and M.'s to join Stanley Seddon† and myself already aboard with the boy. One or two ominous clouds scudded across the bay. No bother! Three men in a boat with a boy trained to instant command—what are the odds?

We were not more than a mile out when a sudden ferocious squall flattened us. The gunwale went under. When all seemed over for us, somehow the mast came over and we were on an even keel loaded with water. John managed to go about. Stanley and I seized the first objects to hand for bailing. They were his brogue shoes. We went to work with a will. It was going dark as we rounded the pier, still bailing.

John's next letter home must have contained a facetious account of the incident. His father's reply was devastating. He had sailed

---

* This firm's long trading history in Far Eastern waters includes the running of opium from India into China in the early 19th century. As a consequence, the British Navy's role as a protector of national interests overseas was fouled by the Opium Wars. Are we now reaping the whirlwind as narcotics pour into Great Britain and Ireland despite every effort to stop them?

† Husband of Sonia of whom more later. Stanley had played hockey for India— enough said! India were often world champions. He worked in B.P.

Bombay harbour in his day and knew the hazards. John was criminally at fault to chance uncertain conditions of all places in Bombay harbour.

Long years later I spent a night at the Seddon's house in Kensington. One of the family had acquired a tape-recorder. He demanded: "Record something in Hindi about our guest." Whereupon Stanley poured into the mike the drama of the Bay, not forgetting his brogues: for my sake the family dubbed English into the replay.

He died in 1984 at their cottage in Norfolk. Soni's wifely devotion throughout a long illness was supremely characteristic of her heroic mould. Looks, voice, energy, invention, leadership combined in her to fashion the contemporary Valiant Woman of Proverbs 31, 10. I arrived too late in Bombay to know her in her star role as Hostess of Shandy Tavern, the Services "Home from Home", and her own brilliant creation. I remember her as charging off to Delhi at the drop of a hat to put "Dicky" Mountbatten right on emerging problems. She made sure I had swimming at Breach Candy, that delectable British enclave where even the kites penetrated with difficulty, though I retain a vivid memory of one pouncing from an unbelievable height to claw a cake from a woman's hand. Another sharp silhouette against the pitiless blue sky and sea remains of a pensive little girl. She, Soni's middle daughter Nicola, is now the mother of four strapping sons. Then it was her sixth birthday. A festive gathering at the Seddons introduced me to Mr and Mrs Joe Booth of Rocky Hill. I can never render adequate thanks either to the Lord or the Seddons for this event. The Booths matched the Seddons' Angela, Nicky and Sandra with Ursula ("Teddy"*), Mary Bridget ("Midge") and Anne.

Throughout the war Joe was Food Minister for Bombay Presidency and universally recognised as having done a very good job. His earlier I.C.S. career was mostly, I think, in Sind. There he became an authority on General John Jacob, founder of the city of Jacobabad. I suppose that fearless agnostic who fell entering the impregnable Red Fort in the storming of Delhi must have inspired at least one decent biography. If not, Joe was the man to write it. For literary taste and skill I have rarely met his equal. He would in turn have inspired a finer film than a glorious technicolour effort I seem to remember. But I shall have the joy of returning Booth-wards after the partition of India when Joe finished up in Karachi from which port I, too, took my farewell of India.

In the meantime my service of the port of Bombay continued to be diversified and strengthened by ever-widening circles of friends, men and women who despite all the exasperations the sub-continent bristles with, knew and cherished India and, more surprisingly, knew and cherished me.

Undoubtedly Susan Bliss, shipmate on the *Strathnever*, and printer

* Ursula is Latin for Little Bear.

of my tardy thesis, was the Queen-post of the edifice. Years as manager of the Examiner Press* had schooled her in the "do's and don'ts" of life in India. She lived handily next door to the Cathedral in the convent of the Poor Sisters of India, where all of us emigrés were sure of a noggin and down to earth advice. She recruited my loyalest helpers among whom pride of place must go to Evelyn and Jack Cox. Their son, Derek, was an officer in the British India Shipping Line. He was a lineal descendent of the Venerable James Duckett, himself scion of an ancient Westmoreland family who became a Catholic while an apprentice in the London book trade. His martyrdom at Tyburn on 19 April 1601 was remarkable for three details: first the jury at his trial acquitted him only to reverse their verdict when the bigoted judge made an impassioned appeal for reconsideration; that travelling with him in the same cart to the gallows was the man who betrayed him, bookbinder Peter Bullock, a renegade Catholic whose treachery had failed to save his own skin; lastly on the way to Tyburn someone handed a cup of wine to our maryr, who drank and urged his wife to drink to Peter Bullock, and freely forgive him. He kissed his betrayer, begging him to die a Catholic.†

The Coxs delayed their departure for Sydney until I was due to go home. It was typical of them and deserved a better reward than the cold shoulder Sydney seems to have given them. They moved on at once to Hong Kong where Jack was soon employed and both found friends. Either they or Susan Bliss about this time put me in touch with a legendary old gentleman whose time in India was running out. How many years he had exercised his profession (the Law, I think) in Bombay, one forebore to ask. Pin-striped, secured to his pince-nez by a silk lanyard, he daily drove, *adagio molto*, back and forth from his chambers. His vintage car was in mint condition. It had a Hotchkiss engine whose indestructibility very soon forced the makers to drop that model. No one, the owner told me, had ever driven or cleaned his Pegasus but himself. He had informed the firm of his intention to repatriate both the car and himself. In this solid, shining old-timer, the old gentleman picked me up one Sunday for lunch at the Bombay Yacht Club of which he was probably the oldest member. For me this was exquisite pleasure, not merely because of the B.Y.C.'s Sunday curry (famous in song and story) but for an event in my Roman days.‡ At last I was to enter this fabled sanctum! Memories of the curry are vague. Not however

---

* Publisher of the weekly *Catholic Examiner* (modelled on the *Tablet*) and a prestigious general printing-house. Bombay University recognised there was no alternative if they wanted examination papers to confront examinees *unseen*.

† These details are all from an account of the martyrdom written by the martyr's son, Prior of the English Carthusians in Flanders. Fathers Page, Tichbourne and Watkinson died with Duckett.

‡ A Beda student who had written the "Prince of Wales' Big Game Hunting in India" and later became Game Warden in Baroda joined me on a night journey to Orvieto. Early next morning he gained entrance to the episcopal palace and premier places in the Corpus Christi Procession by flashing his Bombay Yacht Club membership card.

those of my legendary host's courtesy in the ideal setting of B.Y.C.'s spacious dining-room.

At last Archbishop Roberts was back. His resignation had not won favour *in altissimo loco**. He had, I believe, counted on powerful support which either failed or in the event was not forthcoming. The issue was indeed complicated. Portugal, at this juncture of the long-drawn conflict over ecclesiastical jurisdiction in the Far East, alternated with Great Britain in providing an archbishop for Bombay. The arrangement was designed to do away with "double jurisdiction". About 35,000 Goans were living in Bombay and were personally exempt from the Archbishop's spiritual authority. They came under the Patriarch of Goa who acted through his suffragan, the Bishop of Damão.

The first Portuguese to be appointed under the alternating scheme was followed by Archbishop Roberts. He was well aware that in the interim the Indian clergy had petitioned Rome for one of their own. An unpleasant encounter with certain lay representatives may well have strengthened his conviction that the only decent way of burying the controversy between the Padroado and Propaganda† was the appointment of a Goan as Archbishop of Bombay‡. He had his man in Valerian Gracias and saw his own resignation as essential to the good estate of the Church in India.

Despite his deep disappointment Archbishop Roberts, like a good Jesuit, allowed no sign of it to escape him on his return. He had chosen to sail in an Anchor Liner. Many of the crew were from the Isles, superb seamen and devout Catholics. Before their ship turned round, a run ashore to Bassein was arranged. The Archbishop included his port chaplain in the party. He was in excellent form. Among the diversion for passengers on the way out was "Hunt-the-Slipper" which, in this case, was not a slipper. The Archbishop was saying his breviary when the door of his cabin flew open and a breathless American junior blurted: "Is there a lady's bra in here?" A gentle shake of the head brought the door to with a slam. This was one of many shipboard-yarns spun that day among the ruins of what from 1512 for a couple of centuries was one of the most flourishing Portuguese missions in India.

We picknicked on the heights above the fishing village from which came moving evidence that the ancient glory had not entirely

---

* i.e. Pius XII had turned it down.

† Sacred Congregation *De Propaganda Fidei* or since Vatican II: "S.C. for the Evangelisation of Peoples". Founded by Gregory XV 1622.

‡ Portugal was awarded the Padroado (ecclesiastical patronage of the East Indies) by the Pope in the 17th century. Certainly the vitality and success of missionaries from the Peninsula deserved the signal favour of the Holy See. A century later, however, both the colonial and missionary vigour were spent forces. Propaganda perforce by-passed the claims of the Padroado in supplying the deficiency, erecting and staffing new dioceses. The honorifics accorded to the Archbishop of Goa: e.g. "Patriarch of the East Indies" and "Primate of the East", despite constant protest, remained *Tituli sine re*—empty titles. Bombay which became British in 1661 saw the expulsion of all Goan clergy in 1720.

departed. All afternoon the villagers in long lines scaled the escarpment. Eyes with the trick of focussing distance had not missed their Father in God though our approach had not been through the village.

One by one they knelt to kiss his ring. We watched in silence for the most part. I think I partly understood what lay behind the Archibishop's comment during a brief lull: "One gets very deeply attached to them."

The other side of the conflict is illustrated best perhaps by a snatch of table-talk treasured at Cathedral House from the days of Archbishop Goodier* who, like one of his predecessors, George Porter S.J.† wrote copiously on spiritual subjects. It seems a particularly irksome exercise of Goa's personal jurisdiction in Bombay territory came up for discussion at lunch. Goa's immediate agent in the affair was a certain Monsignor Pera. The Archbishop's distress prompted the cathedral wag to ask: "Isn't it time Your Grace changed his episcopal motto?"

"Suggest me one," said the Archbishop.

"SINE PERA."‡

The two words in essence encapsulated the present Archbishop's purpose, which despite the recent set-back, ultimately prevailed in the appointment of Valerian Gracias, a Goan born in Karachi, as his successor. With hindsight Pius XII's Fabian tactics appear remarkably providential.

The days of the British Raj were numbered despite Churchill's determined words about "a half-naked rebel on the steps of Government House". In 1942 Stafford Cripps' ingenious proposals for a new constitution failed to please either Congress or the Muslim League. I had arrived in India about the time of the "Great Calcutta Killing" (16 August 1946) in which 4,000 died in three days. Both Nehru and Gandhi at that time were opposing any partition of India. The danger of Civil War, however, was only too evident. The viceroy, Wavell, pressed Attlee for urgent action. Attlee reacted, sacking Wavell and sending out Mountbatten in March 1947. His Plan for the two new dominions of India and Pakistan received British Government sanction June 3, 1947 and became a reality on the Feast of the Assumption, not without appalling loss of life.

Many condemned the partition line as inconceivably reckless in cutting through neuralgic points such as temple precincts; others were favourably impressed by the famous Mountbatten drive and whole-heartedly praised him; others again put the blame on the endless manoeuvring of Congress and the Muslim League. I suppose there is some truth in all these views.

Partition precipitated a stampede across the new frontiers. An

* Archbishop of Bombay (1919-1926) in his day best-seller of English Catholic spiritual writers.
† Archbishop of Bombay 1886-89.
‡ "Without a scrip" (Vulgate: Luke 22, 35.)

estimated seven million fled from either side. An estimated 200,000 perished in the attempt to leave Pakistan for India. This latter figure, I was assured at the time, was an underestimate. So I also believed, partly on the evidence of systematic slaughter of whole train-loads of Hindus*, partly from my own observation of the refugees who survived this worst journey in the world. Thousands of them were bivouacked on the large open space alongside the Heart and Anchor. Night after night my windows forced a heart-rending panorama of human misery on my conscience. I was involved. This was the outcome of solemn decisions sanctioned by the Mother of Parliaments and implemented by the brisk master-mind of a great R.N. commander. It wasn't that I gained from this experience any new statistical evidence of the magnitude of the pogrom. Rather it was a hardening of one's prejudice and shame at the way the thing had happened and a readiness to listen to axes being ground by fellow-countrymen who deplored not only the way devolution had gone but the fact that it happened at all.

Latterly I have seen things in truer perspective—particularly with subsequent evidence of what Civil War in India can mean, and not merely to two hundred thousand.

Mahatma Gandhi spent that Assumption Day fasting and sorrow-ing, of all India's leaders the only one unreconciled to its partition. One hundred and fifty-two days later, on January 20, 1948, he was shot by one of his own Hindu disciples in the streets of Delhi as he maintained his changeless message of peace and reconciliation. No one in India that day can ever forget it. Archbishop Roberts wrestled long over the statement everyone expected of him. It may well have betrayed the process of excessive cerebration, but of one thing I am persuaded. It was supremely right that it should come from an English archbishop, as, again, it was right that neither Goan, nor Mangalorean, nor member of any one of the multiple ethnic strains composing the Church in India should offer Pontifical High Mass for the peace of India in Bombay Cathedral on the Feast of the Assumption 1947.

Hence my earlier surmise that Pius XII's Fabian tactics can with hindsight appear remarkably providential. I have, alas, laboured too long in getting to the point, but allow one last memory of the end of an epoch—the day British soldiers left India, marching with their colours, regimental bands and matchless drill to the Gateway of India. Shades of Outram, Clive, Warren Hastings, Havelock, Jacob, the Wellesleys, Kipling, the Widow of Windsor, Kim, Gunga Din *et al!* Surely they crowded round the Gateway for the send-off. Doubtless, too, they later trooped across the road into the Taj to mingle bitter tears with their pink gins. Nor shall I ever forget Bishop Gracias' comment on that occasion: "You have to look hard through universal history to find a parallel. A nation yielding

---

* You had to see how trains in India could over-load. Better still travel on one. A Roman bus at rush hour pales in comparison.

possession of a continent not to force of arms, but out of respect for reason and common-sense." He was exaggerating. India is a *sub-continent*, but without any doubt that day the brightest Jewel fell from the Crown.*

* As I write they are repeating *The Jewel in the Crown* on television. The universal acclaim accorded to this saga is in many ways more than justified. May I wonder if others who were there at the time find it strangely trivialising?

CHAPTER XXX

Farewell to Mother India

MY OWN appreciation of India was not based only on Ballard Pier and Bombay. In the way of duty, friendship, recreation, or an amalgam of all three, I was lucky enough to move towards the main points of the compass: N. the Himalayas, S. Bangalore, E. Calcutta, W. Karachi*.

Calcutta and the Himalayas were in fact one and the same trip which I made in response to our port-chaplain on the Hoogly. He was also recruited by Archbishop Roberts but in a more comprehensive way than by post.

Graham Langford was a C. of E., R.A.F. Chaplain in India whose conscience left him no option but to seek admission into the Catholic Church. The night before he was received, who should join him at the table in the mess but a truculent Catholic padre. Greatly relishing the irony of a last fling, he sturdily countered with what he regarded as the best apologia for Anglicanism he had ever heard. As they parted he whispered in the other's ear, "Pray for me. I'm being received tomorrow." So he was, and after appropriate delays for study and preliminary minor and major orders, Archbishop Roberts ordained him for Bombay, drafting him later to Calcutta in pursuit of his plan to provide Eastern ports with chaplains R.C.

It must be 1,000 miles from Bombay to Calcutta as the crow flies: as the train steams, by Agra and Delhi, the distance doubles. Complete with bed-roll, I joined my train at Churchgate Station and met the three chaps with whom I was billeted for the next three days, all seasoned travellers of Indian rail-roads.

Kipling records a conversation among locomotives of India during a night's rest in the shed. It is a marvellous *tour de force*, a descant on the liveries and routes of the vast system linking all parts of the sub-continent. If only I could lay my hand on it to quote *my* engine! It was a monster indifferently pounding away through irrigated plains and deserts where yet another cyclopean monster must have flung open all the furnace doors of Hades. Oh, the blessed cool of night! The mouth-melting glimpse of hill-stations and the mouth-searing bite of the excellent curries!

Father Langford ferried me from the station to his chaplaincy through broad streets thronged from wall to wall with pedestrians

* Karachi-W. is a "con" really. It's more N than W and I got there not by land but by sea.

142

all going the same way. We passed the thirst-quenching area which gave its name to that famous unofficial Campaign Ribbon, the Chowringee Star. At that time somewhere in Calcutta a young Loreto Sister from the Balkans was preparing with God's grace for world service of the poor. I refer to Mother Teresa.

The Himalayan trip was never in similar danger of becoming blurred in memory. A valiant little engine hauled us up to Darjeeling. It appeared to me no bigger than the one that used to go back and forth, burdened with kids, mums and dads, on the Miniature Railway alongside the Marine Lake at Southport. Perched on the cow-puncher of the Darjeeling model sat a skilled craftsman with a box of sand. Judicious handfuls, spilled on the wheels at the stiffest gradients, ensured their grip on the track. The occasional threat of aimless slithering was decidedly ominous when you looked back.

The Jesuits have a theology house at Curseong near Darjeeling. They might well claim theirs is not just high thinking but the highest in the world. They put me up. I have never enjoyed such high living. From their sports-ground day after day I raised my eyes to the eternal mountains. Everest always remained shrouded in cloud. The reward came suddenly one noon. A rent in the cloud, and hey presto! There was Everest? No, Kanchenjunga, the consolation prize. Not at the level to which I had meanly raised my eyes, but towering high, high beyond. My head went back with a jolt, mouth opening in a gasp of astonished incredulity.

I went walks with the students. Walking-sticks were not just for decor. One of my companions confessed his professor was on his track for over-dosing Existentialism. What did I think? Alas, I was little help to him—too long away from the Schools. He was clearly a brilliant lad.

Darjeeling market place became my mecca. There rosy-cheeked men and women from the Shan States sat smiling behind their wares, cocooned in thickly padded trouser-suits. They exuded an infectious merriment. Later when a Salesian friend of mine from those parts became Archbishop, I was delighted to send him the results of a generous whip-round. It was a way of paying my debt for the fun in Darjeeling market. And something of that same sense of "noblesse oblige" binds me ever since to the Sisters of Loreto. Their Darjeeling Convent School claims a unique corner in grateful memory for two unprecedented experiences.

A laywoman admitted me. I gave my name and waited. A sister, obviously distracted about many things, put her head in to say: "Kindly wait a little. I'll get the little girls for you as soon as possible." She was gone. She returned some minutes later. "Your daughters, Mr Holland, will be here immediately." For this trip to the Himalayas I had donned my old dark blue battle-dress which partly covered the clerical collar. The point was, I assure you, much needed warmth. "But sister—" and I pulled the clerical collar into full view. It was a natural, if somewhat novel, clerical error. There *was* a chap called Holland, a tea-planter, about my size. He had two daughters at Loreto. But the Sister made swift amends. The object of my visit was to meet Mother Marie Antoinette. We met half-way in the corridor. She was yet another component of Susan Bliss's vast mosaic of friendships in India. The *Bombay Examiner* circulated widely. Something I'd written there prompted Mother Marie Antoinette to write. Our correspondence continued for at least a dozen years after I left India. At this, our first meeting, she was already in her seventies, young at heart, brimming over with hilarious but far from hare-brained schemes for bringing people to love the Lord.

She was an Australian but had clearly migrated well before the Motherland, for the average Digger, produced only "B----y Poms". The G.H.Q. of our retaliatory offensive against the Japs was for some time based on Darjeeling. Loreto kept open house for Brasshats and all ranks. Mother Marie Antoinette's warm-hearted motherhood embraced the lot. After the elegant tea or the nosh-up, she led all parties into chapel, said a brief formal prayer and sat them down. She was mistress of all their names and background. With her inimitable turn of phrase and digger informality, she then yarned away about them to the Lord. Her letters to me later in England recorded further approaches among her former friends of all ranks to both Faith and Priesthood. She was in touch with them all, including many who made no such approaches but remained her very warm confidants and admirers. She asked me to call on one of her generals who was facing the last enemy in a Grace and Favour cottage at Windsor, a man of international acclaim. I am still beating my breast. I let her down through cowardice.

She died in her nineties, all the trumpets sounding for her on the other side, many a Chindit bugle among them. Please God, a great soldier was also there to beckon her home with his field-marshall's baton.

Father Langford and I parted but only for a brief interlude. We were destined to work together on the same job again, not, however, a thousand miles apart this time, but side by side in the Catholic Missionary Society.

I broke my return journey at New Delhi. Lutyens was Archbishop Downey's choice of architect for Liverpool's Metropolitan Cathedral. His plan had come in for a lot of criticism. Here in Delhi was a chance to see his work in three dimensions. I was greatly impressed but forced to wonder who paid the piper. All I had of Agra and the Taj Mahal was the view from the train. They would have to wait another twenty-five years, and came with the unforgettable bonanza of a visit to Mother Teresa's Refuge for the Poor.

Once again Ballard Pier and the docks claimed my undivided attention. Father Roper had resumed his cure of souls at Colaba. Always a phrase-maker, he spoke of life somewhere in England as 'wading in stagnant pools of reminiscence'.

Family group taken in 1908. Standing: John Holland. Seated left to right: John Holland Jnr., Aunt Hannah, Hannah, Uncle John with Mary Winefride (Mamie), Mary Holland with the infant Thomas.

Upholland Cricket XI, 1926. Thomas Holland was wicket-keeper.

Street frontage of St. Alban's College, Valladolid.

The College patio, Valladolid.

Chaplain in the Royal Navy:
at Antwerp.

50th birthday, 11 June 1958,
with brother, Father Joseph,
and dog Teddy.

Above:
With Archbishop
Gerald O'Hara,
c. 1958.

Right:
Leaving Portsmouth
Cathedral after
consecration as
coadjutor Bishop,
with Bishops Dwyer
(Leeds) and Healy
(Gibraltar).

Above:
Archbishop Beck
enthrones Bishop
Holland in Salford
Cathedral
12 September 1964.

Right:
2nd Vatican Council,
1962-65: entering St
Peter's for one of the
sessions, with Cardinal
Heenan.

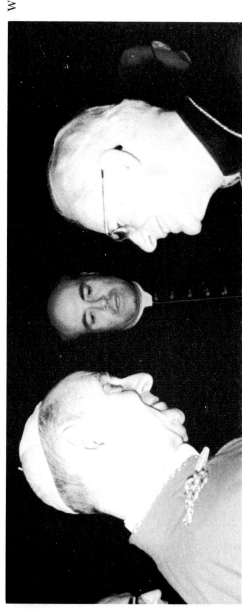

With Pope Paul VI.

In St Peter's during one
of the Council sessions
(front row at left).

Above:
Bishop Holland and
Bishop Burke welcome
Pope John Paul II to
Manchester, 31 May
1982.

Right:
Blessed Sacrament
Procession through
Manchester, mid-1970s.

"I would love to be remembered for loving the children." (Radio interview, April 1983).

Celebrating golden jubilee of priesthood at St Alban's, Blackburn, June 1983. Left to right: Mgr. Bruno Kresing, VG Paderborn; Canon Michael Fitzpatrick; Bishop George Gilson (Le Mans); Bishop Holland; Archbishop John Joachim Degenhardt (Paderborn); Bishop Burke; Canon George Hughes.

Susan Bliss hooked me for an event in Bangalore on the irresistible plea of "noblesse oblige". I had come to know within her closer circle of friends a remarkable widow who along with her husband had spent many years among the poor of India as a Medical Missionary. (She too had played international hockey in her day.) Her ardour was by no means confined to sport. She became a Catholic and it was no surprise to Susan and others when she discovered a late vocation to Carmel. She entered at Bangalore. Susan insisted we flew down for her 'clothing' ceremony. The ceremony attracted wide attention and a distinguished gathering met afterwards for sumptuous refreshment provided by the Nizam.

My last distraction from Ballard Pier was Goa. It had to happen. I could not leave India without paying homage at the greatest of all shrines in the East. Hadn't the Pope just sent the Golden Rose there—the most eloquent token of a desire to be there? One of the cathedral priests due for a home-break invited me to join him. I jumped at the chance. We sailed by night and woke as our ship slowly threaded the River of Goa between well-wooded banks to tie up at Panjim.

Old Goa in its day (which began with the Portuguese colonists in 1510) boasted fifty churches, with convents, hospices and other institutions attached. The lethal miasma of the jungle fens began killing first people and finally the city which was abandoned for Panjim five miles away. It was totally deserted by 1759 and the relentless jungle moved in to strangle and topple the glory that was Goa. Our eerie visit of the site allowed at least the mind's eye to pencil in the outlines of manueline basilicas. Only overgrown stumps of masonry and broken ridges remained.

The Patriarch invited us to lunch. A day or two before, we had an unconvenanted preview of the great man and his sister swimming in the secluded lagoon below the palace. The vision was not sought but thrust upon us as our bus rounded a corner of the corniche road. They were both charming, even commending my ghastly Portuguese. How many years the Patriarch had spent in India (he was bishop of Mylapore before Goa) I forget. His last years and they, too, were not few, passed decorously in Rome as a Cardinal in Curia. I saw him from time to time but never ventured to speak.

The Faith and culture of Portugal's golden age interpenetrated her conquests. Goa's was the achievement of restoring the Malabar Thomas Christians to Catholic Unity. The Grandees of Portugal proudly sponsored mass-baptisms, giving their surname to everyone of the neophytes. Hence today's de Sousas, de Mellos, Vasconcellos and dozens of other noble patronymics. Open your eyes in any Goan church, you would think yourself back in rural Portugal. Open your ears on any street or hamlet, you are likely to hear from many directions stringed instruments of every kind but Indian playing the sacred and profane music you might hear at Braga or in Tras os Montes, played too with consummate skill.

145

Goa attracted other visitors than the returning native and the pious pilgrim. The Congress Party had succeeded in banning alcohol in Bombay state. Their achievement went much further than the British colonial closure of all grog-ships on the night the mill-hands were paid. Medical evidence of need or a foreign passport were about the only legitimate titles to a monthly ration. Needless to say comedy lurked in the wings. Trains north from Bombay to the military terminus at Deolally paused briefly there before heading back to Bombay. It was not uncommon to see travellers whip off their white Congress caps, dash to the bar, swallow a couple of "burra pegs"* and resume their seats along with the virtuous insignia of their political affiliation. The station was the other side of the Bombay border.

I said Mass at St. Francis Xavier's shrine, content, indeed thrilled, to be there though this was not a peak period when the incorrupt body was exposed and the world gathered in homage. That experience was to come sixteen years later at the time of the 38th International Eucharistic Congress.

Back in Bombay the Archbishop had chosen my successor for the post of Port Chaplain, a Goan priest friend who was later to become Bishop of Baroda. Alas, he was not to enjoy the facilities and amenities of Ballard pier. The Port Authority for their own good reasons had given advance notice of closure. Sixteen years later I made a pilgrimage to the Port. I wish I hadn't. Possibly fond memory had changed all my geese to swans. What remained with me (and ever shall) bright, colourful and bustling, now appeared drab and lifeless. Pier and docks no longer hummed with traffic. Had the airport stolen the spidery cranes and gantries along with the passengers? M. & M.'s no longer fringed the water-front with stout hulls and canvas. Their great business-house looked empty.

My last view of Bombay Harbour in mid-1948 was from the bridge of a ship flying the flag of the Anchor Line, the one Archbishop Roberts preferred to all others. Military Transport very decently treated my homeward voyage as delayed repatriation for demob and sportingly fell in with my intention to spend a week or so at Karachi and pick up a later ship. The Booths had insisted I join them in their new home.

The six hundred miles voyage from Bombay had been agony and I had felt very unwell. Freya Booth warped me into harbour up the outside stairs on the right front of their lovely house. A self-contained flat welcomed the sailor home from the sea to dreamless repose. The next day began with the stamp of hoofs below. The syce had Joe's horse at the gate for the early morning canter on the maidan. Joe later described his mount as "a decent old horse", and I was moved to wonder if there was another one like it. Apparently this was not thought to be a good idea, but I recovered well enough to play a decent round of golf with Joe and crew with him in the

* Doubles.

146

Sunday regatta. This was memorable for the encounter with the outrageous woman.

The course selected for the day included a narrow channel connecting two stretches of open sea. Joe was clearly favourite but at this point appeared a craft coming from the opposite direction. Joe moved over to his side allowing ample passage. Sulphurously he denounced the oncomer's failure to follow suit. There was a palpable hit. It was the outrageous woman at the helm.

Our time was easily the best. We were, however, automatically disqualified for contact with a competitor. She boldly presented herself on the steps of the Club-house scantily clad, whisky glass in hand, as though nothing had happened.

Joe later threw up his cabinet post, unable to go along with prevailing methods, and took Freya and his family back to Ireland, I was to see the youngsters grow up year by year in their new home above the sea at Dalkey, named after the house on Malabar Hill, "Rocky Hill". Already they were very dear. My accolade came as I waved good-bye from the towering side of the Empress liner outward bound for England. Freya's and three other tiny arms raised handkerchiefs but Teddy needed hers. She had dissolved in tears. My last clear sight of Mother India was Freya bending to comfort her.

CHAPTER XXXI

Uncharted perilous Seas

"A life on the ocean wave," chant the matelots, "is better than going to sea." Believe me, even nonsensical parodies can apply to actual cases. Boarding the *Empress* that night in Karachi, I was all agog to be homeward bound yet so daunted by the prospect of what confronted me on arrival that I could have wished the voyage to continue endlessly, or at least till the vision faded. What confronted me once ashore was, paradoxically, uncharted perilous seas.

Was that the old "yellow streak" diagnosed by a discerning Vice-Rector twenty years ago at Valladolid? From that same consultant, now Bishop of Menevia, I had received a letter in the previous March. He had wind of my return. Would I consider seeking release from my Archbishop and joining him? He intended to found a Catholic Missionary Society in Wales. The Jesuit holiday house at Barmouth was available as G.H.Q. You could have knocked me down with the proverbial No. 13 bus. In a daze, and no doubt influenced by our former relationship, I obediently answered "Yes" and wrote to the Liverpool Curial Offices for the necessary permission. The Vicar General, Monsignor Alban Atkins, replied very promptly. Petit, learning I would not be available for a few months, favoured the suggestion that Welsh would come in very handy. Appropriate manuals had arrived from Wrexham cathedral through the good offices of the administrator, Canon Adolph Evans, a contemporary at Valladolid and a native Welsh speaker.

Intermittent application ashore now went into high-gear once aboard the *Empress*. The Captain and a Padre going home on leave, both Welshmen, supplemented the bookwork with not exactly conversation, but intonation, phonetics. By the time we were half-way home I was sanguine about my chances of coping with the language.

We made a non-stop passage to Liverpool and were warped into dock in the late evening. Some favoured passengers were allowed off promising to return. Customs were not operating until morning.

I looked forward to that particular hurdle uneasily. Never before or since have I travelled with so much impedimenta—crates, sacks and suitcases. The chances of strict or generous treatment at Liverpool in my case would turn not on the *rouge et noir* but the orange and green. (Ulster Protestant or Irish Catholic Customs Officer.) My stuff made a bulky pile by which I stood awaiting my

148

turn. The chap next to me was in trouble with a service revolver. The Customs Officer reeled off the grim alternatives and left him to make up his mind. My turn had come. Would it be "Father" or—? "This your lot, padre?" I feared the worst.

Susan Bliss had masterminded the major packing, numbering each stoutly corded case or sewn-up bale. I held ready her detailed list of contents. "How long have you been away padre?" I told him. Without more ado he chalked each of the pieces and moved on. "Oh me of little faith!" A couple of "whackers" came forward. "Where do you live, Father?" I gave my address—a good twenty miles away. "We'll deliver this afternoon. Five quid?" They were as good as their word.

I came ashore that morning side by side with the Rt. Reverend John Forest Hogan, O.F.M. He was returning to Friars Minor H.Q. in Forest Gate to be consecrated Bishop of Bellary. Two years earlier he had taken over the territory with the non-episcopal rank of Prefect Apostolic. Bellary in the meantime had been up-graded from Prefecture to Diocese. As port chaplain I had welcomed him to India in 1947 along with his companions, half-a-dozen fresh young "Frats" raring to complete the unfinished labours of St. Francis Xavier. They all came out to Colaba for an evening before entraining for the south. Their Prefect's sunny countenance, I remember, clouded somewhat as I recharged the young men's glasses with a generous drop of the cratur. But this was welcome home: "Did he not know that even Jesuit scholastics, under doctors' order, for years, centuries perhaps, had conditioned themselves to the insidious climate of Mother India with a 'sundowner'?" What that dear man certainly could not know was his own unique place in the history of the 21st General Council of the Catholic Church, Vatican II. Fifteen years later he obediently took ship from India to attend the First Session which began 11th October 1962. He died on arrival in Naples, the Council's first casualty, or better, Protomartyr.

It was as I emerged from the Customs Shed that I came face to face with family. Both were in good form, all agog to point out what a picture of misery was coming down the gangway in contrast to the happy priest at my side. Mother who was now seventy-four chose to welcome me at home. Mamie confided to me later the reason for her unusual emotion on this occasion: "Mother had come to think she would never see you again."

The two "whackers" arrived, shouldered the white man's burden into the house, family meantime very suitably impressed. I regret to say foodstuffs claimed prior attention. What I thought would be their pride and joy, a great red carpet from Karachi, was partially unstitched from its sacking to be then relegated to the out-house for later consideration. Three or four years later it was rescued and laid. A much smaller Bokhara rug won universal acclaim and pride of place in our modest home.

Time had marched on in my absence. Canon Turner had died in

his ninetieth year, Father Pat Cahill in his sixty-ninth, honoured with the dignity of Domestic Prelate long beforehand. I owed and still owe them an incalculable debt.

I 'phoned the Vicar General, Monsignor Atkins, to tell him I was back. Would he be in touch with Bishop Petit about the future? Ought I, perhaps, to see the Archbishop? He was very sure I should. In fact the Archbishop wanted to see me. I would be informed shortly when to appear.

Ominous overtones came over the 'phone. The Archbishop began by saying he had just heard of my going to Menevia. The idea was plainly ridiculous. Forty years ago, he and Father Joe Howard* had preached through the Rhonda and the Rhymney Valleys. Considerable numbers gathered to hear them in the village squares and institutes. They had the same reaction everywhere: "Come back speaking Welsh and we'll listen."

"Your Grace," I ventured. "I have done some spade-work in that direction and feel I could qualify, given time."

"Absurd! You would speak a Mandarin sort of Welsh like the old man down there in Cardiff* I 'phoned Monsignor Atkins. He was apologetic but stuck to his guns. He had most certainly cleared the matter in March. He would remind the Archbishop and be in touch later.

I was due to meet Bishop Petit at the Albanian Society Meeting† in Manchester the following Tuesday. Could the V.G. clear the issue finally before then? In the meantime rumours had reached Bishop Petit in Menevia. It was agreed mutually that Tuesday was *Der Tag*. The V.G. rang the day before. "Definitely off." I shall never forget crossing the Grosvenor‡ lounge that morning. We met half-way. He knew. He knew I knew. "Spilt milk, Tom." And that was that. A few days later I was appointed to the London Catholic Missionary Society, Superior Father J. C. Heenan.

---

* Archbishop McGrath, a recognised Gaelic and Welsh scholar. He and Archbishop Downey were both Freemen of their native city, Kilkenny.
† O.B.'s of St. Albans' Valladolid Annual Meeting: Tuesday nearest St. Alban's Day, June 22nd.
‡ The Grosvenor Hotel faced Manchester Cathedral at the corner of Victoria Bridge Street and Deansgate. It disappeared in a post-war development.

Pause in Midstream

Teamsters, I believe, when fording water-ways of any kind, were warned never to pause at any such point. And now I am a teamster, member of an outfit re-vitalised a year before I joined. Forced off the road throughout the war years, the old chariot seemed unlikely to roll again. A word in time from the Apostolic Delegate* just saved it. He suggested the demise might give a false impression in Rome as though we were no longer interested in direct approaches to our fellow-citizens with the Catholic Faith.

The C.M.S registers among my earliest memories. In 1912 we at last got a chapel-of-ease at our remote end of the parish of St. Marie-on-The-Sands. A legacy for a Mass-centre had been provided early in the nineteenth century. Long before the railway made Southport, a colony of fisherfolk from Ireland had settled among the sand dunes at North Meols, alongside the marshes fringing the Ribble Estuary. Hesketh Golf Links now cover the site.

The fisherfolk sailed away and the legacy lay dormant. Southport, however, developed other links with our Doomsday village of Churchtown by rail and tramway. Where ours had been one of the first Catholic families to live there since the Reformation, gradually a congregation gathered, large enough to justify activating the dormant legacy. The choice of a site on Marshside Road where another community of fisherfolk lived a few furlongs from the earlier colony of Little Island†, for all I know, may have been dictated by the terms of the original pious bequest. In the event it proved to be at the same time both Magnificent and War.

The "Little Islanders" were Catholics, the Marshsiders Primitive Methodists. Over the entrance to their Social Centre hung a painting of fishing smacks afloat with a legend to this effect: "Water is all we need". Their ardent dedication to total abstinence may have been one reason for their detestation of us Catholics. There were also theological and historical factors which, it seems, their Marshside Chapel did not let them forget.

Our Marshside Chapel, St. Patrick's, as I often heard my father say, could never have got above ground but for the clerk of works, an inspired choice: a Churchtowner, probably therefore a worshipper at St. Cuthbert's‡. More to the present purpose he was a recognised authority on racing pigeons. That won the day for us.

* The Most Reverend W. Godfrey, then Apostolic Delegate to Great Britain.
† I confess I never learned which was right: Little Island or Little Ireland! Anyway, one or the other was the local name for the former site of the Irish colony.
‡ By tradition built on the spot where the bier carrying the body of St. Cuthbert rested during his Community's flight from the Danes. There are others either side of the Ribble. All are dedicated to the great monastic founder. Churchtown's is the oldest in North Meols and "Mother Church of Southport".

Religious animosities dissolved in the local white-hot passion for tips likely to accelerate the homing of Marshside's favourite birds.

Archbishop Whiteside came for the laying of the Foundation Stone in 1912. Seated at the faldstool delivering his *fervorino*, did he realise the magnitude of his achievement? Crowded behind the waist-high walls, East met West, Catholics and Primitive Methodists, shoulder to shoulder, listened intently. Archiepiscopal magnetism? or simply pigeons? One thing he certainly did not know. His feet rested on the white woolly rug from my old perambulator.

St. Patrick's opened with a C.M.S Mission. (At last I am toeing my starting line.) Catholic men went round all the houses delivering personal invitations. The preachers were Dr. Downey, the future Archbishbop, and Father Joe Howard. My father was deeply impressed, as were, I believe, the majority, by the powerful manner and matter of the latter. Our Welsh neighbour, headmaster of the village Council School, wagged a disapproving finger, "The little fat man is the one to watch. He'll go far." He did, fifteen years later, but don't imagine this percipient critic saw his way into the Catholic Church. His mentor was Bertrand Russell. Later his profound researches into Vedantic philosophy earned a doctorate from a Hindu University.

My father was already "factotuming" at St. Patrick's aided by the family. He never allowed us to forget that C.M.S. Mission. The friendship he then formed was a constantly recurring theme. My ordination at St. Marie's "on the Sands" fulfilled an earlier promise made in virtue of that friendship.

Perhaps my posting to the original C.M.S. in preference to the Bishop of Menevia's Welsh facsimile could be dimly derivable from the Mission which launched our chapel-of-ease thirty-six years earlier? Liverpool sent two recruits to the C.M.S. in 1948. My companion, Father John Callaghan, had considerable experience of out-door speaking in the Catholic Evidence Guild. In view of the nomadic life ahead he had the extra advantage of owning a car. It was in immediate demand for our journey down. We met on the apron of the old L.N.E.R. station in Wigan. There began an eight-year comradeship-in-arms and a friendship ending only in "Jack's" call to higher things. Then, very surely, once again, "all the trumpets sounded on the other side".

He was a natural crowd charmer, a short, dimple-dumpling of a man with a welcoming smile and golden hair. Luckily in his case, the normal priest's stock-in-trade had not been complicated by continental degree courses or domestic higher studies. Not that he lacked the necessary resources. His mastery of the basics went with an easy expository style and shrewd judgment of his audience's capacity and needs. Their reaction was to be neatly conveyed on an occasion when Jack was paired with a famous C.M.S. speaker. "Father X is a highly educated priest. But we've been working all day. We can follow Father Callaghan better. We think he's tops."

M-roads were far away in the future in September 1948. We were often to travel together between London and the North in that bull-nosed car on the A1, tediously crawling through the heart of busy little towns.

We had our moments, good and not-so-good. Jack had a nose for good pull-ups for C.M.S. men, old-fashioned hostelries with a good simple table and the right accompaniments. He was rarely without the right smoke for post-prandial relaxation. One's nerves could need that kind of assuagement. Once in desperation Jack pulled out from behind a slow coach and accelerated into the other lane to be confronted with an oncoming lorry. Mercifully both of us ground to a halt within feet of each other. I waited for it. High up in his cab the man at the other wheel looked down at us—two shamefaced dog-collars caught *in flagrante delicto*. His contorted features relaxed. Instead of a well-deserved shower of imprecations, we were treated to peals of hilarious laughter as we shambled away in reverse. Not a word passed between us.

C.M.S. Prothalamion

At some point in my youth the life of Cardinal Vaughan, I remember, provided our refectory reading. He, the founder of the C.M.S. and so many other good things, including Westminster Cathedral, that have stood the test of time, dreamed as a very young priest of travelling the mountains and valleys of Wales to bring the lost sheep back to the fold. He was a Border man, born at Courtfield near Ross-on-Wye. I think he rejoiced, among the angels, at Bishop Petit's gallant enterprise as in no way a challenge to his own far-sighted provision but as a sensitive response to his own first missionary romance.

Bishop Petit's plan did in fact succeed later. We trained Father Pat Crowley, his first priest-in-charge, at our London H.Q. For good measure, it fell to me to preach the first mission from Courtfield, the home of the Vaughans then recently acquired by the Mill Hill Foreign Missionary Society, Herbert Vaughan's earliest foundation and the first of its kind in our post-reformation history. It is now a busy centre for retreats.

CHAPTER XXXII

Roll the Old Chariot along

IN 1940 Gerry destroyed C.M.S. H.Q. in Brondesbury Park with a land-mine. The priests were already dispersed. Black-out and bombs were incompatible with normal C.M.S. targets—large concentrations of people in town and city churches, market-places, and village squares. The Superior, Father Owen Dudley*, bivouacked for a time in the ruins and eventually resumed his apostolate of the pen in new pastures north of London. A young priest of the Brentwood diocese replaced him at the end of the War.

John Carmel Heenan was a burning and a shining light. Before his appointment as Superior of the C.M.S., his shining in pulpits, on radio, with Barbara Ward in the Sword of the Spirit, round his parish, at prisoner-of-war camps, during air-raids, and up and down the columns of the Sunday Express (Irish edition) was steady and at times, blinding. As for burning, many a well-wisher rued his inevitable self-incineration. After wrapping his car round trees during air-raids through lack of sleep, he said early Mass for his people as usual "with dignity and devotion". He could and did fire others with enthusiasm, both ways. A secretarial job he gave me in connection with Cardinal Griffin's General Mission to all parishes after the war, proved to be definitely not my scene. He fired me with unconcealed enthusiasm†.

The new Mission House at Golders Green nestled alongside Golders Hill Park, a winsome wooded domain with a lake, and enclosures for animals likely to rejoice young hearts, bambies, wallabies and bunnies. The Park itself is an enclave of Hampstead Heath. Heenan could not have found a home more likely to refresh the weary missioner returning from the weeks of leg-and-voice work round the houses, in the pulpit, the confessional, schools and, in the summer, campaigns on the shores and village squares of England's green and pleasant land where Catholics are few.

I slept my first night at Mission House lulled by Heenan's kind

---

* Author of *The Masterful Monk, Will Men be like Gods? The Last Crescendo*, etc. He had his fan-clubs in U.S.A. and the odd doctorate thesis dedicated to his work.
† Not, however, before my learning his use of hieroglyphics to guide the secretary's replies to correspondence, e.g. "BYFS" = "Out of the question." That king of weight-lifters, Sandow, once performed before a proverbially apathetic Berlin audience. He increased his load to *two* ladies playing *two* pianos. No response! Down at the footlights he asked: "Anyone here speak English?" A hand shot up. "BYFS" said Sandow— "Blow you for a start." But, it is alleged, he didn't say "Blow".

assurance that the new boys would have a week or two to settle in, learn the ropes and prepare sermon material before taking the road in company with a seasoned missioner.

The week passed amiably with study sandwiching social calls until Friday morning when Heenan burst into my room with a letter in his hand.

"Dutchy, you're on the road *solo* tomorrow. Our Lady's, Lincoln. There's been a hitch. You'll revel in it. One week Mission. Just right for you—new parish, young P.P. All the best!" With that, England's busiest priest was on his way. "In the bright lexicon of his youth, there was no such word as fail."

The people of Our Lady's Lincoln responded nobly to the Mission. It was, I think, the parish's maiden. Heenan was again on course to this extent: it was "just right" for a perfect beginner. If I had not hidden my L-plate status, they would have guessed it anyway. They seemed to be determined to make things both easy and memorable. There would be assignments infinitely tougher in the next eight years, times when one crawled home battered and somewhat bent. That maiden mission, however, had a lasting effect on one's morale.

Cardinal Griffin had accepted Heenan's suggestion that the General Mission of 1949 should include not only all parishes in England and Wales but all H.M. Prisons*. I was soon back again in St. Mary's, Lincoln, lodging with Father Connell. Lincoln was my first introduction to civvy "cells". There were others to come: Lewes, Birmingham and the Scrubs. I find it difficult now to allot experiences to their appropriate *locus*, but not in the case of the one that awaited me when I turned the key and made my maiden entry into a civvy cell. That was certainly Lincoln. He was a cockney, bright as a button. As I adjusted the safety-catch†, my host said: "Not to bother, Father. I can open it for you. Let me show you," and he went forward with the haft of his spoon turned outward. The conditions on which I had been admitted scarcely allowed me to encourage demonstrations of that kind. I stopped him, though I longed to call his bluff. He countered quickly: "But I'm a 'stick-man'!" and went on to describe his gift.

The "stick", it seems, is a metal rod. When applied to objects like the tumblers of a lock in certain sensitive hands, the probing registers the correct combinations, digit by digit falling into place. Such hands are in very short supply which accounted for my host's extraordinary list of convictions. No sooner was he out, than the gangs were after him for their next job. "They have to have me," he said.

"But what are you really in civvy life?"

"I'm a thief, Father—never done anything else."

* Heenan' immense heart was most vulnerable to prisons.
† Once you let the door swing to, you too were imprisoned. The key only opened on the outside.

This was not quite true. During the London air-raids he as a lad had organised free cups of tea in his local tube-station. The ingredients were all "borrowed", but he had become the darling of the neighbourhood—a life-saving Robin Hood for distressed old ladies. So much so, when he was next up before the beaks the court was crowded with clients pleading his outstanding contribution to the war effort. His record as a juvenile delinquent was unique, but he left the court that day free as the wind.

I can't leave out one other side-light on his career. He had his principles. "Snowdrifers"* and "Smash and Grab" men, he held in contempt—no art or finesse about them. On one occasion he was persuaded to join a break-in where his charisma with the "stick" was the key to success. As soon as his job was done he left the premises, as usual, to sit in the get-away car. The underlings appeared with the swag breathless with enthusiasm. "Gold and silver cups. Lovely stuff!" they said dashing back for more. His suspicions surfaced, a chord vibrated from his early days as an altar server. "Show me." They brandished the booty. He leapt from his privileged seat. "Back everyone. The lot!" He leapt from the car. One by one he forced them to replace the chalices, ciboria and monstrances. When all was back under lock and key, he snatched the soap from the sacristy lavabo, wetted it under the tap and scrawled on the window: "Sorry! Wrong house!"

Late visiting in another gaol found quite a few of the inmates already bedded down for the night, but still ready for a chat. In those days new arrivals were relieved of all personal items, including rosaries and medals† which brought a surprising number of fingers and thumbs into play. I was assured that night that a lot of prayer went up in the silent hours. "Porridge"‡ doesn't reveal everything. Cells were "Peters" in the prison slang of those days. The reference is to a famous prison release (Acts 12, 3 and following) when "prayer was made without ceasing by the church unto God for him" i.e. St. Peter.

Another poignant experience came my way, when a rather superior young man who had attended my talks approached with a problem. "Is it part of Catholic teaching that restitution must be made before absolution from serious theft is given?" "It must at least be firmly promised," I said. He went his way like the young man in the gospel (Mt. 19, 22). I couldn't shake him.

Reformatory schools afforded lighter relief. I'd a string of lads one morning, one after the other posing the same problem: "Could

---

* Invaders of back-gardens who run under clothes-lines detaching the week's washing and disappearing with their haul.
† Archbishop Downey used to tell the story, possibly from his C.M.S. days, of an old lag going carefully through his personalia the morning of his release. His scapulars were missing. He stood to attention. "I will not leave this prison without my scafulaars." Apologies were of no avail. They turned the office upside down, goaded on by dogged repetitions of "My scafulaars." They found them.
‡ The popular TV serial.

God make a stone so heavy He couldn't lift it?" A remarkable number of "vocations" to the religious life or the priesthood sprang up in the somewhat hot-house atmosphere of the boys' mission. I never conducted one for girls in similar circumstances. In those days before women's lib and pop-stars got under weigh, the seed had a better chance with them. It's likely now to fall equally on rock (and roll). I hope I need not have to make the point that one's efforts were directed towards no other vocation but the one all Christians share in whatever walk of life. One can't of course close any doors on the divine initiative. "The Spirit breathes where He will." Even those spontaneous urges to higher, even the highest, forms of Christian living however mistaken, are not just good for a laugh. They are precious evidence of the "excelsior" germ implanted in every lad, doomed, alas, only too often, to premature death.

One of those reformatory engagements took me out to North Sea Camp in the bad-lands of the Wash. The chief warden was a truly estimable fellow. He kept his troops in good heart. The lads were up against a formidable task, that of creating revetment banks on the north shores in the teeth of North Sea gales. I can see them now setting off to work whistling a popular song of the day—one that unexpectedly hits a high note in the minor-key.

The school was in the parish of Boston. A former C.M.S. star, Dr. Bernard Grimley, whom I called on, was the P.P. He had preached a retreat at Valladolid, half-way through my course there. Many of his powerful phrases are still with me. Later I assisted at a Nottingham Diocese Eucharistic Congress in Bishop John F. McNulty's time at which two papers were read by Dr. Grimley: "The Eucharist and the local heretic, Wycliffe", "The Eucharist and the Social Question". The Bishop rose to speak after the latter: "There were to be comments and questions", he said. "I know I am interpreting the sense of this meeting when I suggest we disperse and give ourselves time to reflect on what we have heard and let it sink home." He read all our minds. I had never heard anything so profoundly moving. Some little time after my courtesy call Dr. Grimley caught a bad cold in Rome and chose to make tracks immediately for home. He arrived only to die at St. Hugh's Nursing Home, Cleethorpes.

In the first decade of the Society consoling news crossed the Atlantic from an outfit engaged in similar work to the C.M.S. The Paulist Fathers had developed a new technique for direct approach to rural areas in that vast country. They possessed themselves of a rail-car. No doubt the idea originated with the Presidential vehicle and Whistle-Stop tours of the electorate.

In 1909 the Paulist Superior of the Apostolic Mission House, Washington invited Dr. H. Vaughan, the Cardinal's nephew, to study their forward missionary movement. Father Vaughan was prematurely called home. Our first superior, Father Charles Rose Chase, a convert clergyman and former cavalry officer, King's Hussars, had died. Vaughan succeeded him. He had however, studied the prototype for increased Missionary mobility, the chapel rail-car, and shrewdly adapted it to English conditions with the Motor-Chapel in 1911. It was constructed at Saffron Walden, a clumsy hulk with doors opening wide at the stern to reveal a handsome altar.

In September of that year the first non-Westminster members joined: Dr. Richard Downey and Father Joseph Howard.

John Carmel Heenan's revival of the C.M.S. in 1947 made all things new: new house, new staff (Franciscan Missionary Sisters from Littlehampton), new missioners, and new rolling stock. The chapel was wholly and entirely itself. It was a trailer opening on the side. The two panels carried the simple legend: "Jesus Mercy" (left), "Mary Help" (right). The only flaw lay in the traction supplied by the Ford Pilot, a fine car and the best available in those days of stringency, but not quite up to the job on hills.

Alongside this flag-ship Father Harry Martindale and I stationed ourselves in Lincoln Butter Market. The Summer Campaign that year covered parts of Northants and Nottingham dioceses. The previous evening we learned to our dismay that the use of microphones was forbidden in the Butter Market. However, we sought out a City Alderman, an affable, easy man sitting behind the counter in his shop. "Aye—there is a by-law, but"—(looking kindly at our clerical collars) "it's meant to cut out 'ad-libbing'—hucksters, that kind of trade. You'll be all right. Refer anybody who objects to me."

We began with the usual record of the Vatican Bells, somewhat muted*, out of respect for by-laws and aldermen. The crowd gathered and with the sign of the cross and greetings to the bystanders, we launched into the deep. I was at the mike eventually for questions. There was stormy weather a-brewing—interruptions occurred particularly from one determined wrecker. Now was his chance: "What right have you to talk about marriage—you celibates . . . ?" A hackneyed gambit, to which I gave the usual treatment. The nub, of course, was birth control.

Father Harry, however, had something to add and relieved me of the mike. "I was born," he began "in Poulton-le-Fylde". He pinpointed the location for the sake of the crowd. "There we have brought poultry-farming to what is recognised as the highest level of efficiency in the country. I know quite a few of the top men—wizards in the line of egg and chicken production. The point I want to make is this. Not one of those men has ever laid an egg in his life."

Screams of vituperation from our dissenter! Harry proceeded calmly against wider rumblings of pandemonium. Someone tugged at my sleeve. A large Irishman whispered in my ear: "Do ye want him out, Father?" "Not particularly—he's using his rights." "Not if I

---

* At full-blast we could be heard over a wide area. It was a comfort on occasions when the villagers were too shy to be seen anywhere near us, to be told that all their windows were open. I hope the photo survives of Heenan at the mike—total audience one little girl and a dog.

can help it" and he was off. A moment or two later as I was looking at the neuralgic point in the crowd, a strange phenomenon occurred. The heckler suddenly descended out of sight. Sunk without trace from then on!

Four Irishmen came to wish us well at the end of the session. "We dumped him, Father. He'll be alright later."

CHAPTER XXXIII

Jonathan succeeds David

"HOP OUT, Dutch, and get that book on English pub-signs. I'll just see if "The Wings of a Dove" is in the trailer."

Heenan and I were off for an open-air week in Welwyn Garden City. The parish priest's name was Dove and Heenan foresaw broad smiles in the crowd if we played the aforesaid record. In the event no one noticed. The pub-sign book was an even damper squib. The chance of pointing across the village green to a "Lamb and Flag", "Crossed Keys", or a "Green Man" and unravelling the Catholic history behind the name, was just not on. There were no pubs!

On the way there I listened with mounting apprehension to a mastery treatise on the theme: "How to hold a crowd without a rope" in the open-air. It finished ominously with, "I'll tell you afterwards where you go wrong." And, of course, he did.

Our first chore was to find a powerpoint for the loud-speaker. There was the very thing on the perimeter of the green where we parked. The premises so thoughtfully sporting this amenity on the outside wall, received us kindly. St. Peter's bells and a couple of other discs soon assembled a very satisfactory crowd. Heenan said a prayer and deftly went on to hang them on his every word. The "Dove" record relaxed the attentive listeners with the matchless voice of Master Lough. Though Father Dove was conspicuous in the front row, I don't remember citizens rolling in the aisles as I went to the mike. What I do remember is firemen emerging from their station on the other side of the road behind the crowd and standing to attention. Did they sense a firebrand?

Heenan's own style, effortless and unhurried, was in fact the fruit of an infinite capacity for taking pains. Everything he said on formal occasions in public had been dictated after careful thought, typed by Mrs Williams, princess of stenographers, and committed word by word to memory. He reckoned twice as long for the memory-work as for the composition, and sought to form the rest of us in the same mould.

Each January we were off the road for a retreat, a course by a visiting lecturer and a strenuous week of self-exposure. This last exercise involved each of us composing a ten minute address on the same theme for delivery in full season. Each member in turn then commented, the emphasis being mainly, though not exclusively, on shortcomings, and no pulling of punches.

I remember Heenan being roasted for his statuesque rigidity throughout his piece. Next time round he meekly responded with animated gestures. With one voice all of us shouted him down: "Stow it Jack! For heaven's sweet sake!" He was not clowning. In his case there was simply no medium between statuesque and grotesque.

George Patrick Dwyer* also had to take it on the chin—and from Heenan: "George, of all present members yours is the most strident pulpit voice of all." But their friendship, the fine flower of half-a-dozen years together in the Venerabile, is unique in my experience of priestly "David and Jonathan" relationships. Matrimony is not the only sacrament that can fuse two souls into one. A single word, even a glance, was enough to revive shared memories and judgments. When Dwyer was in full flight, Heenan took second place, pretending, of course, to stem the flood, but impishly widening the gates. I have never known such mastery of sustained invective. After lunch one day a distinguished guest who was next to me as we left the table, said: "Tell me, is the priest who was facing me always as good as that?" In all simplicity I had to say: "No. He's usually better."

He had read everything and forgotten nothing. Cambridge awarded him travelling scholarships which he spent at the Cheval Blanc in Chartres consuming tome after tome, occasionally sallying forth to go over a famous battlefield with a Belloc in his hand. Our seminary generation was lucky. We were suckled on a common diet of Chester-Belloc, and easily *en rapport* from whichever Catholic school we originated.

George and I were in Clermont Ferrand for the feast of the Assumption one year. The Curé invited him to preach at the *Grande Messe* in the patronal church. He had prepared, despite Heenan's example and training, only half his prone, and woe was in his heart as he mounted the high pulpit and gazed on the vast multitude. I hadn't seen his text which, like the subject of his doctorate thesis at the Greg, was *"Opus Imperfectum"*.† Nevertheless I knew exactly where "prep" petered out and filial devotion ranged free. The language warmed, and changed key from studied eloquence to popular idiom without loss of intellectual content. Later, at the Curé's festive table, the compliments homed in mainly on that second part.

There was no doubt in Heenan's mind, nor in mine when I had heard him a couple of times, who was the star pulpiteer of the C.M.S. Ill health interrupted Father Coyne's studies as a youth at Upholland. He resumed his preparation for the priesthood at Oscott and later joined the staff as professor of Church History. He was one of Heenan's first recruits. The Society would be hard put to

---

* The Most Reverend G. P. Dwyer, later Archbishop of Birmingham, who succeeded as Superior of the C.M.S. when Heenan became Bishop of Leeds in 1951.

† "Unfinished Work". He chose this important fragment of St. Augustine as the subject for his S.T.D. I remember someone pointing him out to me at the Greg. in 1933, the year he was doing his degree. We met for the first time in 1948.

find another like him. We all felt our loss when he resigned on medical advice.

One other C.M.S. member who joined before Father Callaghan and me has already appeared on the Butter Market at Lincoln, Father Harry Martindale from Poulton. Rumour had it that the Boss gave Harry a rough welcome. He arrived with golf clubs. Dear Heenan like the rest of us could fly off the handle quite devastatingly. Despite his welcome a remark of Harry's comes back over the years: "When the Boss is at home this place is different." We all felt the effect of Heenan's light-hearted approach to the most formidable undertakings. About this time one of the Government Ministries launched an anti-reckless driving campaign in the Press with the aid of devilish winged *agent-provocateurs* whispering "Chance it!" in the motorist's ear. Heenan stood this one on its head and practically made it our C.M.S. watchword, accompanied always with an expression of fiendish glee.

Dwyer, however, had much the harder head and far better judgment of character and capacity. He edited and managed the *Gazette*, and held the general purse-strings. Redoubtable encounters ensued between our David and Jonathan—no holds barred, no quarter given. Dwyer, however, was not always on the home beat to avert domestic mayhem. He once returned from a fortnight's mission, dropped into the office where the account-books were kept and emerged minutes later brandishing a bill, anything but speechless. During his absence Heenan had welcomed a toilet-roll salesman, and typically put some large business his way. But who wouldn't? This was a former Polish officer of distinction. Our Boss more than once cleaned out his own personal bank account to save a reputation and job.

On a lighter note may I be forgiven by his admirers for recording an incident, typical again of his open-hearted response to people which, needless to say, could be at the same time as shrewd as the proverbial sack of monkeys? I am confident he would not object.

Genuinely, though I think he was human enough to enjoy some of the by-products of ecclesiastical preferment, for Heenan the supreme joy of his life was being a parish priest. Better *for him* to serve in Manor Park than reign in Westminster. We turned one afternoon into Golders Green Park. As we skirted the lake the words: "Oh! Farver 'Eenan!" came over the waters. "No doubt one of my old parishioners." he remarked as we closed with an ecstatic mother pushing a perambulator. "Hello," he said. "Hello, at last!" This was not enough. "Don't you know me? I'm Pam". "Of course I know you, Pam. Couldn't forget you, Pam." Far from enough!" "I mean, Farver, I married a fellow called Pam—I'm now Mrs Pam!" There was a house-phrase for situations like this: "One bound and Jack was free!" I forget how he escaped this time. *He* certainly was not allowed to forget.

Heenan saw the C.M.S. as the spearhead of England's conversion.

All his innovations were designed simply to sharpen and polish the instrument and, as far as he could, associate others in the process. Appropriately on March 12th 1951, Feast of St. Gregory the Great, Apostle of England*, he was ordained Bishop of Leeds. Our old Boss emerged from his first Episcopal Conference in Low Week 1951 to tell us that George Dwyer was his successor.

He and I were vesting for Mass the following morning. Through the window blinking a couple of times, my eyes rested on a phenomenon to which I drew the new Superior's attention. "There, George," I said, "is your first problem as Superior. Posterity will judge your tenure of office, perhaps, by the way you address it." Below in our garden a lovable wallaby was browsing the odd plant. One look and Dwyer delivered this *"sentitentia digna Joanne"*.† "That, Holland, is a highly mobile marsupial. It has cleared all conventional fences. By the time we do anything it will be in somebody else's garden. *Ergo!* We do nothing."

And with that he went to the altar, and his six years C.M.S. servitude as Superior.

Changes followed rapidly. Three new recruits, Fathers F. J. Ripley, J. Etherington and G. White, swelled the ranks, the last named in the capacity of resident chaplain to our precious community of Littlehampton Sisters and general manager of finances, always, needless to say, under the relentless oversight of Dwyer. I succeeded him on the *Gazette* in May. The big change came some months later with the arrival of Father Michael O'Connor and the inauguration of the Catholic Enquiry Centre.

Michael hailed from a Kerry village called Causeway where his father was the school-master. Causeway is near Tralee. If I were asked to name a masculine counterpart of the famous Rose, I should not have a moment's hesitation. Physically and temperamentally this young priest radiated confidence and joy. Fleet Street ad-men, I believe, never saw anything quite like him. Their immediate response was such as to save the new-comer years of experience in that gimlet-eyed milieu.

It was of course Dwyer's eye for talent which foresaw and made actual the possibilities ranging far and wide into the future. He met Father Michael when giving a mission at Our Lady's Carlisle and saw for himself the resounding success of the junior curate's new approaches to the city's non-Catholics. No doubt the parish priest, Monsignor Dick Smith, offered advice, though it must have been a heroic sacrifice for him to let Michael go.

As was only fair, our new-comer first learned the basic C.M.S. skills, accompanying senior missioners and widely familiarising himself with his future target, the British "grand public". He very soon setttled down full-time to the creation of the Catholic Enquiry Centre. Female office staff escalated from one, the inestimable Miss

* September 3rd in new Calendar.
† "Sentence worthy of (St.) John."

Barnard, to ten. Nine new stenographers now worked in the new Catholic Enquiry Centre. Cardinal Griffin, accompanied by a Monsignor Derek Worlock, formally inaugurated the new venture with an address in which he pledged his support and allowed himself to surmise we should be needing £40,000 a year to keep the ship afloat. This historic event took place in our large common room-cum-library which the C.E.C. would occupy until the new custom-built premises were available.

C.E.C. technique was brilliantly simple and has continued so in essentials for the past twenty-five years. Press adverts, striking in phrase and illustration, carry the C.E.C. address. Readers are invited to write if they wish to know more. A course will be mailed if requested. Questions will be answered.

Father O'Connor and his professionals designed the ads. Dwyer wrote the course which so far impressed a top journalist he confessed Fleet Street could not do better. I came in at question time as Director of Studies with solutions and advice on further progress. Dictating at a table clacking with half-a-dozen typewriters, I found, is not conducive to exact theological discourse. Thankfully the first separate instalment of C.E.C. premises restored sanity with a quiet end-room just about big enough for a table, typist, dog ("Teddy") and director. But I could not have had a better typist. Miss Audrey Knighton was "slumming". She had worked with distinguished men of letters: regimental historians and so on. Her C.E.C. work was nothing but letters, flawlessly typed as the unsung Director chatted with correspondents at a little less than conversation speed. He was quickly put in his place on a point of order. Punctuation was her concern. She was not having top-typist territory invaded by dictators. Had I noticed she kept out of theology?

In fact the C.E.C. mail-bag posed few brain-teasers in that particular area. The main problems were numerical and personal. The mail-bag was heavily loaded. We had a lot to learn about tools for the job. The same questions recurred time after time. Laboriously one dictated and redictated more or less the same answers. In the end of course transatlantic techniques came to the rescue with automatic typewriters and standard answers to be slotted in at appropriate points in one's reply. First of all one had to grade questions according to the frequency of their appearance. That took time. The system only got into top gear after I left by which time the volume of correspondence had swollen considerably.

Even so I remember dashing back from a mission at Our Lady of Victories to dictate eighty-three letters before returning for the evening service at Kensington. Miss Knighton prudently allowed it could be a record.

One's work of course did not escape the relentless Dwyer eye. His was no idle skimming through carbon-copies. He was soon able to judge which questions would come up most frequently. There were surprises: for instance, the denial of the chalice to the laity for a time was well ahead of the field. But there was just no way of computerising personal problems. Who would have wished one? The writers let one into spiritual impasses and labyrinthine ways which often called for considerable thought and delicate treatment, as well as prayer. You were more than half-way there in most cases, however, if you could get *them* praying. Many, of course, were already men and women of deep spirituality. Often I think the exchange profited you more at your end than those at the receiving end. At least it would have done if you had responded to the countless stimuli to praise and thank the Lord provided by C.E.C. correspondence. Naturally we had press-ganged a number of religious communities into sharing that responsibility. When our clients got in touch with a priest they could talk to, or joined a regular Enquiry Class, and particularly when they finally made harbour, we shared the joy. Then the simple formula "Welcome home!" tripped merrily off the typewriter. It was my star standard answer, and D.G. ever more frequently in demand.

From the beginning the C.M.S. apostolate was never confined to the spoken word. A life of the first Superior, Father Chase *From Hussar to Priest* was reviewed in the first number of the *Catholic Gazette* in January 1910. Father B. Maturin*, like Father Chase a volunteer from the Beda, wrote *The Pearl of Great Price*, the story of his own conversion. I thought it the best conversion story I had ever read at the time. Since then dozens have come my way. This is where the C.E.C. richly cross-fertilised the *Gazette*.

While Editor, Dwyer had recruited a brilliant team of writers for the *Gazette* from the Seminaries: Fathers Gerard Culkin, History Professor and Chris Maguire, Science Professor from Ushaw, Father Alec Jones, Scripture Professor at Upholland. Each of them found willing publishers for their collected articles.

I hope the *Gazette* was in no way responsible for their early departure to a better world, though I once drove Father Chris to fury over the daft title with which I headed his article on psychiatric states. Specialists in this particular branch of medicine I believe are irreverently named "trick-cyclists" or "head-shrinkers". With possibly three minutes to catch the last post for the printing deadline, down went the fatal title: "How to Ride a Tricycle".

I must resort to the *Catholic Gazette* to introduce the doyen of all C.M.S. writers.

"Dr. John P. Arendzen joined the C.M.S. in 1902. He had graduated in foreign and English Universities. Along with his singularly persuasive word from the pulpit and the platform, there came a written output in his adopted tongue that makes one think of Challoner's. Many have nourished the faith and

---

* One of the first five members. He was drowned in the sinking of the Lusitania. Another C.M.S. pioneer, Father T. Byles suffered the same fate later in the Great War. This gave birth to the quip: "Early members of the C.M.S. had a habit of sinking in luxury liners."

devotion of this half-century in England . . . We cannot think of a contribution more solid and steady than Dr. Arendzen's. He has written thousands of weekly sermons (in the Catholic Times). They are always fresh . . . He has a series of books about Our Lord's times. You might well say there is no more vivid background to the Gospels in English. He has illuminated dogmas of the faith for the modern layman: e.g. "The Blessed Trinity", "The Incarnation" etc.

"Then there is the Question Box. How many thousands of answers Father Arendzen has penned for that curious receptacle . . . always clear and to the point! Any month they do not appear (in the *Gazette*) we are sure to receive letters protesting that the paper is bought only for them . . . "*

On the cover of the Golden Jubilee Number of the *Gazette* (December 1952) we published his picture. He is seated, robed in his Westminster Canonicals, holding a scroll. Alongside appears this legend: "One man has come with us all the way: *Canon John P. Arendzen, CMS 1902-1952*"

We asked three questions: "Your fifty years with the Society, Canon?" "A life well-spent without regret . . . An offering to God." "Your jubilee message?" "May God make the Society what its founder, Cardinal Vaughan, intended it to be." "Your memories?" "Old names, the old story—old and yet so fresh. May God continue His blessing as indeed He has done in days gone by."

Two years later, at 2.45 p.m. on July 21st 1954, the veteran campaigner went to God. While full-time C.M.S. missioner (he never in fact severed his link with us and often returned in the role of elder statesman) he preached over a thousand missions, retreats by the dozen and published thousands of sermonettes and Question Box answers.

I have good reason to remember his passing. Our beloved "Doctor of Faith" lay ill in the Sainte Union Nursing Home in Quex Road†. After lunch that day Miss Knighton had a breather. I bussed to Kilburn. Sister showed me upstairs: "He hasn't long to go," she said. I had never heard breathing so loud and laboured. Just as I was finishing the Litany and the Penitential Psalms, suddenly all was quiet. I resort once more to the *Gazette*‡. "I kissed his right hand as he died to honour both the gift of the Spirit and the aureole it had won for our beloved Doctor of Faith. His own spirit still warmed the

* *Catholic Gazette*, vol.43, No.1.
† Next door to the Arendzen family home where I once visited the aged artist father at a critical moment for him. We had scarcely exchanged a word or two when the Angelus Bell rang across the road at the O.M.I. Church. Various clocks around the house joined in, and Miss Arendzen wheeled a curious wagon into the room alongside her father's chair. We recited the Angelus. As the sign of the Cross concluded the prayer, Mr. Arendzen reached busily into the wagon. It was a smoker's Aladdin's Cave. The artist's approach to smoking matched his wide-scale scope as an etcher. Both were under strict control: cigars, pipes, the lot remained untouched until the midday Angelus was said.
‡ Vol. 45, No., 9 (Sept. 1954), p.205, Cf. ibid. (Aug. 1954) No. 8, p. 174.

clay but would move it no more. He was a long-continued blessing from God for the C.M.S. It is hard to think he belongs now to 'days gone by'. Thank God there is no need to think he does."

As I came down the path, there at the gate was the Canon's younger brother Leo*, P.P. of Grantham, Canon of Nottingham Diocese. I broke the news. "I am eighty today," he said. Confessors are well used to the phrase: "I'm hard of hearing, Father" for stone-deafness. Canon Leo's answer to my second louder communication was: "I'm eighty today."

Looking back now at the years 1948 to 1956, I can honestly say we were a team. Any two of us could and did pair together effectively and harmoniously over the whole range of C.M.S. assignments. They *were* assignments: you went where you were sent. Nor have I known merriment on such a high and sustained note in any other outfit. Peak moments come crowding back. Since I came in with Jack Callaghan, I'll take my English leave of the C.M.S. in his company.

We had come through a tough fortnight together. The presbytery was spartan to the point where Jack needed all his *esprit de corps* to resist dropping into the local chippy. He wasn't sleeping either. The last night came with the usual crowded church. Jack dealt with the Question Box: sermon and Benediction followed. Bags already packed, we had decided to leave that night. One last duty remained and we hastened to stand outside the church, available for all who wished to meet us. The last client moved away and we were alone on the steps.

Only for the moment, however. A young man appeared. "You didn't answer my brother's question" he said, with an unfortunate hissing vehemence. This was Jack's territory. "What was your brother's question?" he said rather too silkily. "What about the Monophysites?"

I turned away quickly. Even C.M.S. courtesy can be strained beyond breaking-point. Jack's little car rattled with immoderate mirth most of the way home.

---

* The four Arendzen brothers became priests and members of Cathedral Chapters, two in Westminster, one in Nottingham and one in Cardiff.

CHAPTER XXXIV

Last Fling in Paradise

ENGLAND and my final farewell to the C.M.S. were literally poles apart. Dwyer and I flew half-way round the world to get there. We went in answer to a very cordial invitation from the Bishops of New Zealand to spend six months in their dioceses.

If I may for a moment see the C.M.S. as a pantomime (which it often was) then this was the Transformation Scene. If only New Zealand were fourteen hundred miles away instead of 14,000, it would be everyone's favourite recreation ground. The fiords of Norway, mountains of Wales, glaciers of Switzerland, gold of the Klondykes, stags of the Grampions, lakes of Canada and no place more than forty miles from two great oceans fringed with golden beaches, teeming with fish.

Kiwis love England. They call it "home". England has good reason to love New Zealand. Dwyer I very soon knew why.

We landed at Auckland. Archbishop Liston's secretary, Father John Flanagan, met us at the airport. From that moment onwards there was to be never a dull moment in our six-months tour. Much of the fun was traceable to the original source, Father "Flan".

A letter awaited me in Auckland from the Apostolic Delegate in London, Archbishop O'Hara, inviting me to join him as a personal secretary. I wrote at once regretting my inability to accept owing to a long commitment in New Zealand. I took it that was the end especially when no reply came. To my surprise, some months later there was a reply. The Delegate would expect me when the New Zealand tour was over. Of course Dwyer learned of the suggestion immediately I received it. This was my second surprise: "Good idea," he said. "I think you've shot your bolt in the C.M.S." John Flanagan was equally quick off the mark on the subject of my new appointment. Some days after it was public knowledge, I began to receive telegrams from places and ports I had lived in, half-a-dozen or so. For instance from Bombay: "Samantha and children excited new London job. Expecting higher monthly allowance." The rest were variations on the same theme. Each apeared to be perfectly authentic. The one in Italian, perfectly phrased, called me "everything in the farmyard but a duck"* for not revealing my new income-bracket. It was only later I discovered that "Flan", as well as a brother in the police, had a relative in the post-office.

* One of Dwyer's phrases. Father Flanagan like many N.Z. priests studied in Rome.

Archbishop James Liston* had been a very young rector of Holy Cross College, Mosgill, where all New Zealand priests entered for some part of their training. Clergy and laity alike of both Islands recognised him as the far-sighted Nestor of the New Zealand Church, the Pompalier of the twentieth century†. The Catholic population of the four dioceses was more or less the same as that of Salford‡, yet spiritual resources (Retreat Houses, Congregations of religious men and women, both contemplative and active) matched those of whole countries including our own, thanks in great measure to the Bishop of Auckland.

A young priest, Father Reginald Delargy, was commissioned to ferry us down to meet Archbishop McKeefry in Wellington.§ We stopped the first night at Rotorua famous for its hot springs. An expert priest-geophysicist had recently taken a look. He ran back at once to his car, scared stiff. "Those springs could lift the crust off the earth without any warning," he cried.‖ Reggie and I bathed in the hot swimming bath. Our supper that night, a huge ham, was cooked very simply by inserting it in a hole in the presbytery garden.

In the parish hall, Archbishop Liston was presiding at an unusual ceremony, a reception of Maori debutantes. Singly they moved the length of the hall, each accompanied by the same solemn music, each beautifully gowned, each rhythmically adjusting her steps to the intricate saraband measure. Thunderous applause broke out as each young lady sank to kiss the Archbishop's ring. He raised her, taking both her hands and gently holding them as she listened to his fatherly welcome.

We swam that night to the oft-repeated music from the hall. We ate our supper to the same. When we eventually entered the hall there were still dozens of debutantes to be received. Two or three hours on his feet for a far from young prelate, repeated on similar occasions in parish after parish, is some measure of his pastoral concern. Even more telling is the origin of the ceremony. Formerly, it seems, the Governor General used to preside at the coming out of all Maori maidens. I forget now why the custom was discontinued wholly or in part. There was, I think, considerable indignation and the ugly word "discrimination" was heard. Archbishop Liston announced his decision. At whatever cost he would himself save an occasion so dear to the Maoris.

Our last visit that night took us along a narrow lane to a recess in the hedge which could only be the ante-room to Fairyland. The moss-grown rock pulsated with tiny points of light, thousands upon

* The honorary rank of Archbishop, in those days awarded pretty generally after twenty-five years as a bishop, in his case was never more richly deserved.
† The first bishop to evangelise N.Z., accompanied by fellow-Marists.
‡ Territorially the smallest diocese in England at that time.
§ Father Reggie was to succeed him as Cardinal Archbishop some years later.
‖ In fact there *was* a famous eruption there some years before. Vestiges of the violence were still visible: e.g. the outline of a sewing machine stamped deeply into the trunk of a tree as a house burst into space.

thousands of them. Once only near Rimini on the night train to Venice have I seen anything to compare with such a concentration of fireflies. Then it took the form of a golden frieze endlessly unrolling along the edge of the track.

The next day more marvels—Lake Taupo teeming with trout, deer roaming in vast herds out of the trees. Sad news awaited us at Wellington. That day Father Francis Thompson, University Chaplain, and universally recognised as the most brilliant priest in New Zealand, was killed in a road accident.

Archbishop McKeefry, later New Zealand's first Cardinal, received us at a Nursing Home. Whatever his own state of health, he was an absolute tonic for immigrants still reeling under the impact of new and exciting experiences, and not so sure, for all our years in the C.M.S., what challenges we were expected to meet in New Zealand. Archbishop Liston had partly prepared us for this first one, our meeting at the Nursing Home.

"He is a true leader," he said. "No nonsense, a clear head, afraid of nobody." This from the man who had long kept him as his secretary, appointed him editor of *Zelandia*, the country's premier Catholic newspaper, and, I believe, was mainly responsible for McKeefry's elevation to the primatial see of Wellington.

"No nonsense" was the keynote of our interview. I had never heard a great prelate speak in such unparliamentary terms. And no arrangements! We were to play it by ear. He would start us off with two weeks in Wellington Cathedral. A three-line whip would alert the clergy of both Islands. We were to do whatever we did in England. In churches, halls, universities, retreat-houses, on radio. But keep rolling! He assured us there would be a lot to talk over with priests. Our C.E.C. had attracted a lot of attention in New Zealand. †

The fortnight in Wellington Cathedral began in the heaviest downpour of rain I have ever known. What's more, about the same time each evening the phenomenon recurred. People in the pews were of heroic mould. The line was thinly held but gathered strength. A little altar boy must have put a question to me. Twenty-nine years later (1985) he declared himself* and quoted my answer to me.

For the next six months Dwyer and I pursued our separate ways, occasionally meeting for a double-pulpit, academic debate, and school retreats. We passed one another on airstrips, moving from North to South Islands.

I found my spiritual home at Wanganui where a Marist Grammar School harboured me during a mission. The fathers were brilliant over-worked men; housekeeper, super-over-worked Connie Wear.

* The following year Father Michael O'Connor, master-mind of the Catholic Enquiry Centre, was invited to New Zealand to preside over the actual foundation of the N.Z. C.E.C. It is still going strong there.

† Father Michael Gaudoin-Parker now in charge of the John Paul Centre in Middlesborough.

Wanganui River flowed through sacred ground. The famous pioneer Mother M. Aubert peopled both banks with orphanages, schools, convents. Biblical names sprouted into the bush, the chief settlement being Jerusalem. The navigation of this trickiest of rivers* was in the hands of a Maori coxswain who twenty or thirty years earlier had aspired to the priesthood. His skill as a pilot, however, was judged indispensable. The first Maori priest was ordained, if I remember rightly, the year we were there.

Other memories crowd in undimmed by the years: orange groves at Tauranga in Christchurch diocese and Father (now Monsignor) Ted Ryan; a few days rest at a sheep farm in Central Otago where my host and I in the dark moved a thousand sheep from one paddock to another and woke to find another two thousand bawling their heads off as they struggled to get at their mothers' teats. He, too, a McCarthy, son of an Irish immigrant at the time of the gold rush, was, like Harry Hawke the tea planter in Ceylon, an assidious and expert student of Catholic apologetics. The first morning under his hospitable roof news came of the death of Cardinal Griffin. I began an appreciation sitting at the large dining-room window. As I wrote, the snow line which at first was very near the crest of the mountain behind the house, slowly came down to the lawn outside the window and covered it. We went for a drive in the afternoon, calling for tea at a roadhouse in the middle of nowhere. The view was splendid but strangely daunting. Gaunt ranges hemmed us in. Down below, a dark river flowed through the valley, the only moving thing in the whole panorama. My host pointed to signs of human habitation on the far river-bank—a cottage and outside sheds all in ruins. "That belonged to a relative of Archbishop Masterson", said my host. "He settled there with the idea of felling the woodland and floating logs down to the timber-yards. His wife fell ill. They were miles from medical resources. She died. He abandoned the place. There are still Mastersons somewhere around. The Archbishop came over here at the time of the Sydney Eucharistic Congress."

Cardinal Griffin and Archbishop Joe Masterson were fellow students in Rome. Their friendship was akin to the David and Jonathan union of Heenan and Dwyer. Why on that day of all days and in Central Otago of all places, they should have come together so closely is, for me at least, passing strange. I can only fall back on the "more things in heaven and earth than are dreamt of in my philosophy".

At Invercargill, colonised by Scotsmen, the nearest city to the South Pole, the mission was diversified by talks to the juveniles in detention and a couple of memorable broadcasts. After the first, an old Presbyterian who had listened with great reverence rose from his chair, raised his hands, gave thanks to God, and fell back dead.

* Navigation at night was accomplished without lights by reference to the narrow strip of sky visible between the tree-tops on either bank, the stars governing the movement of the rudder to avoid the rocks.

This news was passed on to the studio by his relatives for my benefit. I need not tell you what the theme of my next broadcast was. Its genuinely warm ecumenical approach surprised many citizens. Not so far away there was a town called Cromwell in which the Catholic Church was dedicated to "The Martyrs of Ireland".

Quite a lot of our broadcasting was beamed over a wide stretch of the surrounding seas. We had with us the first record to arrive in England of the Gelineau Psalms*. Requests for further information were not confined to the mainland.

My plane north from Invercargill bore the mortal remains of a Maori girl on the way home to the burial ground in North Island. I was seated next to her sister and had a unique opportunity to appreciate the dignity and deep Catholic Faith of their family.

One of the saddest pages of our Church history in those Islands is the failure of the early missioners to work together. Had they done so, I was assured, the entire Maori people would have embraced the Catholic Faith. Yet, even so, Bishop Pompalier and the Marists in New Zealand were as true to the heroic pioneering traditions of France as were O.M.I. priests and brothers on the paddy fields of Ceylon or the ice-floes of Alaska. The New Zealand Marist brothers were more popular than the priests. I was informed by the latter that the motor car was partly responsible. Brothers for the most part taught in schools and lived over the shop. Priests caring for wide tracts of country had to be mobile. The people, however, drew their own conclusion: priests were not as loyal to their vow of poverty as were the brothers. Alms went more generously to the brothers—at least so the priests told me. Certainly the brothers worked hard. In more than one of their many schools I saw brothers teaching classes of over one hundred pupils. So they got poor results? Not a bit of it! Standards were high, results likewise.

At this point to honour the sons of the Venerable Benedict Marcellin Champagnat, let me record a little footnote to history. In a sandy stretch of woodland on the edge of Hawke's Bay† there are vestiges of a little vineyard now run wild. My companion pointed to a shabby bastard shoot: "There is a descendent of the original vines brought from France by one of our pioneer fathers," he said. I believe Tennyson once on a woodland stroll gripped his companion's arm saying: "On your knees, man. Violets!" My moment of truth was even more compelling. There before us was the fountainhead whence the Chalice of Salvation was filled for New Zealand's early offerings of her Saviour. At another level, there was the foreshadow of a now cultured and generous wine-production under the Southern Cross.

So far nothing has been said about the wonderful *esprit de corps* of the diocesan clergy and their bishops. At some point in my criss-

* Given me by my old Normandy friend, Abbé Graindor.
† The original landing ground of the first Marist missioners. There was the home port of their sailing ship, the ecclesiastical version of Captain Cook's *Endeavour*.

cross progress from pulpit to pulpit I put up late one night at a local hotel. This was anathema. Somehow the local priest got wind of my solecism. He stormed into the room, furiously re-packed my bags and hauled me to his presbytery. I had sinned against the code of honour.

I happened to mention in some place that Group Captain Leonard Cheshire had joined us on a summer campaign in Cornwall. I fear we used him unmercifully, even hiring a loud-speaker van to tour the streets during the day and ensuring the citizens knew who would be speaking on the square that evening. In his quiet unassuming way he electrified Redruth, Truro and other towns with the simply story of his conversion to the Catholic Church. Shortly afterwards we had reason to examine our consciences. It was discovered he had trouble in both lungs and had to retire to that lovely Services Hospital at Midhurst for a long-drawn-out convalesc-ence. There I visited him regularly and was privileged to guide him in the deeper study of theology which he felt he owed to the Church and to himself.* Among the students who have suffered at my hands, he would qualify for a special award *hors concours*.

On the strength of this contact an enterprising priest decided to take the town hall for a Cheshire Night. Practically the entire population turned out. He more than covered his expenses. I shouldn't be surprised if that night did more spiritual good than many another in the conventional church setting. Certainly one night comes painfully back to memory when my pulpit appearance definitely produced a "nil return". I made the sign of the Cross, addressed the throng and simply went speechless. Not a sound would come, struggle as I may. Down I came. Weeks without a break of daytime talks in schools and evenings in the pulpit had taken their toll.

Even night-time had its hazards. One Saturday, after a late finish in one town, I was scheduled for an early morning debut in New Plymouth many miles to the north. Supper was arranged *en route*, and a relay of vehicles and priest drivers. The second change involved us in near disaster. At the wheel was a priest with the kind of reputation I once heard defined as: "Give him the job and he'll finish the tools". The car suddenly ran its nearside wheels up a bank and we overturned. I spilt out to the accompaniment of an agonising cry from the driver: "I've killed him!" A tractor happened along and pulled us into shape again. I was in the pulpit at the 7.30 a.m. Sunday Mass at New Plymouth.

* Providentially about this time there came for review in the *Gazette* the collected works of Abbot Vonier in three volumes. Manna from heaven! The perfect basis for our discussion and advancement. At this time Leonard was exercised with the idea that he might found an ecumenical brotherhood. He had learned many of the Do's and Don'ts from his experiment with a community designed to continue the comradeship of wartime into peacetime. His destiny however was "Cheshire Homes" and union with Sue Ryder. Our generation can lift its head for once and sing loud and clear.

Our last month in New Zealand was devoted to retreats for the priests of North Island. Dwyer had two in the Wellington area and one in Auckland; I had two in Auckland and one in Wellington. Once again we passed like ships in the night.

One of my last public appearances was in Auckland Cathedral. The talk was broadcast. Archbishop Liston picked it up somewhere, and commented favourably. He was clearly living up to his role as the perfect host. Nonetheless, I could not have wished the compliment from any other source. During that week a gentleman arrived at Cathedral House in a wheelchair, asking to see the English preacher. "I felt it my duty to call on you," he said. "My name is Holland. I also come from Lancashire." He was a native of Preston. His family had emigrated in the 1890s; he had only a little boy's memories of "Home"*. They were nonetheless remarkably vivid and detailed. I wish I had been able to record his description of the "knocker-up" tapping the windows with his wand and the clogs battering the pavements on the way to the early shift at the mill.

The bishop of Fiji's invitation to us to spend a day or two with his priests decided our return route to England. We had flown out West to East via Rome, Cairo and Bombay. Now to my great delight, we were to box the compass via Suva, Canton Island, Honolulu, San Francisco, Chicago and New York to London.†

The local flight from Lautoca to Suva passed over a vast area of tidal sands to the north of Fiji. Far from *terra firma* a dozen little boys as brown and shining as the sands splashed away in the pools gesticulating skywards. Very decently our pilot spiralled down for a closer view. This animated the boys into an ecstatic dance of joy, more than enough to convince any pilot his services were not needed immediately. Wisely, however, he reported the incident on arrival in Suva.

From the cathedral we sallied forth to meet the clergy. Our stay being short, they gallantly listened and questioned us a whole livelong day. The venue, a schoolroom in a palm grove, had I imagine, induced many generations of schoolchildren to yield to the warm shafts of sunlight and dream. Not so the clergy of Fiji. They probed us, comparing our milieu with theirs, wondering aloud how far our techniques would pay off in Fiji.

It was the time a remarkable American Jesuit was visiting Fiji at the invitation of the Governor General who had seen him at work in South America. His line was the creation of co-operative mini-banks in which workers could pool their resources, administer their own

---

* I have earlier remarked New Zealanders speak of England as "home" whether or not they had ever been there. The test matches were being played in England that summer. Kiwis, all I met anyway, were on our side. The Australian Redemptorists with whom we lodged during our first fortnight in Wellington slept very little. Short-wave sets registered the progress of the games throughout the night.
† 22.11.56: "Frisco", Thanksgiving Day. Chicago-N.Y. 27.11.56. 27.11.56 over Toledo, Ohio. N.Y. 28.11.56. Brooklyn 6.12.56. All verified from the margins of my Greek New Testament.

loans and so escape from the toils of the money-lenders. The Fiji fishing community had become inextricably caught. At last the net was broken and they were free, thanks to a Governor General with a good memory and a generous Jesuit Provincial who, in response to his request, had released the liberator from the other side of the Pacific.

We joined Bishop Foley at a general meeting of the fishing co-operative. The Jesuit Father from U.S.A., in the role of elder statesman, intervened judiciously, on the whole leaving the members to run the meeting. Individuals reported on their personal accounts. Each speaker produced a bank-book. I was greatly impressed by a young woman who summarised several weeks, succinctly demonstrating how her affairs contrasted with the hopeless debts of other days. Then the members sang the musical salute* composed in honour of their benefactor.

The Bishop invited one of the men to come nearer. He sat cross-legged a few yards away. "His wife was killed a few days ago. I'll ask him how it happened," said the Bishop. As the story unfolded the Bishop *sotto voce* translated for Dwyer and me. We were sitting either side of him. Crosslegged and leaning forward a little, the husband spoke very softly, pausing now and then: "Three of the women went diving for shells outside the coral reef. It's safer inside: the sharks don't get in there. But our women are wary and generally are not in any great danger from the white ones. That day there was one that was different, a black one. It attacked them suddenly and caught my wife. The others made every effort to rescue her. This shark was too quick for them and mauled her badly before they got her clear. I am happy to tell you," he said to the Bishop, "my wife was at Mass and Holy Communion the Sunday before this happened."

Despite the brevity of our stay, the Bishop was convinced we needed a break and booked us in for a night at a holiday hotel. I have a note of it in my New Testament: "KORO LEVU. Fiji: 19.11.56. O GAUDIUM!" There are thousands of places logged in the margins of that New Testament which has travelled everywhere with me for close on fifty years. No other wins the same simple accolade.

I suppose that was in large part due to our relief at coming to the end of our assignment as well as the physical decor. Our chalet, however, was across a lawn from the hotel in a narrow belt of palms fringing the beach, a matter only of yards from the warm, silken sea whispering on the shingle. One had similar technicolour backgrounds in Ceylon at Mt. Lavinia, with the extra phenomenon of the famous green flash at sunset. But there is no record of these in my Greek Testament.

* There is a technical term for the musical strophes composed to honour a chief or benefactor. It begins with a short intonation by the cantor. The chorus take it up on a higher note from which they come crashing down the scale like a house falling. Along with the Jesuit's name I have forgotten the name of this musical tribute, though I can still sing (without words) the antiphon and verse.

More than any physical surroundings I think our own bodily and mental condition squeezed that *"O Gaudium"* onto the sacred page. The night before we had done our last stint together, a double pulpit effort in Suva Cathedral. It was my last C.M.S. appearance. Afterwards in the parish hall, the undershaft of the cathedral, we met the people. I found myself at table with a modest Fijian whom, for some dotty reason, I began to enlighten on the subject of cricket. He listened to me with great attention. Later that night I learned he was an Oxford blue. His subsequent career in politics has been equally brilliant.

Travelling on from Fiji, we had the inside of a day in Honolulu, met Bishop Scanlan, said Mass and visited Pearl Harbour before the evening flight to San Francisco. If I were asked what rating I would give to Hawaiian maidens and their flowery gyrations, my strictly non-professional verdict would be: give me the Maori "poi" dances and take the rest. But let me quickly balance that mean statement with this other.

Never before or since have I seen an earthly city so beautiful as San Francisco apeared that morning at 6 a.m. on the 20 November 1956. The sun rose behind it as we approached, endowing spires, domes, tower-blocks with a radiant sharpness one associates with Grecian cities of Parian marble famed by poets for just that unearthly splendour. We were in the observation area under the plane. The hostess advised us an engine had ciphered. That didn't seem to matter as we came in past Alcatraz and over the Golden Gate to be welcomed by our hosts, the Columban Fathers.

"Frisco" at ground level did not quite live up to the first elevated vision from the plane. A film actor who appeared with Bing Crosby in "Going My Way" offered to show us the sights. Dwyer, however, opted for an early night. Chinatown impressed me. So did a roving figure wheeling a little cart. He was dressed in a Franciscan habit to impersonate Father Junipero Serra O.F.M., the apostle of the East Coast, founder of so many Missions whose lovely Spanish names live on for ever.

Night had fallen when we broke our journey at Chicago to spend a few days with our fellow missioners of the Chicago Mission Band. They had sportingly volunteered and fielded two priests for Heenan's first Summer Campaign in Oxfordshire in 1948. We visited Mundelein Seminary where for the first time in the history of the Church each student had a self-contained suite. The archdiocesan Catholic population of two and a half million is served by 3,400 priests. Cardinal Mundelein built full and plenty. In the quaint quadrangle of the seminary there is a sizeable lake over which cars pass after entering the *porte-cochère* on their way to the main entrance. As they mount the bridge the headlights throw their beams on the upper windows of the façade.

One of our Mission Band hosts who gave us all his time during our stay recounted his own experience as a student in one of those upper rooms as we stood together on the bridge. I repeat it as he told it for no other reason than this. It is, at least for me, a touching example of the different temperaments which exist within the one priesthood and more or less the same language. "I used to lie awake in bed waiting for the Cardinal's car to return from the city, however late. Once the lights hit the windows and touched the ceiling, I said to myself: 'All's well. Daddy is home.' and fell asleep at once."

The next leg of our journey took us to the New York headquarters of the Paulist Fathers, with whom our C.M.S. had links from its earliest years. There must have been forty or fifty priests in residence. Inevitably, with all the comings and goings we failed to find the intimate *rapport* we had experienced in Chicago though every facility was available for studying their methods. After a few days we moved through the Holland tunnel into Brooklyn to stay with the Columban Fathers. As well as a tree in Brooklyn there was the largest school I have ever entered close by the presbytery. There were thousands of children. Bells rang and the whole place revolved in perfect rhythm.

My get-away route from New York went NNE to Westchester, Millionaires' County, to the extremely desirable residence of the McWeeny family whose daughter was married to a nephew of Heenan.* There I put in a strictly non-missionary spell examining strange sea-shells on the sea-shore. True, Mrs McWeeny, a formidable matron recently widowed, proposed I should address her confraternity. I demurred on the grounds that my visa did not allow me to work in the U.S.A. This was of course discounted as paltering balderdash. As a result I came to know and greatly admire the local clergy. They were in their own way moulded in the "Chance it!" tradition we in the C.M.S. learned from Heenan— ready to try anything.

Before we left New York, Dwyer had a letter from the Bishop of Leeds, our lost leader. Cardinal Griffin's successor would shortly be announced and in Heenan's view it could only be Archbishop Godfrey of Liverpool. The next day the news broke, and so it was! But who would succeed in Liverpool? Of course Heenan was the man. What may have surprised him, as it did me, was to be told the news officially, and *sub secreto*, by one of his old troopers.

On 17th December 1956 I presented myself at the Apostolic Delegation, Parkside, Wimbledon. My next four years, on the fringe of Vatican diplomacy, had begun.

* Dr. Brian Reynolds.

CHAPTER XXXV

Mission Service with a Difference

THE CLOCK strikes 4 p.m. It is mid-winter and the room darkens. A white object next to the clock is still dimly discernible as I sit wondering how to pick my way through the next four years* at the Apostolic Delegation as private secretary to Archbishop O'Hara. It was all very much *terra nova* then. Now, with the lamp lit, the white object next to the clock reveals itself as a shapely porcelain goblet bearing the arms of St. Pius X†. It is one of few surviving pieces from a famous dinner-service which along with tapestries, pictures and a fine sculpture of the Gran Duca Madonna Pius XI ordered to be moved to London when that intrepid man of faith closed the Vienna Nunciature in protest at the Anschluss.‡

The Apostolic Delegation in London was established that year. Pius XI died as Archbishop Godfrey, the first Delegate, was actually on the way to take up his post. The porcelain came into my possession as a farewell gift from Archbishop Bruno Heim, last Delegate and first Papal Ambassador to the Court of St. James, shortly before he retired from Vatican service. I shall keep the blue and gold stemma of Pius X steadily in view from this point onwards. That Viennese porcelain could supply more than physical "comfit" in this rather tricky enterprise.

Pius X owed his election on August 4th 1903 to yet another indiscretion of a Cardinal of Vienna who rose in the conclave to announce that his imperial master regarded Cardinal Tindaro de Rampolla, Leo XIII's Secretary of State who was well set to get the decisive vote, as *Persona non Grata*. Rampolla at once withdrew his candidature but went on to denounce the intolerable invasion of the freedom of the conclave. *Felix culpa!* The Patriarch of Venice, Giuseppe Sarto, was elected as Pius X. The new Pope incurred considerable criticism for his lack of diplomacy particularly in dealing with Modernism. Indeed the story runs of his sitting before

---

* To the day, 17 December 1956 to 17 December 1960.
† The piece is a comfit dish i.e. sweetmeat container probably owing its survival to contemporary non-usage at the English dinner-table and its consequent escape from accidents and the lethal effect of detergents which played havoc with the beautiful gold, red and blue motifs. Now in the enlightened era of After-Eights survival would be impossible.
‡ 10 p.m. 11.3.38 Germany invaded Austria. 13.3.38 Hitler declared Austria "a province of the German Reich". 10.4.38 a plebiscite approved the Anschluss by 99.7% of the votes cast. The Cardinal of Vienna incurred the extreme displeasure of Pius XI by publicly recording his agreement.

a tough decree which awaited his signature and addressing his youthful Secretary of State, Merry del Val, to this effect: "What can we do about this, Eminenza? I, an old parish priest—you, a young seminarist, as they say? Be! Facciamo così*" and taking up the pen he boldly signed: "Pio P.P. X".

Bernard Von Bülow, Kaiser Wilhelm II's Chancellor, who knew all the diplomats worth knowing and had run rings round quite a few of them, had this to say about the "old parish priest": "He is the most spiritual man I have ever met." If the inference was he didn't need anything else, I award Von Bülow high marks. The man whose policies logically led to World War I cannot, however, be easily credited with such discernment.

Archbishop Godfrey chose to establish the Apostolic Delegation well away from Belgravia and the embassies. His appointment had met with considerable opposition from both Church and State, despite being bereft of diplomatic status. (It was going to take another forty-seven years to achieve that, though the Catholic Union of Great Britain† had the issue early on its agenda and the Holy See recognised a British Minister with full diplomatic honours at Rome.) Even when a house in Belgravia was offered to Archbishop Godfrey by a noble lady, the Delegate continued to live in Wimbledon. This was surely very wise. It meant, inter alia, fewer casual visitors "dropping in", and the magnificent common just across the road for exercise and clean air.

Our Head of Mission, Archbishop Gerald Patrick O'Hara, accepted a considerable reduction of status in coming to London from Dublin in 1954, where, as Nuncio, he had enjoyed full ambassadorial status, indeed was doyen of the Diplomatic Corps, and lived in the Phoenix Park next to the President. His first diplomatic appointment was to Rumania already under the Soviets, where he had to deal with a Foreign Minister in the person of the redoubtable Anna Pauka. Relations were strained so far that in the end his only effective mode of communication was to dash up the steps of the Foreign Office, lodge his protests firmly on her desk and dash out again before they could be stuffed into his hand on the usual stonewall policy of *fin de non reçevoir*.

He cherished the memory of heroic bishops in prison like Bishop Aaron Marton all of whom in various ways he sought to sustain. Once his chauffeur under torture finally yielded information which led to the Nuncio's expulsion. It says much for the charity of Archbishop O'Hara that he would have given that chauffeur his job back if he had stayed *en poste*.

Morty, our London Delegation chauffeur, was in no danger of being displaced. As a former London bus-driver he was endowed with the safest pair of hands and rare knowledge of the high-ways

* "Right! Let's do it like this!"
† A non-political association of members of the Catholic laity to watch over Catholic interests. Recruited from both Houses of Parliament etc.

and by-ways of the metropolis. Once he got to his bed above the garage, often at the midnight hour, he slept so soundly that one night the old Rolls was literally stolen from under him. But who could hold that against him? The police assured us there was no problem—the car would turn up in a couple of days, abandoned. So it did. I was not surprised. Rodents were already colonising the back seat upholstery.

Altogether a baker's dozen of us served at the Delegation in one capacity or another under the Chief of Mission: four Medical Missionaries of Mary, two Irish house-maids, later supplemented by girls from Spain, the Eccellenza's man-servant, Buss, whom he had inherited from the paternal home in Philadelphia, Eileen a London typist (who sweetly found time to type my MS despite her full-time employment in a busy London office), Father Joe Jones CSSR, the canon lawyer and Monsignor Egano Righi-Lambertini, the Counsellor, and the only one of us to be *di ruolo*, i.e. an enrolled member of the Vatican diplomatic service. I stoutly bring up the rear with the gardener.

The Archbishop's diocese of Savanna-Atlanta included the whole state of Georgia. His two Cathedrals, door to door, were three hundred miles apart, a distance he normally covered in five hours flat. A large block of ice on the floor of the car provided a primitive version of air-conditioning in the sweltering heat of the Deep South. His diocesan lawyer, a devout Catholic, was the brother of the authoress of *Gone with the Wind*. For including a O'Hara in the novel, she had the professional assurance of the legal researchers that there could be no chance of libel suit since there was no one of that name in the State of Georgia. Why, I wonder, did she not consult her brother? Alas, the dear lady had ceased to practise as a Catholic. Her tragic death crossing a city square moved the only Gerald O'Hara in the State, her bishop, to plead, not in any earthly law-court, but before the court of heaven for her eternal rest.

My predecessor at the London Delegation, Monsignor, later Bishop, David Cashman, once accompanied his chief on a pastoral visit to Georgia. In the absence of the Bishop, auxiliaries ran the diocese. David heard someone wonder aloud why the Delegate did not resign his diocese since his Vatican service kept him away so long. To which the Vicar General at once replied: "The guy has to eat." It seems that Vatican salaries fell far short of the American norms. My own remuneration, on the contrary, was thirty-one pounds in excess of anything I'd "touched" before, apart from my time in the Navy. I needn't say our big-hearted Delegate felt constrained to lift me off what he considered the bread line from his own resources. Frankly I have never met his like for splendid giving.

According to David Cashman, building in Georgia erected by G.P.O'H covered every aspect of social need. In the teeth of fierce opposition he pioneered integrated hospitals. On this issue, the Archbishop told me he had sought the advice of Cardinal Stritch, recognised by his peers as the brains of the North American Bishops' Conference, whose first diocese was in Tennessee, home of the Hillbillies. When it was a question of drafting a text after debate, they put him in a quiet room from which he never failed to emerge with the perfect formula. No wonder Pius XII called him to Rome to be Prefect of Propaganda. But he died within days of his arrival.

My work as private secretary to the Delegate only gradually became clear. It was governed by one or two negative principles: I was under the general restrictions regarding secrecy which obtain, I suppose, in all diplomatic missions. Since I was not *di ruolo* I was not to be initiated into the use of the ciphers though occasionally entrusted with the movement of the machines.

Shortly after my arrival, the Delegate journeyed to the continent leaving me to write a report on the General Election which was due in the New Year. "Don't hesitate, Tom, to send it yourself to the *Secretaria di Stato* when you have it finished." Typical of him, that vote of confidence had me walking ten feet high. I had the nous, however, to wait for his return. He liked it, but my ignorance of certain Vatican idioms was gently supplemented in time to save my face.

With Father Joe Jones, our Canon Lawyer, I got on famously. He was a Mancunian, a fount of that teasing, slightly cynical humour which complements, but by no means coincides, with the "whacker" wit at the other end of the Ship Canal. He was irreplaceable as the shrewd unraveller of the canonical problems addressed to the Delegation. The Delegate's jurisdiction at that time in addition to Great Britain covered Gibraltar, Malta and the Bahamas.

Monsignor Righi-Lambertini, the Counsellor, came to us from Paris where he had served under the future John XXIII. His family gave the Church one of the great scholar Popes in Prospero Lambertini, who reigned as Pope Benedict XIV from 1740 to 1758, a great canonist and *litterateur*: Voltaire dedicated a play to him. A nineteenth century mathematician with a European reputation figured in the Counsellor's maternal line. His grandfather was the moving spirit behind the confiscation of the papal states in the Romagna. Egano's career in the service of the Vatican was clearly seen by him as an act of reparation. More than once I heard him say he would otherwise feel it his duty to return to his diocese of Bologna where, if I remember rightly, there were more than forty parishes without a priest.

Our counsellor had a remarkable ear for languages. He had gone to Paris without a word of French, yet in the briefest period acquired fluency and a perfect Parisian accent. Similarly at Wimbledon with English. He refused to answer any telephone calls until he possessed English at the same demanding level. As a Bolognese he also had an equally refined palate. Through his agency the Apostolic Delegation received olive oil from Lucca, wines of the Romagna, sparkling wines from Moet et Chandon and cheese from Lombardy. When

Egano left us to be Head of Mission in Korea*, I meanly switched from Italy to Spain for wine at 3s 6d (white), 4s 0d. (red).

Our Counsellor's diplomatic career peaked at the summit of Vatican Service in 1969 with his return to Paris as Nuncio in France. Ten years later Pope John Paul II created him Cardinal Deacon in his first Consistory. So I can claim to have rowed the Thames with a Cardinal: better still, to have heard a masterly commentary from him on the English licensing system. We drove down to Brighton late one Sunday morning for a breath of air and dropped into a hotel on the front for a bite of lunch. The waiter served us but minus the wine. He explained that the bar closed as he approached with our order. Egano realised with a shock that the man was serious, and looked to me for help. "Our fault," I said, pointing to my watch: "It's gone time." He simply could not believe it. England, he had always understood, was a free country. That men should sit at table without wine, particularly on a Sunday, could only be of their own choice. Any other way violated personal liberty. That men should be forced (as the waiter was) to invade personal liberty in virtue of a State Law disqualified any country's claim to be free. That was tyranny. †

Monsignor Righi-Lambertini had two successors during my time in the Delegation both of whom have since served as heads of mission around the globe. London proved a handy staging-post for acquiring English which now would appear to have displaced French as the medium of diplomacy. Appointments to Wimbledon came nonetheless in Italian, with the highly diplomatic phrase *"per perfezzionarsi in inglese"* which could mean "to add the finishing touches to his English". The Delegate, however, groaned inwardly, well aware of the likelier meaning. Luckily next door to the Delegation the Ursuline Sisters had a house of studies. Egano was proof enough of their ability to move the pupil from zero to perfection.

* Impressed, I think, by my younger brother's excellent French, Egano asked his archbishop (Heenan) to release him for service with him in Seoul. The answer: "Positively No!", drew this wry comment from the new Capo Missione: "So my very first demarche is an *insuccesso*. Oddly enough, I have reason to believe G.P.O'H chose me on Heenan's recommendation, yet neither of my two C.M.S. superiors saw the point of Vatican Diplomacy and regarded me as a lay-about.

† The idea that such a law might exist to prevent greater evils does not come easily to an Italian in the matter of drink. From classical times the figure of fun in Latin comedy is the glutton, not the drunk. A coterie of young artists whom I knew of during my student days in Rome would slip into a trattoria on their late night stroll not for a drink but a kilo of spaghetti.

CHAPTER XXXVI

My beloved Boss

INWARD groanings of Archbishop O'Hara were usually prompted by his own remarkable blend of humility and sensitivity. The latter not infrequently can be the adversary of the former. Not, however, in his case. He suffered often and acutely from real or imaginary pin-pricks. In a sense he was made to be hurt having no protective shell or skin. Yet this happened without any shift on his part from a down-to-earth appraisal of his own virtues and merits. He was conscious of the respect due to him both as archbishop and personal representative of the Holy Father and fearless, indeed scrupulously exacting, in upholding the honour of Holy Church and the magisterium, but his own abilities he honestly rated very low. I say "honestly". There was no trace in his self-depreciation of that expectant: "Come on! Do tell me I'm wrong."

In fact he was considerably wrong. It was from his brother Ed I learned of his youthful reputation. Using a conventional American assessment of greatness, Ed quoted the number of times in his early years as a bishop Gerald had "made" *Time* magazine. The sum apparently worked out at top-rating. What Bishop Cashman told me about social provision in Georgia chimed in: "All the plant there is Gerald O'Hara."

From Gerald O'Hara himself I heard only of set-backs: for instance how he floated his diocese on the Stock Exchange but had to drop the idea when diocesan shares were quoted alongside of corsets etc. He came under criticism for investing in Coca-Cola, but on that issue was unrepentant. Dividends were too good. He sent many candidates for the priesthood to Mundelein and other seminaries. They all dropped out. Anyway he found himself aboard a plane next to a prominent actuary and raised the question of insuring against his heavy losses on fruitless seminary fees. "No chance" said the expert. "Where a free-will decision is the dominant factor, we wouldn't touch it."

It was also from one of his former auxiliaries in Savannah-Atlanta I learned of his deep attachment to Cardinal Dougherty of Philadelphia despite the almost inhuman workload imposed on him in the Cardinal's service.* It was this bishop who brought him news of the

---

* On return from Rome Cardinal Dougherty placed him single-handed over the diocesan tribunals whose very existence O'Hara had pioneered. He was succeeded by a team of ten priests.

Cardinal's death. "He broke down at once and wept bitter tears for his old boss."

Cardinal Dougherty sent a party of students from St. Charles Seminary, Philadelphia, to Rome in 1917 despite the hazards of U-boats in the Atlantic. True, we had pretty well the measure of them by then and no doubt the Cardinal was anxious after three fallow years to resume contact with the source of his future seminary professors and canon lawyers. Gerald O'Hara was now twenty-two.

The party got safely through to Barcelona where they met delay. The French frontier was closed. Spanish influenza raged in Barcelona. The delay meant the students' money was low and, as a consequence, so were their lodgings. All fell ill and three died before the British Consul heard of their plight and brought the survivors to be nursed in his own house.* They completed their journey to Rome by sea and rail, arriving in a cab at the door of the North American College in the Via dell 'Umiltà late one evening. It was opened by the Vice-Rector in total astonishment. Nobody had advised the college of their coming: there was room only for two of them whom he indicated and invited to alight with their luggage. The other two must go elsewhere. Thus two weary travellers, the future Francis Cardinal Brennan and the Apostolic Nuncio, Eccellenza Gerald P. O'Hara, without a word of Italian between them made their midnight entry into the Seminario Romano where they would hear no English for the next three years. As ordained priests, they would move on to the Apollinare Faculty of Canon Law and finally emerge as Doctores Utriusque Juris (Canon and Civil Law) years later.

Certainly both orphans of the storm owed much, indeed their whole future, to the room found for them at that particular "Inn". They acquired fluency in Latin and Italian, were taught the sacred sciences by professors already prominent in the central government of the Holy See. Their Prefect of Discipline, Tardini, a future Cardinal Secretary of State, was in fact O'Hara's Chief of the Vatican Diplomatic Service†. Fellow students, promising youths from all over Italy, would later fulfil expectations as members of the Italian hierarchy or in the Central Administration of the Catholic Church. I think, however, of all the benefits he derived from his years at the Lateran O'Hara cherished, far more than his first-name relationship with the powers that be, a particular quality I once heard him praise in Cardinal Dougherty. "He was always *Romanissimo. Ubi Petrus ibi Ecclesia.*" In fact he was describing himself. He would be mystified,

* This Catholic gentleman's son became a priest of the Southwark diocese.
† In the goodness of his heart my dear boss insisted once I should go in with him to report at the *Secretaria di Stato.* He introduced me to the great man, and sat me near to him. I could see a certain displeasure mantling his chief's face as the interview began. The storm broke, and I was summarily dismissed. My presence, it seems, was totally irregular. Later the Eccellenza apologised and tried to comfort me. "He clearly thought you *un pretino qualunque*, Tom." It was no good. I should have had the gumption to excuse myself, having had previous experience of the Eccellenza's big-hearted fidelity to Abraham Lincoln's (Gettysberg): "All men are born equal".

but by no means silenced, by the bad press this quality now "enjoys" in his beloved England, and even more so in his native U.S.A. Mercifully for him, he died in the interval between the first and second Sessions of Vatican II before the alternative theological magisterium really mounted its cathedra.

Our English neo-Cisalpines who would trace back their ancestry in a continuous line to A.D. 597 and the rejection of St. Augustine of Canterbury's heavy-handed attempts to impose Roman usages on the Celtic bishops, are no doubt motivated by genuine concern for ecumenical relations. If they confined their dissent within disciplinary, and, up to a point, liturgical areas, they might argue something more like a logical case. Those areas, however, happen to be just the ones in which the Holy See has shown itself to be remarkably conciliatory, as for instance with the convert episcopalian ministers in North America. Today claims for freedom and flexibility can over-run the frontiers even of Catholic Faith. They are implicit in the rejection of papal teaching on marital issues, the source of the ministerial powers of the priesthood and so on. Sadly dissent itself can have bogus origins, for instance, an inflated idea of traditional British resistance to Roman authority or a no longer tenable presumption of out-dated or rough-shod treatment by the Vatican curia.

For the first of these aberrations I would propose careful meditation on Letter 74 of St. Thomas of Canterbury†.

"Who would dare to doubt that the Church of Rome is the head of all the Churches and the source of Catholic teaching? . . . Is it perhaps not true that the whole Church is built on the faith and teaching of Peter, 'until we all come to the perfect man in the unity of the faith and the knowledge of the Son of God'? . . . It is for Peter to give judgment on the major issues. They must be examined by the Roman Pontiff and by the judges of Holy Mother Church whom he appoints, since, in so far as they share his care, they exercise the power which he confers on them . . . "

Here the patron saint of the secular clergy of England is both witness and advocate of the genuine English tradition.

On the second assumption, namely, that the Roman Curia still operates on Byzantine principles, The Ratzinger Report throws considerable light*. It has been howled down on various pretexts in more places than England, significantly always by those who are ill at ease with the central magisterium as recognised and welcomed by St. Thomas of Canterbury.

* PL 190, 533-536 or, more accessibly, the revised Roman Breviary Lesson for his feast on the 29th of December.
† Fowler Wright Books Ltd., especially "Rome, despite everything" pp. 66-69.

CHAPTER XXXVII

The Heart of the Matter

BY GRACIOUS courtesy of Mother Mary Martin, their Foundress, Archbishop O'Hara brought from Dublin Sisters whose devoted services he had enjoyed at the Nunciature in the Park. Her Sisters if not the first, were among the first to break the canonical barrier which for centuries prevented religious women from practising as midwives. As their title—the Medical Missionaries of Mary—indicates, they are destined to serve in the missions where long ago such skills could have been what the Ministry of Defence used to call "a Number One Key Commodity".

Benedictine spirituality endowed Mother Mary with PAX, that is, with ceaseless but tranquil service. On visits to her community at Wimbledon, when she wasn't praying, interviewing, writing, or reading, she was, like Teresa of Avila, with the Lord who "moves among the pots and pans". Laurita, one of our Spanish maids, could not get over her surprise when "so fine a lady" joined her at the sink to wash the pots. *"Que monja!"* said she.* Certainly the spirit of their Foundress transfused her daughters who welcomed me at the Delegation in midwinter 1956.

Papal diplomatic missions throughout the world differ essentially from all others, despite their frequent co-incidence of the day to day tasks that confront them. In some respects there is a similarity here with the two priesthoods, the ordained and the universal. Lay people can and do perform certain priestly ministries. Priests can serve in positions normally held by lay people. Yet the two ministries are different not only in degree but in kind.

Vatican Service does not represent the Vatican State of which the Pope is head, but the Holy See, the supreme spiritual authority over the Catholic Church which the Pope has as successor of Peter. The pocket handkerchief of terrain over which he has temporal authority comes to him as the only sure safeguard in these days of the free exercise of the spiritual. Ambassadors therefore are appointed not to the Vatican but to the Holy See. They continued to be so appointed when Pius IX lost all temporal power. It is significant that our present Holy Father chose to omit the crowning ceremony. Whatever spiritual significance it once had, undoubtedly it was all too easily associated in the popular mind with the glamour of temporal power and sovereignty. Milton's "Triple-crowned Tyrant" is a classical example of the "all time low".

* "What a nun!"

"Vatican Service" is fair enough as a description of what we were all about at the Delegation but only in the sense that our authorities were located there. Our service in fact was to the Holy See. We were instruments, channels, of the Holy Father's spiritual authority to teach, rule and sanctify as exercised over that part of the Universal Church committed by him to his Delegate in London. Canon lawyers may elucidate how the services of a papal representative dovetail with those of the diocesan bishops. It is a delicate synthesis and they have been known to clash. Pius XI's teaching ascribes to the Pope's appointment the source of a local bishop's jurisdiction. Once appointed, however, he exercises his powers to teach, rule and sanctify, not as a delegate of the Pope, but in his own right. The jurisdiction of papal envoys on the other hand is always exercised in the name of the Pope and only indirectly affects the local Church in so far as it relates to the Universal Church over which Peter and his successors alone have divinely committed authority. The point is simply this. You can't just lump together the Excellencies, Counsellors, Attaches and Secretaries of secular diplomatic missions with those of the Holy See, however much their tasks may coincide, or their status be seen as *de facto* two of a pair.

There is an essential difference. Even the lowest form of diplomatic life in the Service of the Holy See, even that of a private secretary to a Capo Missione, is a spiritual, yes, even a "Petrine" service. Going further, and at last arriving at the point towards which I have been groping, I would contend that the services of the M.M.M. Sisters, of Eileen my typist, of Morty the chauffeur—all, in their measure and after their fashion, came within the early morning radiance of an encounter by a lake in Galilee at breakfast-time, and the gift of a world-wide spiritual service.

Certain words I remember hearing the Delegate repeat with emotion may perhaps help to bring down to earth this apparent flight of fancy. They came from the lips of the Nuncio, Archbishop Cossulo, he replaced in Bucharest, the night he arrived to take over in a difficult situation. At the end of the evening meal during which no doubt a daunting prospect opened up on the work ahead, the two men together made their customary visit to the Nunciature chapel.

It should be remembered that the Bishop of Atlanta-Savannah was called to Rome out of the blue to find himself destined to serve the Holy See as Head of Mission without the normal years of training and experience behind him. In fact he went through a crash course at the Secretariate of State under the prefectorial eye of Monsignor Tardini and that was it. To the seasoned Vatican Diplomat who received him that night in Bucharest, the newcomer must have seemed an unlikely match for the Communist Goliath to whom he was accredited. Perhaps that explains the somewhat dramatic climax with which he felt their meeting should conclude that evening. After all he was Italian. As both men rose from their devotions in the chapel the outgoing Head of Mission took his successor firmly by the arm. Pointing to the tabernacle, he said with emphasis: "Eccellenza carissima, THERE is the source of our diplomacy in the service of the Holy See." This was his own single-sentence crash course. In fact the neophyte treasured it as an all-inclusive Magna Carta.

Logically therefore the chapel at 54, Parkside, S.W.19 was the power-house of our work for the Holy Father in London. We made our morning meditation there, said Mass, gathered after lunch and supper to pray there for Pius XII, and there said the Rosary together each evening. For greater convenience the chapel was moved downstairs. O'Hara devised stained glass behind the altar for each of the sovereign units within his jurisdiction.

He instructed me to look out for an organ. Remembering their regular advertisement in the *Catholic Gazette*, I called in the firm of Mander. They installed one of their miniature masterpieces as a pilot effort. Even at pianissimo, however, the ceiling threatened to crack over our heads. Whereupon the Eccellenza bethought himself of the organ he had commissioned for one of his cathedrals in Georgia. As he described it, Mander's face underwent a sickly sea-change. "Sir," he said, "you must not mention an instrument of that nature in my hearing as an organ. I protest." Only too clearly the instrument in question which filtered its dulcet tones from behind the high altar in Savannah, was electronic. I fear we got no further.*

When a sticky problem† faced our Chief of Mission, you could count on his fidelity to the basic principle he learned that first night in Bucharest. His influence was not confined to the top brass at the Delegation. The M.M.M.s went about their onerous duties, Sister Marie to her typewriter, Sister Bibi to her kitchen‡, drawing new strengths from that secret source, the "hidden room" in which G. K. Chesterton locates Pope Pius V during the battle of Lepanto, which ended the Turkish expansion on the high seas§.

* I was able to make it up later with Mander when the organ at Portsmouth Cathedral needed renovating and resiting.
† e.g. Before an interview with Archbishop Makarios in the interests of certain minority groups in Cyprus; or the approach to the Home Secretary to protest at the performance in England of Hoccuth's play *Der Vertreter* which vilified Pope Pius XII.
‡ Bibi is an affectionate Irish substitute for Adalberta Simacova. She was a trained nurse who somehow managed to emigrate from Czechoslovakia after the war to join the M.M.M.'s. When Archbishop O'Hara was appointed to London, Sister Bibi, who had made herself indispensable in the kitchen, was chosen to go with him. The difficulty was her lack of an acceptable passport. Archbishop O'Hara dropped in on the Irish Foreign Minister. They chatted amicably together while his staff prepared the document which made Sister a citizen of Ireland. After a dinner at the Apostolic Delegation I well remember the French Ambassador taking me aside to ask who was responsible for the cuisine. Was there any chance of her moving from her present post? I explained her life commitment, prefaced with the strongest negatives I could command. Was it subtle Gallic blarney? I am still not at all sure. If he was serious, clearly Sister Bibi's continental touch beguiled him. He thought she was French?
§It is an historical fact that the fleet of Don John of Austria clinched the issue of that crucial sea-battle when the Ave Maria bell had assembled the faithful of Rome for the evening Rosary. Pius V's miraculous vision of the event is a tradition, which I am not competent to pronounce on.

Despite the Delegation's formal lack of diplomatic status, courtesy generously accorded much of the substance. Thus the Queen invited the Delegate to her levees, receiving him in a room by himself before moving on to the Ambassadors. Our mail went and came in the diplomatic bag via the Foreign Office. The Eccellenza was included among the guests at Embassy dinners. This particular courtesy could stretch Sister Bibi in the preparation of many a reciprocal occasion, particularly when through the Delegate's absence or his secretary's ineptitude, they had to be bunched close together instead of decently spread through the year. Like all great artists, Sister became incandescent once her culinary designs went into production. As the critical hour approached, her assistants depended more on gesture than the stream of middle-European instructions which gradually replaced her normally fluent English.

My part in the proceedings was by comparison plain sailing: for each occasion I had to prepare a list of about ten others to accompany the principal guest and issue the invitations. All too often, one was 'phoning around for replacements at short notice. People prominent in public life can be hard to get. Luckily there was a noble band of diehards prepared to cancel anything rather than let down the Delegation. They saved my bacon more than once. Names like Dormer, Semphill, Crichton-Stuart, Cheshire are for ever engraved in grateful memory. There were, however, mornings when poor Eileen rang through the list of standbys, only to hand me each time a grateful but fruitless receiver. Had I too been born elsewhere, I fear my language would have been more impenetrable than Sister Bibi's as the morning wore on.

Each year the Holy Father's Day called for a massive reception either at 54 Parkside or at one of the London hotels. Here, as in so many other areas, I entered into the excellent pioneer work of Monsignor David Cashman. His lists of invited guests ruled supreme. The preliminaries for this event were in the capable hands of Sister Marie and Eileen. I came in behind the scenes as a floor-walker. Both H.M. Government and Opposition were well represented on these occasions. Church and State mingled "as thick as the leaves that fall on Vallombrosa".

The Delegate's first duty, as his appointment indicated, was to the Catholic Church of Great Britain. Until the Papal Representative was accredited to the Court of St. James and the Delegation became a Pro-Nunciature, contacts with government and the diplomatic corps though valuable, and even indispensable, were a secondary acquisition. Archbishop O'Hara needed no prompting. Invitations from dioceses or even parishes instinctively found him willing. Unfortunately the energy which had won him his reputation in Georgia as a young bishop was no longer available. I got used to his sad phrase: "Tom, you'll have to get me off the hook." That was not always so easy.

He was very clear on one thing: the main duty he owed to the

Catholic Church in England was logically the main reason for his being in England at all. Since that duty involved the presentation to the Holy See of suitable candidates for the episcopate, that for him came before all other claims on his attention. Once he had shaped up his terna* or secured the assent of the candidate chosen by the Holy See, he could not settle until Rome had all the facts. The hustle, so characteristic of his younger go-ahead country, contrasted sharply sometimes with the more leisurely Roman approach.

Within little more than a month at the Delegation I was entrusted with a gratifying secret mission. Heenan's in-laws, the Reynolds, invited me to dinner. Heenan would be there. The Delegate agreed I should go. Just before I left the Delegate called me in. He had received a cipher. The Holy See's choice for Liverpool in succession to Archbishop Godrey was Heenan. Was he willing? "You must get him on his own, Tom. If he says yes, simply 'phone back 'He *will* come to dinner'." Heenan stood by me as I 'phoned this message. We then went in to our own dinner. As usual Heenan was the life and soul of the party. Later I learned he did not sleep that night.

I arrived back at the Delegation to find the Capo Missione locked in debate with his Consigliere, who had just come in from his English studies. The issue was how urgently Heenan's acceptance should be transmitted. Egano was quite sure tomorrow was right. Anyway, who wanted to get a cipher together so late? Argument ceased dramatically. Egano bowed his head, as O'Hara firmly said: "Tonight!" The point of this episode is that Heenan's translation to Liverpool was issued on 2nd May 1957, two months after a late night cipher probably woke someone up in the Secretariate of State.

Archbishop Godfrey, the first Apostolic Delegate, had carefully assembled his dossier on episcopal candidates, the fruit of wide-ranging confidential research. He then *appeared* to let the process drop until a day came when he locked himself with his typewriter in the common room, to emerge some hours later with the completed *terna*. But there was nothing gradual, or phased, about Eccellenza O'Hara's process. A certain *slancio* (all-round dash) characterised his approach. No less, I am sure, than his predecessor, he accompanied his enquiries with constant prayer to the Holy Spirit for light. There was, however, no apparent withdrawal of the issue *"in pectore"* until the day of decision arrived and the dossier was completed. He would have us with him the whole way in a shared continuous process. After all, we were all sworn to the strict secrecy demanded by our service.

Other things being equal, the Delegate favoured a candidate from outside the widowed diocese. There are advantages in assuming authority elsewhere than among one's former friends and equals. A diocese can, however, have good reasons for wanting "one of its own". The suggestion that any other choice would adversely reflect on its resources is not, however, a good reason. There are occasions

* List of three candidates: "most worthy, worthier and worthy".

when a diocese which has received a bishop from outside has later supplied priests for more demanding responsibilities elsewhere.

I was only once with O'Hara in Scotland, but not on the occasion when the Provost and Bailies of Edinburgh illuminated the city to honour the visit. It must have given Pius XII a certain consolation to know that the City Fathers of "Auld Reekie" courageously voted this gesture because so many of them had been warmly received by him in that constant stream of audiences he gave for our troops after Rome was liberated.

I was, however, with the Delegate when the train pulled into Cardiff station to a tumultuous reception. A famous actress emerged from the next compartment to stand with precipitate delight at the window. As the train came to a stop, the station roof trembled to the strains of *Faith of our Fathers* in four-part harmony from hundreds of Welsh voices.

Our Delegate had an inescapable engagement in Yorkshire the night before the funeral of his successor in Dublin, Archbishop Levame. The Bishop of Salford came to our rescue with a bed at Wardley Hall. They held up the 'plane at Manchester the following morning, Barton Bridge having held us up for the vital ten minutes. At Dublin Airport the Delegate was received with the honours of his former status.

I made myself scarce in the Pro-Cathedral choir loft some time before the Requiem. Where else in the world would one's eyes be blessed with the vision below? Few mourners were yet in their places. The front bench, however, was solidly occupied by the Prime Minister and his Cabinet silently telling their beads.

Mother Mary Martin found room for me in her coach for the long journey to Glasnevin Cemetery. We made our way through drab streets at a very brisk pace immediately behind the bier. The six colonels flanking the mortal remains kept their places only by dint of a superhuman effort. It was a classical demonstration of forced marching if ever there was one. The remains were laid to rest far from the bright shores and blue seas of his native Monaco. I take it this was his own decision, If so, could it be a classical instance of his cheerfulness breaking into solemnity and at the same time a profound exercise of Faith? His episcopal motto as a servant of the Holy See, a neat heraldic pun on his surname, Levame, was *"Leva me, Domine"* ("Lift me, Lord"). The device was the Elevation of the Cross on Calvary. No doubt as Eccellenza O'Hara learned so dramatically from his predecessor at Bucharest, diplomatic service of the Holy See imposed on him, too, burdens which only the Lord could lift.

The scene changed to joy that afternoon when O'Hara took me over to the Presidential Lodge, two hundred yards from the Nunciature to meet his old friend, Shaun T. O'Kelly. The Lady of the Lodge was a sister of Cardinal Brown, a classical theologian much esteemed by Pope Pius XII. She was herself, I believe, highly esteemed in mathematical circles. My thoughts, however, were with the Booth family ten miles away in Dalkey. The Chargé d'Affaires, Monsignor Gerarda, lent me a car. Alas, Joe was absent. With a promise to return in the summer I shot back to the Nunciature in time for dinner. Whether I kept that promise or not I was certainly with the Booths at Rocky Hill in October 1958. Pope Pius XII had recently died. His last public appearance was at Castel Gandolfo when Sir John Barbirolli conducted part of Elgar's *Dream of Gerontius*. Among the singers were members of the Dublin Pro-Cathedral choir. Sir John later recalled with emotion the words with which the Pope had thanked him: *"Figluolo, questo e un gran capolavoro"*.* A door closed behind him and the world saw him no more. Speculation as to his successor was perhaps most acute and best informed in papal diplomatic circles. By the time I left London for Dalkey, the Patriarch of Venice was well to the fore. News of the white smoke came on 28th October. We gathered to the radio for the Cardinal Deacon's announcement. Slightly ahead of him I articulated the Patriarch's name. It coincided perfectly. The Booths gasped. How did I know? I had to confess I didn't: it was a guess with a certain amount of human inspiration behind it.

Descending from the sublime to the minuscule, may I note that two years later to the day, October 28th 1960, my own name came over the 'phone as Coadjutor to the See of Portsmouth. The date sticks. It happens to be my mother's birthday.

* "My son, this is a great masterpiece." The words appear on the sleeve of Barbirolli's HMV recording of the *Dream*.

CHAPTER XXXVIII

Annus Mirabilis

1960 proved to be *Annus Mirabilis*, a Year of the Lord with a difference. The 37th International Eucharistic Congress in Munich and the 19th centenary of St. Paul's shipwreck on the Island of Malta were celebrated at the heart of 1960's high summer. Malta was in the London Delegation's sphere of responsibility, whilst the *Universe* invited the Delegate to lead our National contingent to Munich for the Congress.

Pope John XXIII chose his legates carefully for each of the two great events. If only he had reversed the appointments! Muench, a shy, withdrawn man, was drafted from his archdiocese of Milwaukee into diplomatic service as Nuncio at Bonn during Adenauer's time. He went to Malta. Testa, a Bergamasque like Pope John, whom Pius XII appointed Nuncio in Berne, was affable, outgoing, and prodigal of endearments. He went to Munich*.

No sooner had Muench settled into his car at the quayside of the Grand Harbour than the police cordon broke, and a swarm of excited well-wishers avidly seized his hand to kiss the Legatine ring. How he managed to get the arm back into the car, he himself was not clear. He thought he had lost it. It was the end. An Italian Cardinal deputised for the visit to the sister Island of Gozo. Cardinal Testa on the other hand, in Munich, encountered just the reception that would have put His Eminence Cardinal Muench at ease. His warm approach froze the undemonstrative Bavarians who looked elsewhere as he advanced glad-handing all comers, all, that is, who stood their ground.

An imposing reception awaited our arrival in Malta. Malta for me was the quintessence of the Midi—heat, honey coloured stone, and centuries back in the Ages of Faith. Happily for us we were

---

* A note on the contrast of local styles of celebrating from *Adoremus* the quarterly of U.K. Priest Adorers: Spring 1984:
"Malta was a riot of spontaneous joy from that first unforgettable moment when the Papal Legate's Yacht (placed at his disposal by our C.-in-C. Mediterranean) rounded the headland into the Grand Harbour at Valetta. There alone at the stem stood the Cardinal, his hand raised in blessing, *cappa magna* in full flow. All round the vast land-locked water, dozens of Church belfries, rockets, brass-bands, sirens, flags and streamers burst into clamorous, colourful orbit."
"Munich also offered splendour to eye and ear, but controlled, rehearsed and harmonious throughout. There were gorgeous uniforms, crowd formations, massed choirs and, unique to this Congress, an inspired preview of liturgical features which two or three years later found their niche in Vatican II's Constitution on the Sacred Liturgy, *Sacrosanctum Concilium*."

conveyed to a house on the sea at Sliema within half-a-minute of the early morning plunge in the briny and under the hospitable roof of Mr and Mrs Joe Gasan.

Our arrival in Munich was marred by an unseemly wrangle about where the Delegate should stay. Both contestants, a Bavarian Count and the Burgomeister of Peiting, claimed him as their official guest. Neither would yield. I moved away, the Delegate's German was more than adequate. He must have closed the bout in favour of the Burgomeister who with his officials had driven a considerable distance to be at the airport. Moreover Peiting was certainly appointed to accommodate congressists from England, and an official reception of the Delegate in the village church was awaiting our arrival.

We piled into the huge mayoral car, already late, only to be caught in a police-trap within the first mile. Earnest appeals were reinforced by reference to the dignity of their passenger and the shame the village, already waiting in the square, would incur. All to no avail! The official procedures went on unhurriedly. We were on a main street, the pennant of Peiting flying bravely on the bonnet.

Once again on arrival I made myself scarce in the choir loft with the men of the village. When the last resonant hymn was over, my neighbour shook hands. At last I could study what had been a distraction throughout, the buttons on his jacket. He was a hunts-man. He himself had carved some heads of his quarry on those polished segments of horn. My mother, who loved cameos, would have been keenly interested.

Priests lodged at the main inn. There at our table was our one-time New Zealand chauffeur and future Cardinal Archbishop of Wellington, Father Reggie Delargy. Conversation at table was largely in German. I am delighted to recall Reggie was even worse than me but far more determined. The parish priest of Peiting who lived at the inn and dined with us had a distinctly rough time. He was, he proudly assured us, a "Kunst" chauffeur whose "artistic" skill at the wheel must have been fully exercised as a truck-driver on the Eastern Front. On our free day he drove the Delegate at speed over great tracts of beautiful country, dotted with onion-domed churches and occasional rococo interiors.

Elsewhere* there is an account of Malta, Munich and other International Eucharistic congresses following Munich finishing with Nairobi in 1985.

The Delegation soon settled down again after the glory of the high summer. By mid-October O'Hara thoughtfully suggested a break since for more than a year I had been continuously on duty. "Let us know, Tom, where you are," were his parting words.

I hired a car and 'phoned my sister in Paisley that I was coming. Ominous engine noises soon counselled a deviation from the high

---

* *Adoremus*, the magazine of the Priests Eucharistic League in England and Wales: Spring '84 and '85.

road to Bonny Scotland. I 'phoned Heenan in Liverpool inviting myself for lunch and requesting a professional survey of my hired car's innards. Both were vouchsafed. We watched Heenan's favourite game on the telly while the expert tinkered away. "You've been sold a pup", he said, adding a grudging assurance it could last out the week.

Both driver and car needed a rest at Carlisle. Monsignor Richard Smith provided tea and more sympathy at Warwick Square. But his ever brilliant chatter met with unseemly noises-off. They were sawing trees down in the garden. The shades of night were falling as the car chugged into the bright new Lowland town of East Kilbride. I pulled up at the bright new hotel. They politely took charge of my hand luggage, begging me as a favour to wait a while downstairs. A bright new bride was changing into her going-away outfit in my room. The banquet had just finished.

After dinner I sallied forth to arrange for Holy Mass in the morning. Church and presbytery were both bright and new. Gratefully the three priests were old-style Caledonian. The malt emerged and the guest's half-hearted modesty met with "stern and wild" dismissal. They certainly had their work cut out forming a displaced population into a close-knit worshipping community.

A message awaited me at the FCJ convent in Paisley where my younger sister lived. Bishop Black of Paisley, a recently created diocese, expected me to lunch. Who should open his door there but Father Harry Leonard, former R.N. chaplain aboard the aircraft carrier *Glory*.

O'Hara had 'phoned the bishop that morning. I was to be at the convent 'phone at 7.30 that evening. The Delegate began in excellent Latin. Would I accept the Holy Father's decision and go as coadjutor to the See of Portsmouth? "Libenter"* simply said I. With a blessing he rang off. It was the 28th October 1960. The matter remained *sub secreto* until published in the *Osservatore Romano* midday 8th November. That day I was giving a day of recollection at the Sisters of Charity Convent in Carlisle Place for a group of priests belonging to the Society of the Little Flower. Their founder Monsignor Vernon Johnson was not present and Father Gordon Albion presided. At lunch he was called to the 'phone and returned to announce that the Apostolic Delegate wished them to know that their conferencier was Coadjutor Bishop-elect to the diocese of Portsmouth. Further reading of *The History of a Soul* was suspended and wine was called for. I noticed a priest making for the 'phone. The whole diocese of Portsmouth, I believe, had the news within minutes of his initial call. He was the only Portsmouth diocesan priest there that day, Father Dermot McDermot-Roe.

Since Vatican II all coadjutors have the right of succession. I must have been one of the last to be gazetted *"sedi datus,"* that is, given not to the bishop but to the diocese and *"sine iure,"* with no right to

* "Willingly."

195

succeed the present bishop. In fact he was Archbishop, a personal honour conferred by the Holy See on the occasion of the golden jubilee of his priesthood. I had never met him, a fact which moved the ever-ready Bishop Cashman to supply my deficiency. "Tom", he said without a moment's pause, "he looks very like God the Father only slightly older." Very soon I received his invitation to lunch at Winchester.

I fear my first appearance in those parts cannot have brought the old man much comfort. Badly bungling a change of trains, I was well over an hour late for the meal. On the other hand Archbishop King fulfilled all expectations. Dave Cashman's inspired forecast corresponded uncannily with an impression of God the Father I have carried through life since babyhood. In our parents' bedroom hung a print of Murillo's Christ and John the Baptist as children, the latter with lamb and a slim cross aslant. God the Father, accompanied by baby angels looks down from the clouds, robed, if I remember rightly, in blue and red. The old Spanish master might have had John Henry King as his model. Sanguine complexion, bright eyes, flowing beard—all were there in anticipation. Not, however, the frequent pursing of the features which synchronised with a gusty release of breath ending in a deep chuckle.

Over lunch we discussed my consecration. It was mid-November. The then feastday of St. Thomas, Apostle, 21st December, proved agreeable to all. Chief Consecrator? I suggested the Apostolic Delegate, knowing this was his wish. The Archbishop assented, not so the Vicar General. All subsequent Portsmouth bishops derived their episcopal orders from John Vertue, the first of the line, he urged: priests would take it amiss if Archbishop King were displaced by any other prelate whatever his rank. The old man pulled on his pipe and said nothing. A further complication emerged in the background. Cardinal Godfrey as Metropolitan of the province which included Ports-mouth sensed his was the right to consecrate rather than the Apostolic Delegate. Mercifully the wretched candidate knew nothing of this at the time. But in the event John Henry was the ordaining prelate assisted by Bishop Healy of Gibraltar, my *quondam* confessor at Valladolid, and Bishop Dwyer of Leeds. The Apostolic Delegate preached.

I bade farewell to 54 Parkside, Wimbledon on December 17th, four years to the day after moving in from Mission House. It was a Saturday. The canny administrator of Portsmouth Cathedral was sure it would greatly please the parishioners if I appeared there on the Sunday before the consecration and *of course* preached at all the Masses. Priests and people carefully hid their inevitable misgivings at least in the presence of the unknown North countryman. Indeed they made me feel Pompey was home from home.

Civil and Service notables rallied to the ceremony on the 21st December. The luncheon at Southsea, however, prompted me to wonder if it was my turn to have misgivings.

I unvested in the sacristy, taking, I suppose, an inordinate time to do so. It was my first struggle out of full episcopal panoply. Upstairs I had a similar challenge getting into a bishop's *abito piano* for the first time.

The house was preternaturally quiet when I at last presented myself at the front door. Nobody! Outside, Edinburgh Road was innocent of all transport. I stood helpless, and self-conscious in what U.S. Bishops call "Soup and Fish" attire, looking, like Janus, both ways at once. A milk-van appeared. It was grossly unfair, but I pleaded a lift. Time was running out on me. He opened his door. More, he pronounced himself honoured. We made the South Beach Hotel in record time. They were settling into their places for luncheon. I shall not forget passing my sister (Mamie, the other half of my twosome).

"You look smashing" said she, my normally relentless, down-to-earth critic.

Archbishop King rose a couple of times during the meal to assure my welcome. He used the happy phrase: "Tom will get used in time to our little ways in the South!" I could not resist. When it came my turn to say a few ill-chosen words, I demurred somewhat, instancing my abandonment at the door of Bishop's House which only a milkman could remedy.

The diocesan clergy presented a cheque well calculated, and intended, to put four wheels under me for getting round their parishes.

On Christmas Day at Portsmouth after the last Mass the Cathedral Staff came together for a pre-prandial drink. From my upper room on the front one had a comprehensive view of the Park on the other side of Edinburgh Road. Under the open band-stand a pride of beggarmen had assembled hunched in tattered coats and rags of every sort.

I have mentioned one of R. A. K. Mason's poems, *O Fons Bandusiae* earlier on. The festive drink beside a glowing fire turned sour on me as I remembered his "On the Swag".

> His body doubled
> under the pack
> that sprawls untidily
> on his back
> the cold wet deadbeat
> plods up the track.
>
> The cook peers out
> "Oh curse that old lag
> here again
> with his clumsy swag
> made of dirty old
> turnip bag".

"Bring him in cook
from the gray level sleet
put silk on his body
slippers on his feet,
give him fire
and bread and meat.

Let the fruit be plucked
and the cake be iced,
the bed be snug
and the wine spiced
in the old cove's nightcap:
for this is Christ.*

I just hadn't the guts. I stilled but did not smother my conscience by crossing the road with a pocket full of half-crowns.

Down towards the sea half a mile from St. John's Cathedral, alongside R.N. Barracks, Nelson's Flag Ship *Victory* welcomes visitors aboard, a masterpiece of scrupulous restoration and conservation, a treasure unique among all Her Majesty's dock yards.

Occasionally on my way to 7 a.m. early Mass in one or other of Pompey's convents, I would be held up by the wide river of cyclists pouring into the Yards as the siren sounded 6.30 a.m. As one looked at their faces, the conviction grew that it was not the men but the machines that knew the way and pressed on regardless. The wide river has since ceased to flow.

The Navy were kind to the new boy from the beginning. An officer on the Admiral's staff stood in the sanctuary throughout the ceremony of consecration, motionless like the Pompeii Sentinel as Vesuvius rained its fire. My Pompey guard of honour rivalled his heroism. At the end of the ceremony he discovered a pinnacle of red wax mounted on the shoulder of his No.1 doeskin jacket. He had placed himself under a dripping candle.

C.-in-C. Portsmouth graciously complied with the request of our Senior R.N. Chaplain, Monsignor Cyril Fay, to present me with the chalice subscribed by the Chaplains and Catholics in the Service. I use it still every day marvelling at its beautiful lines. It was the work of the silversmith whose design for the new Ascot Cup was commissioned that same year.

One great moment came with an invitation from the Admiral-in-Command Dock Yard to dine with him on the *Victory* in Nelson's Day Cabin.

As a tail-piece may I add yet another maritime moment which I cherish for reasons which may be clear from earlier pages. The Spanish Sailing and Training Ship, *Sagres*, called in at Pompey. Her Captain accompanied by his First Mate paid a ceremonial visit to Bishop's House. Would I honour them next morning with a visit? They were returning via U.K. from showing their flag in U.S.A.

* Penguin Book of New Zealand Verse, first published 1960, p. 166.

naval ports. But he cautioned me with considerable emphasis about my "rig of the day". American Bishops had failed him grievously. They went aboard dressed in street-clothes, short coats and trousers. "To my lads," he said, "that kind of bishop is unknown. Would you honour us by wearing everything that goes with your rank."

I promised. To my surprise the ship was dressed over-all and the boys, well over a hundred of them, manned the masts and rigging. Bugles and pipes sounded as I went aboard.

That afternoon I had an engagement at the top of the diocese in Berkshire. I began by saying: "This morning I was in Spain." Surprised but grateful glances passed to and fro. It's not a bad thing to surprise an audience at the beginning, and leave them with a smile at the end.

CHAPTER XXXIX
A Venerable Archbishop

ALREADY before I left the Apostolic Delegation the tide of documents flowing via Wimbledon to and from the Vatican was rapidly mounting. Pope John's appeal for matters worthy of conciliar treatment and names of suitable candidates to serve on international commissions produced a massive response. The Vatican Press later published *sub secreto* the *"Vota et Desideria"** expressed by bishops, superiors general and Catholic Universities—9,520 pages in fifteen volumes†: a pretty comprehensive record of the ferment in the Church.

My own nomination to Cardinal Bea's Secretariate for the Promotion of Christian Unity came out of due time after its first plenary meeting. Heenan had found himself the only English member of that august body among a considerable number of continental bishops. Anyway one bound and Heenan was in to see Pope John. Another English bishop, newly consecrated, was made a member.‡

Let me, however, leave Roman matters aside for a spell to dig myself into the domestic consequences of my consecration or, in the now current phrase, episcopal ordination.,

If ever a Church ceremony faced a man with awesome evidence of "the years the locust ate" it was that "Consecration". Only the elder brother in Cairo was missing from the family round-up. How Hannah Fawcett, Abbess Bonaventure of Ellesmere, emerged canonically from strict enclosure was not for me to question. Our FCJ sister also made an unlikely sortie from her own "hidden garden". Our Benjamin, Joe, paired Father Joe Jones CSSR, the Apostolic Delegate's Canon Lawyer, as my personal chaplains. Their star effort was to hold a massive *Evangelarium* open on my head and shoulders as a long committal prayer was said. My impression was that both, in their ardour to imbue me with gospel truth, were doing press-ups on the rich binding. They nearly broke my neck. I hissed sharply. It was very close to curtains for a would-be bishop.

Contemporaries from Upholland, Valladolid and other days joined the local clergy procession. From Normandy with memories of sterner times came Abbé Maurice Graindor and his cousin. He was now a member of the College de France and a geologist of European fame.

* "Hopes and Options".
† cf *Vatican II* ed. A. Stacpoole, OSB Geoffrey Chapman 1986, p. 81.
‡ cf *A Crown of Thorns*, John C. Heenan, Hodder and Stoughton 1974, pp. 261-2

One of my 1961 New Year resolutions was to keep a diary. Herewith the first fruits of a diminishing harvest which peters out a couple of months before the end of the year. But look how earnestly the diarist began:

"Sunday 1st January 1961.

00.00 hrs.	Clear sky: full moon: a few singers (Auld Lang Syne).
	One of the cocks in the park in full voice. Ships' sirens.
00.15	All quiet but for odd siren.
03.00	Utterly quiet and peaceful.
05.45	Ditto
06.45	Rose: wrestled with sermon. Said Lauds.
08.00	1st Mass: assisted and preached: Prime.
09.00	2nd Mass: Terce: preached.
	Consecrated a chalice.
	It is a glorious golden day: still! A pity so few at Mass.
	For the 1st time, no *Confiteor* etc. at people's Holy Communion
10.00	Preached
11.00	Pontificated and preached.
p.m.	Boarded the Victory.
5.30	Carol Service: preached.
6.30	Said Evening Mass and preached. Very tired.
	Supped with Father Gerard Dwyer of Corpus Christi. He is keen on ITV—alert, painstaking. We are to have two weeks of Epilogues.
10.00	Programme of instructions arranged. I may do the last week in December.
	(4 mins to 11 p.m.—not so good!)
11.00	"

From there onwards, piece by piece, a large mosaic begins to form of priests and parishes, brothers and institutions, sisters, convents, schools and children. I begin to get the "feel" of the Catholic Church in Hampshire, Berkshire, Isle of Wight and Channel Islands.

I begin to make contacts with other Churches. Pretty soon the word is around that I am a member of Pope John's Secretariate for the Promotion of Christian Unity. Bishop John Phillips of the Anglican diocese of Portsmouth finds we have much in common: wartime service in the R.N., a taste for wine, daily prayer to Our Lady. He startles me with: "The big moment, Tom, in my consecration at Lambeth came when your 'Old Catholic' Bishop from Holland placed his hands on my head with the words: *Accipe Spiritum Sanctum*." I envied him "Bishopswood", once the silvan home of one of Nelson's admirals, and for good measure poised above the sea at Fareham.

The Nuffield Club was just down the road from our Bishop's House. It compensated somewhat for our lack of woodland and seaside amenities. In addition to the usual Club facilities, membership admitted one to County matches played on the excellent cricket ground. Clearly for my benefit, the Hampshire v. Lancashire home fixture was played there each year. I usually managed a morning session with a pint of the excellent Club beer. Even so it was a schizophrenic experience, tangling the old love and the new. Marshall, the Hampshire batsman, thrilled me with his mastery at the crease. Red Rose Winston Place applied the balm with a century two years running. He hadn't scored one in between.

Further evidence that bishoping was not allowed to be all work and no play comes through in the diary even in the early months: for example "19.1.61 went on holiday (inside of a week in Eire at Joe Booth's Dalkey.)"

Every Saturday I spent a long afternoon with Archbishop King at Winchester. When his predecessor Bishop Cotter died in October 1940, John Henry, his V.G. and Auxiliary, faced what for him was a fate worse than death. If he succeeded his chief, the pressures were on forcing him to live at Bishop's House, Portsmouth. He had built St. Peter's Winchester, the first Catholic Church I had ever seen surrounded by such a spacious garden. But far more than bricks, mortar and roses bound him to Winchester, He had a rare sense of history: King Alfred's capital was still for him the capital of England. ("We never resigned!"), and the Catholic cemetery had never passed out of Catholic hands.* He was a natural research student, the first, I think, to tackle County Archives for the rich seams of Recusant Rolls in which our forbears loyal to the Old Faith were listed for the purpose of fines during penal times. His own family's loyalty was amply demonstrated in the prayer-books handed down over the centuries with names and dates inscribed on the fly leaves. He could cite Mayors of Winchester whose daily rations during imprisonment for Popery in London were supplemented by grants from the City Council.

On the strength of his pioneering research he early became President of the Catholic Records Society. Unfortunately, through lack of time and perhaps of that extra gift, the scribbler's itch, his published work is minimal. His exercise books crammed with pencil jottings have proved to be quarries for the edifices of other men. This would in no way have worried him, so long as truth was the winner.

What developed over the years as the main staple of conversation was a North v. South struggle for the honour of saving the Faith in England. He had facts at his finger tips for Hampshire, Berkshire and Wiltshire. I had nothing like his detailed evidence for Lancashire, but more than matched him with a barrage of impregnable convictions.

* He was to be buried there (March 1965) in the last available plot.

He proposed that we cover the diocese by road together in criss-cross diagonals. If only we had had a tape recorder aboard. Effortlessly he filled in the Catholic associations of the manor houses, farms, schools, village greens we passed en route. Some-where, I think in the Southampton area, he indicated yet another recusant cemetery. The family name of Steptoe, I am sure, came into the narrative and I have some recollection of a high wall sealing the property from prying eyes. It was an experience that certainly opened my eyes. Nor did the Old Man let up with cursive glances through the windows of a fast-moving car. He held me with a glittering eye as we smoked our pipes together in that ancient presbytery in Jewry Street. As he yarned away his beloved Winches-ter emerged through the haze aureoled with a Catholic nimbus.

The Bishopric of Winchester was the richest benefice in the medieval church, often bestowed on very distinguished continental prelates. Did I know that Winchester in the 1790's became the home of seven hundred French Emigrés priests? "Look through that window, Tom. The hostelry there at the back. That's where the Vicars Apostolic passed our famous Theatre Law. John Lingard's mother lived down that street. Didn't John Milner, priest on the mission here at Winchester 1777-1800*, startle the old lady with the news that her beloved son had written a "Bad Book"?† Very few of our chapels were open at that time in the whole country, Tom; Winchester's was, *all the time.* Despite the rigours of the Law, they never touched us."

Best of all was the Old Man's saga of his own family background. His father had farmed on the Arundel estates in Wiltshire. John Henry first heard Mass in the chapel choir loft, standing knee-high to Farmer King who sang tenor. Sunday dinner over and the pots washed, women and children gathered round Grandma in the flagged kitchen. She began her devotions, appropriately seated in her grandmother chair. The others, including the young John Henry, knelt upright on the flags, inevitably sinking on their haunches. Grandma was anticipating visitors for tea. Hence evening devotions were early as possible after lunch. She led them from the *Garden of the Soul* compiled by Challoner: the five Glorious Myster-ies, the Litanies of the Saints, the Seven Penitential Psalms and so on.

Grandma was born before Waterloo. She had learned her prayers kneeling upright on the flags from her early eighteenth century Grandma. *The Garden of the Soul* appeared in 1740. Has any book of devotions—apart from the Psalms of David—exercised so wide and deep an influence on a besieged community or appeared in so many editions?

* Later Bishop of the Midland District, implacable opponent of Cisalpines of every degree. Credited with restoring the pastoral clergy from the dependent position of chaplains to noble families to free-standing status as missionary rectors.
† The 1st volume of his *History of England*. He was our first English historian to base his works on the original MSS in national archives.

Challoner s services to the Catholic Church in England especially as Bishop of the London District during the middle forty years of the eighteenth century were matched by Newman's in the nineteenth. That great Oratorian was now at last in the splendour of the Sacred Purple, having been created Cardinal Deacon of St. George in Velabro in May 1879. The future Archbishop King, born in 1880, was reborn at the font John Henry. He told a story of his boyhood when he and his sisters set out from the farmhouse for a day on Salisbury Plain. It was high summer. The dog days of August are still reflected, after a fashion, in the church calendar by the feast of St. Lawrence and his grid iron on 10th August. John Henry was then nearly ten years old. He had shoved a bottle of lemonade into an inside pocket leaving his hands free to help with other items. They chose the picnic site and were settling down when the cork flew out of John Henry's lemonade bottle with a loud report. Immediately from behind a nearby hillock a head appeared glued to the sights of a long rifle. Inside John Henry's jacket hot lemonade coursed its way down to his shoes.

It was mid-August 1890. The Cardinal Deacon of St. George in Velabro died on 11th August 1890, the day after the feast of St. Lawrence. That year military manoeuvres were in progress on Salisbury Plain in the blistering summer heat.

At that time there was a diocesan boarding school at Woolhampton near Reading. Later, when the French anticlerical Associations' Law of 1903 forced the Benedictines to relinquish their college at Douai, the diocesan school became their home and the nucleus of a flourishing Public School. John Henry studied humanities there as an aspirant to the priesthood in the early 'nineties. The first Bishop of Portsmouth, John Vertue, chose the English College Rome for the further studies of his promising aspirant. In the eyes of the priests and boys of the little diocesan school this was, in Newman's famous phrase, "a portent worthy of a cry". The whole community headed by the school band, with John Henry shoulder-high in the van, marched down the Berkshire lanes to the local railway station to cheer him off to Rome. As he revived the memory, gusty chuckles escaped through clouds of smoke and his eyes glittered with the fun of it all.

He was in Rome for the last five or six years of Leo XIII's twenty-five as Pope. Perhaps he too was mystified by the odd behaviour of one of the dignitaries in the procession issuing from the conclave to announce the new Pope? The man was miming something with both hands. Italians got it at once and before the Cardinal Deacon could announce the name they were shouting "Sarto".*

At the request of the Venerable English College the Old Man donated the Diary he had kept of his student years in Rome. When

* "Guiseppe Sarto", Patriarch of Venice, St. Pius X, Pope of the Blessed Sacrament, Reformer of Church Music, Hammer of Modernists etc. etc. comes through in English as "Joseph Tailor".

I came to know him he was the last surviving *Venerabilino* of the nineteenth century. His return to the College as ordaining prelate in 1957 is recorded in the *Venerabile* Diary somewhat on these terms: "During his visit he, from the fulness of the priesthood, shared the gift he received from his *Alma Mater* with these, her present sons."

As a student he was to leave Rome when already the Modernist crisis had developed a dangerous head of steam. Perhaps John Henry's first-hand report influenced his bishop, John Baptist Cahill. Anyway, Portsmouth students were recalled from Rome to escape the cross-currents of a troubled Holy See. Sixty years later when Vatican II was getting under weigh and the world's rivers were about to flow into the Tiber, John Henry remembered his predecessor's action. "Tom," he said, "the atmosphere in Rome is going to be too heady for our young hopefuls. We will send them to English seminaries until the Council is over."

I was already up to my neck in the ante-preparatory phase of the great assize and staying at the English College whenever the Secretariate for the Promotion of Christian Unity met in Rome. It was "All quiet on the Venerabile Front", so far as I could judge at that time. Moreoever, I had in mind a youth of excellent promise whom I may already have encouraged to prepare for Rome. John Henry yielded at once. It was typical of our relations over the four year I was with him, and probably very bad for me, that he so easily deferred to the greenhorn.

I have a treasured memory of the opening moments of my consecration. John Henry, seated *en Grand Prelat*, asks for my credentials: *"Habetis Bullam?"** The Officialis, Father T. D. Walsh in austere black ferraiuola, reassures him. "Let it be read," replies John Henry.

The Officialis begins to read John XXIII's instrument of appointment. While still reading the Latin he becomes a pianissimo second fiddle to the text in English on another microphone. (Who said Portsmouth was a Dead See?) I shall not forget dear John Henry straining to hear what precisely were the duties and powers of this Coadjutor *"sedi datus"* from the North. Of course he had every opportunity both before and after the ceremony to find out. I don't think he bothered. Again I must salute his all-inclusive acceptance of a person rather than a juridical complication. Whatever Canon Law might say, we were for him simply "King and Son Ltd." Together we should "roll the Old Chariot along". And no "hanging on behind".

Some part of his warmth towards the stranger may have come from knowing he was now for ever safe at Winchester. He owed his first escape from Bishop's House Portsmouth to Enemy Action. Between the death of Bishop Cotter and John Henry's appointment to succeed him, Portsmouth was devastated by the Luftwaffe in January 1941. Bishop's House was completely straffed and the Cathedral badly damaged. The sacristan was drowned when the

* "Do you have the Bull of Appointment?"

mains burst in the cellars where some of the staff had taken refuge. The tabernacle of the bishop's domestic chapel was found intact some days later on the Cathedral roof. That night a cathedral curate, Father Abbon Quin, experienced the phenomenon one often hears about but never sees: his hair went completely white. A great Cathedral treasure, the arm of St. Edmund of Abingdon encased in a silver sleeve, disappeared for ever. Harpies were soon on the site. A voice was heard to say: "But we're Catholics. If anyone has a right to the stuff it's us."

Luckily John Henry had already moved the most treasured items from Bishop's House library across the Solent to Quarr Abbey. A timely gesture which deserved some kind of reward. It came but not the way he would have wished: there was now no question of his moving from Winchester.

Nine years later he warmly invited me to be the first epioscopal resident in the new Bishop's House built by courtesy of 'War Damage'. To my intense surprise within weeks he suggested a move to Maidenhead. Could there have been, unconsciously latent perhaps, the germ of an idea which twenty years later just failed to win support after long and arduous debate, namely the creation of a new diocese in the Thames Valley? Anyway I begged off. True, Portsmouth was on the uttermost edge of the mainland. The Diocese, however, did not end with the land. Beyond the Isle of Wight, the Channel Islands sprawled deeply south. I had every intention of launching into those sea-girt depths. With the best will in the world old John Henry's visits there could not have been frequent. But in fairness to his unrelaxed concern for his diocese, let it be recorded that any letter from a priest was sure of his hand-written reply by the next post. He had striven during the war years to cope with confirmations and visitation of parishes, travelling on public transport with two heavy bags, often crushed in corridors of trains chock-a-block with service personnel. He was already in his sixties when he succeeded as bishop of the diocese. I had joined him when he was eighty. How often, particularly at priest's funerals, I was to hear him say: "My trouble is I can't die. But, Tom, I'll be next." He was still going four years later when, feeling an awful cad despite the thrill of returning north, I left him. He died within the year.

His earth rests now, one with Winchester's, in the consecrated acre which, in harmony with his family background through all the years of discord, heard none but the old familiar prayers. That the last and noblest burden to be laid there was kindred clay, seems to me yet another "portent worthy of a cry".

Towards the end of John Henry's long life he received a letter from a landowner in the diocese whose family gave two Venerable Martyrs to the Catholic cause in the first years of the seventeenth century. Assuming that the Archbishop was thinking of a successor, the letter ventures to offer the name of one "who would be supremely faithful to the spirit in which their beloved father in God had hitherto ruled the diocese, the spirit so admirably expressed in his motto: *"Amor vincit omnia."*

May I leave that as his panegyric? I cannot remember if one was preached at his funeral. It would be like him to have forbidden it. I do remember being told that he chose his motto, thinking it was from Holy Writ, and cheerfully stuck to it when he learned the source* was not so edifying. That, too, would have been very like him.

* Chaucer's Canterbury Tales: Prologue.

CHAPTER XL

Sisters Far and Wide

ONCE the clergy, despite all appearances to the contrary, rumbled the essential "Tweedledum-Tweedledee" relationship between John Henry and the northerner, I was home and dry. The handsome clergy gesture which equipped me, all unseen, with the means of circulating the diocese, is evidence of their loyalty to the Holy See. It was not long before I experienced what every bishop would prize as the most valuable and the least deserved of all his assets, namely, the personal loyalty of the priests. I hope I have made it abundantly clear that in my case this was an overflow from their devotion to John Henry.

Territorially the diocese was big and very beautiful. I was to leave it for one a quarter of the size, which despite smokeless zones still showed the effects of the Industrial Revolution more pitifully, perhaps, than ever in its decline and fall. But both dioceses had roughly the same total population, about two and a half million, and the same ratio of priests to people. The difference was Portsmouth over an area four times the size of the Salford diocese had half the total number of Catholics served by slightly more than half the number of parishes. Portsmouth however was well ahead in the number of religious Sisters and for a number of reasons I decided to give them priority in visitating the diocese. One way or another John Henry had maintained contact with his priests. I could also count on their approaching me for all manner of occasions connected with their parishes, schools and deaneries, and not least, given the hospitable nature of the two mainland societies of priests*, warm-hearted conviviality.

I mugged up on Canon Law (never my *forte*) on the visitation of religious houses, and gradually worked around them all. At that time, noviciates teemed with lively aspirants, convent chapels over-flowed with supplementary accommodation. A single day, however long, would not always sufficce for all one needed to do.

I remember moving to a convent chapel for the closing ceremony as the shades of night were falling. A famous film of the Normandy Landings was circulating at the time. As I staggered up the middle aisle the Sisters rose to their feet and from one of the novices' benches came a crisp whisper: "The Longest Day". It is, I think, the only time the congregation has come to my rescue with the right text at the critical moment.

Active Religious Orders and Congregations male and female

* Entitled respectively "Berkshire Boars" and "Hampshire Hogs".

assured the diocese of an enviable response to educational and social needs. Nor were the claims of contemplation less generously met. Three male Benedictine Congregations were matched by three different families of Benedictine Sisters; Clare of Assisi and Teresa of Avila rejoiced the local city of God with their daughters' prayers and penances.

The French Revolution and subsequent rabid anti-clericals like M. Combes had endowed the dioceses along the South Coast with emigré religious foundations which we in the North never knew. Our compensation came by way of immigrant laity from Ireland in the "Hungry Forties" and a vast network of new parishes. By then of course, but only a dozen years earlier, in 1829 Catholic Emancipation had transformed us from a *"gens lucifuga"** to a community of broad day church builders, bell ringers and school openers. Missioners from the continent were actually walking through English cities and counties in religious habits.

As typical of earlier penal days I recall a brace of emigré communities in Berkshire. They had met for the first time on a dark night in mid-Channel when their vessels collided. The instinct to avoid observation in a country still hostile to all they stood for brought them together again as owners of properties at Hungerford and Goodings only a mile or so apart in an area of farms and forests.

Like the Lanherne Carmelites in Plymouth diocese, Goodings possessed a remarkable treasury of relics of the English Martyrs, including one of Blessed Thomas Holland. One's old colleague of C.M.S. days, Father Frank Ripley, was chaplain to Goodings at that time, allegedly taking things easy after an operation. Trust Frank! He delivered to the Sisters a series of "Elevations"† on John I, 1-14— the "Last Gospel" of the pre-conciliar Mass. He later published them‡. They are very good indeed. It was from him I learned of a curious detail concerning the Goodings property.

Enclosed convents on the continent usually contain a very large garden area within their high walls. Without it the health of the community could be in jeopardy. I don't know how the nuns at Goodings were accommodated abroad but when they settled in Berkshire they wisely acquired a property in its own spacious domain. Whether or not they ever hoped to build the surrounding wall, they satisfied Canon Law theoretically by declaring the property *en bloc* to be Canonical Enclosure. Thus Sisters driving tractors some distance from the convent were still, it seems, at least *in voto*, within canonical limits. Once a year, however, "enclosure" would be invaded by public spirited men in Norfolk jackets. I hasten to say their sole purpose was to safeguard ancient rights of way which would have lapsed for ever without their determined annual effort.

At last the wind of change was rustling through our national

* "A people shunning the light": Newman, *Second Spring.*
† Bossuet's word.
‡ *The Last Gospel,* The Catholic Book Club 1961.

system of education at this time. The earliest and most copious entries in my diary are to do with schools: discussion with clergy about new schools, new patterns of existing schools, visits to schools and local and county Directors. These last I found, despite our modest percentage of the scholastic population, extremely fair-minded men. The County Deputy Director, a Mr. Birtwhistle* from Lancashire, was in full command during his chief's frequent absences abroad as adviser on our national system of education. I remember once coming away from the Deputy's office, having agreed with him a large comprehensive school to be sited equidistant from several nuclei of population, itself, however, in rolling country. Access by bus for all the pupils to be met by the County was fine and dandy. How the diocese was to meet our share of the capital cost (15%) was another matter. I left the office marvelling at myself. It was the first time I had heard hundreds of thousands of pounds tossed around. Later, in Salford, one was to sleep easily o' nights under school debts running into seven figures of money.

The Portsmouth Director, a Mr. Barnard, was equally open-handed. We got a fine senior school on programme in no time. One of the parish priests proposed we should add from our own resources a swimming bath of standard championship size. He quoted the cost. "You must be joking", came from many mouths. Far from it. He argued a powerful case. Many clubs in Hampshire were looking for a championship bath. They would pay big money for training sessions and big events. He persuaded all but the local parish priest. No child of his would co-operate in such folly by using the thing. The vote, however, went against him and the bath was built. On completion it was found to be short of the international length by a matter of inches. Automatically disqualified.

"Stakes", St. Michael's Convent Grammar School over the hill at Waterlooville, drew these comments in the diary: "Modern. Forward-looking. *Very* large community. Rolling country. Grammar kids now coming through. More building required. Physics Lab. already open." I have a horrible memory of a Sports Day I was to open there at 3 p.m. one year. Whatever went wrong at the northern end of the diocese to delay me, it was gone 4 p.m. when I arrived. Clearly I should have 'phoned telling them to get on with it. They were still waiting and no sooner had they begun than the cataracts of heaven opened and the whole event was washed out.

The Ladies of Mary ran a very fine Teachers' Training College in our neighbouring diocese of Southwark. Their presence, again up the hill from Pompey, greatly strengthened our educational re-sources not least, I think, by way of the extra goodwill prestige wins from local administrators. Our priest in that area, Father Troy, was pressing hard for a City Youth Club. So were the younger priests.

* Not, it seems, a familiar name in the deep south. The wife of one of Birtwhistle's staff told me of the horror with which she heard her husband, the first time they met the new deputy addressing Mr "Whistle" by his first name.

Enquiry Classes for people interested in the Faith and a diocesan Youth Rally also figure on the agenda. My diary records meetings and discussions galore. Indeed it was good to have been there in that particular time. I can't say all our objectives were taken. What came home to me was the keenness and the competence of the clergy. In a diocese physically so beautiful and relaxing, one might have expected a certain tendency to sit back in sleepy hollows and eat the lotus.

John Henry's diamond jubilee as a priest greatly surprised the old man. He had no idea of the esteem and affection in which he was held by clergy and laity alike. The celebrations alerted him to resources any bishop might hesitate to claim. He just could not believe he had so much talent and energy behind him. The cheque he received completely bowled him over. One anonymous well-wisher put in £10,000. In fairness, however, I must testify he was more moved by the boys and girls of the diocese who gathered round him with little more than their love and their joy plus an illuminated scroll assuring him of both. I can see him now straining to catch the words as it was read. I don't think he got many of them.

All this time I was working through the Ceremonial of Bishops as an absolute beginner: confirmations, professions and receptions of religious, blessing of foundation stones, consecration of churches, altars and chalices. The liturgical reforms of Vatican II have simplified them out of all knowledge, in some cases no longer reserving them to bishops.

At the consecration of our new church in south Oxford, the bishop began with the recitation of the seven Penitential Psalms in the sacristy. I was still far from the end of the ceremonies in the church when out of the mouth of a small boy came: "Oh mummy! It's too long." I think he spoke for many more than himself.

A lot of Oxford clergy had previously gathered for the blessing of the foundations of that particular church, an evening ceremony under a menacing sky. Shamefully I had prepared no sermon but at least was honest enough to ask for a volunteer. One of the Dominicans agreed at once. As we emerged, once again the cataracts of heaven broke and down came the rain. I decided to see it through. Clergy and people sought shelter under the eaves, in sheds and anywhere and sang at appropriate moments. The M.C. alone accompanied me round the rising walls, back and forth, blessing and praying. We left nothing out. I was wearing the white mitre for the first time. It proved to be the last. The whole thing was pulped beyond repair. Archbishop O'Hara replaced it with one of his which I have now worn on white mitre occasions for more than a quarter of a century. I have just looked for the name of the Chicago firm which was stamped in gold letters inside. It's not there. The band, no doubt disfigured by honest episcopal sweat, has been replaced. Nuns do these things so secretly. As with God's providence, one doesn't say thank you.

CHAPTER XLI

Voyaging South

THE DIOCESE, I remarked earlier, does not end with the mainland, a fact which added weight to my choice of anchorage on the Solent rather than the Thames, as suggested by John Henry.

During the Marian Year 1954 Father John Troy, then parish priest of Ryde, invited a C.M.S. priest to give a week of talks on Our Blessed Lady. Hence my first visit to the I.O.W. I arrived at Ryde pier after dark, well content for once to finish my journey by sea and by starlight. A good omen: the week went well.

Six years later Father Joe's curate, Father Dermot McDermot-Roe was to gallop from lunch to warn the diocese of my appointment to Portsmouth. The three of us that week were mercifully free of all such worries, free, too, since this was not a parish mission, of the arduous duty of flogging round the houses. Only now do I realise it must have been the most relaxed week I ever spent in the diocese.

Who was the statistician who calculated the whole population of the world could stand on the I.O.W.? Certainly they couldn't choose a lovelier site to wreck. I can't say that week opened up all the island's beauty-spots between Alfred Noyes' Orchard Bay on the East Coast and Squire Ward's Totland Bay on the West. I still have to pay homage at Tennyson's Faringford for all I own to the kindred pleasures of poetry and cricket. I am presuming here that the heroic Hon. Lionel Tennyson, Captain of Hampshire and England half a century ago, had some link with that noble house.

I was delighted to discover on the island priests ordained for other dioceses whose harsh winters they could no longer safely stand. Their presence witnessed to a benign climate and a benign bishop who gladly welcomed them and made them parish priests. A bomb fell in the chancel of one of our churches in the middle of the island. The only benign interpretation of that phenomenon is a shockingly bad shot for Portsmouth Naval Yard. But as a contrast to war and its rain of destruction the island offered consoling evidence of success in one important sector of the endless duel between life and death. Huge T.B. hospitals on the east coast were now empty.

I have very muddled memories of our numerous religious foundations in the island. The two O.S.B. Abbeys are exceptions. Quarr over the years has gallantly let me back for retreats which were never complete without the interlude at St. Cecilia's Ryde which was always sure to surprise.

On my first visit (ever memorable for the swelling sound of bells as I approached) a member of the community handed me a letter at the grill. The handwriting was familiar. It was mine alright: a thank-you letter for "sheltering" me in 1944, addressed to the good nun's mother. Normandy? A storm in Devonshire? On another occasion a bevy of postulants from India came forward to be presented. They would return after appropriate training to the sub-continent with the Pax which civilised Europe. Twenty-five years later I still receive greetings from Lahore and Kerala, O.S.B. monasteries. Finally there was a profession I was privileged to preside at in which the daughter of a well known non-Catholic family received the veil. An attractive career opened before her in the world. Now behind her lie twenty odd years of the Rule of St. Benedict and ahead the Peace which surpasses all understanding.

Abbot Tissot of Quarr had a hobby by which I was soon to benefit. It was on my first visit to Quarr I learned that in tracing my ancestry as a bishop he could get no further than Cambrai in the early sixteenth century. This was not because there was any fatal gap. Cambrai was just not answering his letters. This is not to conclude that the abbot was a dessicated scholar on the evidence of this quaint hobby. Two other tracers of episcopal pedigrees have since spontaneously offered me the fruit of their researches. One, a Viennese, to judge by his copious correspondence has all the warmth and sparkle of his native city. He has compiled the pedigrees of 8,000 bishops. I guess that Tissot was a Norman—small, tough and bright as a button. He went back to Solesmes, his monastic cradle, towards the end of my time in Portsmouth. Well into his eighties he had no intention of putting his feet up. Later on my regular visits to Normandy, Father Maurice Graindor, my host, often proposed a day at Solesmes. Abbot Tissot, one discovered, had become chaplain to the neighbouring monastery of Benedictine nuns, his great joy being to sing their early community Mass. He must have been little short of a century by this time.

The whole Solesmes community was evicted no less than four times from their monastery between 1883 and 1905. The fourth time involved, along with robbery under law of their monasteries, the eviction of religious from France. Hence the transmigration of Solesmes to the Isle of Wight. Their first haven was Appuldurcombe. Father John Henry King was then a young curate at Portsmouth Cathedral. The exiles welcomed him and his choirboys on the occasion of the Cathedral servers' and singers' annual excursion day.* In all innocence the good monks regaled their guests with the hospitality they would accord on a similar occasion in

---

* I wonder if the trip had anything to do with the revival of Plain Chant which was both pioneered and perfected by Solesmes, not without clashes within the community itself over the interpretation of the musical signs in medieval manuscripts. Two schools emerged each headed by a Solesmes monk. Both Dom Pothier and Dom Moquereau were emigrés at Appuldurcombe.

France. Despite their conviction that a not too distant day would see them return to their beloved monastery in the Sarthe, they determined to provide a worthy setting for the sacred mysteries and the *"opus Dei"** on alien soil. How early came the generous resolve to benefit the land which had welcomed them with a permanent OSB foundation? That is for historians. I have the more congenial duty of rendering homage to the magnanimity of the project. I forget how many bricks were used. Within their own very different medium they have a strength and suppleness comparable with the work of the medieval stonemasons. I wonder, however, why every one of those bricks was floated across the Channel from the Netherlands? Could our English brick so far reflect our national temperament as to refuse the supple uses required by the Benedictine architect's brilliant design? He, of course, was not British.

In God's good time the exiles returned to France. Solesmes recovered its old rhythm in its own native splendour. Indeed the last time I was at Vespers there, the procession into the choir was never so impressive for the ranks of young monks mounting the stalls. Meanwhile Quarr became a priory retaining a nucleus of French monks around whom it was hoped an English community would develop from its own native resources into an indigenous Abbey. The Prior chosen to preside over the process was a remarkable man. For a whole year I sat in the Beda refectory next to a man from Ryde who was a convert of his. He had been active in local politics and was fancied for promotion on his "gift of the gab" and shrewdness in debate. More importantly, perhaps, he had lost a leg in the Gallipoli campaign and proved his physical resources by surviving nineteen operations.

The Prior's reasoning powers as demonstrated in the course of instruction which led to conversion and, not without irony, to a vocation as a secular priest, bowled the neophyte completely over. Nor had the passage of time in any way reduced the impact, judging by the constant theme of his table talk. I learned *inter alia* how the Prior had, again with supreme logic, paced his own progress in researching the English temperament. He regarded this as the key to the successful performance of his duty to recruit and retain aspirants to the monastic life at Quarr. For instance, he crouched at Lords Cricket Ground to study yet another kind of "bowling overs". Some wiseacre had assured him he would there plumb the essential differences between the Gallic and Brittanic temperaments.

The seal of approval on his pioneer work came with Quarr's elevation to the status of Abbey and the appointment of Dom Aelred Sillem as the first English Abbot. Dom Joseph Warrilow, his Prior, has cradled me through several retreats. I could not say how much I owe him and love him.

* "Work of God" in OSB and Church parlance is the divine office. St. Benedict's Rule: "Nothing must come before the *opus Dei*."

CHAPTER XLII

Southerly Airborne

JERSEY clergy welcomed my first landing at St. Helier *en masse* and on the airport apron. Attendance on the Apostolic Delegate had familiarised me with official receptions at airports. This was a different experience. There was no Great Man behind whom I could trail.

Canon Olney of St. Mary and St. Peter, our diocesan senior priest and the OMI rector of St. Thomas, Father Verkin, each headed a fairly equal number of priests. Their two churches stand very close to each other. St. Thomas's represented the French presence impressively enough to be popularly known as "The Cathedral". I had prepared myself for the problem of two different Catholic cultures on the same terrain, and had no intention of broaching it on my first appearance. In fact when I did broach it months later at a Confirmation in the "Cathedral", I burned my fingers rather badly.

It was the Oblates' Superior who advised me that the OMI Council was planning to reduce its commitments in the Channel Islands and that the "Cathedral" might be soon vacated and offered to the diocese. He also thought it prudent to prepare the people. The Confirmation shortly due to take place would ensure an appropriate congregation for the announcement. The amiable theory that the two clergies each had a totally distinct constituency to serve, OMIs native French speakers, diocesan priests English, was only partly true.

A little history may help to see things in perspective. The Channel Islands yielded to the Tudor Reformation with neither a bang nor a whimper. They silently caved in. Catholic life ceased to exist. But later was there not inconsiderable immigration from France, mainly Hugenots? I may have jumped too easily to the conclusion that French surnames in the Islands meant Protestant families. This was very often the case, but on the other hand the drastically depleted ranks of Catholics speaking English swelled in the last century with the importation of Irish labour for the construction of the harbours. Here, too, as in Lancashire and elsewhere the workers settled down for good.

French, it is true, is widely used in the Islands. I wonder, however, if there are any permanent residents who are not bi-lingual? Those perhaps who still use the Old Norman Patois perhaps—but how many are they? But ultimately the issue is not one of language but of the more subtle cultural values of ethos, presence and *Patrie.*

The Channel Islands, oddly enough, came to Britain by way of the Norman Conquest. They came under British rule not as part of the United Kingdom but as fiefs of the Duchy of Normandy of which our sovereigns are Dukes. When Her Majesty is carried through the tide to land in the Islands she is hailed as "Duke of Normandy". Ecclesiastically, the Islands had formerly belonged to the diocese of Coutances. I took it therefore as a singular gesture of goodwill when the Bishop, Louis Guyot, invited me to stand in for him at the *Pardon* of Granville. In those days indifferent health confined him to his bed or forced him back to his home in the Bordelais. Later, as Archbishop of Tolouse, he became a Cardinal. A saintlier or more humble bishop you could not meet even at a plenary session of Vatican II.

The Dean of Granville, Canon Georges Hyenard, was for many years bishop's secretary in the days when letters to bishops began "Votre Grandeur". There was nothing of the today, however, about this one-time palace factotum. What had come through was a sense of good form and a mastery of prompt and efficient response. I have rarely met a man able and ready to serve in so many capacities. In the liberation of France he was a foot soldier under fire at Ste. Mère Eglise. He fired back in self-defence, hoping he had not killed*.

He put up my sister at the presbytery with his mother, a sweet lady in her nineties. She was relieved of all culinary duties by her highly competent son. He is now in his eighties, living retired at Cherbourg, still driving his car, and still active among the pots and pans. For over a quarter of a century my brother and I have profited by his supreme artistry in that department, first at Saint Saveur le Vicomte where he was chaplain to the Mother House of the Sisters of St. Marie-Madeleine Pastel, and latterly at his tiny house in the Rue Emile Zola, Cherbourg. We dare not leave the Continent after our annual holiday by any other port! But who in his right mind would want to miss the best meal in all Gaul?†

To the table he has since invited others for the renewal of old friendships: M. Georges Delange the Pharmacist of Granville who put us up during the *Pardon*, but alas, not the tycoon millionaire master baker M. Madeleine who put up the finance for the more splendid celebration of the *Fêtes* connected with the *Pardon*. He

* My brother and sister accompanied me to the Granville *Pardon*. The three of us were invited by the C.O. to a regimental reception. On the table as I write lies a treasured souvenir of the event: a shapely leather tag for buttoning on the tunic. The metal badge of 'L Rima' is superimposed on an anchor and carrying the *Croix de Guerre* (ribbon gules) at the stock and the coveted *Croix de Lorraine* at the shank. The whole device impaled over a globe. That day Canon Hyenard took us in his little car all round the coast of the Cotentin. We got back to Granville only minutes before we were due at the regimental reception. The Canon disapeared and re-appeared in a flash no longer wearing the soutane, but in the uniform of L Rima. Breathtaking!

† 1986—alas our preliminary phone-call from Argentan failed to raise him. Don't however, presume bad news! Brother and I phoned again from the Place du Voeux in Cherbourg (where we dined simply but surrounded with great courtesy in the local bistro). No answer! However a visit to the great Church of the Vow showed him still on the list of priests. We have been in touch by post since.

made his pile during the German occupation of the Channel Islands, being the only baker allowed by the invaders to supply them from the mainland with the staff of life and "toastes", which, I take it, are the equivalent of our "rusks". So successful was his line of biscuits, that after the war you could see his sign all over Western France. He dined us at La Beaumonderie, his château on the road north to Cherbourg, wearing his wife's bigoudon most of the time. The hope was I would mediate with Bishop Guyot to secure the privilege of regular Mass in the splendid chapel he had built and furnished in his domain.

The *Pardon* came to a lamplit conclusion on the quais after a procession through the town in which the Isles Chaucey fishermen paraded with their boat and their Curé, an unconventional, greatly loved figure wearing a thick jersey and a very thick beard. The liturgical blessings were amplified on loud speakers round the port. At the very end I wished all good night. On later visits I discovered that "good night" had expanded into a brilliant discourse. Sheer legend! All I said was "Good night and God bless". I did speak, however, at the official lunch the following day. The Bishop of Laval was there on this occasion precisely, I feel sure, to spare me the duty of speaking. The blackleg, however, excused himself and left before the dessert. As my brother remarked later, it was a useful object lesson for episcopal greenhorns. The speeches dragged on interminably.

The *Pardon* inaugurated a very happy *entente cordial* with the diocese of Coutances. On one of my later visits I had to get across to Guernsey rather unexpectedly. Who should come to the rescue but Madeleine's son with his executive plane. Canon Hyenard providentially joined us for the trip. We flew down to St. Malo. It seems international flights can leave only from qualified airports. Our instructions were to fly north along the coast as far as Carteret, turn west and seek permission to land as you approach Guernsey.

I was in the back seat wearing the ear phones, from time to time transmitting our Code Sign. Replies came in a totally unknown jargon, basically English I think, but double Dutch to me. We were inexorably closing on Guernsey. Quick as lightning the Canon plucked the apparatus out of my limp control and brought it within reach of our pilot. To his surprise we were being given immediate access and coasted comfortably to the appointed bay. I admit near panic as we were being talked down and all depended on my useless ears. Madeleine's enterprise was eventually swallowed by Biscuits Nantois. Shrewd observers saw it coming: "The son isn't a patch on the father." Thank God he was a jolly good aviator!

CHAPTER XLIII

A Cluster of Islands

A FEW miles north of the Norman town of Argentan, where Henry II uttered wild words leading to Murder in the Cathedral, there is an ancient farmhouse whose origins may well be contemporary with the royal outburst. A brisk stream separates garden from woodland. On the north bank is the tiny chapel where daily Mass is said. The property is named in Greek "House of Mary". Thither each year, by the grace of God and favour of my old wartime friend l'Abbe Graindor, go brother and I. Each evening closes with music. The *châtelaine* is a concert pianist. She rises from the keyboard to pick up violin or sit to 'cello at appropriate moments against a recorded background. Her library contains all Kathleen Ferrier's recordings and much of what has been written about her. Players and listeners are alike regaled throughout the sessions with a local distillation served in tiny shining goblets. Two (or at most three for those who live *fortissimo*) when drunk *adagio molto* enhance musical appreciation: more could swamp it. For this is "Calva". Not the Calvados marketed under endearing titles backed by heavy publicity. This has never moved far from the parent orchard. It has reached this final, general expression of fruitfulness by way of scrupulous fidelity to a very ancient ritual. Years have passed since it was first distilled. Any travel it has since undertaken would be within a tight circle of friends and probably by night and by tractor, or the farm-vehicle least likely to arouse suspicion.

So far this chapter must look like a "moonlight flit" from the work in hand, my years of service in the Channel Islands. It may help to bring things into focus if I first identify the old farmhouse as the home in which my friend, Father M. Graindor, lives now in retirement. The *châtelaine*, of course, is his cousin Dr. Marie Madeleine Roblot.

When Maurice was developing his revolutionary theory on the pre-cambrian landmass of Normandy, his fieldwork broadened at one point to take in the Isles Normandes. The ensuing thesis which embodied years of research upset all previous conclusions*. Recog-

---

* The final link came to light as he waded downstream searching for the tell tale outcrop of rock in the river bank. In his knapsack along with the hammer etc. lay the day's rations. Suddenly there it was. His hunch had not misled him. He clambered ashore, extracted the wine and poured out the lot in a thanksgiving libation. It went of course down his throat; he is a Norman. Later geologists now lead students to venerate the spot. For Maurice, however, the cherished accolade came when the doyen of European geologists, M. Lugeon, stood at his side and saw for himself. *"Monsieur l'Abbe,"* he said. *"Chapeau!"* and uncovered his head.

nition came domestically with a fellowship at the *College de France*. He has since represented his country at international geological conferences and was in fact so engaged at Prague when the Russian tanks poured in.

Unpredictably he found himself in command of a flotilla of boats in the Bay of St. Malo when called in as consultant on the abortive project to harness the tides with a barrage. Of all the Channel Islands I think Guernsey was handiest from his mainland base. I hope his research there proved helpful. Otherwise I have intruded my dear friend's saga illogically at this point.

Guernsey, however, has a tenuous link with the ambrosial beverage which accompanies the music at Maurice's Norman farmhouse, Calvados. The most widely advertised commercial version is marketed under the trade name of "Pere Magloire". Now Saint Magloire is the patron of Guernsey. The story as told to me by an Irish priest in Guernsey, is that on his feast day, 24th October, they sing an accommodated version of a popular hymn to St. Patrick:

"Hail glorious Saint Maglorious,
dear Saint of our Isle.
On Guernsey's greenhouses
look down with thy smile."

Ben trovato, I fear! This great missioner, one of the Celtic companions of Saints Sampson and Illtyd, remains simply Magloire in English as in French. There is a chapel-of-ease dedicated to him at Lislet.

When visiting Guernsey I usually stayed at Our Lady Star of the Sea in St. Sampson with Canon Francis Phillips, an old boy of the Portsmouth Salesian College for which he had composed the school anthem. One evening when I was to give Confirmation in his parish I suddenly noticed how shockingly unkempt my head was. There was just time to get to a barber. He was shaving and there were others round the walls. "You're next" said he, noticing my hesitation. "These loafers are only here to gas." And gas they did at the expense of the customer in the chair, gravely computing the months, nay years, since his face had been cleared of fungus. He took it in good part as one well used to being the butt. Relieved of the sheet and smiling at them all, he said: "Aye! But this time it's worth it. It's my bishop will see me tonight!" I kept my head down until the sheet in turn covered me.

I got back to the presbytery for lunch one day to be told the Apostolic Delegation would 'phone me at 2 o'clock. My kindly host added somewhat cryptically: "I hope it's not what we suspect." If he was referring to me in the context of the vacant metropolitan see, of course he was up the pole. One had to leave him there. The call was in fact *sub secreto*.

Guernsey's Church of Our Lady and St. Joseph and Notre Dame du Rosaire, Burnt Lane, match Jersey's St. Mary and St. Peter and the "Cathedral" as the Island's main English and French "presence".

219

Both are at St. Peter Port. They serve a remarkable constellation of religious foundations: Les Vaubelets (de la Salle), Platon (Hospitaller Sisters), Les Cotils (Presentation Sisters), Mt. Pleasant (Congregation des Saints Coeurs de Jesus et Marie). The Sisters of Mercy with two communities provided a Kindergarten for girls and boys at Cordier Hill and a Boarding and Day School for girls at Blanchlands, St. Martin's. Each of those names strikes chords of memory. The sound grows fainter with the years. Blanchlands, however, loses none of its resonance. Of all the diocesan sites I visited in these seagirt islands, Blanchlands remains for sheer beauty the freshest and fondest in memory. As you circled the perimeter you had glimpses of the sea below and the shelving cliffs. You heard the rustle of the tide and saw it cream on the rocks.

Blanchlands, however, is more memorable for a beauty which nature may mirror but never rival. I saw the beauty of holiness. This pearl of great price was to be found, by God's good grace, not in one single oyster, if I may so refer to a religious community; honestly, there were no empty shells. Yet, maybe because of her finding time to keep contact over the years by post (no mean achievement for the Mother of the community and principal of a boarding and day school), the memory of Mother Mary Ethelburga continues to be a kindly light and by the same token a demanding one.

The expulsion of religious communities which brought the Benedictines to Quarr and enriched the southern counties of England with religious sisters and brothers, failed to move the Jesuits out of sight of *la doulce France*. They established themselves in the Channel Islands with their schools and professors of the sacred sciences and resumed the dedicated service of scholarship which I had so much opportunity to admire at the Greg in Rome. A challenging study of Hylomorphism by one of the philosophy professors soon appeared to rivet the attention of Catholic Faculties throughout the world.

Once the crude anticlerical laws were repealed, no time was lost in resuming the even tenor of life back on the mainland. In my time only one French Jesuit remained in Guernsey, Father Rey. I imagine his services to the whole community were too valuable to be dispensed with. He was the meteorologist in charge of the observatory. Sprucely dressed, *distingué* in speech and manner, and sporting a trim Van Dyke beard; could France wish for a staff showing the *Tricouleur* to greater advantage?

Be that as it may, it was the recently appointed parish priest of the French church of S. Pierre Port, Maurice Lecluze, who, all things to all men, made the French presence an ever inspiring vehicle of cordial understanding. When the Bishop of Ports-mouth recently honoured his twenty-five years pastoral service in Guernsey with a canonry the trumpets sounded on every side. Before ordination by Bishop Louis Guyot of Coutances he had qualified as a dental surgeon. I seem to remember there were similar instances of this mutation among the late vocations at the Beda. Both dentists and priests have at times to inflict pain to get rid of it. Both must be gentle in manner but firm in fact. If true to their calling, they learn, each after their fashion, to respect the weaknesses of their clients and without betraying or compromising their duty, to temper the wind to the shorn lamb.

The analogy is, of course, not confined to this particular brace of professions. It still allows me, I think, to discern in Maurice Lecluze a certain natural coherence in his development towards maturity, and goes some way to explain why, with God's good grace, he became "all things to all men".

He brought "Maman" with him to Guernsey. On all the festive occasions at Notre Dame du Rosaire, Burnt Lane (or Ruelle Brulee) "Maman" sat in the seat of honour at the great banquet which always rounded off the day, and was graced with the noblest tribute in our host's after-dinner speech and not without tears. On these occasions his guests from the mainland were France's élite, men well-known for their faith and heroic loyalty to *la Patrie*, men one had longed to meet. How Maurice managed to get them is his secret. No doubt the prestige of the French presence and the showing of the *Tricouleur* were major incentives. How otherwise explain the final touch to the re-ordering of Notre Dame du Rosaire, the arrival of the Bells? They left France for Guernsey in no "dirty British coaster with a salt-caked smoke-stack": a shining French cruiser wearing an admiral's flag put them dramatically ashore just in time for their baptism and anointing.

Alderney is the nearest and the smallest of the "big three" Channel Islands. There is only one parish and in my days there was only one priest, Father Jim Murray. The S.C.J. Fathers of Betharam have since taken over on behalf of the Diocese.

Alderney belongs to the bailywick of Guernsey, but rejoiced in possessing its own President and administrative officers. I say "rejoiced" since in those days the President, M. Herivel, a highly festive character, jealously maintained all the island's ancient rights and privileges—indeed all that gave it its own distinctive Norman character. Lawyers in other islands may no longer learn their trade at the University of Caen. If the Herivel tradition survives, Alderney will still dispatch her lawmen there at least for a semester or two. The law of the islands still rests on old Norman customs. I wonder if the *"Clameur de Haro"* is still effective at least in Alderney? In virtue of a law based on old Norman custom an aggrieved citizen could get an instant hearing of his complaint by shouting in a public place: *"Haro, mon prince! On me fait tort!"**

Our early brag that we would not yield an inch of British territory to Gerry was grievously deflated by the occupation of the Channel Islands. Anyone who witnessed our return, even on TV, can never forget those scenes of ecstatic relief. Sixteen years, however, had

* "Haro (hue and cry). My Prince! I am being wronged!"

softened the sharper edges of the ordeal for most people when I arrived. One heard more of the lighter deeds of derring-do: for example the concealment of an Alderney bull-calf itself unaware that the discomfort of years without seeing the light was an heroic and indispensible contribution to saving the island breed. I even heard Gerry being awarded a light pat on the back for daily letting Madeleine's rusks in from the mainland for the children in arms.

I fear I made no visit to Sark, Herm, Jethon, Liton and Brecqhon all, like Alderney, dependencies on the bailiwick of Guernsey, which also claims Ecrehon Rocks and the long disputed Minquiers. Once the diocese did allow a priest to winter at Sark. Never again to my knowledge. I regret to say it was not any effect of Nature's elements that made the experiment unjustifiable.

During World War I sharp eyes took note of suspicious lights on Herm at night. They traced them to a house in which two ladies lived, a Princess and a Countess. They both had the German name Blücher and were in some way connected with the General, later Prince, who made a useful appearance on the field of Waterloo, and who later, at the victory celebrations in London, remarked: "What a fine city to sack!" Nothing was proved but the ladies were "invited" to leave Herm. They moved to an imposing chateau in Guernsey. There Canon Phillips and I were invited to tea during one of my visits. From the entrance hall we were ushered to the first floor where the ladies received us. By this time it was clear that the wide façade screened a very narrow house one room deep. But what a treasure house! It was only too clear that General Blücher had a good day's looting after Waterloo. Archbishop Cowderoy of Southwark, our neighbour, an ardent collector of "Napoleonana" regarded the house in Guernsey as the foremost napoleonic shrine this side of the Channel. I could see why, for against the walls stood rows of chairs, First Empire every one, all upholstered in silk bearing the 'N' monogram, and all as fresh as new. During tea we learned the covers in fact were new. The Princess told the story. It had been high time the originals were replaced. She had sent samples of the material pretty well all round the world. None of the French looms could do the job—not even Lyons. The only 'yes' came from Leningrad. The work was perfect, said the Princess.

And now let me sail hundreds of miles north and more than a few decades back in time to childhood and the Lancashire coast.

On the promenade at the point nearest to the Church* and the School† of St. Marie's-on-the-Sands, there stands a magnificent proof of the enterprise and foresight of Lancashire cotton operatives at the turn of the century when the going was really good. It is a large convalescent home built in the finest materials the county could provide. The long façade faces the sea. The building stands proudly in its own spacious grounds. My earliest memories of it go back to 1914 and the arrival there of wounded Belgian soldiers. We would dash to the Prom from school at 4 p.m. to see them.

Communication was difficult but mutual kindness got through. Witness the little souvenir long since lost: a tunic button cut off and presented *sans paroles* one autumn afternoon by a smiling Belgian solider in a wheel-chair.

The medical superintendent of that hospital some time later was a certain Colonel Dorgan, an Irishman married to a lady of the Stapleton-Bretherton family‡. They rose to fame and fortune in the heyday of the stage-coach and became considerable landowners in Lancashire. Munificent benefactors of the Society of Jesus, *inter alia* they built the great Jesuit Church of St. Bartholomew at Rainhill where the Liverpool to Manchester road bends South.

Mrs Colonel Dorgan's sister married Prince Blücher and became herself a Princess. The Blücher family were the first Germans to be officially "received" in England after the First War.

Was the Stapleton-Bretherton Princess Blücher the lady who came under suspicion at Herm? Was that official reception (I presume at Court) the *amende honorable* for those groundless suspicions and the ensuing displacement to Guernsey for closer surveillance?

At the time we were invited to tea, I was in no position to put questions of that kind to our charming hostesses. Now I suppose the answers could be easily found from a variety of sources. I prefer not to ask. Who wants to imperil a cherished link, however *recherché*, twixt the coast of one's childhood and the Isles of the Hesperides? Not I for one!

* Where I made my first Confession (to Canon Turner), my first Holy Communion, and was confirmed (by the saintly Archbishop Whiteside), ordained priest (by Archbishop Downey), and said my first Mass (19.6.33).
† Where I enjoyed the priceless boon of seven years tuition by the Selly Park Sisters.
‡ The gallant Colonel was dearly loved by patients and the staff of the Convalescent Home. He died there as Sunday evening service was in progress in the room below. They were singing "Abide with Me"—his favourite hymn. He was all heart. My father was at his post as usual at the door of St. Marie's on one occasion when the Colonel entered and drew out his wallet. The collection was for S.V.P. charities. A handful of notes landed on the plate. He was then heard to say "Arrah! Go on with you!" The wallet went back empty.

CHAPTER XLIV

Oversights and Overseeing

ALTHOUGH Vatican II opened halfway through my stint in Portsmouth*, the Secretariate for the Promotion of Christian Unity was early off the mark in the preparatory stages with copious paperwork and meetings abroad. Less time consuming but a distraction nevertheless was membership of C.R.A.C.† Clearly one had to keep an eye or ear open for certain programmes if one was to contribute to the twice-yearly "summit" meetings. Luckily for those of us whose Sunday duties robbed all chance of viewing the more relevant output, the evening before the meeting one could catch up on programmes likely to come up on the next day. But proportional representation on C.R.A.C. gave us few places. Anglicans predominated. Among their clergy I was glad to meet my future opposite number in Manchester Bishop Greer and my former 1944 opposite number at Dalditch Camp M. A. P. Wood, at that time vicar of a well-known evangelical church in London, principal of a training college for ordinands, and later Bishop of Norwich.

"Billy" Greer was a remarkable chairman, always managing to bring the p.m. sessions to a close precisely at 4 p.m. After a pretty wide experience of chairmen at home and abroad, I still name him the master. A happy relationship developed which was to stand me in good stead in the years to come.

There were occasional stormy interludes. Heenan, then Archbishop of Westminster, did an occasional "Athanasius against the World". I found myself once in a minority of one until a comradely intervention of Maurice Wood, whom elsewhere I have hailed as "the glass of fashion and the mould of form", somewhat swayed the adverse trend. A great asset to the R.C. team was John Coulson, the eminent Newman scholar. Beyond all doubt, however, it was the presence in the background of Father Agnellus Andrew which enhanced the status of our numerically modest representation on C.R.A.C. As chairman of our Mass Media Commission I was able over a number of years to appreciate both the supreme contribution he has made to the world of broadcasting and the immense prestige and affection he won there.

To my surprise there was no problem about my assisting at the Hierarchy meetings: at that time assistant Bishops were not invited.

* 11th October 1962.
† Central Religious Advisory Committee for both BBC and IBA

Stories circulated of stern exclusion. One was led to believe that no one but the head of the diocese appeared at this august assize. I made no move. In the event, John Henry simply told me to go. A place was already waiting for me at the righthand corner of the famous horseshoe table in Archbishop's House library. Our Low Week meeting in 1961 began with a moving ceremony. Bishop Murphy crossed the floor from the top place on the right curve to the end place on the left. Cardinal Godfrey at the apex of the horseshoe smiled approvingly, other dignitaries contributed a modulated applause. Within a few months it was again "Bishop's Move" for John Murphy, this time to Cardiff as Archbishop. Applause on this occasion was not modulated except of course in the widowed diocese of Shrewsbury. My own move came at the end of a triple "knock-on" manoeuvre, which shuttled Heenan from Liverpool to Westminster, Bishop Beck from Salford to Liverpool, leaving Salford six months a widow until Pope Paul invited me to drop the titular see of Etenna (a heap of sand and stones in Pamphylia Prima)* in the widow's favour.

Pope Paul's invitation came early in his pontificate and I took solace from the assurance that he had intervened very personally in the decision. I can't deny that I, too, took a rather personal interest. My father was born in the Salford diocese in the time of the first bishop, William Turner. There he met my mother int he last years of the second bishop, Herbert Vaughan. He bought the ring there in the early years of the third bishop, John Bilsborrow. The fourth bishop, Louis Charles Casartelli, professed his first child as a Poor Clare nun at Levenshulme. "Double or quits?" I chose the former and became eighth bishop. Archbishop Cardinale whose evening 'phone call put the issue before me expressed surprise that I did not ask for time to reflect.

I have a duty to perform which I hope is already seen to be basic throughout my time in Portsmouth. Without John Henry at the top, the whole experience would have been vastly different. The same would be true if he himself had been ten or twenty years young. But then, of course, I should not have been appointed to help him, or would scarcely have enjoyed the freedom or the fun which mellow old age disposed him to share with me. His Vicar General, Canon Sidney Mullarkey, lived with him at Winchester. Once see him with his crippled nephew and you thanked God for "a gentle, parfait" priest. One of my first battles was to get him to accept the Domestic Prelacy which Pope John had conferred on him. He gave in only when it was clear he could not pass it up without disrespect to the donor. It delights me to see he has since moved to the rank of

* I was of course relieved to note that my bartered bride went to an auxiliary bishop at Toulon, which like Portsmouth is a great naval base. Doubtless he too was a former naval chaplain and would know how to treat her as Canon Law in those days required: i.e. never go near her under pain of legal electrocution. There must have been a change? I seem to remember Bishop Fulton Sheen visiting his titular see in Wales.

Protonotary Apostolic: I wonder if he has ever used his privilege of wearing the white mitre? It was he who on behalf of the clergy presented me with a chalice "suitably engraved" just in time to anticipate my departure. May I assure him many hundreds of men have since looked devoutly towards it at Mass in our Manchester Night Shelter where it has long remained and I hope will always continue to remain.

I realise these valedictory remarks risk being unbalanced for two or three reasons. To begin with I can't allow the impression to prevail that my farewell was universally deplored in presbyteries, religious houses and the Catholic homes. That doesn't always happen with saints, rarely perhaps with pastors of mature experience, and never with bungling beginners.

I realise that up to this point it has been all clergy with a hint of the debt I owed to religious sisters or religious brothers. In fact, it was as chairman of Governors in the vast range of schools run by Sisters and Brothers that I learned my trade as educational overseer in all branches of the art—an asset of considerable relevance when I went to a diocese with over 100,000 pupils in three hundred Catholic schools. Beginning at the top can be even a short cut to mastering the problems if you listen discreetly. I don't recommend it, however, in the case of what used to be called Reformatories. There were two in the diocese run by de la Salle Brothers. There the Chair can be too hot for the perfect beginner. I look back now, however, thankful for the scorching and deeply grateful to the Brothers and fellow governors for all they taught me. I needn't say I learned also from the lads. I still carry a small torch for the only lad to "scapper" by night across the Solent in a "borrowed" rowing-boat. He wasn't the first nor the last to try.

My chief duty at this point is to carry a big torch and lift it high in praise of the religious sisters who came to our rescue at a critical point in the history of Bishop's House, Portsmouth.

For some months after my arrival the administration of the Cathedral and Bishop's House remained in the capable hands of Father T. Dwyer and Miss Norah, his housekeeper. Those were halcyon days. I was as free as the wind to push around the diocese in my M.G. Magnette which twice collided with other vehicles*. I was sure of a square meal on return; sure, too, that on Chapter Days the Canons' lunch would do honour to the House. But those days were too good to last. The trusty administrator and resourceful Norah left for a vacant parish along the coast. John Henry invited me to take on the Cathedral. Mercifully a providential escape-route opened for Father Peter Wilkie, a curate at Southsea, to move in as administrator. Father Derek Reeve, a convert trained at S. Sulpice, was the third musketeer. I can only hope we were as united, one for all and all for one, as present memories beguile me to believe.

* Oddly enough in both instances the other parties initially admitted they were at fault but later rather changed their tune.

There were difficulties. We survived more or less out of a frying pan. Peter imported a large dog whose lack of house training showed mainly in my bedroom. Derek trained us to drink our breakfast coffee black following his night raids on the fridge. My efforts to recruit female staff proved useless. Even the typist I had engaged failed to appear. This must have been the period when Sir Walter and Lady Campbell offered to come to the rescue, he as doorman, she as mistress of the interior. I could not accept. But in the meantime Mrs. Wilkie gallantly stood in, as I continued vainly writing to Mothers General and Provincial. They were most sympathetic, hoping they might see their way later, but not for the time being.

In desperation I picked up the 'phone. Clearly letters allowed too much time for careful consideration:-

"Is that Mother General of the Franciscan Missionaries of St. Joseph?"

"Yes, Mother Eamon speaking."

I put the case and vigorously pressed home.

"Yes! How many sisters would you need?" Was I hearing correctly?

"I'll come down next week with four."

And so Mother Eamon did, to inaugurate an association which was to last the rest of my time in Portsmouth and all my active years in Salford.

When my departure day came, who was waiting at the end of the road north but Mother Eamon and her F.M.S.J. sisters? I could not have hoped for a kindlier homecoming. All was prepared to meet my known needs and preferences.

A Father Vincent Lang appeared from Manchester to pick me up, bag and baggage, in a huge car. My M.G. remained demurely in its pen. John Henry's vehicle was off the road and likely to be so for some time. At least he would have a back-up, well acquainted with the highways and byways of the beloved counties which to the end were for him the saviours of the Faith in England. Our leave taking was brief. We embraced. He blessed me, turned away and I was gone. Both of us, I think, hid our eyes. As Father Vincent and I steamed up the M6 I admit I felt the need to repeat the same evasive action. My record at the wheel was a mile or two over 80 m.p.h. Father Bert Davey, an old school-mate from Valladolid days, was with me on that occasion. Mock-modestly I invited him to note the speedometer. "That's nothing" he said. "A fellow always takes me down this road at over the hundred."

Father Lang belonged to the same driving school. As Archbishop Beck's secretary for eight years he had sat under one of the greatest speedmerchants of our time. I timed our progress on the measured distance between two staging points. We were travelling at an average of 106 m.p.h. Need I add these were the days of unrestricted travel on M-roads.

As we came to the little bridge* over the infant Mersey, the car ground to a halt. I knelt to kiss the hem of my spouse. Doesn't Manley Hopkins somewhere† speak of his beloved Oxford wearing "a base and brickish skirt"? My beloved Salford's skirt was woven of hard and dusty paving stones.

Why such un-English carry-on? Well I owed my spouse to Pope Paul VI and remembered his journey to Milan where, as freely interpreted by some of his critics, his appointment as Archbishop proved he had forfeited the favour of Pius XII by declining the Cardinal's Hat. On that journey "accompanied by the now legendary ninety crates of books"‡ he stopped the car at the border of his huge archdiocese and kissed the ground. If my imitation of him was void of the heroic resolution which characterised his whole life, could it not pitifully appeal for the Lord to exercise his kindly gift of writing straight with crooked lines?

* Dividing the dioceses of Shrewsbury and Salford.
† "Duns Scotus's Oxford".
‡ *The Oxford Dictionary of Popes*, by J. N. D. Kelly, O.U.P. 1986, p. 322.

CHAPTER XLV

The North Once More

BEFORE I took the high road north Quarr Abbey exercised its gentle appeal on a pilgrim all too conscious of his need to spruce up his spiritual progress with a few days retreat. They were not very successful for two reasons.

I decided to write a pastoral letter to the Church in Salford plus an *Ad Clerum*, submitting both to the judgment of the diocesan Vicar Capitular*. The heart-warming atmosphere of Quarr may have influenced their composition. Vatican II was also two years on at this point and winds of change were in the air. I signed the pastoral "Your loving bishop" and told the clergy I would always be frank with them. The Vicar Capitular 'phoned his agreement. He was also quick to act on the implication I had somewhat overlooked and became from then on my relentless critical *alter ego*. My promise of universal frankness was, I fear, more much honoured in the breech than the observance.

Another distraction was my impending departure. These were my last days in the diocese. My dear hosts must have decided: *"Noblesse oblige.* Here is a man condemned to the salt-mines in the smoky north, far from this 'sweet especial place' he has loved. We must cherish his last hours of sunshine and sea."

They came in relays bearing comforting gifts. In all honesty I had only myself to blame. Quarr Campo Santo had early won my vote as a last resting place for a local bishop. The frequent tides in the Solent, which the Venerable Bede thought worthy of record, rustled close by on the shingle. The sirens of battleships and liners blew anything but faintly through the woodland fringing the Abbey domain. The good monks were well aware of my intention to be finally at rest with them. Now all was over. What could they do but stiffen my courage for the farewell to the South.

It was 8 p.m. September 9th 1964 when I mounted the famous stairs at Wardley Hall, the home of the last three Bishops of Salford, and paused on the landing to venerate the head of St. Ambrose Barlow O.S.B.† Here indeed was a link with the Pax Benedictina

---

* Monsignor Anthony McNulty and I were six years together at Valladolid.

† Born 1585 the year Statute 27 Elizabeth became law making it high treason for a Catholic priest to enter the Queen's dominions. Born into the seigneurial family of the Barlows of Barlow Hall, he was trained at Douai and Valladolid. He joined the Benedictines on return to Douai with other students who had the honour of continuing from Spain the line of Benedictines in England which otherwise would

from which I had emerged the previous day. It was his feast day on the morrow. The secretary judged the moment opportune to call: "Should I get up a bottle of wine?" "No, Vincent, I don't think so," said I primly. How often since have I hung my head over that reply. St. Ambrose was remarkable for his hospitality as well as for peace and good humour. On great festivals he kept open house and regaled his guests with goose and "minch" pies. Each left clad in a new grey coat. There I was with him on the stairs, literally *tête à tête*, so satisfied with myself that the idea anyone might feel differently about the events of the day never entered my fat head.

There was, however, no time for crying over spilt milk or un-poured wine. I arrived on Wednesday. The ceremony of "enthrone-ment" was on Saturday, then the feast of the Holy Name of Mary. On Sunday the flight to Rome was scheduled for the third Session of Vatican II which Pope Paul VI was to open on Monday 14 September, feast of the Exaltation of the Holy Cross. Only Thursday and Friday remained for courtesy calls at Manchester and Salford Town Halls, interviews with the Press and Radio, and presentation of Papal Bulls to the Chapter. Happily everything to ensure the splendour of the liturgy, the accommodation of guests and their warm approval of the luncheon at the Race Course Restaurant was in very competent hands. They left me entirely free from rehearsals and included the ecumenical dimension with exquisite foresight. Archbishop Beck, however, had to rescue me from a last minute hitch. The prescribed Profession of Faith came naggingly to mind as we were going in to the ceremony. I had not made it. "No panic" said this Solomon of Metropolitans: "You've made it on other occasions. You haven't retracted? You're IN!"

I was delighted to see Bishop Greer of Manchester foremost in the congregation wearing liturgical apparel; somewhat stunned, however, but certainly not so violently as Billy, when the thurifer, having incensed the prelates and dignitaries in the stalls, moved out from the sanctuary to incense *him*. It was, I feel sure, the first time he had even entered a Catholic church. He was the son of a Belfast C. of E. minister and a low churchman. To "incense" has two meanings. If the bishop experienced both on this occasion, he heroically repressed all outward signs.

Bishop Moorman of Ripon, official Observer at Vatican II, had felt it his duty to warn me I would find ecumenism hard going in Manchester. Ecumenically Bishop Greer was no front runner. Personally, however, I was at home with him. We knew exactly

have been broken. He was sent to work in England, made his H.Q. at Morleys Hall, in the parish of Leigh seven miles from Manchester. He was apprehended there on Easter Sunday 1641 and hanged, drawn and quartered at Lancaster, 10th September 1641. His head and members were impaled outside Manchester Collegiate Church (now Manchester Cathedral) where his family had a chantry. Francis Downes, his cousin, by night rescued the head and brought it to Wardley Hall where it has remained ever since. Professor Cave, a forensic scientist, identified the skull as male, aged between 50 and 60 and of the 17th century.

where we stood. There was a movement afoot to merge our two Whit Walks. I judged this to be premature and was somewhat taken aback when, without consultation, one of the Anglican dignitaries made a public announcement about it. So I asked the bishop was he prepared to walk with banners displaying our devotion to the Sacred Heart, Our Lady and the Saints. Emphatically he was not. Not was I at that time prepared to change the traditional character of our procession.*

I think nearly all these processions have since disappeared from the streets. Perhaps the only exception is the Walk connected with Manchester Cathedral on Whit Monday. Ours has been replaced by an outdoor Blessed Sacrament Procession on a Sunday in June. Despite gloomy forebodings even from within the Chapter, there has never been a single instance of disrespect though we process through the heart of Manchester. The police assure us it is for them the most carefree duty day of the year. They also enjoy the "hospitable" review of events at the 'Hidden Gem' which rounds off the day†.

At this point I am sorely tempted to divert this narrative from the domestic scene, and carry it with me on the 'plane into the mainstream of Vatican II, but to do so would drop the reader with adequate preparation in at the deep end into the greatest, and in many ways, the most complicated event of our time. We were just half-way when, by the skin of my teeth, I made this Third Session, no longer as Coadjutor of Portsmouth, but as Bishop of Salford. The change registered a major impact when at the English College I moved from being a lodger on Cardinal Heard's corridor into the spacious apartment occupied by my Salford predecessor during the first two Sessions.

Leaving aside the Council as such for later treatment, may I crave space to salute here the memory of Pope Paul VI. Frankly, however sketchily the gesture is made, I can no longer withhold it.

Pope Paul closed this Third Session with his tenth allocution to the Fathers of Vatican II on 21 November 1964. Altogether he addressed us twenty times in the Aula. Faithful throughout to his Predecessor's initial impulse, he outlined the themes ahead of us with exquisite insight. You could sense the ardent reverence with which he touched in the details. As well as furnishing us with a

* From early times, centuries before Manchester became industrialised, Whit Week was all holiday. Vestiges of the tradition survived in the Manchester Races. More colourful features were the childrens' processions, new clothes, banners and bands. The Sunday Schools developed these into festive demonstrations of scholastic and religious loyalties. Anglicans walked on Monday; Catholics on Friday. Walks were not confined to Manchester. Many Lancashire towns had them—always, I think, connected with major religious festivals. Bishop Greer realised their social importance early in his twenty-odd years in the Manchester diocese. We both regretted the efforts of the city Chamber of Commerce to interfere with them.
† The 'Hidden Gem' is Manchester's midmost Catholic church from which the procession originates and to which it returns—so called for its inner beauty and its inconspicuous site on the edge of Manchester's Albert Square.

spiritual *vade-mecum* for the work in hand, all unawares he composed for succeeding generations a shining mosaic of his own tender devotion to Christ and the Church and his total abasement as Servant of the Servants of God without which he could never have accomplished the way of the cross which as yet was mercifully hidden from him in all its painful detail.

I was back in Salford on 22 November 1964, the day after the Council closed. On the 23rd the doyen of the Salford clergy, Father Joseph Fitzgerald, affectionately known as 'Big Mick', died in his early nineties. He had been for more than half his life parish priest of St. Brigid's, Mill Street, Manchester.

Within days of my arrival, I was due to leave the diocese once again. Months ago *The Universe* had engaged me to lead a group from England to the Eucharistic Congress in Bombay. Our rendez-vous was in London on the day of the late parish priest's funeral which I simply could not miss at any price. My father had been an altar-boy at St. Brigid's in the eighteen seventies and eighties when the Missionary Rector, as P.P.s were called in those days, was a zealous young priest from Holland, who later became known as the "Apostle of North Manchester". He founded the parish of St. Willibrord, Clayton and galvanised the Faith of that new development area with his dynamic zeal for souls. With him came Continental pieties and customs. For instance: Latin Sunday Vespers which my father years later could sing by heart. Perhaps it was my father's surname which endeared him to the ardent missionary from the Low Countries which was at that time, and for many years to come, the supreme source of vocations to the Missions. As a boy I listened to the tale of drastic interventions by the yount priest in his determination to keep his favourite altar-boy on the straight and narrow path. I have no doubt he was behind the scheme to send my orphaned father to board at a Brothers' School in Belgium to be trained as a veterinary surgeon. His trunk was packed and tickets bought by our redoubtable great-uncle John, when, not for the first time, their young hopeful absconded and dodged the draft.

It was a singular disposition of divine providence which brought Father Sassen and his altar-boy together again. They had not met for many decades though certainly the priest's memory had always remained evergreen in my father's conversation and in his prayers.

Our eldest sister was to be professed a Poor Clare at St. Mary's Levenshulme. A prior courtesy call on the parish priest seemed appropriate. I am ever grateful that I accompanied my father to Manchester that day. To the surprise certainly of the clergy, Bishop Casartelli had moved Father Sassen from St. Willibrord's to Levenshulme. I forget now if my father was aware of this. Anyway the surprise and welcome of the old priest had to be seen to be believed. They had not met for perhaps forty years, but knew one another at once. Out came the cigars and the port. I rather think the going and coming this involved, as well as fulfilling the requirements of true

Dutch hospitality, had another purpose. *"Sunt lacrymae rerum"!** I escape to the more recent memory of "Big Mick's" funeral. Canon Angelo O'Connell, a former curate of St. Brigid's, pronounced the panegyric. It was a masterly tribute of filial piety towards a true Soggarth Aroon† and a skilful navigational exercise round his well-known eccentricities.

As we followed the bier to the door, once again a white mitre came under the impact of torrential rain. That morning, 28 November 1964, all was just as my father would remember it. On the other side of the waiting hearse stood, arms akimbo, a Mancunian version of Madam Defarges in full view of St. Brigid's main door. Behind her pressed a phalanx of female supporters. As I emerged into the downpour, an Amazonian arm shot point-blank out at me. "That's him!" said she, loud and clear. I waited for it but no rush came. The brass sprinkler in my hand was raised, only to fulfil its normal function of blessing the coffin. I have since wondered whether this identity procedure owed its drama to a memory lingering on in the parish of a lad with my name? The retainers of it would have to be octogenarians. There, however, in the coffin was a nonagenarian who would have known them in their thirties. Father Joseph Fitzgerald by all accounts had a remarkable memory. I dined afterwards with the Canons in the presbytery. They were all agog for first hand news of the Third Council Session which had just ended. It ended in fact with a rather unusual event.

1964 was, as every schoolboy knows, the fourth centenary year of the Bard's birth. Someone had the bright idea of bringing out Stratford Players to act selected scenes for the Pope and the Council Fathers. This mastermind also brought with him a First Folio Shakespeare. Archbishop Grimshaw of Birmingham in whose diocese the Swan of Avon was born accepted the honour of introducing the event with a tribute which would refresh some minds and perhaps initially inform others. The archbishop took his duty seriously, even retiring for a day or two to Palazzola‡ to collect his thoughts. He fell ill, however, with a throat infection. For a couple of days we both sat together at meals, avoiding solid food. Mine was tummy trouble which soon passed. His continued and shortly after his return to England led to his premature death. I can't forget the wan smile with which he accused me of treachery when I went back on solids. In the event Heenan joined Dorothy Tutin and others on the stage and gave the preliminary address. The old C.M.S trooper shone as always. So did the players. They held the Pope and prelates, episode after episode, *sans* rope, *sans* scenery, *sans* wardrobe or green room. Before the Pope left, the leader of the Shakespearian mission stepped forward with the Bard's first folio.

---

* I have never read, or been able to make, a decent translation of Vergil's most pregnant triad. It has to do with our inability to recall certain things without tears.
† Dear Priest.
‡ The English College Villa on Lake Albano.

Heenan and others commented. I think His Holiness could well appreciate what he held in his hands without any commentary†. A secretary relieved him of it. He made a graceful comprehensive thanksgiving, received the players individually and moved towards the exit.

Consternation was followed by despair throughout the Shakespearian embassy. One bound, however, and Heenan was into the breach. Without any sign of embarrassment the treasure was smilingly restored to the hands of those who dare not return to England without it.

I was sitting next to Bishop George Dwyer, then at Leeds, when the ubiquitous George Armstrong threaded his way to our seats. I believe he owed his presence in Rome to the Columbia Broadcasting Corporation as an expert on the Sicilian Mafia. Whether this was an appropriate qualification for covering the Vatican Council, my ignorance of the newspaper world forbids me to judge. Many of us, however, were unhappy with the *Guardian's* reports, and when Mr Armstrong suggested it was time to review the Third Session, I fear my hackles went up and the drawbridge dropped with a bang. Dwyer felt I had badly overdone things.

I mentioned the incident to the Canons at lunch that day. I think *The Guardian* had not yet moved to London, dropping *Manchester* on the way. So I apologised to those present who were still readers if they had noticed any sharpening of criticism in reports on the Council. Whether they had or not, they were all on my side, come hell or high water. One must remember this was the first time we had come together informally and they no doubt wanted me to feel at home. I have no doubt now that Dwyer was right: I had made an ass of myself and did no good to our cause with that outburst in the Vatican theatre. When the Canons knew me better, I'm sure they would agree.

From St. Brigid's I made for the London train, and joined the Congress pilgrims at the overnight hotel. Once again I am sorely tempted to leave home and duty behind and continue this narrative with the exhilarating variation on the Eucharistic Congress theme which Bombay offered to the world in December 1964. I have recorded the experience elsewhere. This was the second of seven such events I have been privileged to attend between 1960 and 1985.

Allow me here at least to reflect some of the highlights which made me proud of the city in which I had spent two happy years as Port Chaplain. Cardinal Valerian Gracias was at the peak of his considerable natural and grace-given endowments. His voice was often heard in the Council, making shrewd comments on well-known proverbs which he usually quoted first in English. To him, as host, must go credit for weaving in and around the Congress

†Is there a similar treasure in the Vatican library? There was one in the College library at Valladolid which the Rector sold to Kansas City for an unspecified sum, partly paid in yearly instalments.

liturgies all that was best and most authentic in the culture of the sub-Continent. Haunting melodies, graceful and dignified dance, colour everywhere, streaming and fluttering around the Cooperage,* criss-cross over the city highways and by-ways.

The climax came with the arrival of Pope Paul in a white Rolls Royce which he later left for Mother Teresa to mint into money for her charities.

I must not forget the commentary of Father Agnellus Andrew. Only one long schooled in the art and endowed with tremendous natural aptitude and stamina could have sustained this vital element so long at such a pitch of excellence. We discussed a curry together at an open-air restaurant next to the prestigious Taj Mahal hotel. Characteristically the old trooper chose the Madras version of India's national dish, the hottest of them all.

My personal highlights were an impressive tour of Bombay's Catholic charitable institutions, the multiple Marriage Ceremony on the Cooperage at which each bishop united numerous couples, a run down to Goa where the incorrupt body of St. Francis Xavier was exposed during the Congress period. May I be forgiven for intruding on a personally depressing note, a visit to my old stamping ground, Bombay Docks. Either their glory had departed or memory had invested them with a light that never was.

Pope Paul's last minute decision to attend the Congress meant there was no longer room for me in Archbishop's House, my former home for most of my time in Bombay. Instead three papal bodyguards found accommodation under that hospitable roof. Major Chris Hennessy of *The Universe*, who was in charge of the trip, had problems apart from pilgrims. At the last moment, our chartered plane was withdrawn from service. He drummed up a substitute from Germany, better and roomier than the first. I award the crew full marks—they could not have been more courteous or accommodating. Inter-com was at our disposal for prayers, hymns and travelogues. We found a place for a hitch-hiker on the first leg, the ebullient Vatican diplomat Monsignor Silvio Oddi, who later, as Cardinal Prefect of the Sacred Congregation for the Clergy, dealt with secular priests' problems the world over.

We returned from Bombay via the Holy Land. As we began our descent to Lydd, now Tel Aviv airport, I alerted the pilgrims to honour St. George, protector and patron of England, of soldiers, scouts, and churches in many lands. "We are now near the birthplace of St. George our national protector", I said. "I shall lead you with: "Arm, arm for the struggle approaches." I intoned the first line. Total silence quelled the uncertain voice within me. Nobody knew it. I changed the hymn. As we taxied over the tarmac our Gerry plane was still ringing with the strains of "Hail, glorious St. Patrick."

As for our "four and forty folk in companee" even Geoffrey

* The large open space at the heart of the City.

Chaucer would have been hard put to it to describe us despite our collective and individual "full devout corage". Aboard we had a "poor persoun of a town" from Barmouth, Father P. Collins, who spent his nights as a student at the Beda relighting the lamp before the Sacred Heart statue outside his room and passed his nights now in his parish visiting patients in the local hospital. On our return journey he was actually observed sleeping in broad daylight on a Sunday morning as we came down by boat from Caphernaum to Magdala. He was still sleeping when a sudden rain storm blew up.

That afternoon taxis were ordered for the ascent of Mt. Tabor. The storm, however, later became so violent the taximen called it off. Before that, when the trip still seemed feasible I was making towards a cab. "You'll need a coat", said the driver. "I haven't one," I replied. Immediately he whipped off his coat and wrapped me in it.

We were all confined to the hotel lounge for a long afternoon. But on our pilgrimage was a character Chaucer never knew: a member of the Magic Circle.* He held us spell-bound for the duration. Tabor remained throughout inaccessible. Far below us the Sea of Galilee drove teams of white horses across to Gergesa.

Another Beda man, Father Sandwell from Southampton, was with us on this trip. He was formerly a chemist. I do not remember our needing him in that capacity. What I have every reason to remember with great gratitude are his services at Southampton docks the morning of my episcopal ordination. On my behalf he met the Abbé Graindor and his cousin, Marie Madeleine, off the nightboat from Normandy and saw them through to Portsmouth. They have never forgotten his courteous reception.

We were back in England 18 December 1964. Despite the inevitable strains and *contretemps* of three weeks complex and demanding travel, all parted "jolly good fellows" and friends. Organisers and air-crew were regaled with a home-spun equivalent of the Carolingian Laudes. At Wardley, a thoughtful Secretary waited with a stack of correspondence and boxes of Christmas cards. There was a letter from Archbishop Mathew in the post. This master-craftsman's book *Our Naval Heritage*, became required reading for naval entrants during the war. Briefly he assured me Salford was the best diocese in England and offered his congratulations.

I have no diary to consult at this point but an old work-sheet records:

December 21 (fourth anniversary of my episcopal ordination).
Opening of a new Church, Nelson.
December 23 Interviews at the Cathedral.
December 24 Pontifical Midnight Mass, Cathedral.

* This gentleman also joined Chris Hennessy's 1973 party for the Melbourne Eucharistic Congress, and rivetted parents and children to the number of 200 with his skill (ably assisted by my Secretary, Monsignor John Allen). The audiences (there had to be two shows) were composed of emigrés from the Salford diocese. We had put out a 3-line whip for any such in the Melbourne area.

December 25 Sung Mass at Strangeways Gaol.
Low Mass at Little Sisters of the Poor.
December 25-29 Breather at home.
December 30 Visitation to Carmelites, Kersal.
December 31 Interviews at the Cathedral.

Grievous entries record the death of Father Louis Hanlon and his dirge and Requiem in the presence of Archbishop Beck, Bishop Dwyer of Leeds and a vast concourse of clergy. My predecessor had appointed Father Hanlon first principal of Christ's Training College at Liverpool. He spent a hard year recruiting staff and setting up plant. Coming back from a conference in London just before Christmas, he was involved in a head-on crash at Warrington and rushed into hospital there. For a whole fortnight he remained unconscious. They moved him to Liverpool for the best available brain surgery. Somehow I managed to be with him every night. I went to Liverpool with the relic of St. Ambrose Barlow. My predecessor, Bishop Marshall of "Martial Law" fame, never allowed this treasure to be moved, not even when bombs fell near Wardley Hall in the Manchester blitz. He had heard stories of strange consequences of any displacement. I was to experience them more than once. They could be drastic and at the time very hard to take. Father Hanlon died the night he was blessed. Everyone, however, specialists included, knew that short of a miracle the brilliant brain of Louis Hanlon could never function normally again.

Some time later, one of our church students at St. Bede's College, son of Ronnie Smith, a classics master at the school, fell grievously ill. Brain cancer was diagnosed. There was very little hope. We visited him with the skull locked in its cedar-wood travelling-case. Father and mother knelt by the bed. My secretary, now Monsignor Allen, proceeded to open the case. In no way would it open, despite protracted application of keys, pressure to left and right, above and below. We blessed the boy with the relic unexposed. The following day came a letter from Sheila, the boy's mother, one of the bravest I have every read. She had read the *Life of St. Ambrose* and remembered his extreme care to look no woman in the face. She wrote: "If I hadn't been there, you would have had no difficulty opening that case!" The boy died. The funeral was on a Saturday morning. Manchester City had a match that afternoon. The team turned out for the funeral. He had been one of their keenest fans.

CHAPTER XLVI

Destruction and Reconstruction

"WHAT'S going to be your line, Bishop? What are you hoping to leave behind you?", one of the pressmen had asked me at the pre-installation conference. I fear the answer came off the top of my head rather than from any profound meditation. "A family united in faith and worship", said I.

In many ways my posting to Salford was a return of the native. True, I was born and bred on the extreme edge of West Lancashire. I was also trained and ordained for the diocese of Liverpool. Salford diocese huddles up against the Pennines, covering the eastern half of Lancashire between the Ribble and the Mersey—*"entre deux mers"*, so to speak, like many a good wine. Our family roots, plunged deep into the good earth of that interior. Even mother's Cumberland merged early into the stream of Manchester memories flowing from both our parents. Vivid stories were told of Salford bishops and priests—like Herbert and Bernard Vaughan, Father Sassen and the great defenders of Catholic schools like Canon Richardson whom Scott welcomed into the columns of the *Manchester Guardian* for many a hard-fought controversy. My father remembered the day when Herbert Vaughan, already installed at Westminster, returned to preach at the Holy Name. His brother, Bernard, was then parish priest, a position he never held while Herbert was bishop. The sermon began with a solemn condemnation of the parish priest. The Bishops had collectively forbidden the custom common in England in the days of Mesdames Tetrazini, Patti, Melba and others of advertising the names of guest singers at the last Mass. Father Bernard had done precisely that. My father was at the back of the church. So was the P.P., packing in the late comers, and taking not the slightest notice of his brother's tirade from the pulpit.

Contemporary Manchester continued to loom large during our youth. Father's business most days took him back there to the Coal Exchange whence he branched north into East Lancashire towns, booking his orders with Co-ops, at times even venturing across the Pennines to customers and collieries. He knew Gracie Fields' mother at the time when the little daughter made her debut as a dancer. In the evenings we children listened to his stories of the day's travel. What so often came through loud and clear was the people's genius in war and peace for pooling their slender resources. The doors of their little terraced houses were constantly open. Neighbours dropped in and out. The sick were sure of a companion. The needy got the crucial loan—the half cup of sugar, a twist of tea, perhaps an egg, all scrupulously returned when the ship came home. Long before the State enlisted social workers and home helps, such services were assured, certainly not with the same expertise or comprehensive cover as today, but as naturally as saying "good morning". And a golden thread of genuine charity was richly woven into the texture of life in the little towns.

The phrase I came up with at the Press Conference was a clumsy effort to emphasise spiritual neighbourliness, so often the source of the community spirit which had so staunchly enabled our people to survive. The religious dimensions were indeed still there, but waning. Gone were the days when after Sunday evening Benediction people gathered in one another's homes to sing hymns sitting on the stairs, and drinking their penny cup of tea. Naive? Forget it! Even as entertainment, they got more out of it than watching "telly" immured in their own homes.

I was not long in the diocese, however, before realising there can be grim casualties from even the most necessary social reform. It was peculiarly depressing to see the community spirit taking some of the hardest knocks.

Manchester was highly praised for its vigorous slum clearance policy. Prime Minister Wilson came to congratulate us in the Town Hall. But at the same time damage was done to some of our oldest and most venerable city parishes. Someone has to suffer. Certainly, however, the courtesy of prior consultation with Church authorities could have been profitably extended. What really hurt was the loss of community as people were moved out into new kinds of housing. Inspiration came, I understand, from the cult architect of the day, and the new South American city of Brasilia. People became cliff dwellers in tower blocks. Old ladies became hermits. The antics of rowdies in the lifts scared them rigid. "Deck access" provided express runways for lightning theft. Drab front elevations quickly earned the title of "Fort". In the *Manchester Evening News* Canon Harry Clarke (then at St. Wilfred's, Hulme) weighed in trenchantly against such regression.

I made a nuisance of myself at the Town Hall. The Lord Mayor eventually arranged a meeting with the City Planners. Already I had questioned the wisdom of tearing the heart out of Manchester to provide a huge university campus. This was one instance when in my judgment policy had done unnecessary harm to parishes, particularly to the Holy Name and St. Augustine's at All Saints. The answer I got was surprising: "We wanted to have something like Oxford here in Manchester." I had two criticisms to make when the interview with the City Planners was arranged. The first, of course, was the unhappy plight of so many people in the new housing. Even slum dwellings without gardens at least gave each family its own little castle at ground level. The neighbourhood was an agglomeration of such homes. Everyone knew everyone else in the same street. How could the huge barracks of people unknown to one another ever become neighbourhoods in the old sense of doors open, sick visited and basic supplies shared? We were creating jungles instead of communities.

The City Planners (give them capital letters—they were distinguished men and right up to the minute) were glad to meet us. I was accompanied by my secretary, Monsignor Allen and Canon Joseph Lakin—a Manchester man through and through. Respectfully but inevitably the Planners regarded us as "fuddy-duddies". Clearly we knew nothing of the vast architectural developments not only in England or Europe but world-wide. Courteously they withdrew, shaking hands, glad to have had the opportunity . . .

My second complaint fell, I think, between two stools. It was no concern of the Planners. No doubt the speed of the city's rehousing operation entailed inevitable problems. I was concerned with what happened to homes when people moved out. Certainly there was a demolition programme. I shall not forget standing outside St. Edmund's, Miles Platting one afternoon with the parish priest, Canon John McCabe, as the houses at a tangent to the church went up in flames. One by one he made his comment: "My mother spent her first night in England in the end one. Bishop Hanlon M.H.M.* was born next door", and so on along the row. One evening we passed a smouldering ruin on the Rochdale Road, not far from St. Edmund's. "That was the Egans' home" volunteered my driver. That house must have rippled with music. Mr Egan was organist at St. Patrick's. The children lived with music. Better still they lived with grace—it was a hallowed home. From it came a future prioress of Carmel, a masterful and musical school-mistress, and Charles a co-Vicar General of Salford. Of him it was said that if V.G.'s were elected by the priests, Charles would be in *nem. con.* I record this as a tribute to my predecessor Archbishop Beck who appointed him.

There were, however, humble streets whose houses were left to rot or fell prey to vandals. There, too, generations of decent people were born, lived, had their families, prayed, received the last Sacraments and died. I still deplore whatever problem withheld the devouring flame from its kindly duty.

Relations with our Town Halls were not by any means all querulous. I began with Jewish First Citizens in both Salford and Manchester and from the outset gained a healthy respect for their community's strong sense of civic duty. Indeed formal contacts ripened more than once into warm friendships which in turn opened up avenues of genuine understanding and co-operation I never thought I should tread.

Come to think of it, I realise now I was only following in the footsteps of my old C.M.S. Superior, Cardinal Heenan. In a broadcast the day he was ordained Bishop of Leeds, he offered his

* Leader of the first Mill Hill missioners in Uganda and Kenya, 1891.

services to the city and specifically to the Jewish community. Montague Burton in reply assured him of a free range of suits. That is the story.

Sidney Hamburger was my second Mayor of Salford. He initiated a series of civic luncheons to which he invited prominent citizens from every walk of life: an excellent shoehorn into the civic scene for a relative new boy. Sidney has gone from strength to strength since then: honorary degrees from universities at home and abroad, the chairmanship of the North West Regional Hospital Board, a knighthood etc. etc. On the Jewish New Year we have recited the appropriate psalms together over running water in the park near his hospitable home. Luckily for us he joined one of our committees in preparation for the Papal Visit to Manchester. We have reason to be eternally grateful to him.

CHAPTER XLVII

Early Times in Salford

PART of Manchester Town Hall (John Betjeman's supreme embodiment of the Victorian era) covers the site of St. Mary's original school and cemetery. The founder of St. Mary's in 1794, Father Rowland Broomhead, had been curate at St. Chad's, the first Catholic church in Manchester since the Reformation if one omits the "Meeting House" in Roman Entry* Church Street, catering for the twenty or thirty Catholic families which then composed our total Catholic presence. To Father Broomhead, Salford diocese owes an incalculable debt for St. Mary's, Mulberry Street and St. Augustine's, Granby Row. There was much more to thank him for, to mention only his annual courses of instruction in the Faith for the immigrants and the long days and nights in the confessional during Lent. There is a vast legacy to be traced in contemporary Manchester to his energy and foresight. As a C.M.S. missioner one came to sense pretty well the state of prayer throughout England and Wales. I would go along with the comment of a more experienced man: "There are more visits paid to the Blessed Sacrament in St. Mary's Mulberry Street than in any other church in the country."

On a stone column now standing at the shallow end of the "Tank"† in the garden of the English College Rome, there are graven three names: R. Broomhead 1774, N. Wiseman, G. Errington. The first one is exposed to the elements and should be glassed in before it disappears altogether.‡ If I have unduly strayed from personal matters back into history, take it as a feeble effort to "glass in" a name which every bishop of Salford must hold both high and dear in benediction.

There is yet another worthy who tempts me back to the past, though I can claim in all fairness he has been with me ever since I met him in the centenary volume: *Salford Diocese and its Catholic Past*, published in 1950. Rector of St. Mary's (1821-37) he succeeded

---

* The coincidence of place name with our return to Manchester as a community is remarkable. Roman Entry was quite recently demolished without our salvaging a single item from the ruins.

† This swimming bath was Cardinal Hinsley's legacy to the College as rector in 1928.

‡ Wiseman went to the English College from Ushaw in 1818—one of the first batch of students to recolonise the Venerabile after its 20 years' occupation by French troops. Errington was ordained the first Bishop of Plymouth along with William Turner, the first Bishop of Salford, by Wiseman in Salford Cathedral July 25 1851. He was Wiseman's vice-rector in Rome and at the time of his consecration administrator of Salford Cathedral. Later Wiseman chose him to succeed him at Westminster. That, however, is another story . . .

Father Broomhead as the principal Catholic figure in Manchester. *Inter alia*, he pioneered the first schools in Salford and later laid the foundation of that city's Cathedral parish. In a way he could never have wished he literally forced the Cathedral's foundation stone to be laid.

The roof of St. Mary's was showing unmistakable signs of collapsing and had to be taken down. Father Henry Gillow was about to engage professional advice for the replacement when the workmen on the site approached him with an alternative: they could and would restore the roof themselves. I am sure it was the compassionate element which won his agreement rather than any saving. The men needed to be sure of the job. They botched it. Early Mass-goers stood aghast one Sunday morning barred from entering. The roof of their beloved chapel had collapsed during the night.

Since for many Salford Catholics St. Mary's was their nearest chance of hearing Mass, it was vital to provide the alternative. The first site chosen at the city end of Chapel Street proved to be complicated by the spread of what is now Victoria Station. Nearly a mile back, however, on the same thoroughfare the ideal site was located and acquired. Thus Salford Cathedral came out of the roofless wailing walls of the Hidden Gem.

The laying of the foundation stone had the whole Catholic community concentrated in the public eye and on its metal. It was, by all accounts, the complete answer to a huge challenge: for long enough Salfordians had been contributing a penny each week towards a church of their own. Ten Manchester Sunday Schools and three from Salford marched, clad in their best, and, as always, ever since, bravely hoisting their banners as the brass bands began to play. The Vicar Apostolic of the Northern District, Bishop Sharples, laid the stone in the presence of six thousand people. It was Whit Thursday 1844.

At that date no one was aware the stone was destined to support a Cathedral. At some time during the building, however, the signal was given for a diocese based on Salford. The architect, Hadfield, rose handsomely to the occasion. The Cathedral spire was the tallest in all Lancashire. But Father Gillow was not there to see the splendour precipitated by his fallen roof. He died at the early age of forty-one, one of fourteen priests to contract typhus in their heroic ministration to a plague-stricken flock in a single year.

I remarked earlier that Father Gillow was "with me" throughout my time in Salford. The following quotation from the *Manchester City News* of 26th February 1837 which I read soon after coming to Salford may explain his ghostly presence. I make no apology for its length or its florid phrasing. Remember this is the year Victoria came to the throne.

"In those days the vicinity of Mulberry Street was foul in every way and the idea of its being the site of a place of worship was to the last degree a glaring and nauseous incongruity. Perhaps as one of the early Catholic worthies of old Manchester, the Reverend Henry Gillow, for pure saintliness of personal aspect, and for a certain pathetic benignity of manner, was the most remarkable creature ever beheld. His silver hair, pure pallid face, gentle compassionate eye, and womanly and touchingly tender voice, exercised in those days a magical spell over the ruder and wilder spirits of the then Manchester Catholic world, and under his sweetly irresistable remonstrances they would burst into tears and fall on their knees before him with wild cries of inarticulate penitence and remorse. No such feeble and ghostly inhabitant of earth ever surely before or since exercised over the untamed human animal, just hovering on the verge of civilisation, such a curiously overwhelming fascination! I remember well the wild sorrow that smote the hearts of the Catholic poor when this pale and sacred phantom gave up the ghost and was seen no more."*

I add Father Bolton's footnote to the *Manchester City News* report. "The angelic charm of manner and appearance of Father Gillow is not an isolated example of the physical and moral beauty that adorned some of the aristocratic families of Catholic Lancashire. In the yeoman classes the same characters were often present but in a rougher form, as it were in plain homespun."

The Gillows, of course, ranked high in Lancashire history and commerce despite their staunch fidelity to the Old Faith.

I wonder whether the *Manchester City News* reporter who found "the vicinity of Mulberry Street foul in every way and the idea of its being the site of a place of worship to the last degree a glaring and nauseous incongruity" lived to see Manchester Town Hall. True the vast expanse of Albert Square lies between the Town Hall and the present Hidden Gem, as St. Mary's is now known.

There is, however, one day in the year when that *cordon sanitaire* fills with the Hidden Gem's procession of the Blessed Sacrament. Benediction is given from the Town Hall steps. There I must have stood a dozen times for the launching of the annual Whit Walk. Lord Mayors stood by me every bit as proud of the sight before us as I was. There were thirty Manchester and Salford parishes, each with their clergy, children, confraternities and sodalities. You could have walked on their heads but for the forest of towering banners tossing hither and thither. The "off" came with the blessing from the steps in which the Lord Mayor modestly took no part. I was, however, delighted when a Lord Mayor asked if he might walk with us. That established a precedent. I learnt what confidences can be exchanged in an hour's walk despite the crashing of sixty bands, two per parish, and the plaudits of the crowds. One dear mayor marched himself back into the Church *en route*.

I forget now if that excellent Lord Mayor, Dame Elizabeth Anne

* *Salford Diocese and its Catholic Past*, Charles A. Bolton, 1950, pp 123-124.

Yarwood, intended to walk with us. As we stood together on the Town Hall steps, the cataracts of heaven opened to release the most awful Mancunian downpour. "Quick," she said. "Look at those children. Let's get them all into the Town Hall for a hot drink." Noble words from a noble lady but there were thousands of them! Moreover my head was on the block. Any bishop guilty of stopping a Whit Walk would certainly have been cashiered by the Pope. I gripped the mike, blessed them and roared, "In the name of the Lord, WALK." "Faith of our Fathers" blared out from the brass, up went the banners! We were "off".

The crowd reaction that day was very special. They, too, were twice soaked to the skin all along the route. They, too, twice dried out in blistering sunshine. The applause on all sides from the crowd was never so overwhelming. In all justice it should have gone into reverse, from us to them.

How many times, I wonder, did this mobile pageant of Faith walk the City from the vicinity of Mulberry Street once so "foul in every way" where the very idea of a place of worship was "to the last degree a glaring and nauseous incongruity"?

One year the Walk appeared on French television. That, after all, was surely natural in a land of supreme couturiers. Our children's dresses, all new for the occasion, were in effect a showcase of our own ability in that respect. I made the point when the Chamber of Commerce complained of the inconvenience our progress through Manchester inflicted on commerce.

CHAPTER XLVIII

All Went Walking

MY FIRST active participation in a Whit Walk came as a mighty windfall in 1958. Bishop Beck, my predecessor at Salford, had invited the Apostolic Delegate for the event. As usual with diocesan engagements Archbishop O'Hara readily accepted once he had the assurance that for him "Walk" meant "Ride". An open landau would be provided. But he was just not up to it on the day and I went in his place as guest of honour. The landau, however, was cancelled. I walked with the bishop and the Cathedral clergy at the head of the procession.

Top hats and Chesterfield suits were *de rigueur* for the clergy. Somewhere I have a photograph of that wide rank of clergy at the head of the procession. George Andrew Beck smiles bravely at the camera. He, of course, wears his green-corded Roman hat and episcopal full rig. That brave smile may have masked mixed feelings. He had every right to feel abysmally let down. As we stood side by side at the saluting base in front of the old Queen's Hotel, parish after parish went past ablaze with colour and sounding brass. Their clergy dutifully moved across from behind the parish banner to kiss the bishop's ring. The parish priest of St. Willibrord's, whose hospital death-bed I was to visit at midnight a dozen years later, confusedly knelt to kiss my non-existent ring. This, I think, completely removed any lingering episcopal regrets about the day. Bishop Beck was all for the traditional top hats. The Canon was a rigorous non-conformist. Of all the clergy he alone stuck staunchly to his trilby even for the Whit Walk.

My sister Mamie stood hidden in the crowd on the pavement opposite the saluting base—"crying my eyes out", she told me later, as she remembered our father's tales of the eighteen seventies when he marched down from St. Brigid's in the drum and fife band. They had a long way to go on only two tunes. He was a drummer.

Bishop Beck gallantly insisted that my sister should join us at the Cathedral for the evening meal. The bishop and I in the meantime lunched at the Town Hall as guests of the Lord Mayor, Alderman Fitzsimons. He had joined in the Walk, not, however, with the leaders in mayoral rig but at the tail-end as a member of St. Michael's Men's Confraternity.

In my time as bishop half a dozen Lord Mayors were Catholics, rather more Jewish, the rest good Christian men and women. I came

246

to expect and invariably received collaboration and courtesy from Manchester's First Citizens and Town Hall staff, an experience which culminated in the all-round supreme effort demanded by John Paul II's visit in 1982*.

An outstanding champion of our Catholic community both locally and at Westminster was Leslie Lever, City Councillor, Lord Mayor and M.P. for Ardwick, who made no secret of his standing on education: "I get my schools policy from Wardley Hall"†.

Leslie attributed his seat on the City Council and later his seat at Westminster to Bishop Marshall. He composed a speech the first time he put up for Parliament. Never again—he always went in on a massive majority. Even so polling-day was a nightmare for him. Round he came begging for prayers. Yet he was totally disenchanted, even disgusted, with what went on at the House. Illogically, however, he was all for getting Catholic bishops into the House of Lords. I can't think any of my colleagues would have jumped for joy at that prospect. Leslie was later honoured by Pope Paul with the Grand Cross of the Order of St. Gregory.

I must pay homage to Lady Lever's heroic dedication in the days of Leslie's decline. He had burnt himself out physically and mentally. No Lord Mayor ever took on more engagements in his year of office. As M.P. he was back and forth to London on night trains while still running his legal practice and his ward. For me what best brings out the quality of the man was his devotion to Councillor Hopkins in his last illness. Neither politics nor religion united them. Yet somehow within every twenty-four hours Leslie was at his bedside. This I learned from Father William Hopkins, the Councillor's brother.

Of course the inevitable breakdown came. Lady Lever learned to drive a car and guided the wheel-chair to places of honour at gala events, anticipating all needs. In this way Leslie continued to attend our community celebrations. No one had a better right to be there. Apart from the spiritual bond of charity such as linked him with the dying councillor, Leslie had established claims to our ever-grateful remembrance, especially for his part in supporting our schools. For that reason alone I make no apology for recording Leslie at length.

Rather late in the day I realise my head is on the block. Only one meagre mention so far of *lady* Lord Mayors! One of the three or four in my time was a Catholic. She and her cousinly Mayoress

* "We would not have this park prepared for you, Holy Father, but for the wonderful collaboration of the City and the Greater County whose chief citizens and chief executives and high public officers for two years have arduously and ardently worked for this day. May I thank them here before you?" (From my welcome speech in Heaton Park.) I cannot at this point omit the name "Brian D. Keneally", Principal Administrative Officer, Town Clerk's Department, without whose drive and mastery of detail from all sources we should never have been ready to receive the Holy Father. May he rest in peace! He died recently at the early age of 48. Though not a Catholic his last request was that his ashes be scattered around the monument in Heaton Park which marks the site of the Papal Mass. *Talium est Regnum!*
† Bishop of Salford's residence.

sought audience with Pope John Paul II at Christmas 1981 to impress on him his bounden duty to include Manchester in his apostolic visit to Britain between 28 May and 2 June 1982. In Rome they lunched at the Capitol as guests of the Mayor of Rome, who showed distressing signs of a cold during the meal. Our resourceful deputy mayoress produced from her bag a "Fisherman's Friend". The Roman Mayor was not seen again for several days.

Of all Lord Mayors Dame Kathleen Ollerenshaw was undoubtedly the most brilliant academic. She had original mathematical formulae to her credit and despite her aural handicap immense services to the Northern College of Music. A tour of the Town Hall in her company was a liberal education. She asked for a Latin motto when promoted to the supreme degree of Dameship. I suggested "Pro Mathese Urbeque", for Mathematics and the City. But, said she, "I want Music to come in as well." I reminded her of the medieval division of studies. Music then came under Maths. Did not Leibnitz define the pleasure of music as mathematics without tears, an effortless awareness of the number of vibrations in every note?

Civic twinnings of towns in the diocese opened doors to new friendships, none more cherished than those formed in Le Mans and Paderborn. Distinguished visitors to Wardley Hall whom I usually introduced to the Town Hall, Rylands' Library and other places, also generated contrasting vibrations. Cardinal Slipyj wore his full regalia for the occasion. The Lord Mayor was aware of his former ducal rank, vast estates and subsequent crunch under the Russian jackboot. Manchester is twinned with Leningrad; the reception was solemn and pardonably somewhat overawed. Cardinal Heenan's visit on the other hand sparked off a scherzo of hilarious good humour throughout the Town Hall.

Before leaving it may I pay tribute to a pair of councillors who well deserved to be our chief citizens.

Martin Flynn was one of a considerable group of Irishmen who by sheer hard work and brains rose to the topmost ranks of Mancunian entrepreneurs. Their loyalty to the Faith owed much to Provost William Sewell of St. John's Chorlton and the Irish Association Social Club founded near that magnificent church.* There with a range of amenities equal to those of any non-residential club in the land, they set standards which paid off well beyond the club perimeters. So also did Monsignor's wit. Manchester comedians had their ear to the ground for the stories Monsignor Sewell told in the Irish Club. He was the star speaker at all manner of festive gatherings. A visiting rabbi on one such occasion proposed a transfer: any three rabbis he chose to name in exchange for the last speaker, the Irish Monsignor. There was thunderous applause from the Chosen People.

* When Sir Matt Busby was well enough to go to Mass after the Munich disaster, journalists preceded him to ask the P.P. to show them Matt's pew. "He doesn't have one. He stands in the crowd at the back when he's lucky enough to get in," explained the Provost. "And," he added with pardonable pride: "it's not that he's late."

He came to us from Killarney early enough to do his humanities at St. Bede's Grammar School, followed by the full course of philosophy and theology at Ushaw. Those fourteen years moulded a great priest and a legendary master of our national games. One of his legendary sixes for St. Bede's crashed through a distant bedroom window. The occupant wrote advising the rector "to curb this youthful Jessop". The rector carefully stone-walled. "There is no boy of that name in my school." Three cheers for the plaintiff who seems to have let the issue drop.

As Provost, Monsignor Sewell rightly felt a certain responsibility for his bishop's welfare. He proposed, for instance, a complete weekly break if only for half a day. When I heard years later he had taken to his bed, I hastened there at once. He had done the same many hundreds of times for others. As a curate at St. Wilfred's he worked in close partnership with Dr. Burke, the father of my devoted auxiliary bishop. They made a formidable team. Leaning back on the pillows he looked back over the years. "I'm 83. I've had a good innings," reflected the old Jessop. He went north to seek the care of the devoted Augustinian sisters at Boarbank Hall where so many of our priests find health and relaxation. Within days he was back again. Chorlton was his home and there he died. A kindly light for bishop, priests and people slowly faded and the diocese mourned a gentle pastor in the great tradition of Soggarth Aroons. One of the chapter canons, John McCabe of St. Edmunds, struggled to the funeral in a wheel-chair. The effort killed him. That he went to God that way says something about both men not all that far away from John 15.13.*

The other councillor, Winnie Carlton, she came to us from Yorkshire via Birmingham University. In her public service of the city she was fearless. Her work for the Church, especially as president of the Catholic Women's League, was outstanding and never-ending. Her last initiative—a sundial recording Pope John Paul's helicopter landing in Nazareth House garden—was completed after her death. Speaking in the first person, as sundials not infrequently do, the legend runs: "I stand here by courtesy of the C.W.L. Salford to record the five hours of unclouded joy between the landing of John Paul II in this garden and his leaving it for York 31 May 1982."

* "Greater love than this no man hath . . . "

CHAPTER XLIX

Ecumenical Meetings

THE MAJOR task of the Secretariate for Christian Unity was accomplished when the Decree on Ecumenism was voted in the second session of Vatican II and promulgated by Pope Paul VI on 21 November 1964. Early in 1966 Father Bernard Leeming, S.J. published his commentary on the text of the decree. I treasure my copy which he signed: "With respect and affection" on St. Valentine's Day. Luckily for one whose memory is short on detail he prints in Appendix IX a pastoral letter "given at Wardley Hall on the Feast of the Epiphany 6th January 1965." There is nothing marvellous about the text which is routine and here and there typically over-cautious. The date, however, fills me with astonishment. I had returned from the Bombay Eucharistic Congress close on Christmas. After Christmas dinner at Wardley I shot off home for a break. The pastoral is inordinately long by present standards, so I am amazed how I managed to "give" the blessed thing in the first week of January.

The pastoral was the prelude to the creation of a diocesan Ecumenical Commission which met regularly at Wardley. I had good reason to be proud of the team. When Cardinal Bea came to Heythrop we were all there to hear the principal architect of the Decree. He lectured in Latin which being interpreted found all of us warmly *en rapport* with the mastermind. We were a "mixed commission", not in the current sense of combined faiths, but of clergy and laity, male and female. I recall with particular pleasure Sister Olivia C.P., and Monica Stalker who on one occasion brought to the "mix" her new-born baby. This ecumenical neophyte kindly abstained from all oral intervention in the debates.

Father Bernard's book furnishes me with yet another cardinal point, and one which concerned rather more than one Catholic diocese. Indeed the whole Catholic world was involved along with the World Council of Churches. "In the third week of May 1965", writes Father Leeming, "eight representatives of the World Council met six Catholic representatives, to discuss 'practical collaboration in the fields of philanthropy, social and international affairs; theological study programmes which have a specific bearing on ecumenical relations; problems which cause tension between the Churches, such as mixed marriages, religious liberty and proselytism; and common concerns with regard to the life of the Church such as laity, missions."

No wonder we went on meeting every six months, year after year. Pope Paul VI had appointed me to this Joint Working Group, but my problem as a working bishop was how to combine the reams of paperwork which mounted on one's desk before each meeting with the pastoral demands of the diocese. Various new "structures" were then in demand. The Ecumenical Commission was closely followed by a Clergy Senate, Liturgy Commission, Social Services and others.

Many of Salford's 215 parishes were overdue for Visitation and Confirmation. Unwisely I had taken on a schedule of three parishes per week, more perhaps than anyone should attempt. "Spring", says a poet, "blesses us with surprise". So did the schedule. Word came that there were thirty-seven candidates for confirmation at St. John's, Rochdale. Undoubtedly ears can lapse as well as tongues. There were 737!

I am ashamed to record I was at times mugging up the WCC/RC agenda on the outward flight to the meetings of the Joint Working Group. Luckily venues were conveniently remote and usually very attractive. The World Council of Churches and Roman Catholic Church took turns to be hosts. We met twice annually.

Crêt Berard somewhere in Switzerland came early in the series. There for the first time I met Visser't Hooft, founder of the WCC. I had of course seen him in Rome. This time, however, it was against quite a different background. Crêt Berard, as the name suggests, is located at a certain altitude. We arrived on a wintry evening. After supper there was a gathering in a somewhat chilly common-room. Duty-free Scotch improved the atmosphere in more ways than one. Before this, however, I had been the recipient of a more delicate compliment by way of coffee. It was the time the leaders of the Catholic delegation, Cardinals Jan Willebrands and Jerome Hamer, were not as yet bishops. Nikos Nissiotis, the darling theologian of Athens university, invited them to join him and Lukas Vischer, Swiss Reformed Church, in the round tower which is such a remarkable and unforgettable feature of Crêt Berard. With exquisite courtesy Nikos sought me out and to my surprise served me with the first cup and a deft Athenian accolade: clearly, however, not for the man but for his office. I was the only bishop in the party.

Geneva, the G.H.Q. of the WCC, had, of course, its share of meetings both in the city and at Bossey, a delightful conference centre close to the Lake on the edge of a huge forest. There I spotted certain species of birds for the first time. It was at one of our Geneva meetings that I heard with something less than joy Visser't Hooft's views on the Vatican Diplomatic Service. He found it irreconcilable with the Church's spiritual endowments and mission. If I remember rightly we had once heard pretty well the same cantilena from one of the Council Fathers. Earlier in these memoirs there is a chapter dealing with the issue and I gave Visser't Hooft the gist of the argument. I fear the great man was not impressed.

Another WCC venue comes happily to mind, this time in

Germany. We were actually inside a forest, housed in a boarding-school some distance from the Catholic church where we said Mass. On the last evening Bishop Kempe of Limburg paid us a visit. This was highly appreciated for more reasons than one. We were in his diocese. He was one of Vatican II's four moderators and personally responsible, I understand, for introducing the technology which recorded all that was said in the aula. Like the Greeks, he came bearing gifts. This time it was not coffee, but wine in generous measure. Before this thoughtful bishop left but after I had sampled the gift, he addressed me in these terms: "Come to stay with us for a holiday. Many parish priests have an excellent vineyard. All their doors will be open to you. Come at vintage time, not for the new but for the old." He departed. Alas, I never went back.

That evening Manchester United were playing in a European Cup Match. We all gathered round the T.V. punctuating the play with shouts of "Hoch!" and quaffs of Hock. I was sitting next to Professor Schlink of Heidleburg University. Luckily Manchester United's adversaries were not from the German Federal Republic. Otherwise could it have been the end of a perfect friendship? Occasionally I rose from my chair to cheer as Bobby Charlton showed his prowess. This must have been an unusual experience for Professor Schlink. He entered generously into the spirit of the occasion though remaining sedentary throughout. At the end, however, he rose to address me: "You are the most unusual bishop I have ever met." I must have presented a somewhat different *persona* from the warm but wary neighbour in the conference room.

Our R.C. choice of venues naturally veered towards southern Europe. One I remember at a monastery off the coast of Naples; another at the Friary in Assisi, and more than one at or near Rome. There one of our meetings climaxed in unforgettable tension. Pope Paul VI had agreed to give the leaders of the Joint Working Group his answer to a problem which was exercising many minds. Within our closed circuit it was at this time constantly near the surface in all our discussions: "Will the Catholic Church, having come so far in dialogue, now move on to accept membership of the World Council of Churches?" We already had permanent R.C. delegates in the W.C.C. at Geneva. The W.C.C. theologians, Nikos and Lukas, had both worked hard on the problem, lecturing and writing, and I am sure, making the most of the fact that Orthodox Churches had accepted membership without compromising their status or independence. That final day we met at the usual time and despatched a number of items still on the agenda. Judging by my own experience, I can't think any of them won undivided attention. All minds, I think, were anticipating high noon. Half-way through the session our leaders left. Tension was palpably too high for further debate. We drifted into amiable chatter, ears alert for the return of the leaders. When they resumed their places at the conference table, Jan Willebrands went simply to the point: "The Holy Father has decided

that the Catholic Church will not become a member of the W.C.C."
I think the disappointment was not wholly confined to one side. Personally I was greatly relieved. Some time later at one of our meetings we were faced with a decision as yet secret. The W.C.C. had decided to subsidise certain liberation groups in Africa with arms. The decision had not been taken without great angst and by no means unanimously. We were asked for our reaction. I gave the reasons why in conscience I had to be totally *contra*. Lukas Vischer who put the question commented with exquisite courtesy. What I said, it seems, more or less parallelled what had also been heard within the W.C.C. itself from certain members. With hindsight one saw how wisely the Holy Father made his decision on the day of the great W.C.C. rejection. Could one argue that had we joined, Catholic votes might have swung the W.C.C. vote against supplying arms? How many votes would we have had? Apparently the Greek Orthodox presence, if indeed they qualified to vote on such decisions, had not turned the tide. And could one count even on a solid Catholic vote on such an issue?

Lukas went on to make much of the change the decision had made to their relations with the freedom fighters, a totally new sense of brotherhood. For the first time it was acknowledged European well-wishers were genuinely on their side. Pope Paul was taking no risks.

CHAPTER L

The Radio Priest—and Ups
and Downs

POPE Paul VI had already confided the problem of Atheism to the Jesuits when Vatican II produced its international Secretariate for Non-Believers. No doubt it was as a bishop of "little faith" that Cardinal Heenan suggested me when the Holy See asked for a member from England. Our chairman was Cardinal König of Vienna. Though I was already up to my neck in commissions and secretariates at home and abroad, this one, however, was a genuine gift-horse. The cardinal's grasp of the agenda, his lucid Latin and good humoured conduct of debate, all ensured a happy ship in which we served with zest and jest. Crewman Fulton Sheen showed to better advantage here than in the Council chamber where I think he overplayed the Bossuet line.

Needless to say at home we had to create a domestic version of yet another Secretariate. Here again I could not grumble. Father John Gaine as secretary took most of the strain apparently in his stride. Our meetings brought together masters from a range of disciplines outside one's normal ecclesiastical studies. Via this new commission I met John Finnis, Oxford Professor of Philosophy of Law. At the Eucharistic Congress in Melbourne, his native city, we arrived too late to hear his splendid address.

After a double dose of time on the Central Religious Advisory Committee B.B.C. and I.B.A., I found myself stuck in the chair of our own Mass Media Commission for the next fifteen years. Far from complaining, once again I reckon the experience a huge bonanza if only for the privilege of working closely with one of the most remarkable churchmen of our times, Father Agnellus Andrew O.F.M. As a young friar he was destined for studies abroad. His future was to be academic life in a chair of Scotist Theology. A providential indisposition kept him in England. He came newly ordained to Manchester, and there, instead of a rostrum, mounted a soapbox every lunghtime in the industrial estate of Trafford Park to hold large crowds with the social doctine of *Rerum Novarum* and *Quadragesimo Anno*. Manchester's Radio 2ZY jumped at him. Bristol provided a chair on the *Anvil*. When the B.B.C. opened its doors to a resident Catholic priest, Cardinal Hinsley with a blessing at once assured him: "Agnellus, this is your life." And so it was, in ever widening circles of responsibility which John Paul supremely rounded off with a Vatican post of all-inclusive concern for the Church's "Instruments of Social Communication". The young friar's earlier destiny to a rostrum in Rome thus came true. But the master was dispensing wisdom from on high over audiences and areas of knowledge undreamt of by Duns Scotus or any of the Schoolmen, Thomist or Scotist.

When I came to Manchester, twenty years after Agnellus left for the B.B.C., his name was still a household word, not so much for his media achievements as for his Greyfriar Players at Gorton and their performances of Gilbert and Sullivan operas under his direction. Wherever they went, and most of our Manchester parishes seem to have welcomed them, the memory persists of an experience out of this world, a celestial irruption of light, harmony and colour into industrial drabness.

I must in pious memory of my predecessor Bishop Thomas Henshaw record an experience Father Agnellus had in the church of St. Francis Gorton. This noble edifice was the scene of his first appointment and, as he once assured me, remained his greatest love. On the night of 22 June 1938 the then bishop of Salford, Thomas Henshaw came to stay at the friary. He was to consecrate the church on the following day which meant he fasted on the vigil and began the marathon ceremony very early next morning. Around midnight Agnellus remembered something missing from the preparations and went down into the great church. Alone in the darkness the bishop was still there prostrate at his prayers.

In those days St. Francis Gorton was one of our most densely populated parishes. Re-housing schemes have now dwarfed it from thousands to hundreds. Drastic clearances make the church by contrast ride like a great ship at anchor, higher than ever. In a sense two of our greatest churches in Manchester, St. Francis and the Holy Name, have returned to their origins. With commendable foresight and heroic trust in the Lord, both were built outside the city. Land no doubt was cheaper and population swelled daily beyond the perimeter. Both are now in effect back in the country again. There are buildings and some people. Not, however, the great clustering Catholic neighbourhoods which those churches anticipated and served so well. With the displacement of people, our down town parishes in all parts of the diocese have been devastated. To reduce the number of Masses was simple enough. The real solution, the reduction of parishes, was dynamite. I just had not the courage to face the wreckage.

There was, however, as a result principally of one man's tireless initiative and drive, copious consolation in New Town Langley near Middleton into which poured masses of Manchester's displaced citizens. Long before I came to the diocese Father Jack Murphy, the parish priest of Langley, had established his claim to my undying gratitude. He was then a curate at the English Martyrs, Manchester, star parish for vocations to the priesthood. The legend runs that in holiday time there were enough students home in the parish to form their own cricket and football leagues.

One morning in the sacristy after Mass, Father Murphy bowed to the crucifix, deposited his chalice and turned to salute the altar boy with these words: "I'm seventeen years ordained today, John, and nothing to show for it!" They made a deep impression, though having seen the priest at work around the parish the lad was puzzled. Nonetheless he declared his own desire to be a priest and in due course it was Father Murphy and fellow curate Father Joseph Cassidy who set the candidate on the way which terminated in his ordination at the English College Rome on the Feast of Christ the King, 1962. It was Cardinal Godfrey's last ordination. English Bishops were all in Rome at the time for the First Session of Vatican II. Most of us were staying at the English College and were present at the ordination.

Whatever grain of truth there was in Father Jack's dramatic statement, that act alone, his sponsorship of the altar boy, handsomely makes full amends.

For all but two of my twenty years in the diocese, John Allen, the altar boy, was to be Bishop's Secretary, Master of Ceremonies, Press Officer, Archivist, chauffeur and the rest, and, best of all, my ever-faithful Jonathan. He rarely left his desk before 11.30 p.m. What he achieved in the preceding two years to meet the multiple demands of the Papal Visit to Manchester remains his finest hour and my deepest debt.

To return to Langley New Town. My predecessor, Bishop Marshall, had made one of his most brilliant bishop's moves when he appointed his fellow Kerryman Father Jack Murphy pioneer of our Catholic presence there. From my days in the Catholic Missionary Society and from the lips of a priest with unique experience of New Towns I had learned the secret of pastoral success in that challenging environment. "Get them as soon as they arrive," was Father B. C. Foley's* advice, backed by his own heroic example. We were campaigning in Essex New Towns—Basildon, Harlow and others. Brentwood diocese was honeycombed with them. We met many a priest committed to old time principles: "Better to ring doorbells than churchbells." "A house-going priest means a church-going people." Certainly England and Wales owe much to these old timers. Alas, they are somewhat under siege in this present era of proliferating committees, courses and con-celebrations.

Langley New Town crowns the hill rising from the busy heart of old town Middleton. Father Murphy stationed himself there astride his bicycle, day after day, as the exodus from Manchester came through, families, furniture and much else mounted on all manner of vehicles. "Are you Catholics?" he shouted. "Yes, Father", was his signal to hitch on with one hand and free-wheel alongside. This way he arrived at the front door simultaneously with the new tenants.

* Later Bishop of Lancaster 1962-84.

Legend has it their names were down for the outdoor collection before they got inside. Certainly he gave them value for money: two churches and presbyteries, five schools, and, at his invitation, convents of teaching Sisters of Selly Park and nursing Sisters of the Assumption. His own church of the Assumption, a massive Norman pile, can be seen for miles around. St. Columba's, now served from the main church also has a community of Sisters of the Good Shepherd. When he invited me to consecrate the church of the Assumption I could scarcely believe it was so soon free of debt. Those uphill cycle rides had harvested not only the pennies but the people. They were there in their thousands all round the walls outside and inside as in the old rite we circled blessing the vast perimeter. Father was younger than me yet I had to modulate my pace to suit him. The demon cyclist was done. It was a merciful providence that he died worn out before the falling birthrate emptied his schools and reduced the congregations in both churches. The night we struggled round his great church of the Assumption I cherish the chance I had to tell him and his people that his personal achievement was unparallelled in the post war parochial history of the Catholic Church in England. After eight years all over the country in the Catholic Missionary Society and four years as bishop in the South, I was not talking off the top of my head.

Yet something must be added to the Langley story if all is to be seen in true perspective and I am sure Father, by now Canon, Jack would be the first to insist it should be said. For all his shrewd diplomacy with local authorities which secured appropriate sites for his churches and other plant, what really put us not only on the physical map but found a place for us in the heart of the New Town was the Sisters' contribution in the schools and particularly in the homes.

The Sisters of the Assumption are, or were, known in France as the "Swallows", I suppose from their black and white habits and perhaps even more so from the radiant springtime they brought into many a wintry home. Rearguard novelist René Bazin wrote a charming piece about them. I think a daughter of his had taken the veil with them. Happily, all the winsome features he praised came with them to Langley. They were often all night with the sick in their homes—any home—Catholic, Protestant, Hottentot, the lot. Breadwinners were able to start the day after a good night's sleep. Likewise the school children.

Canon Jack's festive sessions with town planners and environmental big-wigs of course played their part. Despite advanced work on subterranean telephone cables, one word or maybe two from Leslie Lever, and the whole site was cleared to make room for a Catholic school. It was the comprehensive charity of the "Swallow" Sisters, however, that radically changed the climate of a whole New Town. It is sad indeed to reflect now that the schools closed and the Swallows flew away. Their ever-open haven of peace became a local authority home for refractory youth.

I am only too conscious of my neglect in these pages of those cherished towns and parishes in the north of the diocese. Salford diocese comprises the Hundreds of Salford and Blackburn, divided by moors over Bolton and Rossendale. In terms of parishes and Catholic population, Salford would outnumber Blackburn by three to one. In terms of regular practice of the Faith, however, the northern part would take the Blue Riband. You only have to look at the 1767 lists of Catholics in Lancashire* to see how Faith and native stubbornness can go hand in hand. Visitations and confirmations in these Northern parishes invariably produced their crop of old Catholic names: Southworths, Holdens, Woodcocks, Swarbricks and many others. Perhaps the following story will highlight their quality and make some amends for my omissions.

Many times, passing through Intack on the ring road round Blackburn, I remembered my first encounter there with a valiant woman of the Faith. It was near Old Mother Redcap's and in my C.M.S. days. The parish priest then was Father John McNulty, who more than anyone else in my experience qualifies for Francis Thompson's directive: "Look for me in the nurseries of heaven."

In the course of mission visiting I knocked on a door and was admitted by a lady who went on to tell me of her grandfather's recent death. "He weren't a Catholic, so when he were dying I asked him if he would like the minister, and he said he would. But when his minister came, he turned his face to the wall. 'Don't want him,' he said. 'I want t'little 'un.' T'little 'un' were Father McEnery, so I sent for him and he came. He were with Grandfer for half an hour, and when he came out he said: 'Well, Mary, I've done all I can for him. He's a Catholic now, and I've anointed him and given him Communion. He hasn't long to live, so you go in and say your rosary for him.' So I did. I hadn't been in long when Grandfer opened his eyes and said: 'Mary, 'oo's that woman a'back o'thee?' I looked round and I couldn't see anybody, and I told Grandfer there were nobody there. 'Nay,' he said. 'Hoo's a reet bonny lass. Hoo's wearing a blue shawl.' And then he died."

* Returns of Papists 1767, Diocese of Chester, Catholic Record Society 1980.

CHAPTER LI

Quinquennial Visits

EVERY five years diocesan bishops make a duty visit to Rome with a detailed report on the state of their diocese. They personally present this in writing at the Sacred Congregation for Bishops, formerly known as the Consistorial. Each country has its given year and latterly we have gone as a province headed by our metropolitan archbishop. An alternative and nobler title for these visits is *"Ad Limina Apostolorum"*. They involve a visit to the "thresholds" that is, the tombs or "Confessions" of Sts. Peter and Paul. One used to have to produce documentary proof that one had fulfilled this obligation. In more enlightened times it seems bishops are now trusted to observe this basic piety spontaneously. A welcome *aggiornamento*.

My first visit *"ad limina"* came the year after the Vatican Council's last session, in 1966. With his usual exquisite courtesy Pope Paul absolved us from the drudgery of preparing an exhaustive report. He indicated he would be satisfied with what he called *"un lavoro sintetico"*. After all we had been away from our dioceses for months each year of the conciliar sessions. Even when at home, *"in sede"*, nights and days could be dominated by study documents connected with the Council. This was particularly the case with bishops serving on Commissions. They would also be attending inter-conciliar meetings here and there on the continent from which they returned with yet more *pabulum* for study and commentary.

The Cardinal Prefect of the Consistorial Congregation in 1966 was Carlo Confalonieri. The night before I was due to appear before him to give my verbal report, I chanced on a slim volume among the books in my room at the English College entitled *Un Decennio Aquilense*. It was the story of the Cardinal's ten years as bishop of Aquileia. Early in my interview I mentioned that in his book he recorded the curious fact that his episcopal decade began and ended with the gift of a car from the faithful of the diocese. I am afraid from then on there was very little said about my own diocese of Salford. Was I playing the artful dodger?

The climax of an *Ad Limina* visit is of course the personal interview with the Holy Father. I began the day with Mass at the tomb of the Apostle in St. Paul's outside the walls which I offered for Pope Paul. On the way back to the sacristy a sign was given indicating very clearly that this was to be my great day: I was created a Cardinal! As we passed a group of pilgrims I heard the guide say loud and clear in German: "Do you see the priest wearing the scarlet cap? That is the sign he is a cardinal of the Holy Roman Church." In the sacristy a Benedictine monk produced and signed the document attesting I had made my visit to the "threshold" of St. Paul. I was now all set for the audience. In the event I came home with the document. Nobody wanted it.

It was well after midday when my turn came to enter the papal apartment. I was the last that morning of a long line of clients. Monsignor Roccagiovane* who with a companion was on duty that morning somewhat anxiously enquired was I going to speak in English. There was evident relief when I said I would try Italian. They both romped away at once to their delayed spaghetti. When I entered Pope Paul was bent over the huge *Atlas Hierarchicus*† looking for Salford. "Behold the last cross of the morning, Holy Father" said I, dropping to my knees.

"Ma no!" said he. *"Una gioia!"* *(Bis.)* His finger was on the map of Great Britain and I was delighted to see SALFORD in bold capitals alongside Manchester in small print. "So Salford is near Liverpool," observed His Holiness. It was my turn to disagree. "No, *Santita!* The truth is Liverpool is near Salford." His finger descending a little, he said. "Years ago I remember crossing that big river Mersey and coming to Chichester." Once again I ventured to disagree: "No, *Santita!* It was Chester. Chichester is right down here near the south coast." "Ah yes. Chester. Chester," and he went on to recall two notable features of the cathedral: the colour of the stone and its beautiful *intaglio* work. We moved on to diocesan matters. He listened to my answers with an ever clearer conviction mantling his face. *"Caro"*, he said, "you are making a big mistake. You think you are the only bishop of Salford. You mustn't. The Lord is still Shepherd of all his sheep." So this was the secret. The reason he could generate such light-hearted joy despite the heavy load on his frail shoulders.

Before I left his presence, walking on air, I ventured to say I had offered Mass for him that day at St. Paul's. "Then I shall say Mass for you," he said, as I kissed his ring. There was one last courtesy. "Would you like to be photographed with me?" A panel opened in the wainscotting. There was Signor Felici with his camera.

None of my other audiences during Pope Paul's time come back as vividly as that one. On a number of occasions I broached problems with him, particularly those concerned with the reorganisation of our schools. Looking back I marvel at my insensitivity. As if he hadn't enough problems of his own.

* This member of the papal *entourage* is a descendant of Napoleon I from whose library he inherited books donated by Lord Holland, 1773-1840, a leading Whig politician. Monsignor was impressed by the laconic signature: "Holland". He took it for granted I belonged to the family. *Purtroppo!*
† A superb production covering the world's Catholic dioceses and other episcopal jurisdictions, the work of the Fathers of the Divine Word in Austria under the direction of Father Heinrich Emmerich SVD.

I remember thanking him for the stream of instruction in the Faith he was then channelling through public audiences. He deprecated any mention of them but he was human enough to show that he was pleased. To have given him one moment of good cheer remains a cherished privilege. He had, I think, far more of the other kind, more pehaps than any other pope of our time as Vatican II continued to suffer at the hands of pseudo-experts, and vehement opposition to *Humanae Vitae* continued to grow. The *Times* carried a letter signed by seventy-six laymen and priests deploring the encyclical. Inevitably they go down in story as the "seventy-six trombones". The Saturday that encyclical arrived I circulated a letter to the clergy which I read and commentated the following day in the cathedral. One paragraph read: "In all major issues I stand with the successor of St. Peter, and I call upon my priests to stand with me, because there is no redemption, there is no progress for a particular Church, for the Church of the diocese of Salford, unless we are in the closest and most loyal union with the Successor of St. Peter. I call upon my priests and my people to be with me in these things, to stand firm and to be with our Holy Father."

As I made the point that the Pope by remaining loyal to the teaching of the Church had at the same time spoken for the true happiness of Christ's people, a woman rose from the middle of the congregation shouting, "It's a lie," and swept out of the cathedral followed by her husband. It was my first indication of the odium Pope Paul was to suffer I fear for the rest of his life. At times I have allowed myself to wonder why he had delayed his decision so long. Was it in deference to the well publicised fact that the majority vote of the Commission he set up to study the issue was in favour of change? What I think cannot be denied is that the long silence allowed the dissenters to strengthen both their self-confidence and their propaganda. How else account for Rosemary Haughton's public appeal for prayers that the old guard would have the grace to accept the reversal of their convictions when the Pope announced his decision?

That Sunday afternoon the B.B.C. somehow managed to fly me down to London for the televised debate on *Humanae Vitae* conducted by Malcolm Muggeridge. Needless to say I was not the B.B.C.'s first choice. Five or six other bishops, I believe, had been approached before me. I arrived too late for what Continentals call the "fusion", the highly civilised intermingling of the panel over drinks. There must have been twenty or thirty guests among whom I recognised Peregrine Worsthorne and Charles Davis.

Muggeridge sat me facing the panel, gave me the initial few minutes and promised me the chance to wind up the debate. We agreed a hand signal which would call me in. I opened with little more than words of praise for the Pope who against the tide had had the courage to give his flock the only genuine compassion, the truth. Needless to say, most of the speakers disagreed. Worsthorne, however, was forthright in stating his theoretical agreement with the Pope.

With some anxiety I awaited the agreed signal for my last word, crowded issues jostling through my mind. In fact, somewhat to my relief the signal never came. Malcolm Muggeridge must either have forgotten or decided I was better unheard. Either way he was right. I could scarcely have coped. But the day was not quite over. Two gentlemen from the Press were waiting for me as we emerged from the set. At some point before the broadcast I had unwisely mentioned the morning's bitter murmur in the cathedral. Clearly the incident in the meantime had been passed on to Fleet Street. It duly appeared on the morrow complete with my comment that I would be glad to meet the couple. In due course they appeared. The husband who was not a Catholic remained silent; his partner was less aggressive this time but still unable or unwilling to agree. I felt it my duty on every parish visitation to tackle the issue openly. Only the Lord can judge how far mental blockages on this issue were culpable or not. All I know is that the schools we were building hand over fist in the mid-sixties were within two decades up for sale and a drug on the market.

My last quinquennial visit was in autumn 1982. This time the Cardinal of the Congregation of Bishops received us all together as a province. No sooner had Archbishop Worlock, our metropolitan, introduced us, than His Eminence launched into the audience the Holy Father had given him immediately on return from his visit to Great Britain the previous May. Apparently there had been much in that visit to impress and console the Holy Father. We gathered it both could and should serve as a model for similar occasions.

This was indeed a bonanza for all of us and well worth all the immense effort demanded by the visit. For Archbishop Worlock in particular it was the supreme accolade. No doubt he had already received it personally from the Holy Father. But for his determined defence of the visit which locked him in endless debate with the bishops from South America, the visit would never have taken place. The peace formula which won the day for Britain reflects enormous credit on all concerned. It says everything too for the sportsmanship of Pope John Paul II who lost no time in taking the air again for the balancing visit to the Argentine. For that solution we owe eternal thanks to Cardinal Hume who was the first to suggest it.

Once again my audience with the Holy Father on that autumn quinquennial came towards the end of a long morning. I emerged about 1 p.m. Bishop Foley followed me. After him there were still three East European bishops for interview.

On this occasion I presented an appropriately bound copy of *"A New Creation"*, the illustrated story of the papal visit to Manchester. The Holy Father glanced briefly through it and then concentrated on the other document I had laid before him, my resignation from the See of Salford. Shrewdly he demanded the precise date of my seventy-fifth birthday. It was then nine months away. "We shall deal with this matter in due course," he said. He then read aloud a phrase I had used about "fearing to harm the diocese" as I declined mentally and physically. "Harm?" He repeated the word with relish. But eighteen months were to pass before I was finally released. Before then would come my golden jubilee of priesthood. Like John Henry King, I too was to be surprised by the warmth and compass of the celebrations: liturgical at the Cathedral and St Alban's Blackburn; festive at Hopwood Hall; musical at the Manchester Free Trade Hall, which rang and rippled in a melodious marathon performed by high school pupils from the whole diocese. I had never imagined we were nurturing such talent.

The papal audience was as always the climax, not, however, this time the end of the quinquennial. A "new wave" was now surging through the Vatican. The Northern Province was invited to a papal lunch. Our metropolitan sat facing His Holiness. As senior member I was on the Pope's right. It was Friday with *cuisine polonaise* and a white Cesanese wine from the Castelli. I drank level with my host, two or was it three glasses. Throughout the meal, along with the light-hearted banter, went a skilful pontifical trawling of our news and views on a variety of pastoral issues. Our host listened carefully, clearly storing away his impressions for further reflection. Bishop Gordon Wheeler was attentively heard on certain Anglican matters.

The Pope's visit to the Anglican Cathedral in Liverpool was mentioned along with the winsome detail of the fallen rosary beads which the Pope had picked up in the aisle and restored to its owner. "Our Metropolitan," I informed my august neighbour, "has been picking up people's rosaries ever since!" "Tom Holland has never stopped kissing babies" came the instant metropolitan comment. It was perhaps as well I was too slow to get in with, "Only those frightened by the Archbishop of Liverpool!"

Towards the end of the meal the Polish Secretary brought in a large case from which he extracted a rather special apparatus. I was somewhat taken aback when he announced it was the gift of the Salford diocese. It was a video-recorder which Bishop Agnellus had advised us would be welcomed at the Vatican. It was being seen not only by the Holy Father for the first time. I too had not seen it either. We had picked up the case in London on the way out. From lunch we moved out to pray in the papal chapel. I was comforted to see the altar had not been turned round. Was I perhaps the only bishop then in England whose domestic chapel was "un-reordered"?

Of the dozens of visits I have made to Rome as a bishop only once have I stayed elsewhere than the Venerable English College. On this occasion Bishop Agnellus booked us in at the Hotel Cardinale on the other side of the Via Monserrato. The super-hospitable English College compensated for the lack of beds with the loan of the vice-rector's car.

As we left the Hotel Cardinale for the papal audience dressed in our ecclesiastical finery I whispered to the padrone at the desk, "The next time we stay here we shall both be cardinals." "In that case," said he, "you will be our guests." He paused: "That is to say for the first night."

If I may wind up this chapter on quinquennials with a single overriding impression it would be the incomparable value of that Friday lunch with the Holy Father. There for a relaxed leisurely hour we chatted about our work with the one ultimately responsible for all our dioceses. Far from aimlessly, but without exerting any pressure, I am sure he got a finer appreciation of us and our terrain. Certainly the exercise worked both ways!

CHAPTER LII

Papal Visit to Greater Manchester 31st May 1982

ARCHBISHOP Bruno Heim, Apostolic Delegate to Great Britain, broke the news of John Paul's visit to our country on 31st August 1980. He was on an official visit to the Salford diocese. The announcement came at the end of sung Mass at St. Gregory's, Farnworth, near Bolton. Half an hour later he gave the news to the Mayor and Councillors of Salford at his official reception in the Town Hall. A telex at once left in their name welcoming the Holy Father to the City of Salford, surely the first of many such invitations. The following day Manchester City Council gave a luncheon to the Delegate who repeated to them the good news. They too sent an immediate invitation to the Pope on behalf of the city. From that moment onwards we had both cities and the Greater County of Manchester sharing the long drawn out preparations both "ardently and arduously", as I was able to tell the Holy Father in the address of welcome which began the inaugural Mass on 31st May 1982 in Heaton Park.

In successive Papal audiences during 1981 two Manchester Lord Mayors, Councillor Winnie Smith and Councillor Hugh Lee, both Catholics, personally invited the Holy Father to visit Manchester. In their search for an appropriate venue, Greater Manchester Police surveyed many sites in their area, always coming back to Heaton Park, the largest municipal park in Europe. On 23 January 1981 we met the Chief Constable and his deputy at the Park and made our decision, Mr Anderton actually indicating the best spot for the papal altar. A month later the Northern Bishops approved the venue. All our planning was hypothetical until April 1981. Only then were we given approval by the Holy See for both our proposed dates and itinerary. The Manchester visit would be on the 31st May 1982. Twelve groups* and a co-ordinating committee were recruited to cover the major problems involved in the accommodation of hundreds of thousands of people in what was to be the largest gathering in the history of northern England.†

* (1) Spiritual and Pastoral Preparation. (2) Finances and General Purposes. (3) Ecumenical Contacts. (4) Liaison between dioceses. (5) Liaison between Local Authorities, Consular and other civil groups. Protocol. (6) Hospitality and Reception. (7) Liturgy: (a) ceremonial: (b) construction. (8) Media. (9) Medical. (10) Security. (11) Stewarding. (12) Traffic and Transportation.
† Experts had forecast 300,000 for the Papal Mass in the Phoenix Park, Dublin in September 1979. In the event there were 1,300,000.

In mid-May 1981 I was as usual with the junior clergy of the diocese at the Passionist Retreat House, Ilkley, Yorkshire. Our brilliant theologian, Father Francis Frost, joined us from Lille University. This particular day his afternoon lecture was on ecumenism. His frankly pessimistic view of current progress surprised us: "We shall never get anywhere at this rate," he said. "We need some colossal act of penance, something to jolt us out of our complacency. Something like the murder of Pope John Paul II."

At that very moment I was called out to the 'phone. It was Monsignor Allen, 'phoning from Wardley Hall. "The Pope has been shot in the Piazza," he said. It was 13 May 1981.

For days the stunned Church agonised, for once the world was with us. Mercifully as days passed, it became clear the victim would live. But what kind of life? Could there still be room for the supreme physical effort of a five-day tour of Great Britain? We simply had to hope and go ahead with the preparations for the visit.

Less than three weeks after the outrage, on the 30 May 1981, I had the hardihood to face the pilgrims at Walsingham with this message: "A year tomorrow we shall have the Holy Father with us in our beloved diocese of Salford." Needless to say they were under no illusions about what that would cost in terms of prayer and penance.

There was some mention in the last chapter of the later threat to the visit from the Falklands War. If that had baulked us after Pope John Paul through God's good grace had gained his strength, are there in any language words strong enough to express the pity and the irony of it? Once again I salute Archbishop Worlock's unyielding tactical defence which I believe mainly saved the day. I cannot therefore hold it against the Archbishop that his tactical expansion of John Paul's visit to Liverpool probably hived off a number of people who would otherwise have come to Manchester. If I remember rightly, the original shape of the Liverpool visit was basically the reception and papal address to the sick at Speke airport. Eventually, however, both cathedrals came into the picture, plus a Papal Mass, and supper at Archbishop's House to which all bishops were invited and nobly regaled.

If there was any depletion of the Manchester congregation I am still glad to have rendered a uniquely delicate service of good will to the Liverpool visit. As the Holy Father emerged from his plane at Speke, a gust of wind swept off his skull cap and sent it rolling towards the tail. I set off in pursuit and managed to get a hand to it before it came to rest. The next day I admit to taking considerable delight in the press photograph captioned, "Well fielded, sir!"

Before leaving Liverpool that night I managed to get in touch with Monsignor Martinez who was custodian of the Holy Father's sermons and addresses. Early the following day the Chief Commonwealth Rabbi was to meet the Pope in Manchester with a considerable Jewish delegation. I was anxious: had the Holy Father written a reply to the Chief Rabbi's address? It might raise certain delicate issues. My other preoccupation was with Strangeways Gaol and the largest population of any gaol in the country. Could the Holy Father remember them in his homily?

31st May, "this day the Lord has made" (Ps. 117, v. 24) dawned at last. Despite the nocturnal return from Liverpool all of us at Wardley Hall were up and away by 4 a.m. to Nazareth House. There on the spacious lawn some hours later the papal helicopter would land. John Paul II would alight and there meet the local dignitaries. After the Mass he would return there for lunch and brief rest before taking off for York. Heaton Park, the venue for the Mass, lies alongside Nazareth House. Each of the two was perfect for its different purposes. Their togetherness eliminated all rival options.

On arrival I at once isolated myself at the top of the house, for a very good reason. After busying myself the night before with the Holy Father's speeches, here I was myself still speechless. On a long narrow note book I began to prepare the welcome address. The text lies before me just as I wrote it: "Dear H.F. We can scarcely believe you are here! God be praised for your brave decision to come to us. Your family and friends up here . . . " There is no more. At that point in came my auxiliary, Bishop Geoffrey Burke.

As the Holy Father stepped down from the helicopter the two of us knelt side by side to kiss his ring. I put my arm round Geoffrey. "Holy Father, here is the Vatican's greatest gift to me." How I meant it! "I could not have survived without him." Pope John Paul embraced us both. Together we moved to the long line of disting-uished religious and civic leaders each one of whom received a special word. I marvelled at the Holy Father's fecundity of apt and varied comment. To the ailing former Bishop of Shrewsbury, who was waiting by the door to Nazareth House the Pope said: "I beg you to pray for me."

His homily that day thrilled us with explicit reference to St. Ambrose Barlow O.S.B. and our other Lancashire Martyrs. I would hazard a guess that there were more people present that day who could claim a martyr in their family than at any other papal Mass. And how good it was for us priests that day to hear praise of a custom which, I think, derives from penal times and the close intimacy of priests and people without which priests and the celebration of Mass would have perished in our land: "Visit your parishioners in their homes. This has been the strength of the Church in England. It is a pastoral practice that should not be neglected."

Still addressing priests, the speaker went on with what might be called his *Magna Carta* for prisoners: "I was in prison and you visited me. And remember He did not specify whether they were innocent or guilty. Because you represent Christ no one can be excluded from your pastoral love. I ask you together with your brother priests to take my greetings to all prisons of Britain, especially the large one in Manchester."

One of our prison visitors, Miss Pat McEvoy, played the tape she had made at the Mass to the inmates of Strangeways. They could never hear it often enough. Our principal Prison Chaplain was also quick to press home the Holy Father's words in a letter to every bishop.

Later that year 1982 I was staying with friends on the Costa Brava. Daily and twice on Saturdays there was a TV news programme which opened with three brief action strips: President Reagan at his most vivacious; a yacht somersaulting skywards in the gale; and the Popemobile leaving Heaton Park after the papal mass. The local P.P.'s housekeeper was the first to identify the Pope's companion. "That's the bishop who was here from England last summer," said she. Only very sharp eyes could have done the trick in the few seconds available. The programme had been running for months. My friends assured me I was the best known bishop in Cataluña, Tarragona and the Spanish Mediterranean Islands. "Where can you cash that?" was my mercenary comment.

For the papal lunch at Nazareth House three Manchester hotels had submitted menus. We chose to reserve the honour for two qualified Sisters of Nazareth House. I insisted on Bury black puddings for starters, for Nazareth House lies just inside the township of Bury. Since the Doomsday Book Bury market has sizzled with boiled black puddings. They come in two editions: unrelieved black and handsomely flecked with succulent white wheatlets. I chose the latter. As host facing the Holy Father, I watched as the plate was placed before him. Sliced into two halves the outsize pudding was wholly black. Our guest left half untouched. "Holy Father, don't you like our local dish?" "I have no discernment!" was the enigmatic reply.

Very sportingly Cardinal Hume had insisted that Bishop Burke should occupy his place on the Holy Father's right. At the end of the meal I looked for His Eminence. He was away at the far end of the table. "Holy Father," said I, "I think Cardinal Hume would like permission to smoke." The blackleg went back on me! "No, Holy Father, I gave it up on January the first," said he. Feeling somewhat dashed, I tried again. "Holy Father, may I have permission to smoke?" "I think you *must* smoke!" he replied. Unfairly no doubt, those words have since been twisted to accommodate my addiction to the pipe, when commonsense would have had it otherwise.

During the visit to the chapel after lunch, Sisters, guests and staff were regaled with a lovely little impromptu homily. Archbishop Marcinkus was heard to say as we left the chapel: "Only twenty minutes rest, Holy Father."

When the papal helicopter at last disappeared from view I went into the papal suite. There was neither ruffle nor wrinkle on the counterpane. Having been up and about since 4 a.m. I threw myself on the bed for a couple of hours, never dreaming that two years later I would be sleeping there for the rest of my natural life.

CHAPTER LIII

"Mother Church defends the sacred gift of Human Life"

A FRONT-PAGE headline this morning* runs: "Crime rate up to six a minute." Metropolitan Police Commissioner Newman, commenting on these latest Home Office records, blames parents, schools and church, TV, credit cards, unemployment and drugs. He defends the police: "With virtually static resources in the last five years the police had given 'tremendous productivity'."

When I came home from India in 1948 a new phenomenon was on display: "The Generation Gap". A truer catch phrase, I think, would have been: "The Loss of Parental Grip". How far this was due to the wartime absence of parents from home, how far to the emergence of clashing youth cults like Teddy Boys etc. or how far to unheard of spending money, motor bikes and a new mobility, it is impossible to say. Our super-mobile C.M.S. Superior John Carmel Heenan, asked me to take his place at the monthly meetings of the London Public Morality Council at St. Martin's-in-the-Fields. Bishop Wand was in the chair. He missed nothing despite his apparent absorption in making pencil sketches of the members.

Fresh insights into the cause of declining standards were rare. Reports on the whole were routine and factual. Of course we debated copiously and wisely, wasting no time on complaints about insufficiently clothed tailors' dummies in shop windows!

When an invitation came to us to appear before the Royal Commission on Homosexuality, the Secretary and I were deputed to go. We were not briefed with any agreed policy. Indeed I doubt if the L.P.M.C. could have produced one.

We were interviewed by two gentlemen, one of them a young Catholic peer. I agreed of course on the fact of blameless deviant predispositions but urged the undeniable prevalence of acquired perversions, what someone called "the pursuit of gamey meat". When our interrogators left for a tea-break, they had done a long stint. It was late afternoon and when our turn came I think they had already had enough.

In the parliamentary debate I believe much was made of the opportunity for blackmail provided by the then criminal law. Inevitably good men will agree to differ on that particular line of

* *Daily Telegraph* 17 March 1987.

269

argument. In fact distinguished churchmen of all denominations did so. I believe Cardinal Griffin was impressed by it.

There was at least one Catholic lawyer who deeply deplored our failure to speak with one mind and voice on the issue—Richard O'Sullivan Q.C. English Law and society, he assured me, had consistently and vehemently penalised and denounced unnatural vice. He argued here was a unique instance of collective moral insight which we should abandon only at our grievous peril. He grieved over the failure to respect and cherish a tradition so consonant with the Old and New Testaments, so utterly at variance with the pagan culture of Greece and Rome and so universally upheld by Christendom with the single exception of the Code Napoleon.

Was this momentous change perhaps the first crack in the flood gates? Certainly pressures were mounting on other sectors as well. Way back in the 'thirties G. K. Chesterton identified human life as the main casualty of twentieth century social change. This was prompted by Marie Stopes and her vigorous campaign for birth-control. G.K. was in his grave before our legislators made their U-turn on homosexuality. Events, however, have dramatically con-firmed his judgment even in that respect, providing at the same time, a remarkable commentary on Romans 1, 26-27*.

Altogether apart from AIDS, and with genuine compassion for blameless deviations, the homosexual demo which I witnessed in Utrecht during the 1985 papal visit to Holland served only to highlight the ugly face of moral degeneracy. It did, however, succeed in forcing our conveyance to decant us on the wrong side of a canal at some distance from our venue for a longish walk through torrential rain. By the 'sixties the rot had eaten well into our own society. When I came north in the mid-sixties the campaign for equal rights *a la Hollandaise* was spearheaded from Manchester in the person of an alumnus of a well-known Catholic school. I thought I'd seen everything. But *"facilis descensus Averni"*†. Once the genera-tion gap dams up moral teaching in the home and the permissive society scares school teachers with the "indoctrination bogey" away from "Thus says the Lord" to "How does it seem to you?", the end product is predictable: "Any society which abandons moral teaching is on a suicide course." Homosexual instruction penetrates schools. Town Halls promote Lesbianism. The crime rate soars. Multiply

* "For this cause God gave them up to vile affections: for even their women did change the natural use into that which is against nature. And likewise the men, leaving the natural use of the woman, burned in their lust one towards another: men with men working that which is unseemly and *receiving within themselves that recompense of their error which is meet."* Douai version. First published Rheims 1582.
Or in the version of Dr. H. J. Schonfield: "Consequently God has given them over to their infamous passions; for their females have changed the normal function into the abnormal. The males, too, abandoning the normal function with females, inflamed with lust for one another have engaged in indecency, *duly receiving the reward appropriate to their irregularity among themselves."* Panther Books 1962 p. 259.
† The downward path is all too easy-going.

police, arm them with lethal weapons, rifles, howitzers or whatever. The result will be the same. The crime rate will continue to soar. James Anderton quite early in his career as Manchester's Chief of Police came out with a broadside against pornography. To my great surprise he told me later I was the only senior churchman in the city to support him.

At this point our society was about to lurch head-on, eyes open onto the predictable suicide course. In 1966 Mr. Steel's abortion bill came before the House. Chesterton's prediction of the 1930's was about to be dramatically and literally fulfilled.

In April 1966 Mr. Peter McDonald, a Manchester Catholic lawyer, produced and circulated his first Broadsheet. He wrote: "The attack on human life continues. Only the Church stands four-square for the principle of the sanctity of human life. And only a handful of Catholics are vocal."

There was, however, dissension in the camp. A group of influential Catholic laymen convinced Cardinal Heenan that the campaign against Mr. Steel's Bill was better left to the laity. Otherwise the usual gibes about ageing celibates could alienate all too many of the "don't knows". There was this further consideation. We could only hope to influence public opinion in alliance with non-Catholics. It was still early days for ecumenism in this country. Better keep a low R.C. profile and avoid mass meetings presided over and harangued by bishops in purple.

I fear this ever so reasonable policy failed miserably. The months slipped by without meetings of any kind. Thrust and impact associated with the Albert Hall protests on behalf of Cardinals Mindszenty* and Wyszynski were totally absent from our defence of human life. Yet this was to be the main battle for the rest of the century.

At last in December 1966 the intolerable silence burst asunder with mass protests from Liverpool and Manchester. Ours was at the Free Trade Hall on 5th December 1966. I quote from McDonald's Broadsheet No. 9:

"Two public meetings were held early in December, one in Manchester, one in Liverpool, both instigated and supported and to a large extent organised by Broadsheet readers. Well over 3,000 people heard the case against Abortion presented by such speakers as The Bishop of Salford, James Dunn M.P., Dr. Frank da Cunha, F.R.C.O.G. (Catholics), Canon G. B. Bentley M.A., Gordon Oakes M.P., Leslie Lever M.P., Professor Ian Donald M.D., F.R.C.S., F.R.O.C.G. and Professor Hugh McClaren (not

* Cardinal Mindszenty concelebrated Mass in Salford Cathedral at midday on Monday 16 July 1973. The rain came down in stair-rods but the cathedral was thronged with people long before Mass was due. Some told me they had left their work and would be sacked, but they had prayed for the Cardinal for years and would not miss him for worlds. Canon William O'Leary, Chapter secretary, welcomed him in elegant Latin. His Eminence replied vigorously and off-the-cuff in the same language.

R.C.s). The *Universe* and the *Daily Telegraph* gave the best publicity at least to our first meeting."

I took the decision to go against Heenan's policy with some difficulty despite constant prickings of conscience to do something before it was too late. The decision came during a consultation with Dr. Frank da Cunha. His answers to certain questions of mine cleared any last doubts. I remember it was he who said: "Then you have no alternative. You must mount a public protest." He read my mind. I was trapped by my own logic.

Broadsheet No. 9 continues:

"It may be of help to those organising other meetings to have the wording of the resolution passed by acclamation at the Manchester meeting. It reads:

1. This meeting is acutely aware of the grave social evils which call for an enlightened and compassionate effort of the whole community.

2. We recognise the probity and concern of the sponsors of the Medical Termination of Pregnancy Bill 1966, but register our deep anxiety and alarm at the solution proposed in the Bill.

3. So that nothing be done in haste in this crucial issue, we dedicate ourselves to a policy of sustained and informed opposition to the Bill as it stands.

4. We further call for a General Enquiry under an appropriate Commission with powers to consult all sections of the community and thoroughly explore the large areas of doubt and danger which distress us in the present Bill."

The call for an appropriate commission followed a tip-off "that the one thing Mr. David Steel is convinced will wreck his Bill is the removal of the debate from Parliament into an area where the massive medical opposition to the Bill would have such a telling effect."

Undoubtedly the star speech at the Free Trade Hall that night was Professor Ian Donald's. During it he played a recording of the heartbeat of a ten weeks old infant in the womb. People rose clapping and cheering as the throbs pounded through the vast hall.

Later in 1968, when Pope Paul VI issued *Humanae Vitae*, Professor Donald and another equally famous specialist happened to be having treatment at the same time in the same hospital. Somebody sent Donald a copy of the Encyclical. He read it and excitedly moved down the corridor to share it with his colleague. Looking at one another with a wild surmise both agreed: "The whole thing locks together. This is the key!"

I should have mentioned in the chapter on Quinquennials that at my 1968 audience with Pope Paul VI a Pastoral Letter of mine entitled *"In the Service of Life"* was mentioned. I went on to tell him about the Manchester lawyer, Peter McDonald, to whom we owed so much of the success of the Free Trade Hall and its aftermath. I begged the Holy Father to send him the papal medal of that year.* "If there are any left," said the Pope, "I will see he gets one."

The legend for 1968 ran: *"Mater Ecclesia Sacrum Donum Humanae Vitae defendit."*†

In due course the medal arrived. My secretary was on his way with it as once. No man had a better right to this signal honour than Peter McDonald. In his own words: "I saw *Humanae Vitae* as the Church's first broadside in defence of life. So when I came across a photo in *L'Osservatore Romano* of the 1968 Papal Medal carrying a picture of the Visitation and the Latin legend, I was overjoyed at this evidence that my mind had been in tune . . . I mentioned the medal and the legend at the end of a talk I then gave round and about on 'All life, all holiness'."

Mr McDonald has nobly responded to Pope Paul's munificent gesture with twelve Broadsheets a year ever since, all of them loyal in their support and brilliant in their illumination of the central magisterium of Mother Church.

* Every year a medal is struck recording the number of years the Pope has been in office and an outstanding feature of that particular year.
† "Mother Church defends the sacred gift of Human Life."

CHAPTER LIV
Run in to Vatican II

IN 1986, during his third visit to France, Pope John Paul II directed a short retreat for priests and seminarists at Ars. He made one thing very clear. To invite lay people to serve in areas formerly reserved to priests is not the answer to priests in short supply. He insisted the Church may not relax her quest for priestly vocations. She must have priests and many more of them.

It would be wrong to blame either the Council or Pope Paul VI for the instability which so grievously tried priests and people in the early post-conciliar days. There were, it is true, genuine misunderstandings abroad of Vatican II's intentions. At the same time the atmosphere was not entirely clear of malice and manipulation on the part of some publicists, God forgive them! We must thank John Paul II for his vigorous reduction of valid reasons and conditions for release from priestly obligations. The former creeping barrage is over. Our ranks, however, are more exposed than ever to increased attack from our friendly enemy Old Age.

I remember discussing with Heenan the situation in which a bishop could obtain a priest's release from his burden by simple presentation of the case. He was quite sure such a policy was fatal to the obligation of celibacy. He argued that it was all too obvious that the possibility of facile release magnified even minor personal problems into major crises. Frankly I still find Pope Paul's inaction here very hard to understand.

An industrious American priest, well known for his true life conversion stories published under the title *The Road to Damascus*, turned his hand to true life stories of a very different kind. Their publication is a sign of times more honest, open, if you like, but also much more hard-faced. This series tells the story of priests after release from their priestly obligations. There is no joy or constancy in these accounts: only repeated divorce.

Who then is to blame? The easy answer is the seminaries and those who run them. Seminary training and its equivalents serve two purposes: to recognise and encourage the genuine vocation; to reveal and eliminate the deficient. Both purposes are equally important to the Church. Mistakes either way are tragic. The Church is either robbed of a true pastor or lumped with a misfit. Before apportioning blame for either tragedy it is well to remember that the responsibility of Superiors for a well-informed and impartial judgment of the candidate must be complimented by the candidate's own readiness to seek and accept competent advice on his personal problems. This is, or should be, copiously provided. Within the classical concept, however, of the seminary as *"hortus conclusus"*—a sheltered garden—there was a chance that the candidate, under-exposed to the outside world, might come up against certain problems for the first time. The danger was judged to be remote once regular holidays away from the seminary were introduced. But nothing in seminary life, however freely diversified and open to the world outside, could have toughened candidates for what became the explosion of Vatican II. Indeed the most senior labourers in the vineyard had never seen anything quite like it.

The blame, however, rests not with the Council but with the rogue intepreters who crashed in with their own wishful thinking to make the occasion a supremely severe testing time for many of the faithful; most of all for those committed to the intimate service of the Church as priests and religious. Suddenly it seemed the Household of the Faith no longer had any house rules. A fourth theological virtue was now on display: "Contestation." Promoted into the Decalogue this became: "Thou shalt always contest thy rights and thy wrongs." Captive audiences, such as religious sisters on retreat, were exposed to new gospels. It seemed Catholic Publishers could no longer afford to bring out anything "Trad". Two works I was interested in—Monsignor McCreevy's on Birth Control, and a volume of essays on Seminary Training—could find no takers. Monsignor McCreevy was then probably our premier British moral theologian. He attended all four sessions of Vatican II as a *peritus*. A bleak wind from the left blew mean little news-sheets around the Church. The deposit of Faith was exposed to the blast. Witness the Dutch Catechism—*Concilium** was countered by *Communio†*. Vatican II definitely stimulated a *per se* welcome appetite for theological discourse and dialogue. I attribute this to the Conciliar Commissions which regularly brought together experts in the Sacred Sciences for considerable periods. I think they were also a tribute to a new experience. Where formerly experts knew one another's books they now knew one another. Rival publications varied in allegiance to theological tradition: you could find "trad" teaching on the extent of Our Saviour's human knowledge accepted in one, questioned in another.

The most dramatic sea change in traditional loyalties seems to have happened on the land between the North Atlantic and Pacific

---

* A theological review somewhat inspired by IDOC—a group dedicated to re-statement of the Faith in ways irreconcilable with I Tim.6, 20-21. Their campaign GHQ in Rome during Vatican II was behind the left arm of the colonnade of St. Peter's.

† So named from the valuable concept of the Church as a Communion. See Jerome Hamer's: *The Church is a Communion*. There were several *Communios*, main language groups tending to produce their own often, however, drawing upon one another in translation.

Oceans. The Second Session of the Council in 1963 registered a notable change of U.S. bishops in sensitivity to Rome. First session debates had revealed them as strong traditionalists—more so perhaps than ourselves. Other bishops' conferences were free in their comments and criticisms: one or two missioners and younger existentialist bishops were very free indeed; a certain middle-eastern patriarch, Maximus IV Saigh, outrageously so—in French. This may have impressed the U.S. bishops but surely, however, not so much as the domestic climate to which they returned from the first session. A revolution was in progress fuelled by Xavier Rynne in the *New Yorker*. No one could at that time have foreseen where it might end. Even so if you had suggested that the Pope while a guest on American soil would have his teachings pulled to pieces by American Catholic theologians on a coast-to-coast hook-up, you would probably have been clobbered. That, however, was to happen each night of John Paul II's first papal visit to the U.S.A.

On a rather lower note, I recall that shortly before the Second Session of the Council the teaching of the Episcopal Conference of England and Wales suffered minor dismemberment this time at the hands of a continental theologian, the much acclaimed Father Häring, C.SS.R. Ours was a traditionalist statement on the vital issue of Birth Control. I do not think I am blowing the trumpet too hard if I say we were already declared *Humanae Vitae* men some years before the decision of Pope Paul VI. Häring, however, took exception to our teaching and unwisely, if not unfairly, gave an interview to the egregious George Armstrong of the *Manchester Guardian*.

Heenan and I used to walk every day along the Tiber bank from the English College to St. Peter's for the morning Session. As we turned one morning into the Via della Conciliazione there immediately in front of us was Father Häring. He was at the Council as a *peritus*. Heenan dug me in the ribs. I knew it at once! The old "Chance it!" imps had taken over as of yore. We at once stepped up alongside the great moralist, and exchanged greetings. "Father, we should be delighted to welcome you some evening for supper at the English College. Perhaps afterwards you would address the Bishops?" Thus the smiling Heenan. Häring agreed at once, though he must have realised there could be a rough house in the offing.

In the event there was to be nothing of the kind. We had left the choice of subject to our guest. He decided to give us his personal *apologia* which covered a tough childhood, large family on a tiny farm, deep Catholic faith and early conscription into the Wehrmacht. After this introduction he moved on to his present employment at the Redemptorist faculty of moral theology in the Via Merulana.

I have at times been tempted to regret that I did not walk out at the point where, several hundred years after the event, he psychoanalysed St. Thomas Aquinas, using his famous gesture with the brand snatched from the fire to drive away the temptress as proof that St. Thomas was a misogynist and his judgment in respect of half the human race somewhat flawed. A certain detail came back to me from the Cambridge Summer School on Thomas Aquinas in the 1920s. Whenever he cut a new goose-quill he first tried it in the margin and always with the same word, "Maria".

It was my turn now to psychoanalyse my contemporary, Father Bernard Häring. From his brave, brilliant but somewhat over-heated monologue I concluded he lacked level-headedness, a quality I should think any great moral theologian must exercise at all times if he is not to generate more heat than light.

But I have most grateful recollections of the Alfonsianum and the Redemptorist Fathers in Rome. As a student I frequently in the middle '30s said Mass at their famous Shrine of Our Lady of Perpetual Succour. There, at their H.Q. in the Via Merulana, I made my eight-day retreat before episcopal ordination under the direction of one of the American Fathers, a true master of his spiritual craft. It was in a way a return to one's origins. Nearly all our retreats as boys at Upholland Junior Seminary were conducted by Redemptorists, as also was the Upholland retreat before my priestly ordination. In a way therefore it was only natural that the day before our baptism as Fathers of the Twenty-First Ecumenical Council of the Catholic Church Heenan and I should leave the hurly-burly of the city of Rome to hide away in the Campagna with wine, bread and cheese and a Redemptorist Father from the Merulana, that brilliant professor of Patristic Moral Theology at the Alfonsianum, Father Xavier Murphy, C.SS.R.

October in Rome can open the floodgates and keep them open as I well remember from my first weeks at the Beda in 1933. Anyway on that eve of Vatican II we were hopping on tussocks across swampy ground at some point in our rural progress. Was it only months or years later I realised that one of us was also treading on egg shells for most of that day?

Both Heenan and Murphy were in splendid form. Both shared a lively interest in what was for me an entirely new theme, the identity of the "Xavier Rynne" whose articles on the Council were already appearing in the *New Yorker*. They were to continue bright, author-itative and keen-edged "thru" October 1962 to December 1965 perhaps with interstices, neatly filling each year a popular and piquant hard-back.

It was an auxiliary bishop of New York who eventually cracked the Rynne secret. As Cardinal Spellman's deputy Chief Chaplain to the Armed Forces, Bishop Griffiths had access to RC chaplaincy records. Thereon he discovered a "Father Francis Xavier Murphy, C.SS.R., mother's name Rynne." He commented: "Sometimes it's easy to put two and two together!"

I wonder how far these eagerly canvassed commentaries changed the climate of the American Household of the Faith? On many RCs they must have acted as a sudden douche of cold water, at first breathtaking, finally exhilarating. Top performers in the Vatican II drama appeared in their birthday suits—shorn of the usual protocol and formalities. Astringent analysis and commentary invaded areas of criticism where once only angelic quills dared to be busy.

No wonder ecclesiastical students at the North American College found Rynne intoxicating. They could not get enough of him. Undeniably he was a master craftsman with a pen and supremely well informed. His readers gained a privileged insight into Council affairs uninhibited by courtesies once reckoned essential. He had, of course, every right to claim that this was in no sense letting the side down since his lay pen name absorbed the shock waves otherwise inevitable at that time in the Catholic public.

I have met Murphy a couple of times since Council days. The first, in Toledo Cathedral on the titular Feast of the Assumption, he had just come from interviewing Cardinal Tarancon whom he warmly approved as "having the right ideas".* The other occasion was in Philadelphia during the 1976 Eucharistic Congress, as Monsignor Allen and I sat watching the immense Catholic procession through the city on the Sunday. He joined us in the benches. "What about a biography of Cardinal Heenan?" was his first question. Firmly, to myself, I resolved this one was not for him despite his undoubted talents. However, neither was he looking for it. "George Dwyer and yourself should get together to provide the materials. I know a fine young biographer would work them up." It is, I know, a shame there is still no life of Heenan. Nor in fact was there a life of his hero Cardinal Hinsley until he burned his brief candle at the shrine. Anyway Heenan was not notably reticent about himself—witness *Not the Whole Truth* and *A Crown of Thorns*. They must do for the time being.

---

* Perhaps not, however, on mastering a tipsy thurible which cascaded onto the priceless predella carpet during the subsequent High Mass.

CHAPTER LV

Vatican II

THE TWENTY-FIRST General Council of the *"Sancta, Catholica, Apostolica, Romana Ecclesia"* harnessed all her human resources of mind and heart under the assured guidance of the Holy Spirit with one single intent, namely to explore the mind and respond to the will of Christ her Head for his Church and his world in these supremely challenging times.

Clearly an engagement of such magnitude, whatever demands it may make on the competence and preparation of the human agents involved, depends far more on their attunement to the mind of the Lord. For that, imploration must accompany and permeate exploration.

Logically therefore we gathered for each session in choir dress, the liturgical garments of prayer. The day began with Mass, the Mystical Body's offering of Christ's sacrifice for the life of the world. Predominately the offering was made in the Western Rite. Each Rite honoured in the Church however had its turn. In the Ethiopian Rite we heard Mass to the accompaniment of drums and bells, the words of consecration in Aramaic, the language in which Christ instituted the Holy Sacrifice the night before he suffered. Before our eyes as the Council proceeded the Bride of Christ appeared as he had willed, day by day, *"circumdata varietate"*, in all her irridescent splendour. Nor did she lack the splendour of sound. Famous cathedral choirs came from afar. Most frequently of course we heard the Sistine choir under Domenico Bartolucci.

After Mass we stood for the enthronement of the Sacred Scriptures in our midst. Under the guidance of the same Holy Spirit to whose mastery we confided all our puny efforts, the sacred writers tell of Christ before, during and after his coming. Preceded by cross bearer and acolytes a Council father* bore the sacred burden between the tiered ranks of bowed heads the whole length of St. Peter's and placed it on the altar.

At Trent the Fathers of the Nineteenth Ecumenical Council (1545-1563) also laid the *Summa Theologica* of St. Thomas Aquinas alongside the Scriptures. Neither Vatican I or II followed Trent's example though early in the ninety-two years which separated them

---

* The privilege of enthroning the Scriptures was shared among the hierarchies. Our turn came in the last session. Cardinal Heenan ceded his right in favour of Bishop Parker of Northampton, the only member of our conference who had not missed a single meeting in four sessions despite his advancing deafness.

Pope Leo XIII voiced his powerful recall to Thomism.* The revival reached its high point with the publication by the Sacred Congregation of Universities and Studies of a list of theses† approved by Pope Saint Pius X. The key thesis runs: "It is risky to dissent from Aquinas in a matter of metaphysics."

An issue surfaced in Council debates during the first session of which I am not clever enough to say whether it is a metaphysical matter or purely one of method. I had been asked at our 1963 Albanian Meeting to say something about the first session of Vatican II. Inevitably, since it was then exercising my mind somewhat, the contrast between the essential and existential approaches to our problems came up in my speech; not exactly the best of themes for a celebration dinner. Nonetheless it did spark off some comment. The general feeling with which I agreed at the time was that the two approaches were complementary. Now I am not so sure. I believe it is claimed, however, that valuable theological insights come along existentialist lines

Perhaps experiences in Holland during the liberation in 1944 had prejudiced me. I recognise that existentialist moral judgments don't have to depend only and solely on circumstances. Otherwise we go helter-skelter downhill into consequential ethics. I should still like a latter-day Aquinas to reconcile the two approaches in the same kind of happy union‡ that the original St. Thomas combined Catholic theology with Greco-Arabian philosophy.

I regret posing this minor problem so early in what I have to say about the Council and treating it so turgidly.

Let me begin again with the glorious ceremonial opening of 11 October 1962, the day chosen by Pope John. It was the feast of the Divine Motherhood. The previous night the Piazza was fitfully illuminated from the glory that was Ephesus.‡ A torchlight procession 5,000 strong, organised by the town council, halted below the papal apartments calling for Papa Giovanni. It was already agreed he should appear. He was extremely reluctant to do so. Few of us then knew how ill he was.‖ "Not a good thing for the Pope to show

---

* It swept the Gregorian University clear of stalwart Suarezians like the famous Spanish philosopher Professor Urráburu who retired to his beloved Comillas in Spain. I risk a lighter moment to recall that his voluminous work was our textbook at Valladolid. Our ritual farewell to study as we retired to Country House for the Summer recess was sung to the tune of the Weeping Willow Tree. Only a couple of lines come back: "Adieu, adieu, Urrábura (bis), I can no longer stay with you . . . "
† These theses used to appear, if I am not mistaken, in Denzinger'a *Enchiridion* of Creeds, Definitions and Declarations concerning Faith and Morals. I notice in the 1957 edition (ed. Karl Rahner) they are there no longer.
‡ Fr. Edward Booth O.P. the finest metapnysician I know assures me that in fact St. Thomas has already achieved "the happy union" by way of *ens* and *esse*.
§ The Third Ecumenical Council which in Canon I against Nestorius defined the divine motherhood saluting Our Lady as THEOTOKOS. The people spontaneously accompanied the Council Fathers to their lodgings with lighted torches and acclamations.
‖ See Archbishop Capovilla's poignant "Reflections on the Twentieth Anniversary" in *Vatican II by Those who were There*, Geoffrey Chapman 1986: pp. 106-128.

himself in public again," he said. He had appeared and spoken earlier that day. In the end he gave in. "Draw the curtains bu' I will not speak."

Of course he did speak—wittily and winsomely with a warm welcome for the Man in the Moon "who *had* to look in" and a neat analogy between the rosy moon's radiance and the union of us all in the light of Christ's countenance. His deservedly famous last words were: "Now all of you go home, pick up the baby and give it a kiss from the Pope." Next morning at the crack of dawn the *cortile* of the Venerable English College roared with revolving engines. A swarm of British bishops boarded transport to St. Peter's. As I passed Bishop John Petit, "Tom," he said, "what's going to come out of this lot?" The question was in all our minds. The first working day of the first session of the Council made one thing very plain: the Fathers of Vatican II had a mind of their own.

The first item on the agenda was to elect members of the Conciliar Commissions. Their key responsibility for shaping the texts to meet the mind of the Council as it emerged in the ensuing debate was crucial to the success of the whole enterprise. We needed the best brains the Church could muster. As yet we had no chance to identify them. Each hierarchy knew its own resources. For the overall view there had to be an inter-hierarchy exchange of recommendations and that meant suspending all further business.

Archbishop Garronne of Toulouse had prepared a petition along those lines which he slipped into the redoubtable hand* of Cardinal Lienart of Lille, as they entered the *aula*†. He was first at the microphone when speeches began. The effect was devastating. The twenty-first Ecumenical Council ground to a full stop. The decision was taken to drop everything while inter-hierarchy consultations took place. The assembly broke up. From my place very near the door of St. Peter's‡ I threaded my way up the *aula* to the table where the twelve presidents, all cardinals, still sat, shattered by the turn of events. They made no attempt to hide the fact as I approached.

The Council eventually got under weigh with the key document on Sacred Liturgy, and, as expected the liturgical language was one of the main issues. There were rumours that in certain parts of the Western Church the Mass was already being unlawfully said in the vernacular. Certainly the general feeling was that some loosening up was due. Way back in the 'forties I remember a Belgian Jesuit saying a whole generation was being lost through the rigid use of Latin.

Young Benedictine missionary bishops made a firm but modest appeal for the teaching part of the Mass to be in the vernacular. I

---

* Pope Pius XII rewarded the Bishop of Lille with the Sacred Purple for nobly standing up to the *blitz krieg* and the German occupation of his diocese in 1939.
† The Council Chamber, the nave of St. Peter's.
‡ We sat nearer the altar the earlier we were made bishops. Cardinals, however, topped everybody, and archbishops topped bishops regardless of seniority by consecration.

remember Bishop Dwyer calling for hands off the "dear Roman Canon". It was he again who towards the end of the first session when little progress had been made reminded the council: "We have laboured all the night and taken nothing."

At least this was clear both then and in the next session when the document on Sacred Liturgy was finally passed: nobody foresaw in the generous diversification of language and texts which that document provided, the almost total loss of Latin in our parishes, seminaries and even universities. How many Council Fathers wanted that when they voted? A fair question!

What we all wanted that first session and failed to get was results. Mountains had gone into labour without even a ridiculous mouse being born. This prompted an event unique in history which took place in the library of the English College. The hierarchies of England and Wales, Scotland and Ireland met to consider what advice we could offer to expedite the progress of the Council. This, we felt, was a matter of conscience. Were we not the heirs of a great debating tradition—sons of the Mother of Parliaments?

True, but I fear irrelevant. General Councils and Political Assemblies are very different animals. Politicians do at times go in for "consensus Politics". In national emergencies they even form coalitions. Normally, however, the parties are out for one another's blood. Their debates sunder winners from losers by way of "division". General Councils, on the other hand, work towards victory all round in a final statement agreed by all. The process is laborious. The Commission charged with preparing the text for debate in the *aula* may have spent years on its preparation.* Inevitably its exposure to criticism in the *aula* will subject it to repeated revisions. Each section of the text is discussed and subjected to a written vote. A continous osmosis is shaping the text as the parent commission sensitively reacts to the interventions in the *aula* and the written notes. These record one of three options: *"placet"* meaning "yes", " *non placet"* meaning "no", and *"placet juxta modum"*—meaning "yes if this or that is changed or understood". The final vote on the text as a whole has to be a simple Yes or No.

I have perhaps laboured the point that General Councils and Parliaments work in different ways and with different ends in view. It may perhaps be clearer why, despite our well intentioned endeavours, no wisdom emerged either from the meeting of the three bishops' conferences of the British Isles or the joint working party appointed by it.

Once only†, if I remember rightly, did Vatican II resort to the "win or lose" method and that was on a purely procedural issue, namely: whether to devote a separate document to Our Lady or

---

* In the Secretariate for the Promotion of Christian Unity, seventeen versions of one of our texts paved the way for the final one.
† Mistake! There was another: on whether or not to issue a message to the world when the Council began. The answer was YES!

include her in *Lumen Gentium* on the Church. The matter was concluded in half a morning session with a narrow majority for *Lumen Gentium*. None of the votes on the substance of Conciliar documents produced anything like that. The two thousand or more Council Fathers' final votes were all morally unanimous. Each was the fruit of anything up to six years of hard work if you include the preparatory years 1960 to 1962.

Pressure mounted unbearably in the later sessions of 1964 and 1965. Nothing had been finalised in the first session and relatively little in the second. The ambitious theme: "The Church in the Modern World", a relative late comer to our schedule, was clearly destined to consume the lion's share of the last session. It was, of course, worth every minute of it. Had we left that one out, I think we would have miserably betrayed our maiden effort as a Council, the Message to the World with which we pledged ourselves to the service of all in humble solidarity.

That message was clearly inspired by Pope John's homily at the ceremonial opening of 11 October 1962. In it he disassociated himself from "the prophets of gloom" and launched Vatican II on a mission to the world with "the medicine of mercy" and no anathemas.

A week or so later I was invited to view the Italian TV film of the opening ceremony. We robed in the Sala delle Benedizioni above the portico of St. Peter's and descended the Scala Regia in the longest and I bet the earliest procession ever to tread that noble staircase. As we emerged into the piazza, M.C.s formed us into ranks with the mystic words, *"Seni, seni"*.*

I forget how long the endless river of mitres streamed across the piazza. There were well over 2,000 of us. Eventually even Pope John's patience gave out and he appeared on the piazza leaving the rest of the Fathers to take the interior route into the basilica.

The film of his passage through the piazza was singularly moving. Carried high in the Sedia Gestatoria, and wearing his tiara, he strove to maintain recollection alternating bowed head and moving lips with gentle motions to the wildly enthusiastic people. When he entered the basilica (where some of us had already been waiting for hours) acclamation rippled along the standing serried ranks. His dream had come true. All the successors of the apostles were gathered around him where Peter sealed the Faith with his blood, and he, Peter's successor, was about to guide his brethrens' approach to a wounded world as Good Samaritans.

Though the enterprise began and evolved in St. Peter's, I think bishops from England rightly cherished the fact that John first broached the idea of a General Council in the "English" basilica of St. Paul's-outside-the-walls, where once our kings had their canonical stall. It was January 1959. The suggestion was tentative. John

* "In sixes, in sixes."

283

later recorded with apparent relief the cardinals' welcoming smiles. Heroically, at the end of that first session, the Pope invited us country by country to a farewell audience.

The farewell audience to the first session was also farewell to Pope John. If any of us had wind of his rapidly failing health, so far as I can recall, no mention was made of it. When the end came we were not surprised to discover we had said goodbye to the most popular pope in recent history. Perhaps only the early years of Pius IX (before his prime minister was murdered on the stairs of the Cancelleria) could challenge John XXIII's short five years. At his Requiem in Portsmouth Cathedral my Anglican "oppo" Bishop John Phillips welcomed my statement that he was everyman's pope—theirs as well as ours. I proudly pointed to the restored west window, shattered in the blitz of January 1941, whence Pope John smiled down on us in what I claimed was his first appearance in stained glass in the whole world.*

The Apostolic Delegate, my old superior Archbishop Gerald O'Hara, invited me as a one time employee in Vatican service, to preach at Pope John's Requiem in Westminster Cathedral. Not surprisingly I borrowed for my text the Patriarch of Constantinople's tribute to Pope John. "There was a man sent by God whose name was John" (John 1, 6). Was it the first time the B.B.C. televised a papal requiem at Westminster Cathedral? If so, it would be a fair reflection of mass media's new look at the papacy.

* The artist was a monk of Buckfast, Fr. Charles Norris, who had invented new techniques of glass-firing. He was related to Eddie Blackwell whose artistry has adorned many a church in the Salford diocese and beyond.

CHAPTER LVI

Johannine to Pauline

I DOUBT if ever in the history of the Popes two such widely different temperaments and contrasting styles of government came so close together. Let me try to illustrate the point by way of what each has said of the other:

First, John on Paul (off the record and in familiar converse): "Our dear Hamlet!" Then Paul on John very much on the record in his inaugural address to the Second Session of Vatican II 29 September 1963: "We cannot but bring to mind our predecessor John XXIII whom we greatly loved. His very name revives the memory of that winning, priestly figure. Beloved and venerable Pope John! Thanksgiving and praise be to you for calling this Council together in response to guidance from above in order to find new ways forward for the Church and, at the same time, release from the source of all grace, Christ the Lord, new and as yet undiscovered streams of sweetly flowing water upon the earth."

In that inaugural address, Pope Paul also presented himself: "In a way I now appear in the role of my predecessor Honorius III as he is depicted in the apse of St. Paul's Basilica-outside-the-walls in shining mosaic adoring Christ. The diminutive Pontiff, prone and well-nigh lifeless, kisses the feet of Christ. Immense in stature He presides over the huge multitude in the Basilica, that is, the Church, invoking God's blessing. This vision, it seems to me, is now being realised no longer in colourful outline on a wall but here in our very midst. We too recognise Christ as our fountain-head; we too recognise in the Church here below Christ's veiled features and his continued presence. Our mind's eye is also filled with the vision of the Apocalypse as John describes it: 'And he showed me the stream of the waters of life, shining like crystal as it flows from the throne of God and the Lamb'." (Apoc. 22,1).

That quotation, as you see, goes well beyond the declared purpose of revealing Paul's mind on his predecessor. It reveals his own inmost self at the point where he shouldered his burden.

All these years later, I cannot approach the Council in a cosy or light hearted way. More and more it becomes the awe inspiring event of a life time. I cannot claim that was always my main reaction or that even as the event unfolded I constantly registered profound emotion. Indeed there were moments. Four years, however, is a long time. *"Assueta vilescunt"*.* Even peak moments seem to lose height when they are multiplied. Besides we were tired. Even punctuated with a modest break in Bar Jonah, the morning session at St. Peter's was gruelling. All that oratory! If you were a Commission member you were out again to the Vatican shaping up texts for the aula, discussing written *"modi"* for hours in the evening. I mustn't moan. There were refreshing interludes†. None of us would have missed the Council for the world. Again everyone, I think, would agree, once in a lifetime is enough.

Of one thing I feel sure: the deepening sense of awe Vatican II now inspires owes a great deal to that Pauline address which opened the second phase. But in fairness to John at this point I feel I must balance accounts with the valedictory audience he gave us English Bishops at the end of the first phase.

Those two encounters, John's on 25 November 1962 and Paul's on 29 September 1963, admittedly in very different settings, admirably bring out both Popes' contrasting talents at their best. John began with a salute to the Church in England for sacrifices made for its schools. Then came a repetition of his well-known esteem for Father Faber. Since, he said, every bishop would like to say the Pope addressed him by name he then read out all our names. Archbishop Mathew's responsibility for the Armed Forces prompted memories of his own service in the First War. He had moved up from conscript to moustachioed sergeant and later chaplain. He touched a sensitive chord in some of us with his mention of the spiritual consolation this last of his military roles had afforded him.

Our audience was on his birthday. The night he was born, 25 November 1881, he told us his father ran to the presbytery with the good news, demanding immediate baptism for the son the Lord at last had given him.

"But there's a storm on" said the parish priest.

"I have an umbrella," said the proud father. That very night the boy was born again.

Pope John had great praise for that parish priest. It was seeing him laid out for his funeral that decided the seven-year-old to offer himself for the priesthood. Another great P.P. saw him through to the seminary. As a bishop he later consecrated the parish church which this P.P. had rebuilt.

He asked us, alas, not to repeat the comments he was about to make on the First Session. Surely I am not revealing anything new if I say they were true to form, shrewd, racy and good-humoured. He had carefully followed the debates in St. Peter's on Vatican intercom. He ended with these words: "Thank you for your birthday wishes. Here I am till God calls me. I only know that when my time

* Long-drawn experience becomes commonplace.
† All hail at this point to the Bishop of Chalons-sur-Marne! He called spontaneously at the English College bearing a heavy burden: six bottles three each side of a wide reinforced case. He returned each session. Better champagne is made nowhere outside his diocese.

is done he will call me at once. An invalid Pope is no use to anyone. When I have done my work I hope God will tell me it is time to be off." Bishop Wall* intoned *"Ad multos annos"* which we sang twice rather badly. The Pope, however, was not with us: "Myself, I don't want many more years." He spent about twenty minutes with us after he had seen the Irish and Scots.

When we returned for the Second Session in September 1963, the inevitable groundswell for the immediate canonisation of Pope John lapped round the piazza of St. Peter's. Sheets of papers for signatures fluttered from the kiosks. If this was an effort to canonise "by acclamation", Pope Paul deftly stalled it by linking the "causes" of Pius XII and Pius IX and awarding them priority. Gradually the joannine fervour subsided. No doubt when the right time comes the fact that there was such a phenomenon will make its appropriate impact.

Pope John himself could be very quick off the mark in honouring a saint. During the Liturgy debate one morning three Fathers followed one another with powerful pleas for the inclusion of St. Joseph in the Canon of the Mass. One of them was that heroic Yugoslavian Bishop Cule who during his four years in durance vile learned that prayers were being said for him by the faithful in Scotland. One of his menial chores was sweeping the prison courtyard. A piece of newspaper in the rubbish pile caught his eye. He picked it up. It was from the Scottish edition of the *Universe*. There was his name! He had just enough English to get the main gist and resolved there and then to learn the language well enough to make a thanksgiving visit to Scotland if ever he was free. We saw a lot of him during the Council. He and George Dwyer were close neighbours in the *aula*. By then his English was excellent.

The day those three speeches were made, the Unity Secretariate had an evening work session in the Vatican. We were hard at it with Cardinal Bea in the chair, when in came the Cardinal Secretary of State, Hamlet John Cicognani, his ferraiuola somewhat askew, straight from audience with the Pope. We stood to receive him. *"Il Santo Padre ha decretato che San Guiseppe sia nominato nel Canone!"*† We were the first to know.

Other great moments‡ from Pope John's only session begin to

* He immortalised conciliar highlights in a series of limericks which circulated widely among the Fathers in English and Latin. They make a neat running commentary on Vatican II. Has anyone of its twenty predecessors enjoyed similar treatment? Certainly they gave great pleasure. Among the contintentals stocks and shares in English *"humeur"* and scholarship were never so highly quoted. If only I could find my copy.

† "The Holy Father has decreed St. Joseph's name goes into the Canon!" We had only the Roman Canon in those days.

‡ e.g. the morning Cardinal Slipyj stepped into the *aula* from seventeen years imprisonment—a direct result of Pope John's much debated policy of *detente*. Some East European bishops who had been allowed beyond the Iron Curtain for the Council continued to press for a conciliar condemnation of Communism despite John's ban on anathemas and his insistence on the "medicine of mercy". Clearly they

crowd in now I am about to leave him. Allow me to recall one which neatly links John and Paul and bridges the two Vatican Councils.

During the first session there was yet another occasion for prolonged applause, namely, Archbishop Carinci's hundredth birthday. I remembered him seated at Pius XI's right hand during papal audiences way back in 1933, the year of the extraordinary jubilee of the Redemption. He was born in 1862, in a house on the Via Botteghe Oscure* now the H.Q. of the Italian Communist Party. In fact he claimed to have knelt for his night prayers on the spot where the party boss now sits at his presidential desk.

More relevant to the present purpose is the fact that Signor Carinci took his seven-year-old son to one of the ceremonial assemblies of Vatican I presided over by Pius IX, still gloriously, but precariously, reigning as monarch of the Papal States.

Now for the link. It was the Sunday afternoon Pope Paul beatified Dominic Barberi. In the baptistry of St. Peter's throughout the ceremony business went on as usual. Benediction over, we were dispersing when I saw Archbishop Carinci seated alone some way down the nave. A moment later a young mother holding her newly baptised baby sank with obvious relief on the bench next to the Archbishop. The old man turned to look at his neighbour.

If only someone had held a camera to record that moment! In Italy, as already demonstrated in Pope John's account of his own baptism, the baby might well be no older than a day. The old man gazed across a whole century of eight papacies, the Risorgimento, three Savoyard Kings, a Dictatorship, two World Wars, and a Republic all within the ninety-two years between Vatican I and II.

Somewhat contrary to my better judgment I wind up Pope Paul's three sessions with extracts from what I wrote in *Vatican II by those who were there*.† I offer this first extract in honour of Cardinal Bea and the members and consultors of the Secretariate for the Promotion of Christian Unity with whom I was privileged to work throughout the Council and the years which preceded and followed it—fifteen in all if I am not mistaken.

> "Divided Christendom now finds (and "full in the panting heart of Rome") a bond of union, not yet, alas, in fullness of faith, but in warmest charity, mutual understanding and every-ready service. Ecumenical traffic now ranges to and from the Vatican as wide as Christendom. It was already moving during the Council with the distinguished presence of observers from other Christian Churches, the return of St. Andrew's head to Constantinople and the mutual liftings of ancient anathemas. Again, if I am not mistaken that was the grand finale of Pope Paul's first

---

felt Vatican II was shirking a primary responsibility. Cardinal Slipyj responded to our prolonged applause with a spontaneous *apologia* in flawless Latin which ranged far beyond the statutory ten minutes. For once no bell was rung!
* The Street of the Dark Shops.
† Geoffrey Chapman 1986, pp. 49-61.

session. And who could ever forget Paul's own return from the
United Nations General Assembly in New York? His message,
formally eirenical, nevertheless in truly "pontifical" style*, built
all manner of ecumenical bridges†. Council Fathers gathered
around TVs to watch his approach to the podium with bated
breath. So motionless he was until then, he seemed to be his own
wax-work effigy, incapable of speech.

"Secretary General, Pericles Felici, prefaced the following
morning's work with the news that the Pope intended to come
straight from Rome airport to St. Peter's to be welcomed home
by us. Business finished as usual about 12.30. It was our turn to
sit motionless, all 2,000 of us. Towards 1 p.m. Peter's great doors
parted. We rose and there he was! Our applause rivalled even
U.N.O.'s response to his *"Jamais plus la Guerre!"* He looked
radiant!"

Of the three sessions over which he presided that moment
remains supreme in memory. With loving respect and not a little
cowardice I abandon further effort to chronicle the passage through
the Council of such towering texts as *Lumen Gentium, The Church in
the modern world, Divine Relevation* and our own *On Ecumenism.* I
resort once again with relief, to Chapman's *Vatican II by those who
were there* for an overall view of the Council, which fails, perhaps to
register the awe I now feel but otherwise remains sound and fair:

"What was Vatican II for this one Council Father? It was the
experience of a lifetime, not to be missed at any price, and
(misericordia!) not to be repeated in anyone's lifetime, be he
Pope, Prelate, Peritus or most brilliant of Secretaries General.‡

"It was a *pastoral* experience. Each bishop—in the Aula, at
commission meetings, struggling with texts at his lonely desk—
was accompanied by his people for whom he was both witness
and judge.

"It was a massive *human and humanising* experience. Not just
the Rhine! All the world's rivers flowed into the Tiber. Provincial
minds broadened, naive reactions met their challenge, gas-bags
were deflated . . .

"Last of all, it was a *controlled* experience. At the human level

* *"Pontifex"* literally means Bridge Builder.
† *The Pope's appeal for Peace*, address 4 October 1965, English text CTS S270, 1-12.
‡ Cardinal Pericles Felici died in the mid-seventies as he was preaching in Florence
Cathedral. I have before me as I write his 1966 edition of the *Constitutiones, Decreta et
Declarationes* of Vatican II. He presented and signed a copy for each of us who opted
for the "Latin Group" in the General Synod on Evangelisation, 1974. He wrote:
"Venerationis gratia" (token of esteem) 15.X.1974 Pericles Card. Felici. This great
Latinist, who, each morning opened the Council's day's work with a lucid outline of
what lay before us and announced the voting results in impeccable Latin, describes
this pocket edition as: *"Editio anni 1966 modo anastatico iterum impressa".* I cannot find
"anastaticus" in my Latin dictionary. It must mean "pocket edition". Though there are
1300 pages it is only one inch thick, less than six long and four wide, and comes from
"The studious care" of the Cardinal's beloved "General Secretariate of Ecumenical
Council Vatican II".

superbly staged and firmly paced (give and take a few lon-
gueurs!) despite running four times the length wishful thinkers
(Pope John, I fear, among them)* had bargained for.

"At the deepest level Vatican II was also a striking confirmation of Pio Nono's monitum to the Fathers of Vatican I: 'You will
find the Holy Spirit within the Council, not outside'!"

* In his address to the torchbearers in the Piazza (11.10.62) he did, however, hint that
he might have to recall the Fathers after Christmas. Our superb Secretary General,
Felici, is reported to have replied: "Liscio, liscio!" ("Smoothly, smoothly!") when asked
how the Council would go.

CHAPTER LVII

Back from the Council

VATICAN II solemnly closed on the Feast of the Immaculate Conception 1965. The event was open to the world and lingers indelibly in memory despite the years. Pope Paul was radiant. He preached in Italian addressing himself to "Cardinals, Council Fathers, National Representatives, Authorities and Citizens from every part of the world, observers from so many Christian denominations, Faithful sons here present, and finally all of you everywhere in the world united with us in Faith and Charity." His last salute was to those in the congregation "who are unaccustomed to invoke Our Lady Immaculate. For us she becomes an inspiring model, a source of comfort and hope. That is how we, Brothers and Sisters, think of her, for us and for you. May this above all else come true."

On St. Peter's piazza seven Cardinals in the name of the Council delivered messages to Statesmen, Thinkers and Scientists, Artists, Women, the Poor, Sick and all who suffer, and Youth. Suggestions that the Council should end with a dramatic meeting of Pope and Chief Rabbi in the square to the accompaniment of music and dance had failed.

At the end of the final session, Pope Paul asked to see the hierarchies of England and Wales, Scotland and Ireland. In a strong appeal for *Fidei Donum** priests, he advised us in Britain to think first of Africa. Within six months of our return home we responded to his appeal by sending over fifty priests to the missions overseas.

On the wall behind me as I write leans another form of farewell, a document in a deep oaken frame (24" x 12"). The text of eighteen lines is printed in robust latin uncials. Paul's pontifical arms in gold head the page. Line eight also breaks into gold with two words "AUREUM ANULUM".† With this document, each Council Father received a gold ring. One's name and diocese are indelibly inscribed at the foot. The ring is mitre-shaped. At the peak is a Maltese Cross, below, Christ between Sts. Peter and Paul. Paul's crest is behind them hidden inside. Typical!‡

* Pope Pius XII issued an appeal to bishops to send diocesan priests to the foreign missions for a spell to supplement the efforts of missionary congregations—Mill Hill, Maynooth Missions to China, etc. The document began with the words *Fidei donum* (Gift of Faith).

† Golden Ring.

‡ Some bishop is alleged to have had his ring valued professionally at a surprisingly low figure. However, when my successor, Bishop Kelly, commissioned a pauline ring of the same number of carats, the price was £210. I have heard that the Pope sometime in the last session received an oriental Head of State who handed him a nugget from his own gold mine.

On returning to their dioceses from the Council bishops usually gathered their clergy for a first-hand account of the Council's progress. In a packed Salford cathedral I began by raising my hand with the palm towards me. It would be comforting to record that a ray of sunlight instantly caught the ring. No such luck! Anyway the priests soon got the point that this was Pope Paul's symbol of our continuing union with him.

"I think," said I, probably gilding the lily, "the Holy Father means something more than that. Something to do with being simple and genuine? Anyway I shall wear this ring until I die." A sudden round of applause swept St. John's cathedral, Mother and Head of more than two hundred parish churches. I like to think this was our priests' emphatic pledge of their own spiritual union with the successor of St. Peter.

In his allocution to the Council Fathers on 18 November 1965, Paul had delcared his intention to associate "in so far as possible" bishops the world over in his "apostolic duty of ruling the Universal Church". That was a great moment for our episcopal conference of England and Wales. In its name I had had the privilege of suggesting that very thing in a short speech on 16 October 1963. It was, I think, the first time "Episcopal Synods" surfaced in conciliar debate. Need I say my intervention was prompted by a pretty clear hint, almost an appeal for help, in Paul's inaugural address to the Council eighteen days beforehand on 29 September 1963.

I dare to think my reward came with Paul's own exquisite touch some time after the Council when I was in Rome for a meeting of the Secretariate for Promoting Christian Unity. Having a free morning I decided to attend the Wednesday general audience. At the end the Pope invited all the bishops who were present to join him in blessing the pilgrims. Three or four of us went forward. For each he said a brief word of introduction. Mine was: "And here is Bishop Holland whom we all remember from the Council." You will say my interpretation is both tenuous and presumptuous? Yes, I agree! But it happens also to be very heartening, and if ever a man needed heart of grace it is now as I approach the impossible task of assessing the impact of Vatican II on the Catholic Church. I have only very slender credentials for the task. For the last twenty-five years I have prefaced every part of my woefully distracted recitation of the breviary with Pope John's prayer "For the happy outcome of Ecumenical Council Vatican II".*

I have already noted the phenomenon of theological dissent which at times palpably tangled with the official Magisterium of the Church. This was a new experience. Once upon a time dissent of this calibre entailed honest and open withdrawal from communion with

---

* "Lord may this sacrifice of praise which I offer to your divine majesty '*pro felice exitu Concilii Ecumenici Vaticani II*' be accepted by You. Grant that what we with our Pontiff John humbly ask of You may in the event be given us." As Pope succeeded Pope, their names were added to the text. One "prays humbly" now: "*cum Pontificibus nostris Joanne, Paulo et Joannibus Paulis.*"

the Church. Now, it seems, this is no longer good form. Dissenters now continue in their official appointments. Is this a fair interpretation of Pope John's "medicine of mercy"?

When men like Döllinger broke away after Vatican I they were of course faced with a solemn definition of Faith. Vatican II of set purpose refrained from any such definition. It is nonetheless clear that on certain moral issues the Church has taken an official stand which has all the guarantees of an irreversible judgment. The kind of "respect" this entails is incompatible with the open dissent which now raises its head. Such at least is the conviction I am unhappily driven to hold and record.

In this connection Cardinal Heenan put the cat among the pigeons even within the Council. He fulminated against *"periti"*, theologians everywhere challenging the magisterium. *In omnem terram exivit sonus eorum*—"Their sound has gone out to the ends of the earth", he trumpeted. He was immediately supported by the bellicose Cardinal of Palermo one of whose memorable diatribes climaxed with the words: "Either that is error or I must be thick!"

On my own doorstep I met a phenomenon which continues to perplex and disturb me. Many of our Salford diocesan statistics began to go down steadily from 1962—the year the Council began. Births, Baptisms, Converts, Confessions, Mass attendance, Easter Duties and the rest. The only significant increase was in Holy Communions. All my efforts to keep the line open for regular parochial and conventual Masses in Latin failed miserably. So did the most energetic remonstrances and reminders to preserve a modicum of silence in church when Mass was over. There wasn't the faintest chance of any thanksgiving. The House of Prayer had become a gossip shop.

But these were perhaps minor indications of the deeper change in sensitivity and manners throughout European society. Wherever the hurricane came from, it uprooted even the basic phrases for bad breeding* which always implied conformity, with common standards of behaviour carefully passed on in home and school. Now, it seemed, "creativity", "doing your own thing" had taken over. And not only in home and school, but to a startling degree, within the Church. Liberation came on all fronts! Dutch Catechism for dogma, jeans in the liturgy. Even a mild request of Pope Paul for the retention of Latin at divine office in Benedictine monasteries† met with the response: "We would be living in museums".

One must make allowances. The atmosphere was decidedly heady. Only a few decades before Vatican II moralists had judged it grievously wrong to join non-Catholics even for the Our Father. Memories of Margaret Clitherow‡ still stiffened us.

The recommendations of Vatican II for the renewal of religious

---

* e.g. Italy, "*mal educato*", Spain "*falta de formalidad*", etc.
† Made at the solemn reopening of the restored monastery of Monte Cassino.
‡ She refused point blank at her trial to join the parson in prayer.

life seemed both spacious and safe. How on earth then did leaping over convent walls into lay dress and also, alas, into lay life, become so prevalent? Is this a salutary reminder of the mental exaltation induced by the simple mention of change in institutions governed by strict and time-honoured regulations?

Experimentation with the Holy Rule was legitimate. Indeed the Council called for it. Not, however, as a permanent way of living the religious life. I was assured by certain innovatrices on one occasion that this was the inevitable future.

Episcopal visitations, of course, involve visits, class by class, to our parish schools. The diocese of Salford was well endowed in this respect. With predecessors like Henry Vincent Marshall and George Andrew Beck, each in their turn Hierarchy Secretaries for education, I entered into a rich inheritance. The Dutch phrase for such luck is: "He sat down in the butter!" In this instance it was doubly best butter. The diocesan Schools Commission was the finest in the country. At our monthly meetings I marvelled at the expertise of men like Canons Bernard Greenwood, Joseph Lakin, James Schollick, Louis Sharp, Anthony Carpenter, Messrs Norman Lewis, Bernard Flood and others. In fact the Building Office which houses a dozen other diocesan Commissions in addition to Schools was a cabinet of all the talents. I attended their meetings with a *Te Deum* in my heart. Looking back, I recognise it should have been oftener on my lips.

Open-ended discussion was one of the educational fads of the day; indoctrination was a dirty word. Thank God our teachers in the main were well aware that the Faith is not a matter of "How do *you* feel about it?" but what the Church teaches as divinely revealed. You *learn* that as you learn another language, adjusting yourself, mind and voice, to objective norms. There is of course plenty of room for comment and discussion. Indeed genuine appreciation of beauty cannot flourish without them whether in language, art or divine revelation. I recognise, perhaps somewhat tardily, that canvassing the pupil's spontaneous reactions to what he has to learn can supply a useful basis for broadening and refining his appreciation even in the area of Faith. But there supremely "Truth is great and must prevail!" Open-ends must close. Misconceptions must be corrected. Otherwise Catholic children are robbed of their baptismal heritage and lost for ever in the mist.

CHAPTER LVIII

At Home

I WAS wrong earlier to preen myself on prefacing all parts of my breviary with Pope John's prayer for "The Happy Outcome of Vatican II". Clearly there was nothing wrong with the intention. If, however, appropriate action to make it come true were lacking, isn't there a strong whiff of Luther in the air? Faith without good works? I firmly believed that Vatican II was what today's Church needed. In practice, however, did I do everything to put it firmly within her grasp, at the level of the people?

Certainly we all went home from the Council determined to show we meant business. Our clergy were obviously our first concern. Study courses on the Council documents had to become as obligatory as spiritual retreats. Luckily good translations were soon available. Commentaries on the texts were called for. At this point I am ashamed to acknowledge my own abject failure to deliver the goods after what I think was a genuine effort to respond.

Stately premises opened with the main purpose of educating clergy and laity in the faith and practice of the post-Vatican Catholic Church. She, with an immense effort, had updated herself into the contemporary world where She was whole-heartedly prepared to be of service. The clergy and laity also must be ready and willing to face the task. Anything less would be treason.

Alas for the schemes of church-mice and church-men! The authentic guidance of Vatican II encountered unforeseen rivals. A new breed of theologians, mobile, articulate, ever ready for press interviews appeared on the *aggionamento* circuit. The distress inflicted earlier on religious communities by "with it" retreat fathers was now, it seemed, about to affect the laity.

We bishops should have kept a closer watch on the ramparts. Our great privilege of mediating the genuine teaching of Vatican II surely involved the duty of warding off misrepresentations. Greater use of our authority to teach and correct was clearly demanded. The Sacred Congregation for the Doctrine of Faith had every right to complain of being swamped with complaints that should have been summarily dealt with by the local bishop*.

Of course local bishops could plead all manner of alibis and excuses: they were catching up on parochial visitations and

---

* During the 1974 Episcopal Synod on Evangelisation, Cardinal Seper the then Prefect of that Congregation allowed himself in one of the language groups to express his feelings on this issue very forcibly.

confirmations—confronted by crises in the clergy—still burdened with commission work abroad, and so on. In fact the whole lot fails to add up to a decent case. I must beat my own breast mercilessly. One's paramount duty at that time was surely to make the genuine mind of Vatican II come through loud and clear to priests and people.

I did address myself energetically to what I consider a major problem bequeathed by Vatican II. It is, I think, still unresolved though much more expert hands took it over after I had failed.

Sacrosanctum Concilium, the Council document on the Sacred Liturgy, called for many far reaching changes. I salute the liturgical scholars who so faithfully, so felicitiously and, given the magnitude of the task, so expeditiously, worked to fulfil the tasks given them by the Council.

The Roman Missal underwent drastic changes not only in language but in the choice and arrangement of biblical readings. The single year structure became a three years cycle. The old style interspersed gospel readings were succeeded by continuous readings from each of the three Synoptics. I understand this particular change was vigorously advocated by French liturgists.

Salford, I am sure, was not the only diocese to find itself faced with a difficult problem.

"Preach the gospel; render an account of the Faith that is in you both to those within and those without the Church." That is our Holy Mother the Church's most binding duty.

Originally, of course, the main thrust was towards conversion of those outside her, nor can we ever relax our effort to proclaim the good news to them both in season and out of season. Despite the heroic missionary efforts at home and abroad shall we ever adequately respond to the appeal to preach the gospel "to every creature"?* Here it is good to remember certain words of comfort from our prince theologian, St. Thomas Aquinas: "If inculpable ignorance of the true faith were a person's only disqualification for entering heaven, the Lord would have to supply that deficiency even through an angel."

What, however, of those already within the Church—when do they hear the gospel? For eighty or ninety-five per cent of us, the answer is: only at Mass on Sunday. This puts bishops on the spot. The Faith is a coherent whole to be presented in an orderly sequence of truths. Hence the various diocesan schemes for Sunday sermons and instructions.

My predecessor Bishop Marshall had produced a scheme for Salford related at least loosely, of course, to the pre-Vatican arangement of the epistles and gospels. Clearly the revised Roman Lectionary demanded a new syllabus of Sunday sermons and instructions.

Has anyone—bishop, priest, or catechist—come up with the

* Mark 16, 15.

genuine article? I again failed dismally. My well qualified priest-catechist devoted himself whole heartedly to the problem. Any time I hear we are home and dry on this issue I shall sing a lusty *Te Deum*. I am anxious at this point not to give the wrong impression. I have every reason to honour and thank our priests for their loyal and competent Ministry of the Word. Their duties, however, become heavier as they grow older and recruits to the priesthood are fewer and fewer. Without prescribed programmes for Sunday preaching there could be danger ahead both for the Gospel message and its recipients. Tired men can all too easily fall back on well worn themes. People in the pews then promptly switch off.

Bishop Christopher Butler O.S.B. used regularly to ask how many survivors from the Council were left in our episcopal Conference. He, in fact, was our only non-episcopal representative. He attended the Council as President of the English Benedictines and sat with his colleagues from other countries high up in the tribunes of St. Peter's, whence he often intervened. His Latin (spoken always *"á l'Université Anglaise"* was generally admired not only for its ready flow but for the clarity of thought it conveyed. I think he was the only Englishman who ventured to speak without a written text. Very few Council Fathers had the courage or the competence to do that. Cardinal Slipyj's famous address on his first appearance in the Council remains for ever unique, coming to us, as he did, straight from seventeen years in prison for the Faith.

Next, I think, must come Cardinal Ottaviani. What a morning that was when Secretary Pericles Felici announced: "The next speaker will be Cardinal Frings." It was late morning but if any fathers were nodding in their seats they woke up with a jump. Frings was making an out-and-out attack on unfair procedure, so he alleged, current at the Supreme Congregation of the Holy Office. He sat down. The Cardinal Prefect of the Holy Office at once went to the rostrum. *"Altissimo protestor!"** he began. "The most eminent Cardinal Frings has spoken—*"non ex ignorantia sed ex nescientia"*.†

It has since come to light that the text from which Cardinal Frings spoke was composed by the well-known professor of Sacred Theology, Joseph Ratzinger. Seventeen years later, on the 25 November 1981, Joseph Ratzinger was appointed Prefect of the S. Congregation for the Doctrine of the Faith formerly known as the Holy Office or, from its standing among the Roman Congregations, *"La Suprema"*.‡

* "I most profoundly protest!"
† "Not from ignorance but nescience". The point being that ignorance implies lack of knowledge you should have had whereas nescience implies you could not be blamed: the truth was not available.
‡ For his *amende honorable* see *The Ratzinger Report*, Fowler Wright 1985, pp. 66-69. It is a noble tribute to the Italian influence in the central government of the Church.

But let me take up Bishop Butler's oft repeated: "How many of us are left, Tom, from Vatican II?" It is some time since he himself moved over to the larger number of those who are always with the Lord.

Ten of us are still *"inter vivos"*, of whom two are on the active list, Archbishop Worlock, whom Pope Paul appointed to Portsmouth in the last days of Vatican II, and Salford-born Bishop Gerald Mahon, now auxiliary in Westminster, who attended the Council as Superior General of the Mill Hill Missionary Congregation. Among those retired there is one archbishop, John Murphy of Cardiff, and one Apostolic Exarch, Augustine Eugene Hornyak, who has worn a crown of thorns courageously for years. His retirement is still *sub secreto* as I write. The other survivors are all retired: Bishops Cyril Restieaux, Charles Grant, Brian C. Foley, Gerard Tickle and Gordon Wheeler.

We have still to celebrate the Month's Mind for George Patrick Dwyer who died at the Alexian Brothers nursing home here in his native Manchester. He might have worn the Sacred Purple in succession to his *"dimidium animae"*†, Cardinal John Heenan, or as head of one of the Roman Congregations. Both promotions, I believe, were supposed to be *sub secreto*.

The remaining episcopal survivors of Vatican II continue to include somewhat surprisingly this present random gleaner of a harvest of memories. He would, I feel sure, have done himself and his readers more good looking forward to where he is going rather than looking back on where he has been. May Light Perpetual shine on all who have gone and all those who have still to go. We can't have long to wait.

† "Half his soul".

Nazareth House, Prestwich.
4 April 1984—19 October 1987.

Laus Deo Deiparaeque
SEMPER

Index of Names

Abelard, Peter 25, 27
Alacoque, St Margaret Mary 18
Alastruey, Don Gregorio 44, 50
Albion, Fr Gordon 195
Alfonso XIII, King of Spain 41, 75
Alfred, King 202
Allen, Mgr John 236n, 237, 240, 256, 266, 278
Almond, Miss 8
Anderton, James 265, 271
Andrew, Bp Agnellus 224, 235, 254-255, 263
Aquinas, St Thomas 24, 25, 27, 45, 83, 276-277, 279-280, 296
Aranda, Conde de 67
Arendzen, Canon John 30, 165-167
Arendzen, Canon Leo 167
Armstrong, George 234, 276
Arnou, Fr, S.J. 50
Atkins, Mgr Alban 148, 150
Attlee, Clem 71, 139
Aubert, Mother M. 171
Augustine, Bp, of Canterbury 185
Augustine, Bp, of Hippo 19, 24, 51, 161n

Balaguer, Fr 130
Ballesteros, Manuel 67, 68
Balthasar, Fr H.U. von 24n
Barberi, Bl. Dominic 288
Barbirolli, Sir John 107, 192
Baring, Maurice 29
Barlow, St Ambrose 229-230, 237, 267
Barlow, Harry 8
Barnard, Miss 164
Barnard, Mr 210
Barroso, Bp Florentino 72
Barry, Fr 97, 99
Bartolucci, Mgr Domenico 279
Bazin, René 257
Bea, Card. Augustine 61, 200, 250, 287, 288
Beatty, Earl 107
Beck, Abp George Andrew 191, 225, 227, 230, 237, 240, 246, 294
Belloc, Hilaire 33, 161
Benedict XIV, Pope 181
Bentley, Canon G 271
Bernanos, George 71
Betjeman, John 242
Bibi, Sr MMM 188-189
Bilsborrow, Bp John 225
Billot, Fr. SJ 49, 50
Birtwhistle, Mr 210
Black, Bp 195
Blackwell, Eddie 284n
Blanco, Maestro 44
Bliss, Susan 123, 136-137, 144-145, 149

Blücher 222-223
Bolton, Fr C A 244
Booth, Fr Edward OP 280n
Cipriano, Don 45, 75
Booth, Joseph, Freya & family 136, 146-147, 191, 202
Borrow, George 32, 36, 44
Bossuet 254
Bourdon, Abbé 107, 114
Brennan, Card. Francis 184
Brennan, Fr. OMI 123, 130
Brennan, Fr Thomas 123
Brewer, Fr Henry 19
Broomhead, Fr Rowland 242-243
Brown, Card. 191
Brown, Fr Joseph 22
Bulliard, Fr Pierre OMI 116n
Bullock, Peter 137
Bülow, Bernard von 179
Burke, Bp Geoffrey 249, 267
Burke, Fr 249
Burton, Montague 241
Busby, Sir Matt 248n
Butler, Bp Christopher OSB 297-298
Byles, Fr T 165n

Cahill, Bp John Baptist 205
Cahill, Dean Patrick 11
Cahill, Fr Patrick 11, 12, 150
Callaghan, Fr John 152, 162, 167
Campbell, Sir Walter & Lady 227
Campion, St Edmund 35
Campo, Don Justo del 32-33, 75, 79
Capello, Fr, SJ 50
Capovilla, Abp 280n
Caraman, Fr Philip SJ 36n
Cardinale, Abp 225
Carey, Capt. 98
Carinci, Abp 288
Carlton, Winnie 249
Carro, Prof. Venancio 64, 79
Carpenter, Canon Anthony 294
Casartelli, Bp Louis Charles 225, 232
Cashman, Bp David 180, 183, 189, 196
Cassidy, Fr Joseph 256
Cauchon, Bp 110
Cave, Prof. 230n
Cervantes 84
Challenor, Bp Richard 165, 203-204
Champagnat, Ven. Benedict 172
Charlton, Bobby 252
Chase, Fr Charles Rose 157, 165
Chaucer, Geoffrey 207n, 236
Cheshire, Gp Capt. Leonard 173, 189
Chesterton, GK 63, 161, 188, 270, 271
Churchill, Sir Winston 109, 139

Cicero 25, 27
Cicognani, Card. Amleto 287
Cipriano, Don 45, 75
Clarke, Canon Harry 239
Clitherow, St Margaret 293
Coke-Harvey, Dr R 74
Collins, Fr P 236
Columba, Mother 8
Columbus, Christopher 37, 83
Combes, M. 209
Conde, Don Felix 38, 39
Confalonieri, Card. 259
Connell, Fr 155
Conrad, Joseph 129
Cook, Capt. 172
Cooray, Card. Thomas 125n, 128
Copsey, Fr Cyril 53
Cordeiro, Card. Joseph 130
Cossulo, Abp 187
Cotter, Bp 202, 205
Coulson, John 224
Cowderoy, Abp Cyril 222
Cox, Evelyn, Jack, Derek 137
Coyne, Fr John 161
Crashaw, Richard 46
Crichton-Stuart 189
Cripps, Stafford 139
Crosby, Bing 176
Crowley, Dr 83
Crowley, Fr Pat 153
Cruz, Don Daniel de la 45
Cuello, Pinto 83
Culbertson 9
Cule, Bp 287
Culkin, Fr Gerard 165
Cullen, Mgr John 63, 82-84, 93
Cunha, Dr Frank da 271-272
Cunningham, Fr Bernard 21-22

Davey, Fr Bert 227
Davis, Charles 261
Dean, Mgr Joseph 11, 15
Delaney, Dr 58
Delange, Georges 216
Delargy, Card. Reginald 169, 194
Delbare, Fr 118
Delvaux, Mgr Jean 61, 62
Dewey, Mgr 95, 99
D'Herbigny, Fr, SJ 56, 58
Dickens, Admiral 118
Dickens, Charles 16, 101
Dickinson, Fr Bernard 20, 21
Döllinger, Bp 293
Dominech, Fr 130, 132
Donald, Prof. Ian 271-272
Dorgan, Colonel 223
Dormer 189
Dove, Fr 160
Dougherty, Card. 183-184
Downes, Francis 230n
Downey, Abp 12, 15, 45, 49, 58, 95, 144, 149-150, 152, 156n, 158, 223n
Downey, Capt. 108
Dryden, John 93

299